BED & BREAKFAST GOES HAWAIIAN:

a DIRECTORY AND GUIDE BOOK

by Al Davis and Evie Warner

1993 edition

Published by Island Bed & Breakfast
PO BOX 449, Kapaa, HI 96746

Copyright 1985, 1986, 1988, 1990, 1992
Island Bed & Breakfast

ISBN 0-9615970-3-8

Printed by
Consolidated Printers,Inc.
Berkeley, Ca.

Every effort was made to ensure
the accuracy of prices and travel
information, but the authors do
not bear responsibility for
errors or price increases

CONTENTS

INTRODUCTION

Bed & Breakfast Hawaii started as an idea when we first visited Kauai in the winter of 1977-1978. Until that time neither of us had entertained the thought of living in Hawaii let alone starting a new business which we knew little or nothing about. But as so many visitors to Hawaii discover, a vacation in Hawaii seems to stir up a longing to live in the Islands.

One day, while hiking along the Na Pali Coast on the way to Hanakapai Beach, experiencing more beauty than we had ever seen in one place, we began toying with the idea of finding something to do that would allow us to live in this tropical splendor. What better thing could we do than have a home, take in guests, and share Kauai with them? Two or three days later we bought a home we felt was perfect for our needs.

From that point on it was simply a matter of returning home and getting everything ready for the big move. That simple task took about twenty months, and by August of 1979 we were settled on Kauai. By then we had even contacted a B & B organization out of Princeton, New Jersey, which we felt sure could supply us with plenty of guests. We anxiously awaited their answer. We did not have to wait long, and by September of 1979 we knew that neither they nor anyone they knew of was interested in bed & breakfast in Hawaii. Keep in mind that in 1979 bed and breakfast was a relatively new thing springing up in the U.S., and when we told people what we were doing they envisioned we were serving breakfast in bed!

Yes, necessity is the mother of invention. In October, 1979, we formed our own Bed & Breakfast group by running an ad in the Kauai paper asking people to become members of **an island network of homes.** *The* **network** *at that time consisted of one home, ours. Now it is 1993, we have over ten years experience behind us, and our network has grown to over one hundred and fifty host homes, each one personally inspected, with homes on all the Islands including Lanai. We have met hundreds of fascinating people and are more convinced than ever that B & B is a great way to travel, especially in Hawaii.*

At first we believed that the main benefit of going the B & B way was cost. Guests can stay in a home for anywhere from $45 to $125 a night, whereas most hotel prices start at $125, with many well over $150 and some of the newer ones well over $200. But cost is only one factor, and perhaps not the most important. As people become more and more experienced with B & B travel, cost becomes less of a factor. The prevailing opinion has become that B & B is more personal and more enjoyable. A visitor gets a first hand chance to see what living in Hawaii is like and receives a more informed idea of what to see and where to go, or where not to go, from a B & B host than from someone working in a hotel. After all, what can they say if asked about the best restaurants in the area, or where the best beaches are? Right at the hotel, naturally.

Also, staying in a private home can be more enjoyable. Many B & B guests and hosts have become friends, and though the guests may not return as often as they like, many keep in touch. One guest who experienced Hurricane Iwa on Kauai in 1982 and spent Thanksgiving with a local group of around twenty people calls each year on the anniversary of the hurricane.

Admittedly, bed & breakfast is not for everyone. Some people just do not feel comfortable in someone else's home. They feel it is too personal in spite of the fact that most hosts are very experienced at making people feel at home, and many of the accommodations are separate from the main home and can be very private. Bed & Breakfast is for people who are open and adventurous, people who are tired of the hotel/motel experience and are looking for an alternative way of travel.

But this book is about more than Bed & Breakfast. It is our opinion that Hawaii is the best tourist value in the U.S. Where else can you get good accommodations with a continental breakfast (which we like to call an Aloha breakfast since our hosts emphasize Island fruits) for somewhere between $45 and $125 a night? Or rent a car for as little as $120 a week, unlimited mileage? And in spite of what you have heard, eating in Hawaii, at restaurants or at home, is not much more expensive than on the mainland if you know where to go. Also, in Hawaii entertainment isn't necessarily expensive since the main attractions, swimming, snorkeling, hiking, relaxing on the beach, cost nothing at all.

The ultimate purpose of our book is to encourage people to visit Hawaii. Many people who have never been to Hawaii have distorted ideas. First, many think you have to be well off, if not rich, but budget travel is possible. Then, some think there is nothing to do in Hawaii but lie on the beach and bake in the sun. This is also a fallacy. There is much to do and much to see, and we hope our book helps more people realize that.

First and foremost this book is a guide to our host homes. We have tried to be accurate in our descriptions of the homes, hosts, and locations. We also want to help our guests in other things such as restaurants, points of interest, beaches, sports activity, and night life where there is any. No guide book that we have seen covers everything and this one is no exception. We do not cover hiking trails, although we realize that hiking can be an important part of a trip to Hawaii. For information on hiking we recommend Robert Smith's Hawaii's Best Hiking Trails, published by Wilderness Press, Berkeley, Ca. Nor do we have much to say about shopping, which is an important part of vacationing. We say nothing at all about other accommodations in Hawaii, and we want everyone to know that there are many small, and some not so small, hotels and motels that offer very attractive rates. We intend to update our guide each year or so, and we urge guests and readers to supply us with tips and ideas about travel in Hawaii. We hope the homes described in our book appeal to you and that the information presented will be useful. We hope to see you in the Islands soon.

ACKNOWLEDGEMENT

When we started Bed & Breakfast in 1979, we had the idea for a guide for our guests. At that time we had only Kauai in mind, and our thoughts ran more to a few pages of helpful hints than a book. As Bed & Breakfast has grown, so has our concept for a guide. No longer could we be satisfied with one Island and a mention of a few special things a guest should not miss. This growth did not occur without some big boosts from some very special people.

Our first big boost came from Jerry Hulse, the Travel Editor of the Los Angeles Times. *In November of 1981 Jerry did a feature story on our new B & B Venture. That article changed our lives. Until that time we had about twenty hosts, and we worked out of our home. Four days after Jerry's article we received 184 letters. We had a policy then, as we still do today, of answering our mail the day received. Some time around midnight we sealed the last envelope. Then, Jerry was kind enough to review our book favorably, which gave us another big boost. Jerry,* a big mahalo nui loa *for your support.*

About a year later we met Al Borcover of the Chicago Tribune, *and he subsequently wrote an article about us and B & B took another big step forward. In 1983 we had a guest from the East Coast, Nancy Shute. After staying in several B & B homes, Nancy wrote about her bed and breakfast experience and her article was published in the* Philadelphia Inquirer. *So a special thanks to Al and Nancy.*

Also to be thanked is Ruth Ann Becker of Hawaii Business Magazine. *When she interviewed us for an article for her magazine, she asked what our next venture might be. We assured her our guide book to Hawaii would soon be complete. That was back in 1983, but it was that promise that was a big motivating factor in getting us to complete this project.*

We would like to thank all the many travel writers who have written about us over the years. Many times we were unaware of being mentioned until one of our guests sent us word of it. Please forgive us if we have failed to mention everyone by name.

Bed & Breakfast, obviously, would not exist were it not for all of our wonderful hosts, and it is to them we owe a great debt. Our hosts have also been helpful in providing us with information about the Islands. Since it is our policy to inspect every home in our organization, we have come to know our hosts and consider the relationship to be more than a business connection. Hosts, mahalo, not only for all of your support, but also for taking such good care of the thousands of visitors that have selected the Bed & Breakfast way.

Then there are the people who so diligently helped in the proofing of the book and encouraged us to continue when the end seemed so far away. Thanks to Fran for some valuable editing. Thanks to Michael for not only being supportive but for helping to set the format. And a very big thanks to Rocky, who spent his two week vacation making sure the details were right.

Last, but certainly not least, thanks to our office staff, Nancy and Patty, and to their very competent leader, Elvrine Zeevat-Chow, our very dedicated office manager, who keeps things going over a busy tourist season and allows us to work on this project.

GENERAL INFORMATION

BED & BREAKFAST HAWAII
PO BOX 449
KAPAA, HI 96746
(808)822-7771
1-800-733-1632
FAX (808)822-2723

WHEN TO VISIT HAWAII

We once asked a Hawaii resident, "When is the best time to visit Hawaii?" He paused for a few seconds and then queried, "When is it cold where you are?" Without a doubt most people visit Hawaii during January, February, and March, and then secondly during June, July, and August. Many people would not dream of coming to Hawaii in the summer months, thinking it might be too hot. Summer months tend to be warmer, averaging a little over 80. When the trade winds blow, summer days are comfortable. There are advantages to visiting Hawaii in the off season. There are fewer people and prices might be less. Off season does not mean dead season as is true in many Mainland tourist areas after Labor Day.

WHY BED & BREAKFAST

When we started B & B in Hawaii in 1979 price was the most important reason for people staying B & B. We have seen a big change over the years and now while cost is almost always a factor in deciding where to stay, it is no longer paramount. What we have noticed lately is that people are looking for a different kind of experience than they can get at a hotel. We must admit that the hotels are more opulent than our accommodations, but in some of them visitors hardly know they are in Hawaii. Be assured that if you stay in a B & B accommodation, you will know you are in Hawaii. Initially the big objection to a B & B stay was the lack of privacy or anonymity for guests. Since most of the hosts we have added over the years offer separate little cottages or studio apartments, complete in many cases with private bath and cooking facilities, we encourage those who hesitate for fear of a lack of privacy to give us a try. Simply make sure the girls in the office realize that privacy is high on your list. Of course, there are travelers who enjoy the luxury of hotel maid service and of having all the facilities right at hand. People who feel that way usually do not enjoy B & B.

BOOKING BED & BREAKFAST

Once you have decided when to visit Hawaii, the next step is to decide where to stay. Let us know as soon as possible which homes you choose, giving more than one choice as some may have prior bookings. When you have made your selections, send 20% (plus 4% tax) of your total lodging plus a $10 booking fee to: B & B Hawaii, Box 449, Kapaa, Hi 96746 to confirm reservations. Should you need to cancel, please let us know at least six days prior to your arrival and half of your deposit will be returned. Keep in mind that hosts lives' change and on occasion a booking made cannot be completed. These events are beyond our control, but every attempt will be made to place you in a comparable host home.

When we receive your deposit, we will send you a reservation form with the name, address, and phone number of your host. This form will also have the date of your arrival, departure and the balance due the host. At the same time we will send your host a copy of the reservation form with your name, address, and phone number. You should then receive a letter from your hosts giving you directions to their home. You should write to the host letting them know the time of your arrival. Our experience has been that the more communication between host and guest the better.

We do accept phone reservations. We now have a toll free number, 1-800-733-1632. Or you can call 808-822-7771. The best time to call is between 9 am and 4 pm Hawaii time, Monday through Friday. Remember that it is always earlier in Hawaii than on the Mainland. When we receive a phone booking, we hold that reservation for about a week, time enough for the deposit to arrive in the mail, or confirm it instantly with a charge card (Visa or Mastercard). When the office is closed, please leave a message on the answering machine and your call will be returned the next day.

STAYING BED & BREAKFAST

B & B hosts except in rare occasions serve a continental breakfast, or what we like to call *an Aloha breakfast*. This consists of fresh Island fruit, juice, toast or some kind of roll or bread that the host might prepare, coffee or tea. In order to serve a full breakfast, ie., bacon and eggs, kitchens would have to be certified by the Board of Health. Now comes catch 22. Kitchens could not be certified since homes are not commercially zoned. Now, if your host serves you more than we have stated, keep it quiet, at least until you get back home and can tell your friends.

If you have specific health needs or certain food allergies, let us know as we will take that into consideration in the booking. Also, let us know if you are allergic to animals as many of our hosts have pets. Some hosts permit use of the washer and dryer; however, since energy costs are the highest in the nation, compensation is expected. Use of the phone is usually permitted and there is no toll charge for on-Island calls. All off-Island calls are toll calls and should be made on a credit card or charged to ones home phone. Hawaii has a 4% excise tax on all purchases including lodging and now they have added a 5% hotel tax; hosts add that to their balance. Some hosts request one night's deposit payable to them and refundable if cancellation is one week in advance.

ON ISLAND TRANSPORTATION

Having a car in the islands is close to a necessity. If you do not drive, there are a few B & B locations that might do; without transportation, one is very limited, and tour buses are expensive. Since 1988 we have been working with Dollar Rent-a-Car which allows us to offer some savings to our guests. We purchase vouchers at a reduced rate and pass that savings on to our customers. Just call the office at 1-800-733-1632. It is not wise to do your shopping after your arrival; if cars are in short supply you will pay a premium or do without especially during major holidays and long weekends (Christmas, New Years, Thanksgiving, Easter, 4th of July, Labor Day and various Hawaii State Holidays) as well as major events like the Ironman Triathalon in Kona and the Merrie Monarch Hula Festival in Hilo both on the Big Island. One bit of advice that may seem silly but we know will prove helpful is to bring a small red cloth to tie to the aerial of your rental car. Recently we returned to the parking lot to find eight white rental cars parked in a row. Had we not had some papers on the front seat we would have had to try the keys in each one, which might prove embarrassing if not dangerous.

ISLAND ACTIVITIES

It has been decided that all B & B Reservation services needed to be licensed travel agents, which we now are. This has proved to be helpful for all concerned because we can now service our guests by making reservations for island activities such as Snorkeling, Scuba, Windsurfing, Kayaking, Canoeing, Biking, Helicopter Rides, Whale watching Tours, Golf, Tennis, Garden Tours, Luaus, Wedding Arrangements, You name it. Just explain to the girls in the office about what you need and they will help you plan and book your activities. 1-800-733-1632.

THE FUTURE OF BED AND BREAKFAST IN HAWAII

As we have already stated, when we started our organization in 1979 we were so low key that nobody paid any attention to us. Well, B&B's have become so popular with tourists throughout the U.S. that the powers that be are starting to pay attention, and, as with most things that government officials do not know anything about, they do not seem to like it. Throughout Hawaii local governments are trying to figure out what to do. Years ago we were approached by the Kauai Planning Department and after much discussion they concluded we were not worth bothering about. On Oahu they have passed legislation that allows existing B&B's but prohibits any new ones. At one time the authorities were of the opinion we needed a real estate license to book private homes. Now it has been decided that all B & B Reservation services needed to be licensed travel agents, which we now are.

We hope that we can continue to do what we have been doing for the last eleven years but who knows. In reality, B&B will go on in Hawaii long after these bureaucrats are gone and new ones have taken their place. It is probably about as difficult to control as garage sales. At least there is one thing one can do in the good old USA without a permit from a government official and that is to write a book expressing ones opinion.

PREPARING TO GO

The biggest mistake any first time visitor makes when visiting Hawaii is bringing too many clothes. Adhere to the travelers' motto of, "Half the clothes and twice the money." Dress in Hawaii is very casual. Day wear consists of shorts or swimsuits, a light shirt or blouse, sandals or thongs. It is a good idea to bring a light sweater, especially in the winter months, as at higher altitudes it is almost always cooler in the early morning and in the evening. If you intend to dine at the higher priced restaurants, men need to bring a light jacket. Most restaurants could care less what you are wearing, and residents of Hawaii give much less thought to their attire than they would on the Mainland. Cotton clothes, long pants for men and women can be comfortable. Ladies may want to buy a muu muu and gentlemen an aloha shirt. Sun glasses, sun screen, mosquito lotion are important items. A plastic bag for wet swim suits is an excellent idea.

GETTING THERE

While flying to Hawaii is not the only option, it is by far the most popular. No single airline consistently has the lowest rate; shop them all to see who is the lowest at any particular time. If stand-by flights are available, take advantage of them, especially in the off season. At the present time, United Airlines has direct flights to all the neighbor islands except Molokai. In the future other airlines will undoubtedly also fly direct. If the airline you book flies only to Honolulu International and your destination is one of the outer islands, be sure to check your luggage through to your final destination. This may not be possible, however, if you are flying stand-by on the connecting flight.

INTER-ISLAND TRAVEL

Although at this printing we have not yet started doing ticketing for the airlines, we are hard at work to find the best way to service guests for the best price. Call our office for more information 1-800-733-1632. There are two major inter-island airlines: Hawaiian and Aloha. Fares are by no means constant, but vary with the number of tourists on the islands. The cheapest way to fly might be stand-by. We recommend this in the off season since the planes are seldom full. If you have doubts, call the airline and ask them how the flight looks. If they tell you it is wide open or looks good, fly stand-by if it is being offered. For more information call the toll-free numbers listed below.

    Hawaiian: 800-367-5320
    Aloha: 800-352-3508

TIME DIFFERENCE

Keep in mind that it is always earlier in Hawaii than on the Mainland. During the winter the time difference from Pacific Daylight is two hours and from Eastern Daylight it is five hours. In summer the difference is three and six, respectively.

HAWAII'S ANIMALS

Perhaps one does not think of wild animals when one thinks of Hawaii but there is quite a variety of wildlife on the Islands. Our guess would be that wild pigs are the most common and pig hunting is a major sport for local people. Axis deer are found on most of the outer Islands and each Island has a short deer hunting season. Wild goat are very common at Kokee and Na Pali Coast area and are also found on Molokai and the Big Island. Mongoose, brought over to keep the rat population under control, are on every Island except Kauai. The plan failed, however, since the mongoose is not nocturnal, rats are. There are also a goodly number of game birds on the Island. Most common are doves which are not really hunted much. Pheasants, though, are common and hunted. Wild turkeys are abundant on Molokai and Lanai and maybe the Big Island and there is a short hunting season for them. Another game bird that we had never heard of until we came to Hawaii which is plentiful on most Islands is the erkel frankolin, which is much like a small sage hen.

HAWAII'S CRITTERS

While we consider Hawaii to be nearly Paradise, we must admit that even in Paradise we have some unpleasant little critters. The most annoying is the mosquito, which was unknown in Hawaii before the white man appeared. You may not see them, but you will feel their presence. One critter you will hopefully not see is the centipede. Most centipedes have been eaten by the buffos, the big frogs you are bound to see, or at least hear. Also, alas, there is the cockroach. Do not run in panic if you happen to see one, just give him a second and he will panic and disappear. Another little critter that bothers some people is the gecko, a tiny lizard around two inches long that makes a clicking sound at night. We never disturb them; they eat a considerable number of mosquitoes and a goodly number of cockroaches. The important thing to remember is that Hawaii has no creatures that will do you serious damage: no snakes or poisonous spiders. You can hike on any trail with out fear of being bitten. We always tell our guests that the biggest threat to their well being is the *monstrous mai tai* or the *creeping chi chi*.

WEATHER

We think the weather in Hawaii is ideal, but since reaction to weather is subjective, we will attempt to describe the weather and let you decide if it sounds ideal. Daytime temperatures at sea level average between 70 and 85, with the summer months having the highs and winter months the lows. Nighttime temperatures seldom fall below 65 and are often in the low 70's. Normal winds, called trade winds, come from the northeast. From around March through October trade winds are usually between 5 to 15 miles an hour, just strong enough to act as natural air-conditioning. At times, usually from November through February, trade winds get a little stronger, but many days in December rival July days. Winds from the south, Kona winds, usually occur in the winter months and often bring foul weather. Rain on some part of every island is almost a daily occurrence. It usually rains at night or in the early morning hours and simply serves to freshen things up a bit. Humidity is a factor, but trade winds tend to mitigate against a high humidity. It is far more humid and muggy in New York in the summer than in Hawaii at any time of the year.

Where else can you find summer days that stay between 75 and 85? Winter is another thing. Most of us who live in Hawaii long for the cold winter snows and freezing conditions found on the Mainland and pine for winter activities such as shoveling snow and putting chains on tires. Oh, sure! And if you believe that we have some diamonds we found on Diamond Head we would love to sell you, cheap.

FOOD

When most people think of Hawaiian food, probably fruit first comes to mind. As the song in *South Pacific* says "...We have mangos and bananas we can pick right off a tree..." and many more fruits could have been included. Hawaii is abundant with fruit, not only mangos and bananas, but papaya, pineapple, coconut, guava, passion fruit, and lychee nut. Some of the more unusual fruits are: mountain apple, Kokee plum, surinam cherry.

Hawaii is distinctive for other delicacies you may not be familiar with. If any food is distinctively Hawaiian it is saimin, which some Mainlanders call Top Ramen. It is sort of a chicken noodle soup with leafy vegetables. Some restaurants in Hawaii serve nothing but saimin. Hawaiians say it is great for a hangover. We are unsure of the origin of saimin; whenever we ask at a restaurant that specializes in it, they end up telling us how it is made. Some say it is originally Japanese, some say it is Chinese, while others say it was first made in Hawaii.

There is, of course, traditional Hawaiian cuisine. If you have been to a luau you know about kalua pig, chicken hekka, lomi lomi salmon, and poi, a few of the dishes you will get at a luau. One need not attend a luau to sample these dishes since each island has restaurants that serve Hawaiian food.

Then there are the multi-ethnic influences in Hawaii, for the most part Oriental (Japanese, Chinese, Filipino, Korean) but there is also the Portuguese and American influence. Few restaurants are exclusively one or the other. This wide ethnic influence is best illustrated by one of the local favorites, Loco Moco, which is a plate of rice, the Oriental influence, topped by a hamburger patty, the American influence, crowned by an egg, the Universal influence, and all of this covered with a heavy gravy.

We could go on and describe the sashimi, the sushi, the kimchee, the manapua, the malasadas, but we will let you discover these by yourself. If none of the foods above appeal to your taste, you can dine in restaurants just like those you find at home.

LANGUAGE

Most guide books to Hawaii present the reader with a fairly full discussion of not only Hawaiian words and their pronunciation but also a discussion of the much more often heard *Pidgin English*. While our discussion will not be as complete, we feel it is all one really needs to know to understand what is happening.

Pronunciation of Hawaiian names can present problems to first time visitors, not because they are hard to pronounce, but because a first time visitor is unfamiliar with the words. Pronouncing Hawaiian words is simple once you get the hang of it. The language contains only seven consonants: h,k,l,m,n,p, and w, and the vowels a,e,i,o,u. A is pronounced *ah* as in ma; E is pronounced *eh* as in bay; I is pronounced *ee* as in key; O is pronounced *oh* as in no; U is pronounced ou as in too. Now, with this in mind if you run across the word PI PE LI NE, you will have no trouble pronouncing it. Easy, isn't it. Or you could put the letters together and just say pipeline.

The first words you will hear on your Hawaii excursion will be *aloha* and *mahalo.* Mahalo means thank you. Aloha, however, is not easily defined. Its simple meaning is hello, welcome, or good bye, but underneath it means much more. People talk of the *aloha spirit* which suggests a caring for people that makes them welcome whoever they are. There is never too much *aloha* anywhere in the world, but it is plentiful in Hawaii.

Two valuable words that are much used in Hawaii are *mauka* and *makai*, which mean respectively, toward the mountain and toward the sea. In this book we use them almost exclusively in giving directions. It is much easier to say "go mauka" or "turn makai" than "go east" or "turn south." Just remember, mauka means toward the mountain and makai means toward the sea. It might also be helpful to know that *kai* is the word for sea water. *Wai* is the word for fresh water.

Another strange sounding word you might hear or see written is *pupus*. Do not get alarmed when you see this on the menu, or a local person asks you over for pupus. It just means hor d'oeuvres. It is also helpful to know *kane* (men) and *wahine* (women) in case you need the men's or ladies' room. Another one you will hear often is *pau*, which means all done.

The most common Pidgin word you will hear is *da kine*, which is used to mean anything the speaker wants it to mean. The extensive use of *da kine* in Hawaii must have some profound comment on the use of language, for it is possible for a meaningful conversation to take place with da kine as the main word: noun, verb, adjective, or if needed, interjection. For example try this conversation.

> *"Hey, Brah, you goin' da kine?"*
> *"Sure. When da kine get here wit da kine,*
> *we pick up da kine and see you bum bi at*
> *da kine."*
> *"O.K., Brah, da kine da beer or we da kine*
> *you lader."*

Then there is the expression *Hawaii Time* which means "whenever we get around to it." If you stay in Hawaii long enough, you will come to know the meaning of *Polynesian paralysis.* When that sets in you may have passed from being a *malahini* (Mainlander) to a *kamaaina* (a child of the land.)

So, aloha all you malahinis, kanes and wahines both. Mahalo for choosing to vacation on our beautiful Islands. We hope your travels both mauka and makai are most pleasant. Fill your *opu* with many delicious pupus, and when your stay is all pau, may your spirit be on Hawaiian time, and the next time you come da kine, may Polynesian paralysis so infect your psyche that one and all will declare you a true kamaaina.

CRIME IN HAWAII

Several years ago much media space was given to a few unfortunate incidents where visitors to Hawaii were attacked by some local thugs, and people began to question how safe Paradise really was. As in all of America today, crime is a problem in Hawaii, yet, to keep things in perspective, if visitors avoid certain places we mention and take normal precautions, most likely they will experience no problems. There is one area of Oahu we would just as soon stay out of and that is the Waianae/Makaha area. For whatever sociological reasons, many of the people who live there do not like tourists, or to put it more bluntly, they do not like "haoles" (a word used to denote a Caucasian). Some of our guests have told us that they did not feel safe when they ventured onto the beach at Makaha. We asked several of our Oahu hosts what they thought and they said they would not go there. Waimanalo is another place where visitors are not always welcome. (see

7

Waimanalo section for more complete explanation). No matter where you are in Hawaii, it is not wise to leave valuables in the car, locked or not. Thieves can open locked cars as fast as if they had a key.

One other area of concern to tourists is the marijuana (pakalolo) growers. If you are hiking, stay on the trails, and you will not have a problem. Growers, like rattlesnakes, get as far from human activity as possible. Hikers would have to be far off the trail to find their patches.

SPECIAL EVENTS

There are so many special events in Hawaii that we will not attempt to list them all but only those we feel are really special. If you want a complete list, write the Hawaii Visitors Bureau, 2270 Kalakakua Ave., Suite 801, Honolulu, Hi. 96815. In this section of the book we will list events common to all Islands and then each Island will have a list.

PRINCE KUHIO DAY (MARCH 26)
This is a state holiday and is celebrated to some degree on all the Islands especially on Kauai.

LEI DAY (MAY)
May day is lei day in Hawaii and every Island celebrates it to some degree.

BON SEASON (JUNE-AUGUST)
Japanese dances that are held to remember those who have passed on. At least one Buddist Temple on each Island will host these colorful dances each weekend throughout the season.

KING KAMEHAMEHA DAY CELEBRATIONS (JUNE 11)
A state holiday celebrated on all the Islands.

ALOHA WEEK FESTIVALS (SEPTEMBER/OCTOBER)
Each Island has a different week so consult each Island for more information.

BODHI DAY (DECEMBER)
The traditional Buddist Day of Enlightenment celebrated at temples throughout the Islands. For more information call Hawaii Buddhist Council, 808-536-7044.

OCEAN SAFETY

While this is the last item in this section, it is not last in importance. Throughout the book we urge caution in swimming in certain areas on each Island. In reality there are certain safety measures that should be observed whenever one is near the ocean. First, never turn your back on the ocean. On Kauai a woman was having her picture taken on the water's edge when suddenly a big wave knocked her off the rocks and she was drowned. Had she been looking she would have seen the wave coming. Second, never swim where there are signs posted no matter how calm the water looks. There may be a rip tide at that spot that will not be obvious to you. Third, never swim alone. Be sure others are around just in case something goes wrong. Last, do not think that because you see surfers way out in the water that the water is easy swimming. Surfers may be able to handle water that could take even a pretty good swimmer half way to Midway. On every Island there are plenty of safe beaches for swimming, so there is no need to risk ones life in any water that is marginal.

RESTAURANT GUIDE

In order for our guide to make sense to you, it is necessary that we explain our method. First, we visited almost every restaurant mentioned and tried to eat in as many as possible over the ten year period we have been researching this book. Where we were unable to do this, we consulted with our hosts who have tried the restaurants. We are not taking the critic's point of view, feeling it necessary to make comments about the culinary arts of the various chefs, cooks, or hash-slingers, whichever the case may be. This year we have included the phone numbers of the restaurants where there is a need to make a reservation.

We feel it is more important to describe the type of restaurant and the food served rather than evaluate their culinary ability. While we know what we like, we do not pretend that our tastes reflect other's tastes. However, at times we will lavishly praise a place we think is special and perhaps damn with faint praise a few others. We will star restaurants that we think offer something special. For example, on Kauai there is a little place in Waimea that serves tasty, fresh baked turnovers. In some cases we will give a spot several stars if we think it should not be missed. We have divided the restaurants of Hawaii into five categories: 1.) fast food, 2.) tourist spots, 3.) **LOCAL STYLE**, 4.) local style, 5.) local/tourist.

Of type 1 we say nothing. They differ little from mainland fast food spots. Of 2 we say little as they are obviously located in the hotels and resort areas and are generally good places to eat and very predictable. Our concentration is on the other three.

First, let us define **LOCAL STYLE**, or what we like to call *two scoop rice* restaurants from their inevitable habit of serving two ice-cream scoops of rice. These restaurants are almost always low in price, and the food is cooked to please local people. Some might call it good stick-to-the-ribs stuff. For example, if you see loco moco (see Food in General Information section) on the menu, you are probably in a **LOCAL STYLE place.** Another **LOCAL STYLE** would be places that specialize in saimin. If you have never tried saimin, do so, for nothing is so universally Hawaiian. Then there are the places that specialize in the typical Hawaiian food. We urge you to try one of the **LOCAL STYLE** places we mention, and if you take a liking to it, you can save a considerable amount of money on food to use on other pursuits, perhaps a helicopter ride, or a sailboat ride to watch the whales.

Then there are the local style restaurants. If you are looking for bargain prices and food that is not as foreign to your palate, these, in our opinion, present the best value. For the most part these are ethnic restaurants, Japanese, Chinese, Korean, Filipino, or a combination of the above, or they are small independently owned short order places that residents of Hawaii use frequently and tourists tend to shy away from, either because they are off the beaten path or they do not look too inviting from the outside. If we define a place as local style, for breakfast you will have a choice of rice or potatoes. If **LOCAL STYLE** you will have a choice between rice or toast, or no choice at all. Also, local style, unless specifically ethnic, will usually have a combination of local and mainland dishes. They will have chicken teriyaki, but also southern fried chicken.

Last are the local/tourist spots. Most of these are modestly priced places, basically depending on residents, with a brisk tourist trade also. In these the food will be more familiar to you; ie., chicken, steak, seafood, fish, and plenty of salad bars. Some do not offer much in the way of atmosphere, but the food is good and priced lower than hotel and resort restaurants. In some you can get a good fresh fish dinner for around $8.00, while the same meal in a hotel/resort restaurant might run between $20-$30.

We realize there are times when price is not the object. You may be looking for more than just a good meal, perhaps a memorable experience. We will not fail to give our opinion on which of the tourist restaurants we think are the best. Many we will not mention, but if you try them, you probably will be pleased. After all the hotels and resorts make it their job to please people or they would not be in business long. Also, keep in mind that the categories are artificial, and while meaningful and helpful, distinctions are sometimes hard to make.

One of the things we have never specifically explained before is the meaning of the word *Okazu* or *Okazu-ya*. One sees this in many of the local Japanese restaurants. Okazu means select from many choices, and Okazu-ya restaurants are always cafeteria style, mostly Japanese cuisine but not always. Another feature of an Okazu-ya restaurant is they usually offer Bento (take out) lunches.

**If you have booked B&B,
do not forget
to let your Host know
your time of arrival**

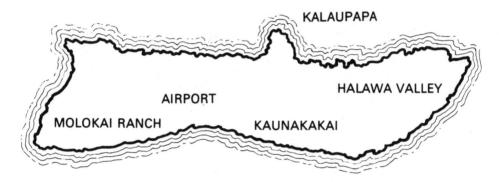

KALAUPAPA

HALAWA VALLEY

AIRPORT

MOLOKAI RANCH   KAUNAKAKAI

MOLOKAI.....THE FRIENDLY ISLAND

.....DRIVING TIMES.....

From Molokai Airport: (approximate)

Kaunakakai...............................6 miles, 15 minutes
To Host Homes....................................8 to 20 miles
Maunaloa (west side)...............10 miles, 20 minutes

MOLOKAI

the Friendly Isle

An often heard complaint about the Hawaiian Islands is that there is too much commercialism and that a place that was once peaceful and serene has been covered with too much concrete and far too many condos. People talk longingly about the *good old days* when one could walk on a beach and the only footprints seen would be theirs. While we know there are still some idyllic spots like this on all the Islands, nowhere are things more peaceful and serene than on Molokai. Also, it is not without reason that one of the names for Molokai is *the Friendly Isle*, for people there are not so hurried that they have no time to smile and chat. We like to think there is Aloha Spirit throughout Hawaii; on Molokai it is very much a way of life.

Obviously one is put in a quandary about recommending Molokai to visitors. It is like seeing your very favorite little known restaurant get a write up in a major paper. While you want everyone to know about it, you want it to stay special and not to become just like every other place. But we are writing for a select group, B & B travelers, and it is this adventurous group that should not miss the special treat of Molokai.

In Hawaiian tradition there are several explanations for the origin of Molokai. The one heard most today is that the god Maui pulled her from the sea as he was fishing. An older myth says that Molokai was born from the mating of the goddess Hina with the sky god of ancient Polynesia, Wakea, father of all the Hawaiian Islands. Since the arrival of the white settlers, Molokai has had several appellations, the Forsaken Isle, the Lonely Isle, and now the Friendly Isle, first called that by the late Senator Harold W. Rice.

Molokai is the fifth largest of the Hawaiian Islands and has a population of just over 6,000. For most of this century the main crop has been pineapple. In years past there were two major plantations, one located on the west end at Maunaloa which was started by Libby, Mac Neil, and Libby, and then taken over by Dole, and one in the center of the Island at Kualapuu, run by Del Monte. Now, pineapple is no more on Molokai. All of the fields have been plowed under. It cannot be long until all of Hawaii's pineapple fields are gone. It will be a strange day indeed when Hawaii has to get pineapple from the Phillipines or South America, since at one time Hawaii supplied 75% of the world's pineapple. There is, however, much experimentation of crop growing taking place and they have had some success with both corn and bell peppers. Independent farmers are doing well with such various crops as watermelon, sweet potato, string beans, onions, potatoes.

Most of the action of Molokai takes place in and around the picturesque little town of Kaunakakai, made famous in R. Alex Alexander's song the *Cockeyed Mayor of Kaunakakai*, sung by the famous Hilo Hattie. Molokai has just recently began a daily paper, The Pueo, a free daily with all the happenings about town. Nowhere in Hawaii is there more local color than in Kaunakakai. Then from the center of town it is just a short walk out to the wharf where everything shipped to Molokai arrives. Local folk use this as a kind of gathering place or a good place to catch a cool breeze when days are hot.

A visit to Molokai is a journey through time and our last visit there so relaxed us that when we returned to Kauai we found the pace almost too fast. We cannot imagine a better place for those whose wish is to experience the *Old Hawaii*, to just kick back, perhaps do a little fishing, and talk story with the local folk. There are three airlines that fly in and out of Molokai, Air Molokai 553-3636; Aloha Island Air 1-800-652-6541; Hawaiian Airlines 1-800-882-8811. The Maui Princess Cruise Boat offers a leisurely 90 minute cruise between Lahaina, Maui and Molokai twice daily on the 118 ft ferry boat. On Maui call 661-5792, on Molokai call 553-5736.

HOSTS

MO-2

This five acre park-like property lies at the foot of Molokai's highest mountain, on the Island's east end where cascading waterfalls and rainbows are often seen. The charming separate cottage is surrounded by lawns, flowering trees and shrubs, and a variety of tropical fruit trees, far enough from the hosts' home to provide total privacy. A small commercial lime orchard adds to the green beauty of the property as well as producing wonderful limes which guests are encouraged to enjoy. Remnants of an ancient heiau (temple or royal residence) and more than 100 species of flora make this a truly unusual, special corner of the Hawaii.

Located ten miles east of Kaunakakai and eighteen miles from the airport; a rental car is absolutely essential. There is no public transportation on the island. Guests enjoy the drive along the south shore where many ancient fish ponds can be seen, arriving at their accommodations just a stone's throw from the ocean but not visible because of the trees in the area.

This studio cottage is fully furnished with everything from frying pans to a Scrabble game. Breakfast items, including fresh home grown fruits in season are supplied for do-it-yourself whenever-you-feel-like-it morning meals. The kitchen is fully equipped with refrigerator /freezer, gas range, and all cooking utensils needed for meal preparation.

There are lawn lounges for sunning, snorkels and masks and a small cooler for days at the beach, books and magazines for lazy hours, and a good selection of Hawaiian records to put on the stereo. Guests in need of quiet relaxation will find it here, and when sight seeing is the order of the day, the central location is especially convenient.

Naturally out going and friendly, these hosts often invite guests to join them when there is a luau or other special event going on. The enjoy their guests but happily respect the privacy of those who just want to be left alone.

The *children of this home* are two friendly outdoor dogs and two seldom seen cats; the dogs become seldom seen, too, when their company does not seem to be appreciated.

RATE: $60 single or double, three night minimum.

MO-4

This Oceanfront home is ten miles from the airport and ideally situated just three miles east of the historic town of Kaunakakai. The cedar log home faces the island of Lanai. Featuring a deluxe quiet bedroom with private bathroom, a private entry and small lanai facing the East Molokai Mountains. The room is warmly decorated country style, including color TV and a small refrigerator. The ocean is precisely 35 steps away. Almost an acre of gardens loaded with tropical fruit trees and plants surrounds the home. The assets include hammocks, lounges, small swimming pool with spa, Bar-B-Q, picnic table, masks, snorkels and kayaks for those experienced in watersports. Continental breakfast including garden fresh fruit is served each morning. For guests traveling with children, there is also a separate accommodation that hosts refer to as the "bunkhouse" which has a private bathroom and can sleep up to four people.

RATES: $85 single, $95 double. ($70 no breakfast)

RESTAURANTS

LOCAL STYLE

OVIEDO'S

At the east end of Kaunakakai on the mauka side of the main street. If you like Filipino food, you should like this. Everything was priced around $7, which we felt was a little high for what you get. The ice cream was good.

RABANG'S INC

In Kaunakakai on the mauka side of the street, look for the Kaunakakai market. Filipino food, very local style.

local Style

KUALAPUU COOK HOUSE

Located in the little community of Kualapuu about three miles from Kaunakakai. They have been in business since 1979 and from the looks of things they will be in business a long time. They have a spanking clean little place, reasonable priced, with the food somewhat local but quite acceptable to tourists. Friday night is pizza night. They are open Monday through Friday from 7 am to 8 pm and on Saturday from 7 am to 4 pm, closed Sunday.

MID-NITE INN

In the center of Kaunakakai. Burned down but they will be back! They were open for breakfast from 6-10, lunch from 10:30-1:30, and dinner from 5:30-9. The most expensive entree was Shrimp at $5.75. Every other entree was $5 or under. Several years ago the sons returned to Molokai and have taken a big part in running the restaurant.

KANEMITSU'S BAKERY

While we realize that breakfast is of no concern to our readers, we mention this spot for those of you who are forced to stay in other accommodation on Molokai since we hear this is the best breakfast spot on Molokai. Recently they have started serving lunch and dinner. We had lunch there and found it very much in the local flavor. One of the patrons sitting near us was very upset when he found out they ran out of poi. Open from 5:30 am to 8 pm, closed Tuesday.

OUTPOST NATURAL FOODS

If you are a health food nut this little store at the west end of Kaunakakai and just off the main street should be for you. They assured us that even the chicken sandwich was made with mock or vegie chicken, very healthful. The Juice Bar has daily lunch specials from 10-3.

JO-JO'S CAFE

Located in Maunaloa Town on the west end of Molokai. Last year we starred this as being of particular interest. This year we tried it for lunch and found the food to be very LOCAL style. The price was very reasonable, $6.50 for Korean style ribs and around $1.75 for saimin. We still recommend it for anyone fond of local style food. The place is clean, there is a nice atmosphere, and it is obvious the owners take pride in how the food is presented. Really fresh fish is available for around $6. They are open from 11 a.m. until 7:30 p.m., closed Sunday. The owner, Gary Patel, has introduced Indian curry to the menu. He also owns Munaloa General Store.

local/Tourist Style

HOTEL MOLOKAI

The best thing about the Holoholo Kai dining room is the location, right on the water's edge with a view of Lanai. The food is fair and the prices are just over moderate, $8-$15. It is located two miles east of Kaunakakai.

PAU HANA INN

Located on the ocean right in Kaunakakai. Prices are about the same as Hotel Molokai, and the food is just as good. They have a soup and salad bar and the soup was great. If you go for lunch, don't be late or they'll be closed.

KALUAKOI HOTEL

This used to be managed by the Sheraton but they sold out and it is under new management. This is the splurge restaurant of Molokai and some say the only place to dine on the Island. Lunch prices are from $5-$8, dinner from $10-$20.

POINTS OF INTEREST

KALAUPAPA

One of our hosts described her trip to Kalaupapa as a *spiritual experience* and this feeling is not uncommon. The story of the *leprosy problem* in Hawaii is a sad and fascinating one. It was late in the 1800's that the Hawaiian Government began rounding up people with leprosy and isolating them on the Kalaupapa Peninsula. Little thought was given to their needs until 1873 when Joseph Damien de Veuster, Father Damien, arrived on Molokai and devoted the rest of his life to those afflicted people. That Father Damien died of leprosy some sixteen years after his arrival attests to his devotion. While Father Damien is the most famous of those who labored at Kalaupapa, he was by no means alone; there are a host of other unsung heroes and heroines.

Since 1946 Hanson's Disease has been controlled by sulfone drugs and patients are free to leave. However, Kalaupapa has been home to these people all their lives and there would be little reason to leave.

Today there are three ways to get to Kalaupapa: walk, ride a mule, or fly. If you choose to walk, you must make prior arrangements for a guided tour as no independent exploring is allowed. To make arrangements for walking or mule riding contact Damien Tours, 567-6171, or Molokai Mule Ride, 567-6088. To fly call Air Molokai 521-0090, or Aloha Island Air 1-800-652-6541. Since airlines seem to come and go on Molokai for the best information call Molokai Airport, 567-6140.

KUALAPUU

This is an excellent example of a company town, where all of the homes were once owned and maintained by the Del Monte Company and rented to pineapple workers. Since Del Monte has cut back on pineapple production, they have been selling these homes to those who worked at the plantation. You will go through Kualapuu on your way to the Kalaupapa Lookout. The most impressive thing in town is the 104 acre Kualapuu Reservoir, which holds 1.4 billion gallons of water. Years ago C. Montegue Cooke, the first owner of the 45,000 acre ranch on the west end of Molokai, predicted that Molokai would feed the rest of the Islands. The University of Hawaii is doing extensive research, attempting to grow corn and bell peppers. Perhaps one day with their efforts and the water at Kualapuu, Molokai will be called the Pepper Island. Another thing of note is the coffee plantation, Coffees of Hawaii. The first harvest was in July 1992, by the end of the year they plan to have the mill up and running. 567-9023.

MEYER SUGAR MILL
Step back 100 years in time and experience Hawaii as it was. See the authentically restored 1878 Meyer Sugar Mill with its mule-driven cane crusher, copper clarifiers, redwood evaporating pans, and colorful steam engine, all in operating condition. Explore Molokai's early history through the fascinating lives of its original owners, Rudolph W. Meyer and his Hawaiian wife, Kalama Waha. For the fee of $2.50 for adults and $1.00 for students, we feel this is worthwhile.

PURDY'S NUTS
If you are a real explorer, you may find this small mac nut farm interesting. It is located on Lihi Pali Ave. off Farrington Rd. about a mile from Kualapuu. You can purchase either shelled or unshelled nuts. Most interesting to us was the method they used to crack the nuts. Open 10:30 - 2:30 Monday through Saturday and on Sundays from 10-1pm.

KALAUPAPA LOOKOUT
To find go four miles west of Kaunakakai on Route 46 and turn right at Route 47 and go to the end of the road. The first time we visited here the fog was so thick visibility was around ten feet and it was hard to believe there was any view at all. But dutifully we walked through the dripping ironwoods to the lookout. As we stood there the clouds suddenly lifted and the experience was beautiful beyond our ability to describe. We have been there several times since and while the experience was different, the view is always spectacular.

PHALLIC ROCK
When you park to go to the Kalaupapa Lookout you will see the sign pointing to the trail which leads to Phallic Rock. Hawaiian legend says that women who were having trouble getting pregnant could bring offerings and spend a night here and they would have no problem from then on. There is a sign there which tells the legend. Magical stones are located in other places throughout Hawaii but none we have seen is as impressive as this or as suggestive.

MAUNALOA
This little town at the west end of Molokai was once the home of Libby, McNeil, and Libby, housing their pineapple workers. Later it was taken over by Dole. Most of the land used for Pineapple was leased from the Molokai Ranch so when Dole ceased their pineapple operation, Molokai Ranch took over and now the homes are rented to some of their workers as well as the people who work at the Kaluakoi Resort or elsewhere. One can see how workers were stratified by viewing the different styles of homes. Highest on the hill were the homes of the managers of the Plantation. At the bottom of the hill are the homes of the field workers. Some might find the gallery and the kite factory interesting.

EAST OF KAUNAKAKAI

ST. JOSEPH'S CHURCH

Just past the ten mile marker on the makai side of the road. Father Damien did not restrict his ministry to Kalaupapa but circled the Island. This little church was built by him in 1876.

HALAWA VALLEY

Whatever you do, do not miss this drive. Halawa Valley is located about 30 miles from Kaunakakai and is one of the most beautiful drives anywhere in Hawaii. For the first twenty miles the road is very good and for the next ten it is rough, but absolutely manageable unless the weather is really bad. Do not be discouraged by a sudden shower as these are common on this side of the Island and go as quick as they come. At about the 22 mile marker the road turns inland and rises slightly, going through meadowed ranch land as lush and green as can be seen anywhere in the world. At about 26 miles you get your first glimpse of Halawa Valley and we encourage you to stop at one of the overlooks and enjoy the view. The road from here on down is narrow and caution is needed. However, there is so little traffic that you should have no problem. Once you see the Valley we feel sure you will feel the trip was worth while. Recently, because of some vandalism to rental cars, a security parking lot has been established. Also, it is possible to rent horses and ride part way to the falls.

MOAULA FALLS

Located a little over two miles into Halawa Valley. While this hike is not as easy as some make it sound, it is worth the trip. As you start up the trail you will be on a dirt road that is driveable and you will pass by several little houses. As you pass the last house, the trail will narrow but it is still good. Not far beyond this you will cross the stream. One tourist we talked to said the book he read said to follow the water pipe and when he did the trail ran out after about a mile and a half and he had to turn back. Once you cross the stream, the trail will be obvious. The water at the base of the falls is cold and refreshing after the long hike. Legend has it that you should throw a ti leaf on the water and if it floats you are safe, but if it sinks, the lizard who lives at the bottom of the pool will get you if you try to swim.

Be sure to take insect repellent as the mosquitoes here are fierce. Also, be careful crossing the stream if the rains have been heavy. When the river is up it is best to wait it out.

BEACHES

WEST OF KAUNAKAKAI

MOOMOMI BEACH
This is a big favorite with the local folks who assured us getting there was no problem. Well, it all depends on what you are used to. Because there had just been a storm and the last half mile of the road was washed out, we didn't quite make it by car. To get there take Farrington Rd., which runs parallel to Route 46, starting at Kualapuu Town, until it becomes a dirt road. After a little over two miles of dirt road, the road will fork. Take the right fork and go about one half mile to the beach. This area is some what protected making swimming safe when the ocean is calm, but it can be dangerous if the surf is up.

SOUTH OF THE KALUAKOI HOTEL
To get to these beaches, take the turnoff from Route 46 to the Kaluakoi Hotel but don't turn in when you reach the hotel. You will drive past the golf course and shortly after that you will see several beach access roads. The first beach past the hotel is called Papohaku and is an excellent beach for visitors since there are picnic facilities and rest rooms. Swimming on these beaches must be done with extreme care, in fact in winter we would not swim here. During the summer, if the ocean is calm, swimming is possible, but remember the advise in the introduction.

EAST OF KAUNAKAKAI

Highway 45 runs from Kaunakakai along Molokai's south and east shore for around 30 miles ending at Halawa Valley. Most of this road is along the waters edge but you will not see many beaches since the south shore of Molokai is scalloped with ancient fishponds, some in very good repair and others barely visible. An especially good example of what these ponds once were is to be seen directly across the highway from Our Lady of Sorrows Church (another Father Damien church) at about the 14 mile marker. After you pass mile marker 18 you will come to many little beaches, very safe for swimming or snorkeling. Right at mile marker 20 you will find a little park, Maui Beach, also called Morris Point, which is an excellent place to snorkel. Unfortunately, the picnic tables that used to be there have been destroyed. In fact, even the sign *Maui Beach* is gone. The water is shallow and the bottom rocky so swimming is not great. Further along you will come to some little coves where swimming is safe and the water is a little deeper. After the 23 mile marker the surf gets a little rougher and this is where the surfing starts. From here the road goes inland and the next place to take a dip is at the mouth of Halawa Valley.

NIGHT LIFE

As would be expected, there is not an abundance of night life on Molokai. People looking for lots of action would be happier some place else. However, Hawaii's top entertainers bring their shows to Molokai but not on any established dates. Basically there are three places where folks congregate after dark: the Hotel Molokai, the Pau Hana Inn, and the Ohia Lounge at the Kaluakoi. At the Holoholo Dining Room of the Hotel Molokai there is Hawaiian music every Friday and Saturday night. Local folks seem to prefer the Pau Hana Inn, where people mostly just talk story. The best place to find out what is happening at any given time is to check the Bulletin Board at the center of town or pick up a copy of the Molokai newspaper, The Pueo.

SPECIAL EVENTS

May Day is Lei Day all over Hawaii, and it seems to be an extra festive day on Molokai. Kilohana School, on the east end, entertains hundreds of people every May Day with lei-making contests; a special Hawaiian show is put on by the students, and there is a Hawaiian plate supper in the evening. This is a rare treat for the visitor.

The Great Molokai Mule Drag has gained a lot of publicity in the last year or two. This event usually takes place in September, but keep *usually* in mind. Teams of people, each team assigned a mule from the Mule Ride Stables, try to see who can pull the mule a block or two through the center of town in the shortest period of time. After the contest, it is party time, Molokai style.

The Molokai-Oahu Canoe Race is probably the best known event, taking place each year at the end of Aloha week, usually in October. It is a unique and stirring experience to stand on the beach at dawn and watch as the canoes are blessed, then carried into the water by their respective crews and maneuvered into place for the start of the race. The paddlers have competed in many races during the summer months, but this is the big one, the real test of strength and endurance. The race across the Molokai channel has become so prestigious that teams come from the mainland and the South Pacific to participate, some bringing their own canoes and others using borrowed craft.

Moloka'i Ka Hula Piko is a celebration of the Birth of the Hula on Molokai. It is held at the Papohaku Beach Park at the Kaluakoi Hotel. There is no admission charge. The festival features performances by Hawaiian musicians and singers and the Molokai hula halau (dancing troupe). Hawaiian crafts, including quilting, woodworking, and deer horn scrimshaw will be demonstrated and available for purchase. Hawaiian foods and Molokai specialties will be sold through out the day. The cultural advisor for the Destination Molokai Association will be conducting tours to historic sites celebrated in ancient chants and hula. A series of lectures on Molokai history and story telling will be presented during the week preceding the festival.

SPORTS AND ACTIVITIES

DISCOVER MOLOKAI
A local guide service for those who want to explore the hidden beauty and rich history that lies behind locked gates and on unknown trails is owned and operated by Ken and Gayle Gibson. They say to call collect for reservations, 552-2975.

BI-PLANE HAWAII
Scenic flights in an open-cockpit classic bi-plane, nostalgia at its best with helmet and goggles. Ten flights daily, weather permitting from Molokai Airport. 567-6100.

MOLOKAI RANCH WILDLIFE SAFARI
One would hardly expect to see African wildlife on Molokai but for the price of $30 for adults and $20 for kids 12 and under they can and will be seen out on Molokai's west end. A small Van leaves from the Kaluakoi Hotel four times a day: 8 a.m., 10 a.m., 1 p.m., 3 p.m. In years past we have always seemed to miss this trip, but this year one might say we got lucky. Then on the other hand...well let's not be negative. We will be descriptive and let you make up your own mind. Trips will be made if there are at least four people, and they could probably handle around ten, but it would be tight. On our trip there were six and even so it was hard not to bounce into the other passengers. Avoid the back seat unless you have a strong back. The animals are so wild that the driver summons them by blowing the horn and the trick then is to keep them out of the van. The guide pointed out that during summer months, the animals must be fed since there is little rain hence little grass for the animals to eat. Perhaps they need some African lions to thin out the population. For more information call 552-2555 which is the Kaluakoi Hotel and they will connect you.

MOLOKAI MULE RIDE
From the topside corral at an elevation of 1,600 feet, mounted on sure-footed mules led by experienced skinner-guides, meander down the Kalaupapa Trail--more than three miles and 26 switchbacks--to Makanalua Peninsula and the settlement of Kalaupapa. Trips are limited to people in good physical condition, weighing no more then 225 and not too advanced in years. Minimum age is 16. The price is $115 + 4% tax and includes a picnic lunch and Kalaupapa tour. Clothing should be slacks or jeans, sturdy shoes, visor or hat, and a light windbreaker. The tour takes around 6 hours. For reservations write to PO Box 200, Kualapuu, Molokai 96757 or call 808-567-6088,1-800-843-5978. If you did not care to ride a mule, a hike in package is offered for $30 + 4% tax. Fly in for $80 + 4% tax.

SAILING/SNORKELING
Molokai Charters offers either a two hour sunset sail for $30 per person or a full day cruise to Lanai for $75. For more information write Molokai Charters, PO Box 1207, Kaunakakai, Molokai, Hi. 96748 or call 808-553-5852.

SPORT FISHING
The only thing we could find was Joe "Captain" Reich who runs a 31' diesel for either fishing or whale watching. Write PO Box 825, Kaunakakai, Molokai 96748 or call 808-558-8377.

MOLOKAI WAGON & HORSE RIDE

Daily at noon a horse-drawn wagon rides through the world's largest mango grove, stopping at an Ancient Hawaiian Heiau (temple), along a lush tropical seashore with Lanai, Maui, and Kahoolawe in view. Learn to throw net and sample local fish and husk coconuts, try Hawaiian games and learn to do the hula. $37 adult, 12 and under half price, 5 and under free. Also, guided horseback rides, 1 and 1/2 hours long for $37. Call 808-567-6773 or 808-558-8380. Ask for Larry.

IRONWOOD HILLS GOLF COURSE

This nine hole course was built by Del Monte to provide more recreational activity for their employees. Now that Del Monte is no longer on Molokai, the fate of this course was in some doubt. However, they turned the management of the course over to the members and the course is in better condition now than ever we have seen it. Prices for visitors have gone up a little, $12 for 18 $10 for 9. If there is no one to take your money, just start playing and before you finish Andrew Luczon, the manager of the course, will find you and collect. Andrew assured us that hand carts will be available for a modest fee and if you want a cart the cost is $7 for nine holes and $10 for 18. They have increased the tees to 27 and added 22 sand traps so the course plays well. It would be hard to find without the following directions. As you drive up Highway 470 toward the Kalaupapa Lookout, .8 of a mile past the 3 mile marker you will see a dirt road going to the left. Turn here and .3 of a mile later the road will swing left up to the course. The course is not fancy but very picturesque and looks like a fun place to knock around.

KALUAKOI GOLF COURSE

Located at the Kaluakoi Hotel. We once had to chase wild turkeys or deer off the green so we could putt out. This is a great place to practice your wind game. Green Fees are around $75, cart included and mandatory.

TENNIS

There is tennis at the Kaluakoi, in Kaunakakai, and at Kualapuu. The two courts in Kaunakakai are lighted.

WINDSURFING

In our last edition we mentioned a company G.S. Enterprise that gave windsurfing lessons. Unfortunately, that is not the case. However, George, who owned G.S. says he would welcome hearing from anyone who had their own equipment and wanted to windsurf Molokai. One can reach him by calling 558-8253. Now is that being friendly, or what?

Chapter IV.....................................LANAI

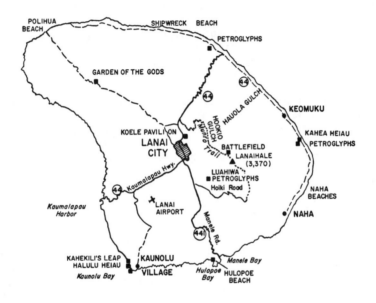

LANAI

the Pineapple Isle

The six of us boarded the twin engine Cessna 402, capacity around ten, at 9:41 am at the tiny airport of Lanai.

"Sit as far forward as possible," the pilot directed.

After cursory safety instructions about exits, life jackets, and seat belts, he positioned his ear phones and cranked over the left engine. It sputtered to life momentarily, but as the pilot attempted to increase the power the engine choked off. With a grimace and a shrug which seemed to say, "come on now, don't start giving me trouble ," he cranked her up again and this time she roared into existence without even a hiccup. The right engine did the same.

The pilot taxied quickly to the runway, poured on the power, and 18 seconds later we were airborne to the south. After about two minutes we hit the south coast of Lanai where the pilot made a sharp bank to the right and headed due west for another minute of so until we cleared the west coast of Lanai. Here he banked again sharply to the right and headed north and a few degrees to the west, a direction that would in around twenty five minutes land us at the Honolulu International Airport. One half hour to go from what some would call the sublime to what others would call the ridiculous. If a journey from Lanai is a step into the present, going to Lanai is a leap into the past. Nowhere in Hawaii is life lived on a slower more leisurely pace.

All of Lanai's 2100 inhabitants live in the ironically named Lanai City, a very symmetrically laid out company town located just about at the center of the Island. Lanai is 98% owned by Castle and Cooke, of which Dole is a subsidiary. For years pineapple has been the only crop grown on Lanai, hence the name *the Pineapple Island*. Other crops have been tried- sugar, cotton, cattle- but it was pineapple that survived. In actuality, pineapple is the only reason Lanai has the population it has. And yet we could not help but notice on our most recent trip that some of the fields that were in pineapple are now either fallow or growing wheat. In fact, Dole has decided to end pineapple production in Hawaii, and we have heard that they will be closing their plants even on Oahu.

Early explorers, including Cook's ships, ignored Lanai, concluding from its sparse vegetation and the meager items the natives offered for trade from their outrigger canoes that paddled out to meet the ships that Lanai had little to offer them. Experts disagree as to the Hawaiian population in the middle 1800's, putting the figure somewhere around 2000 at the high and 800 at the low. In the early 1900's Emory, the leading authority on Lanai, counted slightly over fifty. It is believed that the main reason for this huge decrease of indigenous people was caused by immigration to the other Islands, mainly Maui.

Right now, there is only one topic of conversation on Lanai- **CHANGE.** The big mover and shaker for this change is one David Murdock, the major stockholder and head of Castle and Cooke, hence the owner and land Lord of Lanai. Locals simply refer to Murdock as *he* in much the same way the English referred to former Prime Minister Thatcher as *she*. Murdock, evidently not content to have all his baskets filled with pineapple, has decided that what Lanai needs most are two major hotels, one mauka, one makai.

Both are now complete and ready for guests. The Lodge at Koele, located just west of Lanai City at an elevation of around 1500', has around 150 rooms that start at $295 and go much higher. Their golf course, called the Experience at Koele, is open and, let us assure you, beautiful indeed. The eighth tee is elevated 250' above the fairway with a lake to the right of the fairway. This course was designed by Greg Norman. The green fee is $95. However, golf packages are offered for those who wish to stay three or more days, and if the right time is picked a more favorable rate may be obtained.

The Manele, located at the south end of the island at Manele Bay, is as one would expect, world class and expensive. Their golf course, designed by Jack Nicholas, is scheduled to be completed by the end of 1993. That seemed to us a little ambitious since we could see no evidence of it being started. The two hotels offer quite a contrast in style, with the Lodge seeming more staid, but both are luxurious.

Also quite a contrast is the nine hole Cavandish Course, located to the right as one drives into the Lodge, which was constructed by Dole for the his workers to use. When we were on Lanai several years ago, this course had been let go and looked more like a cow pasture than a golf course. All of the attention was going to build the new course and to maintain the eighteen hole putting course. This year we noticed that it was fixed up a bit. The really good news about the Cavandish is that one can play it for free.

In spite of this development, Lanai is still the sleepiest little place in Hawaii, and Castle & Cooke is working very hard to find employment for the former pineapple workers, those on Lanai as well as the other Islands. One cannot imagine that life on Lanai is as it was five or six years ago, but whether people are better off or worse off, we are not prepared to say. Castle & Cooke has constructed a community park, complete with football and soccer fields and a seventy-five foot swimming pool. The down-side of this is that the pool lacked insurance and could not be used for over a year after it was built. That seems to have been straightened out and the pool is being used. One of the senior citizens told us he had promised to build a new senior citizen center up on the hill. "But even if he does," she scoffed, "nobody will use it. How many of us can walk up that hill?" At times it seems that developers are insensitive to the needs and desires of local folk. For example, we were told that to assure the locals that all that was happening was O.K., Kenny Rogers was brought in to explain how things were going to work. After he spoke reassuring words, he informed all of the pineapple field workers that to show how sincere Castle & Cooke were each and every local was going to get free tennis lessons. Let us hope that in years to come a journey to Lanai will still be a leap back in time. Perhaps there is a need for Honolulus and Lahainas but not everywhere.

HOSTS

L-1

Lucille has retired from her profession as a Registered Nurse in 1985 and now finds time to devote to guests so has decided to offer two of the bedrooms in her home to B & B travelers. One room offers a double and single bed while the other has a queen sized bed. Her home is modest but very comfortable. There is a full bath and a half bath, both of which are shared by hostess and guests. Both of the bedrooms are good sized and well furnished. The hostess is a long time resident of Lanai and quite a fascinating person. She is an inveterate collector of bottles, shells, and other curios, and has made some finds of ancient Hawaiian artifacts that any museum would be proud to own. She is also an artist and at one time had her work displayed in the Lanai Hotel. This accommodation could be ideal for those really anxious to get away from it all. Beach towels and mats are available. Just five miles from the airport and within walking distance of the Hotel Lanai for meals, a car is not really necessary. Lucille can arrange for pickup to and from the airport (or Ferry), $10 back and forth. No smoking inside the house, please.
RATE: $45 single, $50 double, $25 extra person in the same room or on a futon in the front room, if needed.

RESTAURANTS

LANAI HOTEL

For all practical purposes this is the only restaurant in town (except for the hotels where dinner can be had for around $100 a couple). Each night a different special is offered, with Thursday being prime rib. They are also open for lunch from 11 am to 2 pm. The Lanai Hotel, also owned by Castle & Cooke, rents rooms for $95. While we were there things were a mess since they were undergoing extensive restoration. The attempt will be to make it like a early 20th century luxury hotel.

There are two little places in town where one can get a sandwich or a hamburger. One is a little bakery/restaurant, the other is called S and J Properties and is next door to the bakery. The food is fixed for local tastes but eating hear makes an interesting contrast with the hotels.

BEACHES

There are many beaches on Lanai but few that are easily accessible. The one we visited, Hulopoe at Manele Bay, was excellent. If you get there in the morning you will find the beach quite crowded. By 2 pm, however, you will find the place almost deserted since almost everyone there came over from Maui on the windjammer for an afternoon of snorkeling. The beach is very safe for swimming and lots of fun for body surfing. If you really want to get away from it all and you have a rental car or jeep drive to the north side of the Island. To get there go past the Lodge at Koele and go to the end of the paved road. When you reach the ocean, turn right and you will be on dirt road but very driveable, where you can drive along the ocean shore for around ten miles. What was most fun was seeing all the wild turkeys.

OAHU.....THE GATHERING PLACE

.....DRIVING TIMES.....

From Honolulu airport to: (approximate)

Downtown Honolulu.................. 5 miles, 15 minutes
University of Hawaii.................10 miles, 30 minutes
Waikiki.......................................11 miles, 30 minutes
Aloha Stadium......................... 3 miles, 10 minutes
Hanauma Bay...........................20 miles, 45 minutes
Sea Life Park............................24 miles, 50 minutes
Pearl City.................................10 miles, 30 minutes
Kailua.......................................20 miles, 40 minutes
Kaneohe....................................18 miles, 36 minutes

OAHU

The Gathering place

To many people, both those who have been to the Islands and those who have not, Oahu is synonymous with Hawaii. In fact, Oahu is thought of as Honolulu and to narrow it down even further, many people equate Waikiki with Honolulu. In reality Honolulu is much more than Waikiki and Oahu is much more than Honolulu, and the State of Hawaii is more than these put together. Yet, around 80 percent of Hawaii's population live and work in Honolulu. Also, Waikiki gets more visitors by far than any other place in Hawaii. The effect is that many people who have vacationed at Waikiki think they have seen Hawaii and nothing could be further from the truth.

The real meaning of *oahu* has been lost to antiquity. Tourist industry people like to say it means the *Gathering Place*, and for a long time that appellation has been used. Residents of Hawaii refer to it as the *Main Island* since everything and most everyone passes through Honolulu. It is also called the *Capitol Island* since it is the seat of all State Government.

Oahu, the third largest island in the chain behind Hawaii and Maui, is made up of two fair sized mountain ranges: the Koolau Mountains in the east, and the Waianae Mountains in the west. In between is a broad expanse of flatland devoted either to the military or to farmland. Honolulu, the dominant city in Hawaii, sits just in the lee of the Koolau Range.

Unfortunately, when most people think of Oahu they think only of Honolulu and Waikiki and fail to realize that Oahu has as much natural beauty as any of the neighbor Islands. Few drives in Hawaii are more scenic than the drive east of Honolulu, past Hanauma Bay, around the point past Sandy Beach and then a few short miles on to Waimanalo. Nor can the north shore of Oahu be rivaled for its expansive beaches, where in the winter waves twenty feet and bigger crash with unimaginable fury. When this surf is at its highest, even the greatest surfers back off.

By no means do we intend to suggest that Honolulu and Waikiki are places for tourists to bypass. While we have heard the claim that Honolulu is just like any city except warmer, there are enough differences to make a visit here unique. We simply want to urge people who have heard the bad rap (that Oahu is too crowded, just a big city, a tourist rip off) to realize that there is much to do and see besides the Honolulu/Waikiki scene. Do yourself a favor and explore the rest of the Island and we feel sure you will be pleasantly surprised.

SPECIAL EVENTS

CHERRY BLOSSOM FESTIVAL (MID JANUARY)
A Japanese cultural celebration that includes a variety of events and held in Honolulu. For more information call 808-949-2255.

HULA BOWL GAME (MID JANUARY)
Annual college all-star football classic. Aloha Stadium, 808-486-9300.

NFL PRO BOWL (EARLY FEBRUARY)
Annual all-star football game involving the National and American Conferences. Aloha Stadium.

HAWAIIAN OPEN GOLF TOURNAMENT (LATE JANUARY OR EARLY FEBRUARY)
Held at the Waialae Country Club in Kahala. Call 808-526-1232.

ANTHURIUM SHOW (MARCH)
Held at the Ward Warehouse. Call Connie Wright 946-1641.

HAWAII CHALLENGE INTERNATIONAL SPORT KITE CHAMPIONSHIP (EARLY MARCH)
A three day annual celebration since 1982 with competitions, demonstrations, displays, workshops,games and entertainment held at Kapiolani Park in Waikiki. Call Kite Fantasy, 922-5483.

MAKAPUU BODY SURFING CHAMPIONSHIPS (MID MARCH)
For information call Bob Thomas, 808-396-8342.

ST. PATRICK'S DAY PARADE (MARCH 17)
Starts at noon in Waikiki.

HAWAIIAN ADOPT A DUCKIE RACE (END OF MARCH)
More than 15,00 little yellow rubber ducks start at the McCully St. bridge and race down the Ala Wai Canal in Waikiki. A benefit for United Cerebral Palsy of Hawaii, 808-538-6789.

HAWAIIAN HIGHLAND GATHERING (EARLY APRIL)
A gathering of the clans for Scottish games, competitions, Scottish foods, Highland dancing, and pipe bands. Held at Richardson Field, Pearl Harbor. Call Paul Lynch, 808-523-5050.

ANNUAL HAWAII INVITATIONAL INTERNATIONAL MUSIC FESTIVAL (MID-APRIL)
The best high school marching, jazz, and concert bands from Australia, New Zealand, Japan, Canada and mainland U.S. Call Johan Riggle, 800-854-8191.

ANNUAL CAROLE KAI INTERNATIONAL BED RACE (MID APRIL)
A zany race proceeded by a parade from Fort DeRussy to Kapiolani Park in Waikiki. Call 808-735-6092.

SAMOAN FLAG DAY CELEBRATION (MID APRIL)
A parade, Samoan flag raising ceremony, speeches, Samoan dancing and singing held at Keehi Lagoon Park, Honolulu. Call Gus Hanneman, 395-7800.

BROMELIAD SHOW (EARLY MAY)
held at Ward Warehouse in Honolulu. Call Connie Wright, 946-1641.

STATE FAIR (LATE MAY TO MIDDLE JUNE)
Held on consecutive weekends at Aloha Stadium.

ANNUAL FANCY FAIR (EARLY JUNE)
Hawaii's finest crafts people display, demonstrate, and sell their wares. Food and entertainment. Mission House Museum, admission free, call Nina Aymond 808-531-0481.

ANNUAL HAWAIIAN FESTIVAL OF MUSIC (MIDDLE TO LATE JUNE)
Music groups from mainland and hawaii compete in festival of stage and symphonic bands, concert choirs, madrigal and swing groups and marching bands. Held at Waikiki Shell, 808-944-2799.

ANNUAL HONFED BETTER HOME SHOW (MIDDLE JUNE)
Hundreds of food and new products booths plus the latest in audio and video equipment. Held at Neil Blaisdell Center in Honolulu, 808-545-6718.

KING KAMEHAMEHA HULA AND CHANT COMPETITION (LATE JUNE)
Two nights of hula competition both modern and ancient by some of Hawaii's finest halaus (hulA schools). Call 808-536-6540.

MOLOKAI COMES TO WARD WAREHOUSE (JULY)
Held at the Ward Warehouse. Call Connie, 946-1641.

MID-SUMMER'S NIGHT GLEAM (MID JULY)
A moonlight walk with art and entertainment in Foster Garden, Honolulu, call Caroline Dvojacki, 808-537-1708.

ANNUAL UKULELE FESTIVAL (LATE JULY)
Hundreds of ukulele players perform, held at Queen Kapiolani Park Bandstand, Waikiki, call Roy Sakuma, 808-487-6010.

HULA FESTIVAL (MIDDLE AUGUST)
Graduates from Summer Fun classes perform at Queen Kapiolani Park Bandstand, Waikiki, call 808-521-6905.

SUMMER JAM KITE FESTIVAL
At Kualoa Park. Call Kite Fantasy, 922-5483.

ANNUAL GABBY PAHINUI/ATTA ISAACS SLACK KEY GUITAR FEST (EARLY AUGUST)
The best slack-key guitar artists in Hawaii perform from 3:30 to 9:30 at McCoy Pavilion Ala Moana Park, Honolulu, call Milton Lau, 808-522-7030.

ANNUAL PARADE OF HOMES (MID TO LATE SEPTEMBER)
A chance to tour some beautiful Hawaii homes, 808-847-4666.

HONOLULU ORCHID SOCIETY SHOW (OCTOBER)
An exhibit of thousands of varieties of orchids by Hawaii's orchid growers, held at Blaisdell Center, Honolulu, 808-527-5400.

FORD ISLAND KITE FLYERS EXHIBITION (OCTOBER)
In conjunction with the Hydro-foil Races. This year it's rumored that the Blue Angels will perform. Call Kite Fantasy, 922-5483.

KANIKAPILA (LET'S PLAY MUSIC-MID OCTOBER)
Annual festival of Hawaiian music featuring singers, musicians, and dancers from several Islands. Held at Andrews Amphitheatre, Honolulu, 808-948-8178.

KAMEHAMEHA SCHOOLS HO'OLAULE'A (NOVEMBER)
An old style Hawaiian Festival held at Kamehameha Schools, 808-842-8663.

PEARL HARBOR ALOHA FESTIVAL (NOVEMBER)
The largest military festival of its kind in Hawaii. A fair with rides, games, food, and exhibits. Call Frank De Silva, 808-471-0818.

ACADEMY FOLK ART BAZAAR (NOVEMBER)
Sale of folk art items and Christmas ornaments from around the world, held at Honolulu Academy of Arts. Call 808-538-3693.

FESTIVAL OF TREES (EARLY DECEMBER)
A display of one-of-a-kind decorated trees, wreaths, decorations, and gifts. Proceeds go to Queens's Medical Center, 808-547-4371.

DOWNTOWN CHRISTMAS CRAFTS FAIRE (MID DECEMBER)
Over 50 vendors offer one of a kind, hand crafted items including Christmas ornaments. Held at AmFac Plaza, downtown Honolulu, 808-521-2749.

**Be sure to let us know
what we have left out
so we can include it in our next edition!
Or you may want
to call or write for more information.**

**B & B Hawaii
Box 449 Kapaa, Hi. 96746
or call 808-822-7771**

OAHU HOSTS

HONOLULU AREA

O-30
This large family home is located on the hillside of Manoa Valley. It is quiet, cool and surrounded with birds. The guest room has a queensize bed; a child could be accommodated with a futon. The shared bath sports a claw-foot bathtub with a shower. Breakfast is served either in the dining room with a wrap around view of Waikiki, Honolulu and beautiful Manoa Valley or on the spacious and sunny front deck. The hosts are very well informed about what is happening on Oahu and love sharing that knowledge with their guests. The host is the news editor for the Honolulu Advertiser. Both are interested in civic and cultural events. The bus stops one block down the hill. Smokers are invited to enjoy their smoking material outside on the front deck.
RATES: $30.00 single, $45.00 double.

O-22
"Outstanding views and a Diamond Head carriage-trade location on the edge of beach and tourist attractions" are only two of the good things to say about this house. This sprawling, two story family residence is home to your hostess, her housekeeper and one dog. Five adult children with assorted mates and off spring stop by on come & go visits. Even if some of them are "at home", there is still room for B & B guests. Two upstairs suites are reserved for B&B - each with a private bath and outdoor lanai. The 'Mauka" (mountain) suite has a view of Diamond Head and an historic bed that is "larger than some economy rooms". The 'Makai' (ocean) suite has two double beds and a view of the garden plus Waikiki Lights from the lanai. No need for an alarm clock as you wake up to the sounds of birds every morning.The house is furnished with a mixture of local and American antiques. The home is an expression of some of the hosts' interests--Hawaiian History and Contemporary Art.
RATES: $75 single, $100 double.

O-26
Stay in this beautifully situated home in the best part of Hawaii Kai and guests will enjoy a spectacular ocean view from this hillside setting. No matter where breakfast is served whether it be on the lanai or in the dining room, guests can never get away from the views. The whole downstairs level of the house is devoted to b&b and able to accommodate six people altogether. Sliding glass doors facing the ocean run the length of each room.   The Double bedroom has an adjoining private bath, TV, plus appliances for light cooking (refrigerator & microwave). The other two rooms share a bathroom. One offers a double bed while the other has two twin beds and is furnished with a color TV. Across the hall is the hosts' den which has a refrigerator for guests' use. Non-smokers only.
RATES: All bedrooms: $40 single, $50 double. For $10 an additional person can be accommodated in the same room with a portable twin bed. Two night minimum.

O-53

Built on the hillside, in cool, quiet Manoa Valley, about 1/5 miles from the University of Hawaii at Manoa campus, this home has two B&B rooms available for guests. A very quiet and relaxed atmosphere can be enjoyed far away from the hustle and bustle of Waikiki. Guests are encouraged to sit on the large deck and view the city skyline and ocean beyond. Guest rooms are roomy, thickly carpeted, light and airy. One room offers a queen sized bed and private bath with shower. The other offers extra-long twin beds and a private 1/2 bath connected to a shower shared with the hostess. Guests are advised that there is an inside cat. Smoking is not allowed inside the house, please. Children over 8 years or non walking infants are accepted. Three night minimum.
RATES: $55 single, $65 double, $10 extra for one child on a futon in the same room.

O-53A

This quiet, peaceful retreat is only ten minutes from Waikiki and Ala Moana Shopping Center. A separate residence, downstairs from a two story home offers a lovely two bedroom plus large sleeping porch on the hillside overlooking Manoa Valley with a spectacular view of Diamond Head and the Waikiki skyline. **There is no breakfast served or provided here.** 1150 square feet of space includes a living room, dining room, fully furnished kitchen and bathroom. The sleeping porch and one bedroom are furnished with a queen size bed and the other bedroom has a double bed. Amenities include cable TV, stereo, telephone and microwave. Parking is provided. This unit may not be suitable for children between 2 and 5 years of age. No smoking in the house, please. Three night minimum, discount for weekly stay.
RATES: $95 double, $25 extra for 3rd person, $20 extra for 4th person, $15 each addtl person up to 7.

O-66

Guests will enjoy this beautiful Kahala home just two blocks from the Waialae Golf Course, the beach and the Kahala Hilton Hotel. Your hosts, a kamaaina couple of several generations will be happy to help you with dinner ideas or any suggestions on outings. There are two different accommodations available. The one bedroom apartment on the ground floor is stylishly furnished with beautiful antiques. The bedroom has a queen sized bed and a private bathroom with tub and shower. It has a full kitchen stocked with Continental- style breakfast fixings. French doors open to a covered lanai where guests may bar-b-que. The living room is constantly supplied with fresh flowers and offers a TV and a private phone. The upstairs apartment has views of golf course. This two bedroom suite has a king sized bed in the master bedroom and queen sized bed in the other room. The beautiful bathroom consists of a tub and a separate shower. In the living room there is a TV and private telephone. This apartment has a full kitchen that is completely stocked with Continental-style breakfast fixings. Both apartments have central air conditioning. Guests may use the swimming pool. Hours for use of the pool are available. No smoking, please. A three night minimum is preferred.
RATES: $100 single or double, $15 extra per person in the two bedroom apartment.

EAST HONOLULU AREA

O-4

This home is located just three blocks from the ocean in a quiet residential neighborhood just beyond Kahala. The home is handy to stores, the bus line, a beach park, restaurants, and tennis courts. The hosts are happy to provide rackets. The accommodation has twin beds, TV, refrigerator and sliding doors opening onto a small, private garden area for outside sitting. The bathroom is shared. Smoking must be done outside the house. Children are welcome. A continental breakfast is provided. The host is from Iowa and the hostess from Kentucky. They have been in Hawaii since the Fall of 1963. Both have traveled in England and Scotland, have a strong interest in things Scottish, and in genealogical research. They are long time residents of Hawaii who are willing to assist guests with their travel questions.
RATES: $40 single, $45 double, and an additional $5.00 for a child in the same room. Two night minimum.

O-19

"Oh to be in England" which some say is where all this bed and breakfast started in the first place. Well, here the guests can imagine they are in England since our hosts, mother and daughter are from England, and really have learned to combine that old world charm with new world Aloha to make sure that their guests have a good time. In this home there is a spacious, airy bedroom with private bathroom, queen size bed, color TV and a sliding door leading to the swimming pool. There is a smaller upstairs bedroom with a shared bath for another couple travelling, however it is not the primary room. Breakfast is served in the dining room where the hosts join their guests at the table, making themselves readily available with suggestions and advice on places of interest. Non-smokers only, please.
RATES: $50 single, $55 double, $45 for smaller room. Two night minimum.

O-40

This lovely condominium on the water way in Hawaii Kai is hosted by a single lady who knows quite a bit about Oahu and can give guests good recommendations on what to do and where to go while exploring Oahu. The home is located close to Hanauma Bay for excellent snorkeling. There are two single beds which can also be pushed together for a king sized bed. There is a shared bathroom with a tub and shower in the hall next to the bedroom. No smokers, please.
RATES: $35 single, $40 double.

O-54

Spectacular birdseye views of Diamond Head, the Waialae Country Club and the entire Honolulu coastline can be enjoyed from the private deck of this little studio. This is a good location, with Kahala Mall just at the bottom of the hill for shopping and fine dining. The studio is attached to the hosts' main house and yet is totally private as it has it's own entrance along the side of the house. Sliding glass doors off the lanai open into an air conditioned bedroom with king sized bed and a private bathroom. There is also a sitting room furnished with a couch and small table and TV. Along one wall is an apartment sized washer/dryer plus a light kitchenette for snacks and breakfast preparation. Your hosts stock the mini fridge with breakfast fixings. Smoking on the deck only, please. A car is a necessity at this home. Hosts prefer a three night minimum.
RATES: $65 single or double.

O-65

An Artist's Place is great for exploring Honolulu without being in the heart of Waikiki. Swim in the pool and enjoy the views of the ocean and Diamond Head. Accommodations include a two room suite with a full sized water bed and private sitting room that has a single bed for a child or can be used if two single adults are travelling together and need two beds. There is private bath for guests. Breakfasts are usually eaten out by the pool. Two night minimum.
RATES: $ 70 single or double, $30 for extra person.

AIEA

O-1A

This beautiful B&B home is located fight in the center of Oahu with easy access to all the sights and yet in a secluded tropical setting with marvelous views of Pearl Harbor, the mountains and the entire south coast of Oahu. This private apartment is garden level and offers your own swimming pool surrounded by fruit and shade trees and lawn area. Located at the end of a cul-de-sac, in one of Oahu's nicer executive neighborhoods, it is on a valley often filled with rainbows. The apartment has a separate entrance from the main home and tiled private bath with Japanese decor. It is fully equipped for long of short stays with plenty of extras like ice chest, beach mats and chairs ...even wine glasses. The book shelves are filled with interesting books on Hawaii and the hosts, a retire naval officer and wife, who long time residents, are always willing to assist with suggestions and directions. There is a double bed and a futon for third person. Air conditioning and color cable TV are provided along with use of a washer/ dryer. A public golf course is just minutes away.
RATES: $60 single or double, $360/week, $10 extra for third person.

KANEOHE AREA

O-24

Wake up to the cool Kaneohe breeze as birds in the forest back of the guest cottage start to sing. As you step out onto the large deck in order to swim in your own private pool, you will be awed by the majesty and beauty of the Koolau Mountain range which looms just a short distance away. This guest cottage, along with the deck and pool, is located on a separate level just 20 steps up from the the hosts' residence; therefore, it provides a very private accommodation for guests. This unit sleeps four comfortably with one double bed and two single beds all in the same room. It is ideal for a family. The unit has a small kitchenette area which includes a hot plate, sink and small refrigerator. Supermarkets, shopping centers and excellent eating places are located only a few blocks away. Some of the finest beaches in Hawaii are located on the Windward side of Oahu and can be reached in a few minutes from this central location. Two night minimum.
RATES: $55 single or double. $10 for extra person.

O-56

Windward B&B is a luxuriously furnished private home with beautiful views of Kaneohe Bay from the living room, dining room and swimming pool area. Your hosts offer two bedrooms each with private bath. One room offers twin beds with bath across the corridor, while the other is furnished with a double bed and has the bath attached. Ample, relaxed breakfasts are served each morning. Afternoon tea is served in the late afternoon and ice and glasses are provided in the library in the evenings.
RATES: Twin Room: $50 single or double, Double Bed Room: $55 single or double.

O-64

Hula Kai Hale (House of the Dancing Waters) sits at the end of a private road and offers guests a casual atmosphere and hospitality. Guests enjoy their breakfast poolside on the party size lava rock lanai and watch the boats sail in and out of the neighboring Kaneohe Yacht Club. A plentiful breakfast is served from the sideboard in the dining room. Two clean, cheerful rooms are offered each with private bath and separate entrance. The larger suite has a bedroom with queen bed plus the sitting room is furnished with sofa and dinette, TV, small refrigerator and microwave for light snacks or picnic lunches. The other room has double bed and offers a small refrigerator also. Three night minimum.
RATES: Suite $60 single or double, Double room $55. Extra adult in the den, $25.

NORTHSHORE

O-46

A perfect spot on the ocean just 1/2 mile from the Polynesian Cultural Center. Guests stay in the main house in the bedroom with a king size bed or two twins, there is an additional bedroom with a twin bed for one extra person. The bathroom is shared and has tub & shower. Both hosts work yet make sure breakfast is prepared and waiting for you. They suggest dining on the deck by the beach. Their hobby is singing and playing Hawaiian music. Both are well versed in Hawaiiana as host is a local boy and hostess majored in Hawaiian studies in college. They have a large collection of books and music. Hosts prefer non smokers only. Three night minimum.
RATES: $45 single, $55 double, Three people in two rooms $75.

KAILUA AREA

O-6

A great location for enjoying Lanikai Beach. This accommodation in the downstairs area of a beautiful two story A-frame cedar home. There is a bedroom with a queen sized bed as well as a queen sized futon bed with a wooden frame in the living room area. Light cooking can be done from the kitchenette and the dining table with four chairs faces the park which is only down the street about 1 block. A family of five can be accommodated here as there is also a futon for a child. Hostess is a massage therapist. She provides a nice breakfast which usually consists of a fruit bowl, coffee and croissants. Three night minimum.
RATES: $85 single or double, $10 each extra person.

O-8A

Within walking distance to the beautiful Kailua beach and on the canal, this cozy studio apartment is perfect for longer stays. Guests have their own entrance and parking. Inside there is a kitchenette with cooking appliances for light meals and snacks. No **breakfast is served or provided at this location.** There is a queen sized bed in the bedroom area. A large bathroom is complete with a two person jacuzzi tub. An additional queen bed is furnished. Your host family; father, mother, and two young boys have a swimming pool that they encourage guests to share which overlooks the canal and majestic pali. Your hostess teaches preschool and enjoys interaction with her guests. Five night minimum.
RATES: $395 weekly, $56 for additional nights, $65 daily for minimum stays. $20 each additional person.

O-9A

Not only is this a delightful accommodation but it is just across the street from one of the most beautiful beaches in Hawaii. The accommodation offered is a fully furnished garden studio in a tropical setting. Guests have their own private lanai for relaxing after they have tired of the beach activities. The apartment is beautifully furnished with the added touch of Oriental rugs. Since the apartment is fully furnished and is located at a prime spot in Lanikai, this would be ideal for long or short stays. Both host and hostess are true kamaaina and full of the aloha spirit. The unit has a queen sized bed and a large bath. Guests usually eat their breakfast out on the private garden view patio.
RATES: $55 nightly. Three night minimum preferred.

O-12

This accommodation is great because guests can lounge by the swimming pool and enjoy a leisurely breakfast or sit in the hot tub after a day of sightseeing. Just one mile from Kailua Beach in a nice quiet neighborhood area. Hosts offer a choice of two rooms with a shared bath between them. One room has a double bed and the other with a twin bed. Guests can use the hosts' fridge to keep light snacks. Hosts accept children and have a port a crib to use. One night stays are accepted at $5 extra.
RATES: $40 single, $45 double

O-13A

Imagine waking up from a good night's sleep on a raised bamboo-frame, all cotton futon bed and seeing the incredible blue turquiose waters and white sandy beach right outside your windows. This studio in Lanikai offers a private entrance and private bathroom. The sitting area has full ocean views as well as a wet bar for preparing light snacks and picnic lunches. Your host, a professional photographer, uses his own front yard for most of his shooting since it is one of the most photogenic beach scenes around. Three night minimum.
RATES: $125 single or double

O-15A

This hostess has a large property on the ocean in Waimanalo. Two separate accommodations are offered to B & B guests, each a little different. The Mauka Suite has a large bedroom with a queen sized bed done in Polynesian style. It has a small fridge, TV, and a spacious bathroom with tub and shower. It has a private entrance that opens to a fenced secluded garden and lanai. The spectacular Koolau Mountain Range offers a breathtaking view. Also offered is the large and elegant Ocean Suite with sleeping/living room, private bath, and a separate entrance that opens to its own garden and lanai area. Large picture windows offer views over the wide expansive lawn area to the white sandy beach and ocean. Both of the units has a private access to a safe white sand swimming beach. Breakfast is served each morning and guests have use of the host's kitchen.
RATES: Mauka suite $65 one rate, five night minimum. Ocean Suite $75 one rate, five night minimum.

O-16

A gracious home in Kailua on a private access road one half block from a safe swimming beach. For runners, beach or bike lanes are near by. There are two large comfortable bedrooms with adjoining bath -- a choice of twin or double beds. This is ideal for couples traveling together. Two covered lanais (patios) surrounded by tropical foliage are for the guests to enjoy. A separate refrigerator is provided. A neighborhood shopping center and restaurants are within walking distance. Adults only. Breakfast is served either outside on the patio or in the main dining room. Two night minimum.
RATES: $50 single, $65 double.

O-17

This contemporary home, a short five minutes drive from the beach, offers guests two choices, a bedroom with two twin beds or one with a double bed. The two guest rooms share a full bathroom. The home is open and airy and breakfast is often served on the lush and secluded lanai. Your hosts are recently married; the hostess was raised on Oahu and works at the Kamehameha Schools, a private school for Hawaiian students. Her husband is a recently retired math teacher from California and is studying Hawaiian language and the hula. Both will be happy to share with guests their love of Hawaii. They are also volunteer mediators at the Neighborhood Justice Center and enjoy music performances of all kinds. One cat, whose name is Ni'ele, which means 'curious'. Two night minimum.
RATES: $40 single, $45 double.

O-25

This delightful host home in Kailua offers two rooms each with private bath and air conditioning. Hosts have a beautiful garden with covered patio and pool for guests to enjoy. Breakfasts are a treat with something different every day. Guests have a bedroom with queen sized bed private full bathroom featuring sliding glass doors out to the pool area. For two couples travelling together there is an additional bedroom available with a queen sized bed and adjoining private bathroom. Non smokers only please. Two night minimum.
RATES: $65 single or double.

O-27

This home has easy access to the expansive Kailua beach. The hosts offer an attractive studio apartment with a new screened-in lanai. The interior is furnished with twin beds and a loft. It has light kitchen facilities and an outdoor barbeque. This is a roomy studio and could accommodate a family of four. The hosts have outdoor cats and one dog. Smoking on lanai only. Continental breakfast includes: coffee, tea, fresh fruit, rolls and juice.
RATES: $60 double. Three night minimum.

O-31

An elegant ocean front home opens in front on a large pool with jacuzzi and in back opens to the ocean. The home is spacious and has comfortable areas for guests to relax after a day of sightseeing. All the bedrooms with private baths are handsomely furnished with an antique and tropical mixture. Each bedroom has a private entrance from the pool/courtyard area. A deluxe continental breakfast is served. Treat yourself to a luxurious B&B experience.
RATES: $120 single or double.

O-32

This Bed & Breakfast apartment is attached to the host home but has a private entrance with private porch which features a two person swing and faces the older neighborhood, colorfully landscaped with bougainvillea, hibiscus and palm trees. The unit consists of living room, bedroom with a queen size bed and private bathroom. It's equipped with a microwave, refrigerator, toaster, coffee maker, TV and radio and ceiling fans in the living room and bedroom. Kailua beach, where guests can snorkel, wind surf, surf, sail or rent a canoe, is a five minute drive as are restaurants and shopping. Horseback riding is also available in the area. Hostess works at Castle Hospital just three blocks away and also speaks German.
RATES: $55.00 single or double without breakfast, however, coffee and tea are provided.

O-42

These hosts make a hobby out of remodeling already beautiful homes and this one is a gem! A block away from beautiful Kailua beach in Kailua, guests have two newly remodeled bedrooms available. The larger of the two has king size bed and a comfortable setee. The smaller one has twin beds that can convert to king size bed. Both rooms have full private bath, TV, microwave and refrigerator, a separate entrance plus use of the hosts' swimming pool where guests can enjoy a dip or "catch a few rays". **Breakfast supplies and fixings for the first three mornings are stocked to use at your leisure.** The host is a contractor and the hostess is from England originally and finds time to take a few courses at the University besides hosting B&B guests. Truly a charming and top notch accommodation.
RATES: Hibiscus Room: $60 single or double. Pikake Room: $50 single or double. Three night minimum

O-44

Just one block from Kailua beach hosts offer three different accommodations on their beautifully landscaped property. The first one is a separate one bedroom cottage with complete kitchen including microwave and double door refrigerator. The Cottage can sleep up to four with a double bed in the bedroom and a double hide-a-bed in the living area. There is a color TV with cable and a private bath. Guests can enjoy the private outside patio area. The second one is The Studio attached to the house with it's own private entrance. This accommodation can sleep three people comfortably with a full size bed and murphy bed in the studio. There is a kitchenette and private bath as well as a color TV with cable and a private patio area for outside sitting. The New Unit can sleep only two with a double bed. It is also furnished with a light kitchenette and color cable TV. Four night minimum preferred. **No breakfast is served or provided.**
RATES: The Cottage: $65 single or double plus $10 extra for three or four. Studio: $55 single or double plus $10 extra for third person. New Unit: $60 single or double.

O-57

Walking distance to the beautiful, white, sandy Kailua beach a full two bedroom apartment on the ground level of this two story home. The complete downstairs accommodation has white ceramic tile throughout and offers two bedrooms: one with a queen bed the other with two twins. There is a full private bathroom and a complete laundry room and kitchenette with microwave and full sized refrigerator plus a hotplate and toaster oven. The living room is complete with TV and rattan furniture and has sliding glass doors which open out to the patio and fenced yard where guests can enjoy the sun. Perfect for a family of four. Smoking outside only, please.
RATES: $75 double, $100 for a family of four.

O-63

Located just 9 houses from beautiful Kailua beach (five minute walk). A separated cottage detached from the main house offers a full bathroom with tub and shower and a large 23' x 20' room. Private parking, outside shower to rinse off after the beach, full use of the pool, gazebo, deck and gas BBQ. Queen sized bed, TV, clock radio, telephone, refrigerator, microwave, coffee pot and toaster. The cottage is ideal for a couple. Although the hosts do not serve breakfast, they provide fresh fruit, coffee, cereal and breakfast bread, plus goodies for snacking.
RATES: $65 single or double. Five night minimum.

DO ANY OF THE ABOVE MEET YOUR NEEDS?
REMEMBER BED AND BREAKFAST IS A MORE PERSONAL,
MORE AFFORDABLE,
MORE ENJOYABLE WAY TO VISIT HAWAII.
TO MAKE A BOOKING JUST WRITE TO
B & B HAWAII
BOX 449 KAPAA, HI. 96746
OR CALL 808-822-7771
VISA OR MASTERCARD ACCEPTED TO MAKE BOOKING
1-800-733-1632

HONOLULU

Located on the south shore of the Island of Oahu, protected by one of the Island's two mountain ranges, the Koolaus, with the Waianaes far to the west, the city of Honolulu contains more people, stores, restaurants and whatever else is needed to make a city than all of the rest of Hawaii combined. If the population of the state nears one million, seventy to eighty percent reside in Honolulu. It is a large city and has the attendant problems that all large cities have: overcrowding, heavy traffic, crime, and even some smog, but not much. Even with these detractions Honolulu is a pleasant place, easy to get around either by car or public transportation, a city that is unique in many ways.

For anyone with an interest in the history of Hawaii, time spent visiting historical sites in Honolulu is invaluable. Then, Honolulu's Chinatown is small but certainly worth seeing. Even in this bustling city, however, nature's beauty is close by. Just a few short blocks from Chinatown is the Foster Botanical Garden (see Points of Interest below) where tourists can see most of the flora of Hawaii and other tropical climes.

For our purposes we have divided the city into five areas: 1) downtown, 2) midtown, 3) Kaimuki/Kapahulu, 4) Waikiki, and 5) east of Honolulu. For each area as for other areas throughout the Islands, we will list first restaurants, then points of interest, beaches, night life, and sports activities. We do not cover all restaurants in Honolulu by any means but have chosen some that both we and our hosts have enjoyed. Since we intend updating this guide every year or so, we invite your comments and suggestions. If you have a special place on Oahu that we fail to mention, please let us know.

DOWNTOWN

Finding downtown Honolulu can be confusing since the Ala Moana Shopping Center is where you will find most of the major stores, and Waikiki is where you will see most of the tall buildings. The downtown area which for our purposes includes Chinatown is bordered on the west by Ward Ave., the east by River St., the north by Beretania, and the south by Ala Moana Blvd., with the main streets being King and Beretania. It is in this area that one will find the Iolani Palace, the Court House, the King Kamehameha statue, the State Capitol, the Mission Houses Museum, the Academy of Arts, and most of the financial institutions of Hawaii. This area is small and it is best to park in one of the garages and tour the area on foot.

As stated above, most of the department stores and shops are in Ala Moana Center but one good place to shop is in the Liberty Penthouse at the corner of King Street and Bishop. While there are lots of bargains, you need to look to find them. There is also a Liberty Penthouse discount department on the top floor of Liberty House in Kailua. If you are looking specifically for a muu muu, watch for Muu Muu Factory and Especially For You, as these stores present some attractive prices. If you walk up Maunakea St from King to Beretania you will see a host of lei stands where most of the leis sold on the Island are made. One can purchase a lei and have it shipped to any state.

DOWNTOWN RESTAURANTS

There are, of course, more restaurants in the Downtown and Chinatown area than we can cover, and they come and go so fast that it is impossible to keep up with them. We mention only those that we have tried or that hosts have recommended or that looked particularly good to us when we visited them. If you walk through this area, and we suggest you do, you will probably discover interesting little restaurants you might like to suggest we try next time we are in Honolulu.

LOCAL STYLE

PIER 8 CHINESE
Located at Pier 8 under the Aloha Tower. This is LOCAL food to da max. Eat here if you like this style, want to save money, and do not mind getting a few quizzical looks.

NAYONG FILIPINO
Located at the corner of Hotel and Nuuanu. We have been assured by those who know that this is one of the best Filipino restaurants in Honolulu.

MAUNAKEA MARKEPLACE
This Shopping Center which has an entrance on Hotel street and one on Maunakea has a restaurant mall where one can get food from all over the Pacific. Here you can sample almost any food from Pacific nations: Chinese, Indian, Filipino, Vietnamese, Thai, Hong Kong, Singapore, and even Hawaiian. There are also many small gift shops as well as a full market. You will not see many Caucasians here but this is a major market for the local folks.

QUEEN'S PALACE
Located at the corner of Queen and Alakea St., this food mall gives one a choice of five little food stands: Chuck's Bar BQ, King's Okazuya, Ba-le (a chain of sandwich shops on Oahu), Downtown Fast Food, and Nippon Food Takeout (30% off after 3:30).

CUNHA'S ALLEY
Another small food mall that runs between King and Merchant St. The one that we liked the best was Heidi's, located on the Merchant St end.

local Oriental Style

WO FAT LTD.
Located in the heart of Chinatown at 115 North Hotel Street. When we visited here last trip Hotel Street was completely torn up and many buildings were being revamped. Most of the construction is completed and during the day a fun place to browse. Be sure to visit here even if you choose to eat elsewhere. No Chinese restaurant outside of Hong Kong offers a wider variety to choose from. They must be doing something right since they have been serving meals for close to a century. Prices are moderate and the food is good, 537-6260.

SEA FORTUNE
Located in Chinatown at 111 North King Street. We use to think this was the best Cantonese restaurant in Honolulu but we were really disappointed with the last meal we had there. Perhaps the cook just had an off day. If you like Dim Sum, the little stuffed buns, this is the place to go. The waitress passes through with trays and you take what you like. Each serving cost $1.20 and you are charged by how many steamer trays are on your table. They also have an extensive menu. Be careful with the Dim Sum as it is easy not only to over eat but to over spend, 536-3822.

KRUNG THAI
Located at 1028 Nuuanu between Hotel and King. One can get a plate lunch with three selections for $4.65.

A LITTLE BIT OF SAIGON
Located at 1160 Maunakea. This is a highly touted spot that seems to be getting a lot of action from Thai food lovers.

MAXIME VIETNAMESE RESTAURANT
Located at 1134 Maunakea St. When we stopped by here we were sorry we had just eaten because the aroma of tasty food got to us. They are open Tuesday through Sunday from 9 am-10 pm and on Monday from 9-3. The specialty of the house is Pho-Beef Noodle soup, medium bowl $4, extra large $4.50. One can have the meat either in the soup or on the side. Their entrees go from $6 to $8.

ANNIE'S BAKERY
If all you want is a quick snack and a cup of coffee, stop by this little bakery on Hotel St. A cup of coffee goes for $.60 and the pastry items are likewise low priced.

AMERICAN STYLE

THE PATISSERIE
Located at 33 South King St. This is the same as the one in Waikiki or Kahala. An excellent place for a sandwich, very reasonable priced from $3 to $4. There are a few hot dishes available such as Meatloaf Sandwich for $4.95.

AMBROSIA CAFE
Located on the corner of Alakea and Beretania, this is one of our best finds of last year and we still recommend it. To get there it is easiest to go up Alakea, a one way street, staying on the extreme left. Just before you reach Beretania, pull into the parking lot behind the restaurant. They are open for breakfast, lunch, and dinner. Lunch is a very good deal with many entrees between $4.55 and $8.95.

BA-LE FRENCH SANDWICH
This is part of a chain of sandwich shops that you will find in quite a few locations on Oahu. We are of the impression that this store located on N. King was their first.

O'TOOLE'S PUB
This might be a good spot to have a quick lunch. At least it seems to be a favorite watering hole for the local business people. It is located on the corner of Nuuanu and Merchant Street.

HEIDI'S BISTRO
Located on Queen, which is makai of King St. by about three blocks, just a little way up from Bishop. Food is ordered at the counter and taken to tables. From the looks of things when we were there, this is a big favorite with the folks who work in the neighborhood. Best to get there before or after the noon rush.

RON'S PLACE
What caught our eye here was that the most expensive item on the menu for lunch $5. The cuisine is Italian.

FLAMINGO COFFEE SHOP
Located on Merchant St. If you decide to have lunch here, make sure you get there before noon or after one since this is where a lot of the workers in the area eat.

MAGNER'S ON THE PARK
This is a cute little place on Nuuanu St. that backs up to a small park. They serve gourmet sandwiches for $7.25.

MURPHY'S
On the corner of Merchant and Nuuanu. They are open for lunch and dinner and bill themselves as Honolulu's premiere sports bar. This looks to be a popular watering hole for local business people.

JAKES (CLOSED)
Located at the corner of Hotel and Bishop St. this was on e of the most popular restaurants in the downtown area. At the present time it is closed and we could get no information as to when or if it would be reopened.

POINTS OF INTEREST

CHINATOWN

This is one of the oldest sections of Honolulu and one of the most interesting. Located at the start of South King Street, it only goes for about three short blocks. One block mauka is Hotel Street, which has several Chinese stores and restaurants but is much more famous for its night life, for this is where the Ladies of the Evening ply their trade, at least when they are not working the Waikiki area. Chinatown has long been an area for those struggling to achieve the American Dream, and lately there seem to be many Vietnamese setting up shop. The huge market located in the first block of King, where many independent butchers and greengrocers sell their wares is by no means all Chinese. At least half the shops are owned by Japanese. One would think that the newer Maunakea Market place would have drained off some of the business from these old markets but from what we could observe, each market was thriving.

While several mainland cities have larger Chinatowns, few are more interesting, for Honolulu's Chinatown is not geared for the tourist but simply an area where people live and work and where people from all over the Island come to shop and dine. One interesting little shop is the Ying Leong Funn Factory, located in the walk way between Hotel and King, just across from the Maunakea Shopping Center. Do not expect to find the latest in video games. What they produce here are chow funn noodles, made out of rice flour.

Another part of Chinatown that some miss is the Chinatown Cultural Center, located up on N. Beretania, an easy walk from King St. There are several restaurants and many shops to browse through. One might say that this Center is a bit more tourist oriented.

ALOHA TOWER

Located at the Port of Honolulu, at the foot of Fort Street across the Nimitz Highway. You can see the tower from most of the downtown area. Take the elevator located at the rear of the Port Reception area to the tenth floor viewing platform and get an excellent view of Honolulu, Pearl Harbor, and the entire south coast of Oahu. On Saturday, you will get a good view of the cruise ships that travel inter-island.

FALLS OF CLYDE

Located at the Port of Honolulu just east of Aloha Tower. This Museum Ship is open to the public for a fee of $3 for adults and $1 for children. They also cater parties of up to 1000 people for $3 a person.

IOLANI PALACE

Located on King St. just south of Richards. Ave. Open Wednesday, Thursday, Friday, and Saturday. The admission charge is $4.00 for adults and $1.00 for children, but no children under 4 accepted. They give tours starting at 9 am and ending at 2:15. The Iolani Palace has been the scene recently of trouble between native Hawaiians and the authorities. On King Kamehameha Day, June 1992, a group of Hawaiians who are urging that the Hawaiian people be made a sovereign nation, were arrested as they stood on the steps of the Palace. This question of sovereignty will not just go away and we predict that the pressure will get more intense as Hawaii nears the centennial of the overthrow of the monarchy. We realize this is a cursory explanation of what is going to be a very complex event and it is not our intention to treat it lightly. It should give one pause, though, as one visits what is very special to the Hawaiian people. 538-1471.

ACADEMY OF ARTS
Located at 900 Beretania Street. This Art Museum need not take a back seat to many museums in the world. There is no admission charge but donations are accepted ($4suggested) and a receptacle is provided. If one has an interest in Asian Art, stopping here is a must. Since the gallery has a small restaurant, which features home made soup and sandwiches with seating at 11:30 a.m. and 1:30 p.m., it is possible to spend all day here. On Thursday evenings, except during the summer, a light supper is served. It is best to make reservations for either lunch or dinner. Call 531-8734.

MISSION HOUSE MUSEUM
Located on King St. just south Of Punchbowl. Open every day from 9 a.m. until 4 p.m. from Tuesday through Saturday and on Sunday from noon to 4 pm., closed Monday, $3.50 for adults and $1.00 for children. 531-0481.

BISHOP MUSEUM
Located at 1525 Bernice Street. To get there, take the Likelike Highway off H-1 and immediately watch for Bernice on your right. Turn right and go about 1/2 block and you will come to the entrance on your right. The fee is $5.95 for adults and $4.95 for children from 6 to 17, 5 and under free. They have a hula show at 1 pm and crafts from 9-2:30 pm. We feel that it is well worth the price; it tells an interesting story of Polynesian culture. 847-3511.

FOSTER BOTANICAL GARDEN
Located at 180 North Vineyard Boulevard. To find this go up Nuuanu St. several blocks past Beretania to Vineyard, turn left and go about three blocks and you will see it on the right. It takes about 15 or 20 minutes to walk from Chinatown. This is a perfect downtown location for a picnic. The admission fee is $1.00 and that also admits you to the zoo. You will see trees here that as far as we know exist nowhere else in Hawaii. The strangest to us was the Cannon Ball Tree with the Sausage Tree a close runner up.

PUNCHBOWL
This National Memorial Cemetery of the Pacific is open from 8 a.m. to 5 p.m. In this extinct volcano, called by the ancient Hawaiians *the Hill of Sacrifice*, over 20,000 servicemen are buried. To get there take Punchbowl Avenue where it crosses King in the downtown area and go mauka. After you go under the freeway, watch for the signs to Punchbowl Memorial. When you see Puowaina Street, take that right into the crater. From the lookout at the top of the crater there is a magnificent view of the greater Honolulu area. They have recently restricted foot traffic to those who have relatives buried there.

PUU UALAKAA PARK
Located about half way up Round Hill Drive, the first part of Tantalas. This is a good spot to picnic and to get a great view of the south side of Oahu. The day we visited, they were filming *Magnum P.I.* so our view was obstructed by Tom Selleck.

TANTALUS

This drive, starting and ending in the heart of Honolulu, is dramatic, as it goes through what is essentially a tropical rain forest. Just a few miles beyond the noise and traffic of town, one reaches an area as peaceful as can be found in the Islands. This is an excellent drive to beat the heat on a hot summer day as it is always cooler on Tantalus. If you are interested in hiking, there are some good trails in this area. We must point out, however, that in June of 1990 they have had a rash of beatings by young hoodlums up in this area. Perhaps it would be good not to be up here after dark.

QUEEN EMMA'S SUMMER PALACE

Open every day from 9 a.m. until 4 p.m. Adults $4, children under 12 $.50, seniors $3.

SPORTS

GOLF

There are around fifteen courses on Oahu that are open to the public, and for retired military persons, there are another nine courses. There are five private country clubs where one can play as a guest of a member. Many people who stay at the Kahala Hilton are surprised and disappointed when they learn that the Waialae Country Club, home of the Hawaiian Open, which is played every February, is private and unavailable to tourists. In the Honolulu area courses are crowded, and it is a good idea to call ahead for a starting time. The best bet for play is in the rural areas, Makaha Valley Country Club, for example. Do not listen to those who tell you that one must plan to spend close to $100 to play golf in Hawaii. Even some of the semi-private courses are often somewhere between $30 and $60 including a cart. For more information on specific courses, check under sports in the section desired. For complete information on courses in Hawaii we refer you to *Hawaii's Golf Guide*, which sells for around $4.00. To obtain a copy write to Golf Association, 575 Cooke Street, Honolulu, Hawaii 96813.

TENNIS

Oahu has many public tennis courts, both in Honolulu and around the Island, in fact there are about forty different locations with a total of 154 courts, half of these are lighted for night play. For a complete list of these courts, send a stamped self addressed envelope to the Department of Parks and Recreation, 650 South King Street, Honolulu, Hawaii 96813. We will include most locations under the specific areas.

In Honolulu there is Ala Moana Park, 1201 Ala Moana Boulevard. They have ten courts, lighted. For more information call Max Neves, 522-7031. Also, there is Keehi Lagoon Courts, located at 465 Lagoon Drive, which is makai of the Nimitz Highway, west of Downtown. Here there are twelve courts, but none lighted.

MID-TOWN RESTAURANTS

ORIENTAL

MEKONG
There are two of these, the original at 1295 South Beretania, and a second one at 1726 South King Street. Either one serves excellent Thai food at reasonable prices, 521-2025 or 941-6184.

SIAM ORCHID
Located on Keeamoku St. just up from Kapiolani Blvd. right near the Ala Moana Shopping Center. If you like Thai, you will like this. Try the crispy chicken, one serving is enough for two with one other dish. Prices are moderate.

KEO'S
The original Keo's, which is still there, is on Kapahulu Ave. They have opened a new place on the mauka side of King Street about one mile east of China Town, open for dinner only. Keo's has a great reputation.

CHAING MAI NORTHERN THAI
Located in the 2200 block of King on the right hand side (King is one way). This would be our first recommendation for Thai food in this neighborhood. The prices are modest and the food is excellent.

local/Tourist Style

AUNTIE PASTO'S
Located at 1099 So. Beretania. They are open for lunch and dinner, Italian cuisine and, at least for lunch, the prices are not high (Breast of Chicken Cacciatore $7.95), and several specials at reasonable prices. When Frank Sinatra brought his band over for the show that A.T. & T. put on at Aloha Stadium, Auntie Pasto's catered their dinner. They all seemed to like it. 523-8855.

GREEK ISLAND TAVERNA Located at 2570 South Beretania St. and open for dinner from 5:30 to 11 nightly. Dinners are in the $8 to $12 range and feature such things as Kotopoulo Krasato (chicken sauteed in wine sauce-$10.25) and Kolokithakia Yemista (baby zucchini stuffed with ground beef, rice and topped with a egg and lemon sauce. We had dinner here and found the food very tasty and not too expensive. Closed Monday, 943-0052.

FISHERMAN'S WHARF
Across Ala Moana Blvd. at the foot of Ward Ave. They are open for lunch and dinner and have two dinning rooms, the Grotto and the Bridge. The Grotto is open for lunch from 11-2:30 and for dinner from 5-9. the Bridge is open for lunch from 11:30-1 and for dinner form 6-10. Prices in either are not too high, mahi mahi for $8.95 for example.

INDIA HOUSE
Located at 2632 South King Street just east of University Avenue on the mauka side of the street. We love Indian food, hence this is one of our favorite restaurants in Honolulu. We include it only for those who are of like mind. It is not inexpensive; dinners run around $15.00. We were always under the impression that they did not serve beer or wine but we learned they always have. However, they never seemed to object to our bringing wine and have never charged us corkage. You can specify how you like your food, ie., mild, hot, or very hot. Unless you really like it hot, better say mild. On one visit we had Chicken Vindaloo, the hottest thing we have ever eaten, 955-7552.

UNIVERSITY AVE.
Just north of King St. there are any number of small restaurants that look as if they are worth exploring, such as the Sushi Chef or Manoa Pizza.

DOWN TO EARTH
Located at 2525 King St. this little healthfood/restaurant store makes a good salad for the cholesterol counters. One can either get it to go or dine at one of the few tables provided.

PHIL PAOLIS
This is located at 2312 S. Beretania St. We visited here and checked the menu because we were told by several hosts that it was excellent. The decor is nice and the menu is interesting, Italian for the most part. Most of the entrees were over $15-mid $20's.

BUZZ'S ORIGINAL STEAK HOUSE
A bit hard to find so we will give careful directions. As you start down Beretania just past University Ave, look for Kaialiu St. on your right, make a right hand turn and bo on block to Coyne, turn right and you will find it several doors down on the right hand side. Buzz's is an old stand by in Hawaii and always reliable for a good meal.

KIRIN CHINESE
This little place at 2518 S. Beretania serves Szechuan, Hunan, Peking, and Cantonese cuisine. Looks as if they have covered all the bases.

CASTIGNOLA'S
(moved to the Waikiki area) Just about the time this goes to press, Castignola's in the Manoa Shopping Center will be no more. The good news is that they will still exist in a different location.

CAFE BRIO
This is an upscale new restaurant serving "contemporary cuisine" located in the Manoa Shopping Center. To find this center go up University Ave until you come to Manoa and turn right for about a mile.

DANNY'S
In the Manoa Center. This has the feel of a Denny's but the food is fixed more for local tastes than mainland. Their modest prices reflect the fact that locals eat here.

COFFEE MANOA
If all you want is a quick snack, give this a try. From the size of the crowd the day we were there, it must be pretty good. It is also in the Monoa Center.

O-BOK KOREAN
In the Monoa Center open for lunch and dinner from 10 am to 8 pm. Prices here are very modest and the food is fixed for local tastes.

WARD WAREHOUSE
This is located one block mauka of Ala Muana Blvd. at the foot of Ward Ave. There are several places to eat in this center, some inexpensive, some fairly modest, and several more elegant and expensive. On the modest side would be the Old Spaghetti Factory or Benkai Japanese. More upscale would be Orson's. Stuart Anderson's, Dynasty II, or Horatio's Steak and Seafood Grill. There are several small fast food places on the ground floor. We had lunch at Orson's (a bowl of Manhattan Clam Chowder served with sour dough French Bread from San Francisco and a Shrimp Salad, not too expensive, and plenty filling).

WARD CENTER
This is located just a few blocks east of Ward Warehouse and is more luxurious than Ward Warehouse. Both the shops and the restaurants bring higher prices. We would recommend any restaurant in this center as a good splurge spot, but not exactly the place to get an inexpensive light meal. The restaurants here are the Yum Yum Tree, Monterey Bay Canners (they feature an all you can eat soup, salad, and hot potato bar for $6.95), Ryan's Parkplace, Compadres (Mexican), Keo's, Sushi Mara, and Andrew's, or El Fresco which seemed the fanciest of all. One could get a snack at either Moca Java or Crepe Fever.

WATERFRONT PLAZA (RESTAURANT ROW)
If you ask for directions to this, you will be told, "Oh, you can't miss it. It is right on Ala Moana Blvd. just before you get downtown. Take our word for it, you can miss it unless you know where you are going. We will give specific directions since we feel sure you will enjoy stopping by here. Take Ala Moana Blvd. and turn mauka at South St., which is about 1/2 mile west of Fisherman's Wharf, go two blocks to Pohukaina St, turn left and you will see the parking garage on your left. If you are coming from the H-1 Freeway, take Punchbowl makai until you reach Pohukaina, turn left and you will see the parking garage on your right. If you are anywhere in the downtown area, you can see where you want to go by looking for two high tower buildings that resemble, at least to us, huge grain elevators. Once there you will find many shops and restaurants (around a dozen).

If you discover something we missed,
drop us a note
and we'll check it out
for our next edition

WAIKIKI

It is only an area of a few square miles between the blue Pacific and the Ala Wai Canal, but it has a world wide reputation, and while sometimes a tarnished one, people come from all over to be there, summer, winter, spring, and fall. You rarely hear anyone say he likes Waikiki, as if to admit it somehow makes one suspect. And yet, no place in Hawaii packs them in like Waikiki. At the peak of the tourist season, January through March, one must arrive early to insure a good spot on the beach, which is not large by any means. All day and half the night, people parade up and down Kalakaua Avenue, some dressed in outfits that defy description.

As one might expect in a tourist spot like this, just about any kind of action can be found. During the day card and chess players dominate the scene at the tables along Waikiki Beach. Just at dusk, people line the beach and the street to catch a last glimpse of the sun as it drops into the sea. Later, people walk along Kalakaua Avenue shopping, looking for that special place to eat, or watching and being watched.

There are pluses and minuses to all this activity. To some it is exciting and colorful, not quite like anything they have ever seen. To others it stands for blight and they talk about it with scorn. Perhaps because our life on Kauai is so peaceful, we kind of like Waikiki, for the brief time we are there. Everybody should see it, if only once. What is unfortunate in our view is that too many people think Waikiki, and for that matter Lahaina and Kaanapali on Maui, is Hawaii.

The beautiful thing about Hawaii is that it is like its people, variegated and multicolored, and all of it has its own special quality. Many people think Waikiki is nothing more than a tourist trap, but, because of the fierce competition of the place, great buys can be found if you know what to look for. In that way it is a bit like Mexico; some great buys, but, boy can you get taken. Even the restaurants run the gamut. One of the most expensive, and in our minds one of the best, is the Third Floor of the Hawaii Regent Hotel, coat and tie required. Then there is the Salad Bowl at 421 Nahua Street, which has plate lunches for as high as $2.50, and a plain hamburger for $.50, or their special breakfast for $.99, which consists of two eggs, two sausages, and two pieces of toast or rice. There are so many restaurants that we could not cover them all in our book, nor, as far as we know, does anyone else.

RESTAURANTS

As we say above, there are too many restaurants in Waikiki to mention them all. For example, the Royal Hawaiian Shopping Center on the makai side of Kalakaua Avenue has over ten restaurants and about ten other places where you can get a snack. The International Market Place has many little restaurants and fast food stands. Kalakaua Avenue is lined with places to eat. This intense competition, especially during the "off season" drives down prices. What we have attempted to do is pick out a few that either we or our hosts have tried and liked.

LOCAL STYLE

MONGOLIAN BAR-B-Q
At the rear of the International Market Place, it can best be found by entering from Kuhio Street and going to the right. This is the same as the one in Chinatown at the Cultural Center. We tried it and must admit that you get filled up for a low price but some people would find the taste a little strange. Try it if you feel adventurous.

local/Tourist Style

FERDINAND'S
This is located on Kuhio St. near Nohonani. The prices here are very modest.

JOLLY ROGER
There are two of these in Waikiki, one in the 2200 block of Kalakua and one on Kuhio St. Both have a dinner special for $7.95 and the food in consistent.

ONO CHEF
This little place is off Kuhio St. on the west side of the International Market Place. This is the chow down spot of Waikiki; they have an all you can eat spaghetti and salad bar for $3.99. They are open for lunch from 11-3 weekdays and everyday for dinner from 5-9.

KUHIO CAFE
If you are looking for a reasonable breakfast, give this a try. It is located just a few doors away from Ono Chef. They serve a breakfast special for $1.99

DENNY'S
Located on Kuhio Ave.

SIAM INN
Located on Seaside north of Kuhio Ave. They are open for lunch from 11-3 and for dinner from 5-10:30. This has been called "a gem in Waikiki." Their prices are medium.

COUNTRY LIFE BUFFET
Located on Nahua St half way up the block from Kuhio Ave. Strictly vegetarian, neat and clean. they are open for lunch Sunday-Friday from 11-2:30 and for dinner same days from 5-8.

TONY ROMA'S RIBS
There are three of these on Oahu that we know of and for those who love ribs that's good news since getting seated in the Waikiki Roma's takes a little wait. You will almost always see a crowd of people waiting to get in. We have been told that the ribs served here can not be beat.

MINUTE CHEF
On Kalakaua Avenue just west of the Hyatt Regency. Prices are reasonable and they give a 20 percent discount to senior citizens.

THE PATISSERIE
On the mauka side of Kuhio Street just behind the International Marketplace. There are several of these spread around Honolulu and they are all excellent if all you want is a sandwich or the makings of a sandwich for a picnic on the beach. We purchased some roast beef which was as good as any we have ever had, well seasoned and nice and rare.

FISH MARKET RESTAURANT
On the corner of Kuhio and Seaside, reasonable prices for fresh fish and other seafood.

SPECIAL OCCASION

THIRD FLOOR
On the third floor of the Hawaiian Regent Hotel, located on the corner of Kalakaua and Oahu Street. We had one of the best meals here that we have had in Hawaii. It is expensive, and there is a dress code, ie., jacket at least, and they like it if a tie is worn, but that may not be insisted upon.

POINTS OF INTEREST

KAPIOLANI PARK
This park at the east end of Waikiki offers much to visitors and residents alike. Not only does it contain excellent picnic areas, jogging trails, tennis courts, but also a Rose Garden, the Waikiki Aquarium, and the Honolulu Zoo, for which there is a small charge.

ALAWAI CANAL
There are often canoe races along the Alawai Canal that are fun to watch, but if not actual races, there is much practice that goes on here.

DIAMOND HEAD
When the first Caucasian sailors saw this crater, they mistook the volcanic crystals for diamonds, hence the name. To get into the crater, take Diamond Head Road and proceed through the tunnel to the parking area. From here you can hike to the rim of the crater, which is over 700 feet above sea level and affords some great views.

BEACHES

WAIKIKI
Directions are not needed. Somehow we think you will find this. If you intend to have a spot to sit, get there early for after a while it is hard to put a towel down. The swimming is great, and people watching the best.

KAPIOLANI BEACH PARK
Right on Kapiolani Boulevard at the east end of Waikiki. This beach has all the facilities including a defunct Natatorium, the world's largest salt water swimming pool.

ALA MOANA BEACH PARK
All the facilities are here and this park gets much use from locals and visitors. It is located at the west end of Waikiki, across from the Ala Moana Shopping Center.

NIGHT LIFE

There is so much going on in this area that there is no need for us to point out any specifics. There are several different theaters, and at the hotels entertainers of world wide reputation appear. We find it interesting to just stroll through the various shopping malls, where one can often see local performers for free.

SPORTS

GOLF
ALA WAI GOLF COURSE
The entrance to this course is on Kapahulu Avenue. This public course, as you can well imagine, gets an intense amount of play. The fee is $18 weekdays, $20 weekends. Carts are available for $11 but they are not required. Since the course is flat, a hand cart should suffice unless the temperature is up. For more information call 296-4653.

TENNIS
Diamond Head Tennis Center at 3908 Paki Avenue has ten courts, not lighted. To find simply walk to the Diamond Head Side of Kapiolani Regional Park.

54

KAIMUKI/KAPAHULU

This area is mauka and east of Waikiki Beach and for our purposes Kaimuki is along Waialae Avenue between where Waialae starts at the end of King Street and then east to 15th Avenue. Kapahulu runs from King St. all the way down to the east side of Waikiki. Unlike most of Oahu, which seems to be an endless string of shopping centers, from big, bigger, and biggest to new, newer, and newest, these are more neighborhood areas of little shops and restaurants, beauty salons, neighborhood bars, and service stations. For those of us who grew up before the days of the shopping center, areas such as this are refreshing. Without a doubt, the mammoth centers are more practical but just a little short on personality. If you agree, explore Waialae Ave. and Kapahulu St. as we did and we know you will not be disappointed. One little shop to be sure to check out is the Varsity Club Thrift Shop located on the corner of 12th and Waialae. All of the proceeds from this shop go to the Varsity School for the learning disabled. Not only can one make a good buy, the money goes for a good cause.

Also, we realize that the restaurants mentioned are not all of the restaurants in this area. Perhaps you will try one of the ones we fail to mention and will want to tell us about it for our next edition. If so, we will mention it on your recommendation and will try it the next time we are in Honolulu.

WAIALAE RESTAURANTS

LOCAL STYLE

KAL BI
Located on a little alley makai of Waialae Avenue off 12th Avenue. Low prices and the food is tasty if you like the style. Closed Sunday.

SHIRO'S SAIMIN

Located at 1108 12th Ave. They serve 60 different kinds of Saimin and have been around for a long time. We asked them if they knew of Hamaru Saimin on Kauai and they assured us they did and did not take a back seat to them. They are open for breakfast, lunch, and dinner.

local style

TAN-TIEN

Located on Waialae above 12th Ave and across the street from most of the restaurants listed below. This is a small fast food place where one can pick up a French Sandwich for $6.

KIM CHEE 11

Located on Waialae Ave. just short of 12th Ave. Korean cuisine at reasonable prices.

VIET HU'ONG

At 3565 Waialae Ave. For the most part Vietnamese food with a few of the spicier Chinese dishes also available. They are open for lunch from 11-2 and for dinner from 5:30-10. The food can be very hot but if you ask them they will tone it down and then the food is nothing but very tasty. There are places with a lot more reputation but we doubt if the food is any better or as low priced. They do not serve liquor so you are welcome to bring beer or wine.

AZTECA

Just a few doors from Viet Hu'ong, the standard Mexican fare priced in the $5 to $12 range as well as some interesting house specialties in about the same range. A La carte is much less, $3 to $5. They are open for lunch and dinner Monday through Saturday and for dinner on Sunday

NEW KAIMUKI INN

At 3579 Waialae Avenue. This place has been remodeled and is now quite nice. They still serve a wide variety of food at fairly modest prices (Stuffed Pork Chop $10.95, T-Bone Steak $14.95, Katsudon $8.95). They are open for breakfast, lunch, and dinner every day from 6 am to 11 pm. After the dinner hour they open the Karaoke Bar for entertainment.

DUK KEE

On 12th Ave. makai of Waialae. Szechuan style, very reasonably priced, with a nice decor. They are open for lunch and dinner from 10:30-8:30.

HALE VIETNAM

Located on 12th Ave. next to Duk Kee. They are open for lunch from 11-2:30 and dinner from 5 to 9. Most dishes go from $8-$10 and they have Cua Ray Xa Ot (whole dungeness crab) for $17.95. They also serve Vietnamese Fondue.

VICTORIAN INN RESTAURANT

At 1120 12th Ave. Open for breakfast, lunch and dinner. This place has been here for 20 years so they must be doing something right. Meals have a distinctive local flavor but it has the feel of a Denny's.

JOSE'S MEXICAN
On Koko Head, which is one block east of 12th. they are open for lunch and dinner Monday-Saturday form 11-10, Sunday dinner only 5-9.

THE COFFEE HOUSE
If all you want is a light snack, give this new little place a try. They opened in July of 1992. Located on Koko Head just a few doors off Waialae.

local/Tourist Style

VERBANO ITALIAN RISTORANTE
Located on Waialae Ave. between 11th and 12th where Che Pasta used to be. Prices go from $10 for Chicken Cacciatore to $15 for Scampi. They serve plenty of pasta dishes for reasonable prices. If you are not too hungry you can get a light portion for a very reasonable price.

KAPAHULU RESTAURANTS

This street is building a reputation as a restaurant center and in fact has several places that are a big favorite with the local folks. The nice thing is that they are not all fancy and expensive. On the contrary, the funkiest little places on Oahu are on this street. If all you have is a sweet tooth, try Candy Land at 750 Kapahulu.

LOCAL STYLE

ONO HAWAIIAN
If you want to sample Hawaiian food try this place, but you better get there early as the place can get packed and they close when the food runs out. It is located on the west side of the street about half way down. When we passed by there this year there was a large crowd outside waiting to get in. Closed Sunday.

L & L DRIVE INN #7
This is a great chow down spot for the budget minded. It is clean and comfortable. You will not feel out of place. They serve a hamburger for $.95 (we know places where you can get the same hamburger for $2.25 and the place is funkier). Now if you want to splurge, you can get a Double BBQ Cheeseburger Deluxe for $2.45. They serve all kinds of plate lunches (how about the Seafood Platter, Mahi-Mahi,Shrimp, Scallops-$5.75). It is located at 909 Kapahulu.

JOE'S INTERNATIONAL KITCHEN
As far as we know this is the only restaurant in Hawaii where you can fax in your order, 752-4884. Since they serve Hawaiian, Japanese, Chinese, Filipino, and a couple of mainland American dishes, they deserve the name International. Their entrees are $4.25 for a full order or $2.25 for 1/2 order. Their hamburger, however, is $.24 higher that L & L. Located at 1006 Kapahulu.

local style

HELEN'S CHINESE
At 804 Kapahulu Ave. Cantonese cuisine at very attractive prices. The only dishes over $5 was shrimp with pepper and black bean sauce for $6.50 and Bird's Nest Soup, $9.50. Other than that most dishes go between $3.75 and $5. The place is very clean and looks to us like a chow down spot not to be missed.

NEW WORLD CHINESE
Located at the corner of Palani and Kapahulu with parking on Palani. This restaurant received a 23 rating from Zagat for their food, which is high. The rating for ambience was substancially lower. They are open for lunch from 10:30-4 and for dinner from 5-10 every day except Thanksgiving when the owner, Eddie Lee, takes his vacation. Eddie assured us that the policy of the house was that no one left hungry. At the present time they do not serve alcohol so feel free to BYOB.

ON ON CHINESE
We mention this because it is there but the prices are about 20-30% higher than the other Chinese restaurants in the neighborhood. They are open for lunch and dinner from 11-9 pm.

NEW KAPAHULU CHOP SUEY
At 730 Kapahulu. Prices a little higher that Helen's but also a nicer atmosphere.

IRIFUNE'S
This is small little place with a big reputation on the east side of Kapahulu just past Keo's (mentioned below). The food is Japanese style and the prices for most entrees are $8 and $9. They are open for lunch on weekdays and for dinner tuesday-Sunday. We have been told by many people that this is one that should not be missed, 737-1141.

local/Tourist

JAVA JAVA
If all you want is a light snack in a spiffy atmosphere, give this place a try. Not only all kinds of coffee but salads and sandwiches also. Or perhaps you have a yen for a bagel?

KEO'S
This is getting to be one of the most popular places in Honolulu for Thai food, noted for the number of celebrities who dine here. We have eaten here several times and do agree that the food, ambience, and service is hard to beat. The prices are a little higher than some of the other Thai restaurants we mention but the setting that is created makes it worth it for most people, 737-8240.

RAMA'S THAI
Last year this was just a little spot across the street from its present location. They have since taken over what used to be Anthony's Italian. Prices are lower than at Keo's and if one can judge from the menu, authentic Thai dishes are offered. On Wednesdays they have a buffet for $10.50 that amounts to a seven course dinner. They stress the fact that many vegetarian dishes are served. They are open every night for dinner only, 734-3887.

GONBEI JAPANESE
Located at 1018 Kapahulu. If you are looking for authentic Japanese cuisine, plenty of atmosphere, and great service, give this a try. Entrees run between $15-25 or you can get the Combination dinner for $35. They are open for dinner only Tuesday-Sunday, 5-10 pm.

POINTS OF INTEREST

PARADISE PARK
This is a little hard to find and we are not sure it is worth the effort. But if all the ads you see tempt you beyond control, take University Avenue in a mauka direction. When you pass the University this will become Oahu Street. Go about three miles and you will come to Manoa, which you follow to the end where the park is located. Mainly it is a haven for tropical birds, not necessarily ones from Hawaii. Perhaps the most important thing you will learn about Hawaii is that it has many mosquitoes, so bring your repellent. Adults $14.95, children 3-12 $7.95. They are open from 9:30-5 pm. 988-6866.

SPORTS

TENNIS
There are at least three spots in this neighborhood: 1) Kaimuki Recreation Center at 3521 Waialae Avenue, two lighted courts, 2) Maunalani Playground, 4525 Sierra Drive, one lighted court, 3) Petrie Playground, 1039 12th Avenue, two lighted courts.

Remember, mauka means mountain
and makai means ocean:
ie. good for giving directions

EAST HONOLULU

At one time the area east of Diamond Head was farm land and there were fairly large dairy ranches out this way. As the city of Honolulu expanded, the farms were sub-divided and homes were built, and the farmers moved to other places on Oahu, the Waianae area for example. Today, between Diamond Head and Koko Head there are a series of subdivisions, each one supported by a shopping center. Just east of Diamond Head is the Kahala area, where the Kahala Hilton and the Waialae Country Club are located. Further east is Aina Haina, Niu Valley, Portlock, and Hawaii Kai, which is the newest development in this area.

This is a residential area and visitors often simply pass through as they drive from Honolulu to Hanauma Bay. However, since we have some excellent host homes here, we want to point out the restaurants and points of interest. But even if you are not staying in this area, keep in mind the fine restaurants out this way.

RESTAURANTS

KAHALA

local/Tourist

YUM YUM TREE
There are a number of these on Oahu and we have found them to be very consistent in quality. The food is very middle America as is the service and the decor, 737-7938.

COUNTRY KITCHEN
This is small chain with several restaurants in Hawaii: the one we visited was located on the north shore of Oahu. This location had not yet opened in Kahala but will be there by the time our book is printed. Very mainland style food at reasonable prices.

TONY ROMA'S
This is located across the highway from the Shopping Center. As we mentioned above, the original Tony Roma's is in Waikiki. The house special is ribs and they must do a bang up job because in Waikiki they are usually packed with a line outside. Maybe this one or the one in Pearl would be easier to get in to. 732-5505.

YEN KING
This is one of our favorites. Open for lunch from 11-2:30 and for dinner from 5-9:30. The decor is nice and the prices are a little higher than some of the restaurants in China Town. The food is mostly Mandarin style.

THE PATISSIRIE
This is an excellent spot for a sandwich in the $3 to $4 range.

LAM'S GARDEN CHINESE
This is located across the street from the Kahala Mall a little west of Tony Roma's. They serve both Cantonese and Mandarin dishes for reasonable prices. They have a lunch special of $3.50 for two dishes or $4.50 for three.

SPINDRIFTER, CHUCK'S STEAK HOUSE, JOLLY ROGER
These are all chain restaurants located throughout Hawaii and probably on the mainland also. The food is consistent and very much in the mainland style.

HAJIBABA'S
This Morrocan restaurant would be most fun with a group, but there were several couples dinning there on our visit. Lots of atmosphere, something a little different. It is in the Kahala Shopping Center on Kilauea Ave just past the Post Office.

RANDY'S
This is a new restaurant/lounge] in Kahala and a bit hard to find. In is on the far west side of the mall on the north side. It has to be entered from the parking lot, not the inner mall. They are open for lunch weekdays from11-3 on on weekends from 12-2 with sandwiches in the lounge only. Sandwiches go from $5.75 to $8.25. They are open for dinner every night.

CALIFORNIA PIZZA KITCHEN
This is a mainland chain that has two stores on Oahu, here and in Waikiki. The food is good and the prices are moderate. This is a good safe place for a lunch.

BERNARD'S NEW YORK DELI
This placed was packed so either there were a lot of home sick New Yorkers or the locals like this place. they serve dinner entrees all day long (Kosher Knockwurst $8.99, Roast Chicken dinner, $7.99, Nostalgia Plate-cabbage roll, Kishke, Kasha & Potato Pancake.

AINA HAINA

local Style

DORIJI KOREAN
This is a little take out plate lunch place on the east end of the Aina Haina Center. While you order at the window, there is a nice lounge next to it where you can eat. There is just no table service.

local/Tourist Style

DUCK YUN
The food here is Cantonese style with most dishes from $5.25-$7. They are open for lunch and dinner. They have a plate lunch special for $4.75 and a dinner plate for $5.95.

61

JACK'S
Open Monday through Sunday from 7 a.m. until 2 p.m. for breakfast and lunch. Last year we had this in the local/Tourist category; that was before we ate here. It really is pretty heavy local and we mean that in the best sense of the term. Lunch is in the $4 to $5 range, plate lunch special style.

KOMAKATA
The cuisine is pretty authentic Japanese. The decor is very nice and the prices are not too high, unless you get carried away at the sushi bar. Most dinner entrees are under $10 except for the combination dinner which is $15. One can get the Nabe Special where you cook the food at your table for around $13-$14 a person. Lunch prices are between $5 $8.

NIU VALLEY

local/Tourist Style

** SWISS INN**
Open for dinner only from 6:00-10:00 closed Monday. Be sure to call for a reservation as this is one of the busiest restaurants in Honolulu and for very good reason: the food is excellent and the prices are not outrageous, with most dishes in the mid-teens. We did not expect it to be so good in spite of the fact that several people urged us not to miss it. The cuisine is continental. If one is not too hungry, they have a light dinner for around $6.00 which is a really excellent buy, 377-5447.

AL DENTE
This used to be Di Martino, then it was tony Manzo's, now Al Dente. If it had any other names in the mean time we are unaware of them. The one consistent thing is Italian cuisine. They are open for dinner only from tuesday through Sunday. Entrees go from $10 to $20 with several kinds of pasta offered.

LUNG FUNG
Either Cantonese or Szechuan, open daily from 11 until 9 p.m. Prices moderate.

HAWAII KAI

local Style

YUMMY KOREAN B-B-Q
If you just can't wait for some Yook Gae Jang or Bi Bim Bap or some Kal Bi this might be the place. If you don't know what we are talking about, you better just pass on by unless you are in an adventurous mood. Nothing here over $5.45.

local/Tourist Style

CAFE SPLASH
Located where Stromboli's used to be. They had just opened and we did not get a chance to try it and none of our hosts mentioned it either. It looks good as far as atmosphere goes. The menu was limited; they do have Fajita for $9.45.
SIZZLERS
Just the same as the mainland chain.

PACIFIC BROILER
Open now for lunch and dinner with mainland style food priced from $11.95 for pasta to $18.50 for Smoked Lamb chops. Catch of the day is sold Market Price, which usually means the highest thing on the menu.

JOHN RICHARDS
Steak and Seafood is the specialty of the house with prices from $9.95 for Fish and Chips to $17.25 for a 14 oz. cut of Prime Rib. They are open for lunch and dinner. We would think this a good choice for a leasurely dinner.

The restaurants listed below are in a shopping center which can be found by taking Keahole mauka off Kalanianaole Highway to Hawaii Kai Dr. and turning left.

local Style

WONG'S GOLDEN WOK
Food is served cafeteria style and patrons can select 2,3,or for choices: $4.25,$5.10, $5.85. Everything looked good and this would be a good place for the budget minded.

local/tourist

TAIPAN LANDING
Here you can get Cantonese, Mandarin, Hunan or Szechuan cuisine in a very nice setting. They are open for lunch and dinner. Their prices are a little higher (about $2/$3 a dish) than most of the other Oriental restaurants we mention, but the setting and the service is more elegant.

Have we missed something?
If so, please
let us know about it.
We'll check it out
and cover it in our next edition.

BEACHES

KAHALA HILTON

Even though the Hilton "built" this beach, that is, they brought in the sand to create a white sand beach where none previously existed, public access and use of the beach is not denied. We have used the beach many times and have never stayed at the Hilton. In fact, we have used the pool side bar with no problem. Watching the dolphins swim in their pool is almost a tourist attraction.

SPORTS

TENNIS

There are at least four spots in this area: 1) Aina Haina Playground, 827 Hind Drive, two lighted courts 2) Kahala Field, 4495 Pahoa Avenue, two unlighted courts, 3) Koko Head District Park, Kalaianiole Highway, six lighted courts 4) Niu Valley, 5510 Kanau Street, two unlighted courts.

HAWAII KAI GOLF COURSE

This is a private course, open to the public. The fee is $80 on weekdays and weekends, cart included and mandatory. There is also an executive course of mostly par threes with fee of $26.50 no cart required, $35 with cart. This is a nice course to play to sharpen up your wind game.

NIGHT LIFE

KAHALA THEATER

Located in the Kahala Shopping Center. There are nine different movies shown here. To hear a recorded message of what is playing when, call 733-6233; to contact the Box Office call 733-6243.

EAST OF HAWAII KAI TO MAKAPU

For scenic beauty it is hard to beat the drive east of Hawaii Kai to Waimanalo. Many get no further than Hanauma Bay and some, unfortunately, not even that far. Until one reaches Waimanalo, there are no stores or restaurants, although there are a few Snack Vans parked along the road if you decide to spend some time in this area. Below is a list of the points of interest along the way.

HANAUMA BAY
Just after you pass Hawaii Kai, you climb the hill to Koko Head where you find the access road to Hanauma Bay. This is a must stop for any Oahu visitor. Most people think of it for snorkeling, but one need not snorkel to see fish. Simply walk a little way into the water and you will see plenty of fish. Should you have food for them, you will see even more. No fishing is allowed here so the fish are quite tame. If you want to snorkel, the best time to do it is early in the morning as things get a little crowded after 10 a.m.

HALONA POINT
About three miles past Hanauma Bay you may get a chance to see one of Hawaii's Blow Holes. This one is not as consistent as Spouting Horn on Kauai but it is nice to stop here anyway. If it is at all clear, you will see Molokai in the distance.

SANDY BEACH
A mile or so further on you will come to Sandy Beach, a huge stretch of sand where surfers and body surfers come to frolic. This beach is always crowded but if body surfing is your thing, don't pass this one by. Further on the waves are either too rough or once past Makapu, too gentle.

MAKAPU BEACH
Two or three miles past Hawaii Kai Golf course, this is another favorite surfing area.

SEA LIFE PARK
One of Oahu's major tourist attractions. People who live on Oahu say, "Why go to Sea Life when we can watch to dolphins for free at the Kahala Hilton." There is much more to see, however, at Sea Life Park. Admission is $14.95 adults, $7.95 for children 6-12, children under six free. They are open every day from 9:30-5 pm.

FROM HERE OUT AROUND THE EAST SHORE OF OAHU, THE OCEAN IS REALLY BEAUTIFUL. BUT DO NOT BE FOOLED, IT CAN REALLY GET ROUGH AT TIMES. REMEMBER, NEVER TURN YOUR BACK ON THE OCEAN EVEN WHEN YOU ARE GETTING OUT. A SNEAKER WAVE CAN GIVE YOU QUITE A BEATING. ALSO, KEEP IN MIND THAT WAVES COME IN SETS, AND AT TIMES THE HIGH WAVES CAN BE FAR APART. FOR A FEW MOMENTS THE OCEAN LOOKS CALM AS CAN BE, THEN A BIG ONE COMES IN AND WATCH OUT! IF THERE IS A LIFEGUARD ON THE BEACH, ASK HIM HOW THE CONDITIONS ARE THAT DAY. DO NOT CONCLUDE BECAUSE YOU SEE SURFERS WAY OUT THAT THINGS ARE SAFE. THEY ARE VERY EXPERIENCED AT WHAT THEY ARE DOING.

Keep in mind as you drive to buckle up.

PEARL CITY/AIEA

As the plane approaches the Honolulu Airport, the first sight is Pearl Harbor. Anyone old enough to remember December 7, 1941, no doubt remembers exactly where he was and what he was doing on that fateful Sunday morning. Whether one had much of a consciousness of Hawaii before then, from that point on Hawaii assumed an importance in the world that has done nothing but grow.

Since Honolulu Airport is in the Pearl City/Aiea area, most people conclude that this is a part of greater Honolulu, and most guide books treat it that way. In fact, Pearl City and Aiea is spite of being close to Honolulu are as separate from it as Kaneohe or Kailua.

For anyone interesting in shopping the, Pearlridge Shopping Center, Pearl Kai Center, and the Westridge Shopping Center all located just off Kamehameha Hwy. offer just about everything anyone would need. Pearlridge, the largest of the three, is enclosed and air-conditioned. Many of the restaurants in these Centers are listed below.

One of the main supports for this area, as well as others on Oahu, is the military. Except for the Arizona Memorial, a veritable tourist mecca, there is not much for tourists in this neighborhood. Restaurants and stores rely on residents for their success. The net effect of this is that prices in both restaurants and shops tend to be lower than in some of the tourist spots.

There are no beaches here, but there is a very nice park, the Neil Blaisdale Park, which is a good place to picnic or lie in the sun if one does not wish to bother going to the beach.

Our host homes in this area are close to the airport, just a few minutes drive, and it is just a short drive to the center of Honolulu or Waikiki. Pearl City is also a good place to start a trip to the north shore, up through the center of the Island.

RESTAURANTS

LOCAL STYLE

PEARL CITY CHINESE
In the Pearl City Business Plaza, which is on the south side of Kamehameha Highway. Cantonese style, open for lunch and dinner. Lunch runs between $4-$6 while dinners between $6-$8.

SUSHI TEN
Located in Newtown Square, which in on Kaahumanu St. in Aiea, at the back of the Center. Lunch goes from $4.60, where you have a choice of any two of a dozen Japanese dishes, up to $10 for Steak Taishoku. If you like authentic Japanese, you will probably like it here.

LENNY'S RESTAURANT
In the Pearl Kai Center on Kamehameha, which is across the highway from Pearl Ridge. Filipino food at very low prices. They are open from 8 am to 9 pm, closed Monday.

PEARL KAI CENTER FOOD COURT
Located at the rear of this mall. There are a variety of little food stands that serve Pacific Rim Cuisine. From here you can get a good view of the Arizona Memorial while you chow down. As you leave the Food Court you will notice weight Watchers on the left.

WAIMALU HAWAIIAN KITCHEN
This would be a good place to try some Hawaiian dishes. It is located on the north side of Kamehameha Highway in the Waimalu Center.

49 ER
If you can find this in any other guide book we will give you our book free. We are tempted to be more generous but will hold off just in case. This is a real LOCAL place very easy to miss but if you are on the cheap and want a good deluxe hamburger for $1.75 stop by here. It is located on the mauka side of Kam. Highway about 1/2 mile east of Pearl Ridge on the corner of Kam. and Honomamu.

local Style

EDOKKO JAPANESE
Located on the makai side of Kam. Highway across from Pearl Ridge and west of Pearl Kai. This is a unique little place where patrons cook their own food in one of three traditional Japanese methods: 1) Yakiniku- cooking on a grill, enhanced with a special sauce. 2) Sukiyaki- cooking with the traditional sukiyaki sauce in an authentic pot. 3) Shabu Shabu- cooking with water and seaweed in a shabu shabu pot. It is kind of a buffet style, with all you can eat situation. Lunch is $6.50 and dinner is $13.95. This place is getting lots of action from the local folks.

FLAMINGO
On the makai side of Kamehameha in the Pearl City Business Plaza. The most expensive thing on the menu is lobster at $18.95. Many of the dinner entrees are in the $6.00-$7.00 range, with spaghetti at $5.15. Their lunch prices are lower: hot roast beef sandwich for $3.50. They are open from 6:00 am. until 11:00 p.m. every day.

HOUSE OF DRAGON CHOP SUEY
Located in the Pearl City Shopping center at 890 Kamehameha and open daily from 10:30-8:45. Don't let the outside fool you, this place is very nice inside and the prices are good with most dishes in the $5-$6 range. They have a Plate Lunch special (Chicken Chow Mein, Sweet Sour Spare ribs, Pot Roast Pork, Fried Shrimp, Crisp Wun Ton, Steamed rice0 $4.95. The dinner plate special is $5.75.

PEKING CITY RESTAURANT
Located in the Pearlridge Center at the corner of Kamehameha and Kaonohi St. and open daily from 11-9:30 pm. Mostly Cantonese but with a few Szchuan dishes available with most dishes prices $6- $7.50.

PEARL CITY TAVERN & SUSHI BAR
On the makai side on Kamehameha Highway at Waimano Home Road. In some ways we would put this in the do not miss category. Not only is the food good, with a large variety of dishes offered, from sushi to corn beef sandwich, but there is more of interest here. For example, behind the bar is a monkey cage. Patrons can have a drink and watch the monkeys cavort. On the roof is a bonzai garden. Each tree is labeled, giving not only the name but also the age. The restaurant is huge, so in spite of the fact they do a large business you are sure to be accommodated, but if you have to wait you should not be bored. They are open for lunch and dinner every day except Saturday when they are open for dinner only, 455-1045.

BEACON
At 98-108 Lipoa Place which runs makai off Kamehameha Highway across from the Pearl Ridge Center. This is what the local crowd considers the best value in the Pearl City/Aiea area. We whole heartily agree. The food is excellent and the prices are very reasonable. The menu is extensive, not especially geared to local tastes, and fresh fish of several varieties is almost always available. They have a salad bar, all you want for $4.95. The highest entree on the menu is steak and mahi mahi for $9.95. They are open every day from 6:30 am until 10:30 pm. 488-1881.

DARUMA NOODLE SHOP
Located on Kaonohi in the Westridge Shopping Center. Quite new and very attractive little place that specializes in Ramen. There are over a dozen Ramen to choose from, small order from $4-$6 and large order from 5$-$6.75.

CHAMPI THAI
In the Pearl Kai Center. We have been told that the food here is excellent and the prices are not high. They are open for lunch from 11-2 except Saturday and for dinner from 5-9:30. The lunch price is set at $5.75 with a different special every day.

STONE YAKINIKU HOUSE
In Pearl Kai Center. This is a strange little place where one can get such items as Small Intestines Jun Kol cooked with vegetables in a special sauce, $18 for two, or Inner Part of Pork Neck, $12.50., or Spicy Bar BQ Chicken for $7.95. We imagine one would have to have a spirit of adventure to try this out.

KIERAN
In Pearl Kai Center. They claim to be the first Chinese Pizza restaurant in Hawaii. As far as we are concerned they can also claim to be the only Chinese Pizza place. They are open for lunch from 11-2:30 and for dinner from 5-9. A small pizza goes for $9.95 while a large runs $18.95.

MONIQUE'S ALOHA CHICKEN
In the Pearl Kai Center and open from 10-11. Plate lunches run between $6.25-$10.95. They specialize in take out orders so if you wanted to prepare a picnic you could call ahead, 486-0676

local/Tourist Style

DENNY'S
This is across from Pearl Ridge Center on Palimomi and needs no introduction.

SHANGHAI Next door to Denny's. Cantonese cuisine, open for lunch and dinner.

BANDITO'S CANTINA
This is located in Pearl Kai Center. As one might expect this is Mexican food at moderate prices, a combo plate for $5.95 or a chicken fajita for $10.95.

ANNA MILLER'S
If you are driving west on Kam Highway you can't miss this as it is located on the west side of Pearl Ridge and very visible. They are open 24 hours and serve mainland style food with pie as a specialty. They have 21 different kinds of muffins. This is a very popular place and there is often a short wait to get in.

BRAVO RESTAURANT
Underneath Anna Miller's and open for lunch and dinner every day except Sunday when they are open for dinner only. Italian cuisine at prices that are not too high. One of their specialties in Steak Sinatra for $19. If there is a story behind this we failed to get it.

YUM YUM TREE
This and the ones mentioned below are in the Westridge Shopping Center, which is just west of Pearl Ridge. This is always a safe bet, good wholesome food at very reasonable prices.

CHI CHI
Located in the Westridge Shopping Center. There are two of these on Oahu. This one and the one in Kahala. It is Mexican food, cooked in what is called Sonoran style. They have an extensive menu with most entrees under $10, and they advertise that they have dancing every night.

TONY ROMA'S RIBS
Located at 98-150 Kaonohi which runs mauka off Kam. on the west side of Pearl Ridge. If you can't get in the Waikiki or Kahala spot, try this one. Same delicious ribs at any one of the three.

ELEPHANT & CASTLE
Located in Newtown Square on Kaahumanu Rd., which runs mauka off Kam about 1/2 mile west of Pearl Ridge. Named after a very famous English Pub and also styled along those lines. Where else in Hawaii can you play a game of darts? They also have pool tables. Open every day from 10:30 am until 1 or 2 a.m. The food is good and moderately priced, 487-5591.

KYOTARU
Located at 98-1226 Kaahumanu Rd. across from Elephant & Castle. This used to be the Columbia Inn so if you remember that do not be confused. Japanese food at moderate prices, no entree over $12.95 down to Oyako Jyu over rice, Osuimono, salad and pickles for $6.95. The menu is extensive with 40 possibilities plus Okazu and Tokyo style sushi.

STUART ANDERSON'S
Located at 98-1262 Kaahumanu Rd. This is strictly western fare, ie., lots of beef, chicken, shrimp. Prices, especially for lunch, are very reasonable and the food is just like one would find on the mainland, 487-0054.

BUZZ'S ORIGINAL STEAKHOUSE
Located at 98-751 Kuahao Place, Pearl City. To find it drive up Kaahumanu from Kamehameha and you will see it on the left. This is owned and operated by the same people who run Buzz's out in Lanikai. They are open for lunch and dinner. Most dinner entrees go from $10 to $26, while lunch is in the $6 to $12 range, 487-6465.

MONTEREY CANNERY
Located in the Pearl Ridge Center. Open every day for breakfast, lunch, and dinner. The food is not high priced, the menu is extensive, and the atmosphere is nice. Below and in front of the entrance to the restaurant is a small farm totally devoted to water cress, 487-0048.

Whenever you drive in Hawaii,
you must buckle up.
Unlike the mainland,
you can be stopped
for not wearing a seat belt
and the fine is around $20.

POINTS OF INTEREST

U.S.S. ARIZONA
The Visitor Center is located off Kamehameha Highway at Pearl Harbor Naval Station, about a twenty minute drive from central Honolulu. From this Center a boat ride out to the Memorial is free as is the twenty minute movie that precedes it. There is also a museum that tells the story of the attack on Pearl Harbor and some of the story of the war in the Pacific. The Visitor Center is open from 8:00 a.m. until 3:00 p.m. Tuesday through Sunday. There is a dress requirement-shirt, shoes, shorts but no swim suits. We recommend visiting here in the morning as there is often a hour or two wait and there is not too much to do in the neighborhood. Next door is the Bowfin pacific Submarine Museum: adults $7, children 7-12 $3, 4-6 $1, 3 and under free.

ALOHA FLEE MART AT ALOHA STADIUM
This is held every Wednesday, Saturday, and Sunday. If you are in the area you can't miss Aloha Stadium.

NIGHT LIFE

There is often entertainment offered in some of the local bistros or restaurants. Of course, the new rage all over Hawaii is the Karaoke Bar, where patrons sing on stage with the words of the song flashed on a screen. There are probably several of these in the neighborhood. The one we remember seeing was at the Edokko Japanese restaurant. Other than that there is a movie theater at the Pearl Ridge Shopping Center.

SPORTS

GOLF

PEARL COUNTRY CLUB
This is a private club, open to the public. To find, take the H-1 Freeway to the Aiea exit. Take Moanalua Road to Kaonohi Street and turn mauka for about a mile or so and you will see the entrance to the course on your right. On weekdays the fee is $60 cart included and mandatory. On weekends the fee is $65. Club rental is $30. For more information call 487-6140.

TED MAKALENA GOLF COURSE
This public course, located in Waipahu, is a challenge because of all the water holes in spite of the fact that it is short and flat. The fee is $18 weekdays, $20 weekends, 1/2 price for nine holes. Either power carts or hand carts are available for $11 or $2 respectively. For more information call 296-7888.

MOANALUA GOLF COURSE

To find, take Moanalua Road to Ala Aolani Street. The course is located west of Tripler Army Medical Center, a huge pink building that is hard to miss. The course is public, nine holes, with a fee of $20 weekdays and $25 weekends. After 3 p.m. on weekdays the fee drops to $15 and on weekends $17. Carts rent for $9 and clubs for $5. For more information call 839-2411.

TENNIS

There are five locations in the Pearl/Aiea area: 1) Aiea Recreation Center, 99-350 Aiea Heights Drive, two lighted courts, 2) Pacific Palisades Playground, 2292 Auhuhu Street, two unlighted court, 3) Pearl City Kai, 1962 Lehua Avenue, eight lighted courts, 4) Pearl City Recreation Center, 485 Moomaemae Street, two lighted courts 5) Pearl Ridge Community Park, 99-940 Moanalua Road, six unlighted courts.

Did we miss anything?
We're sure we did.
Perhaps you have discovered
something you would
like to share?
If so, drop us a line
or give us a call!
B & B Hawaii
Box 449
Kapaa, Hi. 96746
or call
808-822-7771

AROUND OAHU

FROM MILILANI TO WAIMEA BAY

When one leaves the Honolulu/Pearl City area to get to the north shore of Oahu, there are two different routes possible. One can take either Highway 99 (Kamehameha Hwy.) west of Pearl City through the center of the Island, through Mililani Town and Wahiawa out to the coastal town of Haleiwa. Or one can take the H-2 Freeway, which will miss both Mililani, Wahiawa, the restaurants mentioned below, as well as Points of Interest in the Mililani Wahiawa area.

This great flatland, which lies between the two mountain ranges, the Koolaus and the Waianaes, is for the most part Oahu's farmland. Land that is not growing sugar or pineapple is probably controlled by the military. The first stop along Route 99 is Mililani Town, which is as much like a mainland city as you will find in Hawaii. As one looks at all the tract homes, one gets the feeling that Los Angeles cannot be far away. The only "center" to the town are the shopping centers. In July of 1986 Mililani won the *All American City* award, which is something no other city in Hawaii has been able to do.

Mililani has three shopping centers, 1. the Mililani Town Center located on Meheula Parkway, 2. Mililani Shopping Center on Kamehameha Hwy., 3. Mililani Market Place located on Meheula Parkway. Most of the restaurants listed below are in one of these three Centers. Mililani town Center is the newest, opening in December of 1987. While not every site had been occupied on our last visit, most of them are open.

One thing that interested us was the cooperative farm located on the right hand side of Highway 99 just past Mililani Town. We could see that the land seemed to be separated into many small plots of land with many different crops planted. This land was set aside years ago by Mayor Fasi so that people who did not own enough land to grow their own gardens could raise vegetables and fruit. What makes it most interesting for visitors is that one gets a chance to see some local foods growing that one would hardly get a chance to see on the mainland.

A few miles beyond Mililani Town is Wahiawa, which like Waimanalo on the east side of Oahu is cowboy country. We walked from one end of Wahiawa to the other and could find nothing that would cause us to stop again other than the Botanical Gardens mentioned below.

Just beyond Wahiawa on the right hand side of the road you will see a sign for Dole Pineapple. This is a good place to get a refreshing bite of pineapple and a chance to see pineapple growing, but the pineapple is not processed here and basically this is a gift shop. Since Dole is in the process of shuting down its pinapple operation in Hawaii, this may not be there for long.

Next to Dole is a most interesting place, Halemano Plantation, a number of small shops including a restaurant set in a little mall. The purpose of this project is to provide a place where the mentally retarded adult can be provided education and employment opportunities in an integrated work setting. The Country Inn Restaurant, Gift Shop, Farm, Silk Flower Shoppe, and Used Furniture Store provide a real work environment where special people can work side by side with people from all ethnic, educational, and economic backgrounds. The ten acre complex is made up not only of training and retail facilities, but also a nine unit residential project, providing semi-independent living arrangements for some very special people. Anthony Lapenia, who manages the restaurant, told us they have been quite successful in their venture. When we first stopped by in '87 and chatted with Anthony we wondered if Halemano Plantation would still be there on our next visit. We obviously did not reckon on the spirit of its founder, Susanna F. Cheung and the people who staff this place. Do yourself a favor and stop by here, if not for lunch at least for a visit. We feel sure your spirits will be lifted.

MILILANI RESTAURANTS

All of the restaurants mentioned in this section with the exception of Mililani Golf Course and Halemano Plantation are in one of the three Shopping Centers. If you have any trouble finding them, ask anyone in town for directions.

LOCAL STYLE

HALEMANO PLANTATION
As stated above, this is actually past Wahiawa and before Haleiwa, but this seems to us the best place to put it. It is open every day from 8:30 to 4:30. You can get a buffet lunch for $7.50 and if you like local style food, you cannot beat the value and it is for a good cause. What one should keep in mind, however, is that tour buses stop by here for lunch and it can get quite crowded. It might be a good idea to get there a little early.

INN & OUT
Located in the original Mililani Shopping Center which is located on Kamehameha Highway. Take out only, box lunches. We did not try it, but from the amount of food they were preparing, it was obvious that this spot is popular with the local folks. This might be a good spot to pick up a picnic lunch to take to the beach a few miles beyond. Everything was priced under $4.00.

SUN'S B-B-Q
Located in the same center mentioned above. Korean style food at moderate prices, served cafeteria style.

MILILANI RESTAURANT
Same Center, open from 10:30 a.m. until 8:30 p.m., counter style. The food is a mixture of Oriental and American and the prices are quite low.

MILILANI BAR BQ

This is located in the Mililani Town Center located on Meheula Parkway east of Kam Highway. If you drive out H-2 and take the Mililani exit, you will find it on your left as you drive into Mililani.

PUHI BOWL SAIMEN

Also in the new center. This is a possibility for one who wants a quick snack of local food.

PO SING KITCHEN

Located in the Mililani Market Place Center west of Kam Highway on Meheula Parkway. They are open for lunch and dinner from 10 am to 9 pm and food is Cantonese served cafeteria style.

MAILE CHINESE

Located in Mililani Center off Kam. Highway. Cantonese style food at reasonable prices. They are open daily from 11:00 a.m. until 8:45 p.m. The atmosphere is plain and the place is clean.

local/Tourist Style

MARU-HI RESTAURANT

Located in Mililani Town Center on Meheula Parkway east of Kam. Highway. Open for lunch from 11-3 and for dinner from 4:30-9, they serve Japanese and American cuisine at modest prices. Lunch prices go from $5.95 for Teriyaki Chicken to $11.95 for New York Steak. Dinner prices go up a couple of dollars for most entrees but not N.Y. Steak.

WUNG FU CHINESE

A new restaurant also in Mililani Town Center which serves mostly Cantonese dishes for very low prices.

YUM YUM TREE

Also in Mililani town Center. This is an Oahu chain that has five stores on the Island. They are open for breakfast, lunch, and dinner and are so much like mainland restaurants that not much need be said. Lunch is below $10, in fact the most expensive entree is Sirloin Steak at $6.95. The most expensive dinner is the Seafood Platter at $12.75. One can hardly go wrong if all one wants to do is eat and be gone.

JR'S RESTAURANT

In the same center as Yum Yum and a bit like it only a little more local and a little less expensive. Open from 7 am to 9 pm.

WALDO'S PIZZA

Located in the Kam. Highway Center.

TACO TOWN

Also in the Kam Center.

75

CHUCKS
In the Kam. Highway Center and open for lunch and dinner, this is the fancy dining out spot in Mililani. Most of the dinner entrees are between $15.00 and $20.00, salad bar style. Lunch is a much better deal.

SIZZLER
In the Mililani Marketplace. This may be even a better deal than Yum Yum if you like the style. Hasn't everyone in America eaten at a Sizzler?

MILILANI GOLF COURSE
Open for breakfast, lunch, and dinner, but closes fairly early in the evening, around 7 p.m., unless they are very busy. The food is a mixture of Oriental and American. The prices are low.

POINTS OF INTEREST

HELEMANO PLANTATION
Since we mentioned this above we will not repeat ourselves, but we mention it again since we hope you do not miss it.

WAHIAWA BOTANICAL GARDENS
Located at 1396 California Avenue, which is right of the highway as you come into Wahiawa from Mililani and a little less than a mile off the Kam. Highway. The admission is free for this four acres of tropical gardens and they are open from 9 am-4 pm. This makes a nice stop on the way to the north shore.

FARMER'S MARKET
If you happen to be passing through Haleiwa on a Tuesday, you might like to visit this as there is a lot of local color at these farmer's markets. You will find this about 1/2 mile east on California Ave. To our recollection this begins around 10 am. In fact it may be held other days, we are just not sure. if you find our that it is, please let us know.

MOVIES
There is a theater in the Mililani Town Center which shows first run movies.

SPORTS

MILILANI GOLF COURSE
This is one of Oahu's nicer courses and the price is not as low as last year. It is now $60 on weekdays and $70 on weekends, cart included. For more information call 623-2222.

HAWAII COUNTRY CLUB
To find this take Kunia Road west from the center of Wahiawa. This is an eighteen hole, rather short course, and since it is far out, it is not too difficult to get on. The fee is $45 on weekdays and $ 50 on weekends and we believe this includes the cart. For more information call 621-5654.

TENNIS
There are two spots in Mililani and one in Wahiawa. The two in Mililani are: 1) Mililani Neighborhood Park, 95-245 Kaloapau Street, two unlighted courts, 623-5258, 2) Mililani Waena Park, 95-590 Naholoholo Street, two lighted courts, 623-5258. In Wahiawa at the Wahiawa Recreation Center, 1139-A Kilani Avenue, four lighted courts, 622-4751.

Just a little reminder

After you leave the Mililani area
you will shortly reach the Northshore
where Beaches are about as beautiful
as any in the world.
At times the ocean is calm
and swimming is relatively safe.
At other times, especially in the winter,
waves rise as high as 30
and on rare occasions 40 feet.
Obviously, at times like these,
the ocean is not safe.
But at all times the ocean is powerful
and must be treated with respect.
Never turn your back on a wave
unless you intend riding it in.
Make sure that you do not
get further out than you can handle.
If you are with children,
keep a good eye on them.
Even when the ocean is most calm,
a sneaker wave can come in
and bounce one around like a rag doll.

HALEIWA

When you reach the north coast of Oahu, a right turn will take you to Haleiwa and then east around the north side and eventually back to Honolulu. If you go on, past Thompson's Corner, a short drive will take you to the north west end of Oahu, where there are beautiful expansive beaches that the surfers just love, the glider planes at Dillingham Airfield, and polo grounds at Mokuleia. Polo season opens in March, and matches are held at 2:30 p.m. each Sunday all spring and summer.

Haleiwa is surfer territory and the place resembles areas south of Los Angeles. Little shops and new restaurants open and close with a frequency reminiscent of the tides. However, most of the places we visited last are still there and about the same.

If you happen to be a fudge freak you will think you have died and gone to heaven if you visit the Fudge Factory located next to and in the same building as Jameson's restaurant.

RESTAURANTS

LOCAL STYLE

BONZAI BOWL
On the mauka side of the main highway in about the center of Haleiwa. This is as close to LOCAL STYLE as you can get in a town that is dominated by haoles. Prices are very low. For example, steak and shrimp are offered for $8.95. The food seems to be a blend of Korean and American. They are open from 7 am-2 pm.

COUNTRY DRIVE IN
This is located next to the Bonzai Bowl and in the past has been the action spot of Haleiwa- lots of food for low price, two scoop rice style. However, this year there were no where near the crowds as before.

SUNSET DINERS
This is a few miles east of town just past Waimea Falls Park, a little counter service spot, nothing fancy but O.K. for a quick bite.

CAMELLIA BAR BQ II
Located on the right as one enters Haleiwa from Mililani. They serve plate lunches for $4.95, Spicy Fried Chicken, to $5.50 for Kalbi Ribs. Dinner prices rise about $1.50. They are open for breakfast, lunch, and dinner.

CHINA INN
In the Northshore Market Place just down the road from Country Drive In. One orders at the counter and takes the food to tables. They are open from 9 am to 9 pm and their prices are pretty low with most dishes around $3.50 to $4.50.

BAR BQ DRIVE IN
Located in the little shopping center on the makai side of the highway right in Haleiwa. An inexpensive little place for a quick lunch.

SEAFOOD CHINESE
This is a new little restaurant on the mauka side of the highway just past the main part of Haleiwa. The cuisine is Szechuan at very reasonable prices, a plate lunch for $3.95 or $4.95.

local/Tourist Style

CAFE HALEIWA
On the mauka side of the highway just as you enter Haleiwa. Mostly this is a breakfast place and they are open weekdays at 6 am, 7 on weekends. For lunch, though, one can get a great turkey sandwich for $4.80 or mahi mahi for $5.45.

PIZZA BOB
Next door to the above.

PARADISE CAFE
Across the street from the above and a the rear of the health food store. This opened in may of 1992 and has gotten good acceptance from the locals. Their motto is "... to provide delicious healthful food for the mind, body, souls, and the planet." Now before you devour that fatty, juicy hamburger, maybe you better stop by and read the back of their menu. If that does not make a true believer out of you, we can't imagine what will.

KUA AINA SANDWICH
This small place on the mauka side of the main highway boasts of having the "world's best hamburger." It is open from 11:00 a.m. until 9 p.m. We stopped by here for lunch so one of us, no names please, could devour a fatty, juicy hamburger. We noticed they received a 25 rating from Zagat for food and an 11 rating for decor. That sounded about right to us.

STORTO'S
Located down the street and across from Kua Aina Sandwich. In business here since 1977, serving the same good food they always have, but the names of the sandwiches have been changed to protect innocent ears. No longer can one order any of twenty different sandwiches with "cutesy names" as *Ike and Tina Tuna* or *Joan Livers*. The owner confessed that it just did not work since people simply became confused and besides, no one eats liverwurst no matter how clever the name. Maybe we have mellowed but we kind of liked the names. After all, what better name for a hot Turkey than *Cluck Gobble*? The fact that we got this did not make us feel any younger. At any rate, you can still get a good sandwich here for a reasonable price.

ROSIE'S CANTINA
This Mexican restaurant is located in the same Shopping Center as Steamer's which is mentioned below. Hosts tell us it is good.

HALEIWA BEACH GRILL
This is a new place located several blocks east of Kua Aina that serves authentic Hawaiian food as well as some American dishes.

TROPICAL DREAMS EMPORIUM & GARDEN CAFE
This is located a few doors east of Haleiwa Beach Grill at the rear of a small shop. This might be a god place to get a quick sandwich or salad.

STEAMER'S
This and Jameson's by the Sea are the "hot" spots of the north shore. The food is good but not cheap. The garden like atmosphere is attractive. They are open for dinner every day and serve a brunch on Sunday for $13.95. There is dancing on Thursday, Friday, and Saturday until 2:00 a.m. if you decide to make a night of it, 637-5071. At night Steamer's opens up their patio area (ten tables) under the name Mario's and serves pasta and other Italian dishes. Mario's has an Italian buffet on Tuesday and Saturday nights.

CHART HOUSE
Located on the west side of the bridge at the east end of Haleiwa. There are several of these in Hawaii and the food is standard American prices in the mid-teens. This one has a great view of the water.

GIOVANNI'S ITALIAN DELI
This is a small take out place located just past the east side of the bridge.

JAMESON'S BY THE SEA
On the highway about a mile down the road after you reach Haleiwa from Mililani on the mauka side. Owned by the same people who started Jameson's in Honolulu, this place has much appeal. During the day a light lunch is served on the porch just outside the bar, or, if you don't care to wait, at a table inside. Dinner is served upstairs where the view is the best in Haleiwa. The prices for dinner are not low, but this is the place we would recommend for that special occasion, 637-4336. At night they open their patio area (around 10 tables) and serve pasta and other Italian food under the name Mario's, which has a buffet on Tuesday and Saturday nights.

D' AMICOS
This is located beyond Haleiwa at Sunset Beach. The specialty here is pizza, but also available are a few pasta dishes or a few sandwiches. Spaghetti with meatballs goes for $5.25 while sandwiches are in the $3 to $4 range.

POINTS OF INTEREST

CONGREGATIONAL CHURCH
Be sure to stop and see this small church which is most famous for its clock which was made in England for Queen Liliuokalani. Not only does it tell time but the day of the week, the year, the phase of the moon, and something else we have forgotten. When the clock was made it was mechanical, but it has since been made electric. Behind the Church there is a thrift store operated by the Church.

COUNTY FAIR AND LOCAL CRAFTS
You will see this at the Community Association building as you enter Haleiwa.

WAIMEA FALLS PARK
This privately owned park, encompassing over eighteen hundred acres, and the Polynesian Cultural Center get most of the tourist attention on the north and windward side of Oahu. The cost is around $11.95 for adults and $6.50 for children seven to twelve. If you do not mind crowds, a stop here is worthwhile, and to fully enjoy it, several hours should be allotted. You can either hike or take a free tram ride to the falls and then swim in the pool at the base of the falls.

BEACHES

Except for a few spots, swimming on the north shore of Oahu is never perfectly safe, and during the winter months just playing in the waves is foolhardy. One has to see to believe the size of some of these waves. Keep in mind, too, that the waves are not constant. You can manage them one minute and get knocked around like a cork the next. This huge surf brings surfers from all over the world to try the Bonzai Pipeline, and even they back off when the winter surf is at its highest. At times the main highway is closed as huge waves cascade across the road. Most of this area is *look but don't touch* country.

HALEIWA BEACH PARK
Here is the exception that proves the rule as far as swimming conditions are concerned. It is almost always safe to swim here since this beach is set in Waialua Bay. It is right at Haleiwa so it is easy to find. There are picnic facilities, rest rooms, showers, and a playground for children.

KAIKAKA STATE RECREATION AREA
This spot is better for picnicking than swimming since the shoreline here is rocky. There are picnic and rest room facilities.

WAIMEA BAY BEACH PARK
Swimming during the summer months can be safe here since again there is some protection. The main problem with this beach is that it attracts huge crowds and unless one gets there early, finding a parking spot could be a problem.

SUNSET BEACH
Except for Waikiki this is surely the most famous beach in Hawaii, and around the world Sunset Beach means surfing. There is no time of the year that we would swim here unless the water were too calm for surfing. Yet this is a beautiful spot for sunbathing or beach combing.

SPORTS

GLIDER RIDES
Also at Dillingham one can take a glider ride, one person for $45 or two for $70. It looks like an outstanding trip and the people who take it rave about it. Just watching them soar through the air is an experience worth having, so whether you go for a ride or not, stop by for a look. For more information call Soar Hawaii, 6373147

POLO
We think there are polo matches out this way on Sunday afternoons.

FROM WAIMEA BAY TO KANEOHE

After one passes Waimea Bay going around the east side of Oahu, there is not much civilization with the exception of a few little towns and the Turtle Bay Hilton and the Polynesian Cultural Center. As stated above, the Polynesian Cultural Center, which is owned and operated by the Mormon Church, is a major destination point for tourists. Visitors arrive by the bus loads. Comments from travel writers vary from glowing to insulting. We have spoken to many people who have visited and find that most people enjoy it. The admission is not cheap, around $25 for adults and $12 for children 5-11, under five free, and this does not include the Polynesian show in the evening since this admission charge is from 12:30-6 pm. The charge for the evening show, which includes dinner is $41 for adults and $24 for children. They are closed on Sunday.

The Cultural Center attempts to bring to life seven primitive Polynesian cultures: Hawaii, Fiji, Samoa, Tonga, Tahiti, Marquesas, and Maori (New Zealand). One can either walk among these seven villages, or take the open air train and listen to the guide's talk. At different times of the day, the people from each village get together for a performance, such as the Pageant of the Long Canoes held every afternoon. The Center is closed on Sundays.

RESTAURANTS

LOCAL STYLE

AHI'S KAHUKU RESTAURANT
This is located in the little town of Kahuku. This is a great deal if you like shrimp since they evidently can get a good deal from the shrimp farm up the road. They have four shrimp specials (scampi, tempura, deep fried, cocktail) for $6.95. They are open for lunch and dinner with sandwiches all under $5 and no dinner entree over $12.95, steak and shrimp combo.

JOJEN'S
A small takeout window service place located in the Old Sugar Mill.

LAIE CHOP SUEY
Open from 10:00 a.m. until 9 p.m. The food is Cantonese with a liberal sprinkling of other dishes. Prices are low; for example, a lunch plate goes for $3.50 and dinner for $4.25.

KAAAWA COUNTRY KITCHEN
This is another small window service place with a few tables outside which might be a good place to bet a quick lunch for a low price. You can get Fish and Chips for $3.50 or Fried Chicken for $3.95 or Curry Stew for $3.50.

local/Tourist Style

JAMESON'S AT THE MILL
Just before you enter Kahuku from Haleiwa you will see and old sugar mill that has been converted to a Visitor's Center complete with shops and a couple of dining places. Since this is owned and operated by an old Oahu "stand by" and open for breakfast and lunch, we can be sure you will get a good meal for a moderate price.

RAINBOW BAR BQ
Located just past Laie on the mauka side of the road, they have a take out window or a sit down restaurant inside. Food here has a decidedly local flavor and would offer the lowest prices of the restaurants in this section.

PAT'S SEABREEZE
Located a few miles south of the Cultural Center at Punaluu, they are open for breakfast, lunch, and dinner. The food is mainland style, prices modest for lunch, but higher for dinner. For example, lunch runs between $6 and $10, while dinner goes from $12 to $21. What you get here, however, is a very nice atmosphere, right on the waterfront. Tour buses also stop here for lunch, 293-8502.

PANIOLO CAFE
Paniolo in Hawaiian means cowboy. Actually it is the Hawaiian pronunciation of Espanol. So restaurants that use that name suggest western fare, ie., thick char broiled steaks and lots of fried potatoes. Here you can get that and more; Mexican food, for example, or if you care to you can get some nice fried rattlesnake meat. Prices are moderate with entrees going from $6.00 to $10. When we stopped there this year the waitress informed us that rattlesnake was out of season.

CROUCHING LION INN
Open for lunch and dinner, the Crouching Lion, named for the huge rock off the coast that some say resembles a lion, is popular with locals and tourists alike. Its strong point is the setting, on a bluff overlooking the ocean. Lunch prices are moderate, but dinner prices go up fast, to $20.00 a person. Since tour buses stop here, it can be crowded, 237-8511.

POINTS OF INTEREST

LAIE POINT
From the Laie Shopping Center, take the road that goes makai into the residential area. At the top of this hill, turn right and drive to the end of the road. You are bound to see some local fisherman trying their luck. This is such a scenic spot that we suggest it for a picnic or just a good place to rest for a while. We stopped by here again this trip and were even more impressed with how beautiful the view was from this point.

SACRED FALLS
This is one of the most popular hikes on the east side. It is two miles to the falls and hikers are advised to read the sign at the start of the trail. We stress not trying to cross the stream if it is raining in the mountains or it is obvious the stream is raging. Also, do not start this hike without insect repellent as there are many mosquitoes here. But with all this in mind, it is a wonderful hike.

BEACHES

KAHUKU BEACH
To get to this beach you must cut across the Kahuku Golf Course. This is a secluded spot, very beautiful with a white sand beach. There are no facilities. If the ocean is not too rough, swimming here is safe.

MALAEKAHANA STATE RECREATION AREA
You will come to this just after you go through Kahuku arriving from the north or just after you go through Laie coming from the south. This is one of the good swimming spots on the windward or north side of Oahu. All of the facilities are here: picnic tables, rest rooms, showers. When we passed by this visit we noticed that the park was closed due the large number of campers. It seems that the park is being used to accommodate the homeless the way Waimanalo once was.

HAUULA BEACH PARK
Since this is right on Kam. Highway, just south of Laie, you are not likely to miss it. All of the facilities are here, it is easy to get to, and swimming is usually safe. It is not as beautiful as some of the others.

KUALOA REGIONAL PARK
You will come to this just after you pass Kaaawa. This would make an excellent picnic spot or just a place to rest after a long drive.

SPORTS

GOLF

TURTLE BAY COUNTRY CLUB
Located at the northeast tip of Oahu and part of the Hilton Hotel but open to the public. For non-guests the fee is $99 weekdays, cart included, and $108 weekends. For more information or starting time, call 293-8574.

KAHUKU GOLF COURSE
This short, nine hole course on Oahu's east shore does not get much play in spite of the fact that it is only $14 for nine holes and $18 for eighteen on weekdays and $20 on weekends for nine, $26 for eighteen. For more information call 293-5842.

*Whether you are already in the Islands
or still on the mainland,
keep in mind that our office
can take care of your travel plans
whether it is accommodations,
car rental, helicopter ride,
a golf starting time
or any other activity in Hawaii.
Perhaps in the future
we will be able to
handle your plane reservations as well.*

KANEOHE

Kaneohe is located on the windward side of the Koolau Mountain range, about a twenty minute drive from Honolulu. Most of the people who live in Kaneohe work in Honolulu, and in the morning and late afternoon cars pour over the Pali and Likelike Highway in a seemingly endless line. Like many places on Oahu, there is a military influence here. Kaneohe Marine Base is located along Kaneohe Bay.

Neither Kaneohe nor Kailua are thought of as tourist areas. One indication of this is that there are no hotels, motels, or overnight accommodations of any kind other than Bed & Breakfast homes and many little vacation cottages along the east and north coast. Restaurants and shops in the Kaneohe/Kailua area depend on local trade for their survival, which is a major factor in keeping prices lower than in resort spots. Kaneohe boasts the largest shopping center outside of Honolulu, the Windward Mall. Once inside this mall, it is easy to forget you are in Hawaii. Some of the restaurants in this area resemble mainland places, but there are plenty of ethnic restaurants also, and in both prices tend to be lower than in the typical tourist areas.

At first glance this area may not seem to offer much, but we urge visitors to take a closer look. Beaches from Kailua to Waimanalo are as beautiful as any in Hawaii. Stores which are not geared to tourists sometimes offer bargain prices. At any rate, those who wish to avoid the *typical tourist* locations can do it here.

RESTAURANTS

LOCAL STYLE

WINDWARD CITY MALL
This is one of the largest shopping centers outside of Honolulu. If you are hot and tired from the drive out to the east side, you might want to wander around this air-conditioned enclosed center, which has many fast food dining places. When we stopped by here we enjoyed one of the frozen tropical fruit juices they sell from a little wagon.

CHUN'S B.B.Q.
In the industrial Park area. To find, turn mauka off Kam Highway on Kahuhipa St. and go about two or three blocks to Alaloa St., turn right and it is right there. Prices are low and food is cooked to local tastes.

BOB'S SIAMEN
Located at 46-132A Kahuhipa St. in the Industrial area.

KIKUYA
At 46-148 Kahuhipa St.

KIN-SUN
A small place in the Foodland Shopping Center at the corner of Kam Highway and Kaneohe Bay Rd. If you like local plate lunch style food, you will like this spot.

SANTINO RISTORANTE ITALIANO
Located at 46-138 Kahuhipa St. in the industrial center (in our last edition Wing Sing Chop Suey was here). We may have this in the wrong category; we do so because of location, but since they serve Italian cuisine local/Tourist might be more appropriate. The next time we are in Kaneohe we will eat here and find out.

KIM CHEE
A little Korean style restaurant, not much to look at but if you are starving for some Kalbi ribs this may be the place. It is on the Kam. Highway next to Thalia's, mentioned below.

KOZO SUSHI
In the same center mentioned above, just take out for low prices.

L & L BARBECUE INN
At 45-1106 Kam. Hwy. This is local to da max.

local Style

GOLDEN CROWN CHOP SUEY
At 46-018 Kam Highway on the mauka side of Kaneohe, they are open from 10:30 a.m. until 9:00 p.m. Cantonese style food, with low prices if one selects the plate lunch or dinner, which goes for $3.50 and $4.00. They now have a luncheon special for $2.99.

MUI KWAI
At 45-1052 Kam. Hwy. and open daily from 10:30 to 9 p.m. The fare is strictly Hong Kong Cantonese. The dishes are mostly in the $3 to $5 range. The atmosphere is not fancy.

We realize that our method of grouping restaurants into LOCAL STYLE, local Style, local Tourist Style may sometimes be confusing. Sometimes there is a fine line between them. If you read the Restaurant Guide on pages nine and ten it should beome clearer.

local tourist Style

SMITTY'S
At 46-077 Kam. Highway, across the street from the Windward Mall. Open from 7 a.m. until 10 p.m. daily. The great deal here is the early bird special between 3-6 p.m. One can get a good meal for as low as $4.45, and there are several selections. Another good deal is the all you can eat soup and salad bar.

KOA HOUSE
Just off Kam. Highway on the mauka side of Kahuhipa St. On weekends only breakfasts are served. During the week their menu for lunch and dinner is extensive and the prices are not high, many entrees under $10, 234-5772.

HAIKU GARDENS
We are embarrassed to admit that we missed this in our first edition. We had been told about it, but when looking for it we failed to drive far enough up Haiku Rd. We would urge anyone who is looking for a restaurant in a beautiful setting to be sure to try this. They are open for lunch and for dinner. The food is moderately priced.

KIN WAH
This is a place that both hosts and guests love. We missed it first time around but any of our guests who stayed in Kaneohe or Kailua probably were told. The food is basically Cantonese, servings are generous, and the prices are not high, mostly in the $4 to $5 range, with many even less. They are located at 45-588 Kam. Hwy. which is on the mauka side. They are open daily from 10 a.m. to 9 p.m. 247-4812.

FLAMINGO
This is located in the Foodland Shopping Center at the Corner of King Kam Hwy and Kaneohe Bayview Road. This is a small Oahu restaurant chain that has been around since 1950. They have a fairly extensive menu, mostly mainland style but one of their specialties is Oxtail soup.

THALIA'S FINE DINING
This place has been around a long time and they changed locations from the Bay View Golf Course on Bayview Drive to 46-014 Kam. Hwy. The specialty is Prime Rib $12.50 for large cut and $10.50 for small cut. (Last edition these prices were $14 and $12. Since business has been rather slow they have dropped their prices). They are open for lunch and dinner and lunches go from $4.95 for tuna sandwich up to $8 for Top Sirloin.

CHAO PHYA THAI
Located in the Center at the corner of Bayview and Kam. Hwy. This place is getting rave reviews and from what we hear folks are driving over the Pali to dine here. Considering all the Thai and Vietnamese restaurants in Honolulu that is quite a compliment.

KENNY'S
Located on Kam. Hwy. across from Windward Mall. This has the look of a Denny's but the food is fixed more for local tastes. The menu is a mix-Teriyaki, some Hawaiian dishes, and lots of standard American.

CRABBIES

Once located in Waikiki on Kuhio Ave. they are now out in Kaneohe in the Kaneohe Shopping Center on Kam. Highway near Times Super Market. They are open for breakfast, lunch and dinner and the specialty of the house is all kinds of seafood, which they have flown in for all over the U.S., including oysters from Louisiana. their motto is, "We shuck em, you suck em." Prices are not low and the atmosphere is not fancy, but if you are in the mood for some crab from Maryland, you might want to give this place a try.

SUPER WOK

In the Kaneohe Bay Center across from Windward Mall, Szechuan cuisine for a reasonable price, ie. dinner for four $22.50.

POINTS OF INTEREST

HEEIA KEA BOAT HARBOR

Located on Kam. Highway just before you reach Kaneohe from the north. Fishing boats launch from this little harbor. There are no party fishing boats, but there is a glass bottom boat which would make a nice excursion. The boat leaves at 10 a.m., 11 a.m., 12:30, 1:30, 2:30, 3:30 p.m. The cost is $7 for adults and $3 for children.

HEEIA STATE PARK

As you continue along Kam. Highway toward Kaneohe you will come to the Park on your left. This is a good place to picnic. The facilities are used mostly by the local folks for parties.

KAILUA/LANIKAI

The windward coast of Oahu has a population of around eighty thousand, which is around ten percent of the population of the Island. Most of these people live in the Kailua/Kaneohe area while most work in Honolulu. As stated above, this is not a tourist area as far as mainland tourists are concerned, and yet this is one of the places that those who live in Honolulu come to get away from it all.

Kailua has become a special spot for windsurfers since conditions here are ideal: almost always a steady trade wind, a fairly calm ocean, and enough surf for it to be exciting. Good windsurfers make it look easy, but all one need do to see how difficult this sport is to master is to watch a beginner take fall after fall.

One of the surprising things to us about Kailua is the number of restaurants. Perhaps those living on the military base get tired of their chow line and eat out often. Whatever the reason, the benefit is that there is a wide choice of really good places to eat and the competition keeps prices in line.

It seems to us that the Kailua area is a perfect compromise for those who want to be close to lots of action (Honolulu is about 1/2 hour away) and those who want to get away from it all (either at the beaches of this area or the North Shore, also just a short drive away.) You can take our word for it that nowhere in Hawaii is the ocean any more beautiful than it is on this east shore of Oahu.

RESTAURANTS

LOCAL STYLE

KEANA CAFE

Located at 324 Kuulei Rd., which is an extension of Kailua Rd. This is an excellent place to try authentic Hawaiian cuisine. It is open for breakfast and lunch from 6:30 am to 1:30 pm Wednesday, Thursday, and Sunday, and from 6:30 am to 6 pm Friday and Saturday, closed Monday. For $7.50 one gets Kalua Pig, Beef Stew, Laulau, Lomi Salmon, Pipikaula, Poi or Rice (one scoop), and no one will force you to dance the hula. From our notes we think Hawaiian food is served only Friday & Saturday. If any doubt call 263-0102.

KIM CHEE #5 ONLY

That's the name, folks. It is located at 16 Kainehe St. They are open every day for lunch and dinner and if you like Korean food you will not be disappointed here. You can get a good lunch for around $5.

KAILUA OKAZU-YA

At 440 Uluniu St. just makai of Oneawa St. Very small, open for breakfast and lunch only. In this counter style restaurant, each item is priced and you select as much or as little as you want. Mostly the food is Japanese but there is a sprinkling of other Oriental dishes, also. Very low prices make this a good place to experiment if you have never tried this type of fare.

IN SAM

Next door to Okazu-Ya. Korean food at low prices.

BAR-B-CUE-EAST

This is located in the Kailua Shopping Center on Kailua Ave. You can get very ethnic food, but if you prefer you can get food that is more western. The prices are low and the atmosphere is local color.

NEW CHINESE GARDENS

At 426 Uluniu St. Not much to look at from the outside but our hosts assure us that the food is good and prices are low. Cantonese style. For lunch they have plate lunches that are hard to beat.

DIANE'S BBQ OKAZU-YA

This is a new little spot that serves both Korean and Japanese cuisine. It is located on Hamakua Dr. just south of Kailua Rd.

local Style

DRAGON PALACE
As you enter Kailua on Kailua road, take Hamakua to Keola, turn left and drive about one mile and you will come to the Enchanted Lakes Shopping Center on your right. It is located at the far left corner of the Center. This looked like a good place for a Chinese dinner as it was very clean and the prices were low, 262-2218.

THE SHACK
Across the street from Dragon Palace. This is an interesting little place that offers different specials every day. For example, on Monday and Friday one can get a steak dinner for $5.95, Thursday and Saturday fresh fish for $6.95, on Wednesday Fajita for $5.75 and on Tuesday $1 off all burgers all day.

RON'S PLACE
This small take-out place is located at 201 Hamakua Dr. and open from 11 am to 9 pm. They feature Italian food.

BA-LE FRENCH SANDWICH AND BAKERY
This is a new chain with around a dozen stores all over Oahu. This one is in the Holiday Mart Food Court, where you will find several other fast food places. This seemed the most interesting to us. Sandwiches range in price from $1.50 for a Vegetarian Sandwich to $3 for Croissant Meatball. One could simply purchase the small loafs of French bread ($.40) and Ham or Turkey ($4.50 a lb.) and prepare their own pic-nic lunch.

CHING LEE CHOP SUEY
At 132 Oneawa St. mostly Cantonese dishes with a few of the spicier ones but not many. The menu is extensive and the prices are low, most under $5 and nothing with the exception of shark's fin soup over $5.75.

PRINCESS CHOP SUEY
At 127 Hekili St. (see L'Auberge below for directions). Cantonese cuisine at moderate prices, most between $4-$5 with only a few over $6 in a little nicer setting than the ones mentioned above.

WILLOW TREE KOREAN RESTAURANT
This is located in the Aikahi Park Shopping Center which can be found by driving north on Kalaheo Ave until it runs into Kaneohe Bay Dr. You will see the Shopping Center on your right. They are open for lunch and dinner from 11 am to 9:30 pm Monday through Saturday and for dinner only on Sunday. They have an extensive menu of Korean food with prices from $6.45- $10.95 for dinner. They serve a plate lunch for $5.95.

local/Tourist Style

JARON'S
Located at 201A Hamakua Dr. This restaurant opened up just after our last edition went to press so it has a year or so track record and we feel sure they will have a long run and their food and service is very good and their prices are moderate. They are open for breakfast, lunch and dinner. They have an extensive menu with plenty of appetizers for lunch and dinner. If one simply wants an appetizer for lunch for $1 extra they will serve it with soup or salad. Lunch entrees range from $6.95 for Eggplant Parmesan to $10.95 for Shrimp Lanikai. Dinner prices range from $13 to $25 or one can get a light dinner $13 and under.

EL CHARRO AVITA
Located at 14 Oneawa St. You might have to park a block or so away but if you like Mexican food it might be worth it as prices here are quite modest and we have been told the food is good.

BEACH SIDE GRILL
This is a little sandwich shop at 130 Kailua almost to Lanikai that specializes in sandwiches, "gourmet" burgers, and smoothies. Burgers go from $4.25 to $5.25 and sandwiches from $4-$7. One might like to try their Buffalo Burger.

HARRY'S CAFE & DELI
Their first location was in the Aikahi Shopping Center, but they have closed that and moved to the center of Kailua Town. This is a great place for a super sandwich, salad, or even one of Harry's Special Dinners, or Bombay Curry Dinner for $6.95. Homemade soup. More than one host and guest has told us not to miss Harry's.

ASSAGGIO'S
This is new to Kailua and we did not get a chance to try it. They are located at 354 Uluniu St. between Maluniu Ave. and Oneawa.

L'AUBERGE
At 117 Hekili St. To find take Hahani St. mauka off Kailua, go one block and turn right. This is Kailua's special occasion restaurant, open for dinner only, closed Monday. It is Swiss cuisine at moderate prices considering the quality and they offer a light dinner at $8 and $9. This restaurant won an award for being one of the ten best restaurants on Oahu. That certainly indicates that it might be one of the best in Kailua, 263-4663.

THE NO NAME BAR
On Hekili St. a few doors down from L'Auberge (mentioned above). Open for lunch and dinner, kind of a pub like atmosphere serving most sandwiches which cost between $4-$8.

CISCO'S CANTINA
Also on Hekili St. We were told that this is really good Mexican food at low prices.

CINNAMON'S FAMILY RESTAURANT
This is a little hard to find. It is located in the Kailua Center which is on Uluniu St. off Maluniu. They are open for breakfast, lunch, and dinner. We found the food good and the prices modest. Each day they feature a special from a different Nation. Closed Sunday.

SMITTY'S (WAS PLUSH PIPPIN)
This is located in a new Mall at the corner of Kekili and Hamakua. They are open every day for breakfast, lunch, and dinner. The specialty of the house is pies, all the way from apple to peanut butter. Their prices are in the modest range and they are much like many mainland chains.

GEE A DELI
It is hard to find, but if you are looking for a good sandwich or a nice salad it is worth the hunt. It faces the parking lot behind Mac Donald's, which is located off Kuulei, which runs off of Kailua Road. (The square in which this is located is going to house a retirement home for senior citizens. You may have a little trouble finding it).

LOS ARCOS
At 19 Hoolai St. This is a real sleeper. They specialize in Spanish Food, such things as Bistec Pecado, cut up steak with onions,herbs, and peppers, or pork chops in a red sauce. From the outside the place does not show much, but do not be put off by appearances. They are open for lunch Monday -Friday and dinner every day but Thursday. Prices run between $8.50 and $15. 262-8196.

FLORENCE'S
At 20 Kainehe St. This is an old standby in Kailua, Italian food more or less. They are open for lunch weekdays and dinner every night except Tuesday with lunch being the better value by far. Dinner prices run between $12-$18 except for a pasta dinner which runs $6, 261-1078.

SOMEPLACE ELSE
This is located at 33 Aulike St. which used to be Buzz's Fish House. They have been open for about a year and are going strong. They have a wide variety of items to choose from: Pastas from $6.95 to $8.95, or Seafood dishes from $9.95 to $18.95, or several Chicken dishes at $8.95.

BUZZ'S ORIGINAL STEAK HOUSE
On the mauka side of Kawailoa Rd. as you drive into Lanikai. We were glad to see that this was still in business since we have always enjoyed the ambience as well as the food, 261-4661.

ORSON'S BOURBON
At the corner of Hoolai and Puniu just off Kailua Rd. This is another old stand by in Kailua, open for lunch and dinner. Lunch is not too high, but dinner prices run well over $10 and unfortunately, we have been told by hosts, not consistent in quality. They strive for elegance, 262-2306. We have tried their restaurant in Ward Warehouse and enjoyed it very much. Let's face it, no restaurant is always good, so perhaps the above negative comment should be taken with a grain of salt.

SAENG'S THAI
This has been open in Kailua now for several years, but this owner is not new to the restaurant business. He used to own Sang's Thai in Wailuku, Maui, a place we recommend. The decor is excellent and if the food is as good as what we had on Maui when he owned that place, you will not be disappointed. You will want to give this place a try, if you like Thai food, that is. It is located at 315 Hahani St. which runs mauka off Kailua Road. They are open for lunch Monday-Friday from 11-2:30 and for dinner every day from 5-9, 263-9727.

YUM YUM TREE

To find, take Kalaheo Ave. north from the center of Kailua and go around two miles and you will see it on your right. If you have tried the Yum Yum in Honolulu, you will know what to expect. There is a wide selection of entrees, most at moderate prices, in a very nice setting. We had lunch there and were pleased with the food and the cost. They are open daily for breakfast, lunch, and dinner.

SIZZLER

Located in the Aikahi Park Center (see Willow Tree above for directions).

BEACHES

KAILUA BEACH PARK

To find take Kalaheo Ave. south from the middle of Kailua which will run into Kawailoa Rd. At Alala Rd., turn makai and go two blocks to the beach. There are full facilities here, picnic tables, rest rooms, showers, and the swimming is very safe. This is a good place to start a beach walk.

LANIKAI BEACH

There is beach access all along Mokulua Dr. in Lanikai. This along with Kailua Beach is one of the nicest on Oahu and rivals any beach on the Islands.

SPORTS

GOLF
PALI GOLF COURSE

A Public Course between Kaneohe and Kailua on the mauka side of Kam. Highway. Since this course gets lots of play, it is best to call ahead for a starting time. The fee is $18 on weekdays, $20 on weekends, carts $11 but not mandatory. Hand carts $2. Starting times are given out one week in advance and they start taking calls at 6:30 am. For more information call 261-9784.

OLOMANA GOLF LINKS

This is a private course but open to the public. It is located just south of Kailua on the way to Waimanalo. The fee is $29 on weekdays, cart included, and $35 on weekends, cart included. For more information call 259-7926.

BAY VIEW GOLF CENTER

Located makai of the Kam. Highway on Kaneohe Bay Rd. This is an eighteen hole par three course right in Kaneohe. The fee is $20 every day. Hand carts are available for a $3. For more information call 247-0451.

TENNIS
In the Kaneohe/Kailua area there are three public courts: 1.) Kaneohe District Park, 45-660 Keaahaila Rd., six unlighted court, 2.) Kailua Recreation Center, 21 S. Kaihalu Dr., eight courts, four lighted, 3.) Maunawili Neighborhood Park, Maunawili Valley Rd. one lighted court.

WAIMANALO

This little town, squeezed between the sea and the mountains, gets a bad rap from most of the people in the tourist industry. While we have never had a problem there, we have spoken with others who have. Do not leave anything unattended either in your car or on the beach. Of course, that is the sensible thing anywhere, but we have been told that here things are sure to disappear. We would say just don't bother with the place except that Waimanalo has one of the most beautiful beaches in all Hawaii. Most of the problems occur at the public park where camping is permitted. Some of the people camping there are almost permanent residents.

The above was the comment we made in our first edition in 1985, and, while we would still advise caution as far as leaving valuables in the car or on the beach when you went off swimming, we must say that Waimanalo looked much different now than in years past. First of all, the campers were gone. (On this trip we noticed that the campers were back. This may be part of the homeless contingent that Honolulu as well as other large cities are trying to deal with. On the other hand, this may be Hawaiians exercising what they consider their right of ownership. We are just not sure.) Oh, we saw a tent or two, but nothing like before. Most of the people we saw on the beach were local families having a picnic. Waimanalo seems to be on the upswing; if that is an accurate assumption, we strongly recommend a stop here as this is a really beautiful beach area that is in many ways unspoiled.

RESTAURANTS

LOCAL STYLE

KOLOHE HAWAIIAN
Located at 415F Uluniu St. Unfortunately they are closed on Mondays, which was the day we were there, so we did not get a chance to sample the food. One of our guests liked it so much they ate there several days in a row. Open for lunch and dinner from 11-6:30.

WAIMANALO FISH MARKET
Next door to the above and all of the LOCAL delicacies priced just a tad lower.

95

local Style

BUENO NALO
On Kam. Highway, open Tuesday through Friday from 5-9 pm and on Saturday from 3-9 pm and serve dinner only. As the name suggests Mexican cuisine. You cannot tell to look at the place, but this is a favorite with residents of Oahu. We were told that they drive out from Honolulu to eat here. The prices are fairly low, combination plates $8.95-$9.95.

BEACHES

BELLOWS FIELD BEACH PARK
Because this is on a military base, access is given only on the weekends, starting at noon on Friday and going until 6 a.m. Monday. Many writers call this the most beautiful beach on the Island, and while it is nice, it is really no more beautiful than any beach from Waimanalo to Kailua. Camping with a permit is allowed and, in our opinion, that is what makes this a special place. Also, one feels very safe since access to the beach is controlled by the military. We have read that there is a lifeguard, but when we were there he was nowhere in sight. Swimming is safe and this is a good place for a beginner to learn to body surf as the waves are not too big.

WAIMANALO BAY STATE RECREATION AREA
Just north of Waimanalo. As mentioned above, this is an excellent spot, swimming is safe, and it has the added feature of lots of ironwood trees for shade should the sun prove too hot.

KAIONO BEACH PARK
At the south end of Waimanalo, this grass park makes a nice place to picnic, and it seems to get very little use.

As we have said in another part of this book,
Oahu is an Island that should not be missed.
It is far more than Honolulu and Waikiki,
and if you have taken a trip around
and gotten to this place
we feel sure we agree with us.

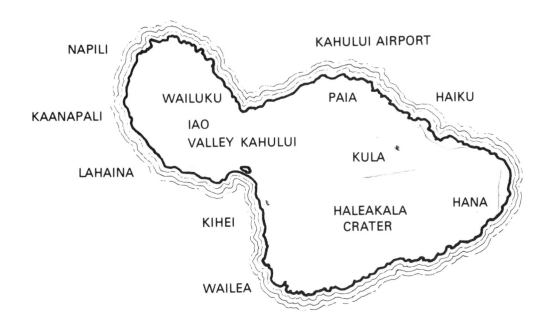

MAUI.....THE VALLEY ISLE

.....DRIVING TIMES....

From Kahului airport to (approxmite)

Wailuku................................ 5 miles, 10 minutes
Iao Valley............................10 miles, 20 minutes
Kihei....................................10 miles, 20 minutes
Wailea..................................15 miles, 25 minutes
Lahaina.................................22 miles, 45 minutes
Kaanapali.............................27 miles, 55 minutes
Kapalua................................37 miles, 65 minutes
Kula.....................................18 miles, 30 minutes
Haleakala.............................36 miles, 90 minutes
Hana.....................................52 miles, 2-3 hours

MAUI

When the average mainlander thinks of Hawaii, it is probably Waikiki and Maui that come to mind; the number of visitors each receives attest to this. Indeed, the residents of Maui intone *Maui no ka oi,* which translates as *Maui is the best.* In fact, it is an old war chant which meant *Maui over all.* But Americans are used to regionalism, the attitude that makes Texans think they have it all when every Californian knows better, and New Yorkers put the Pacific several miles west of Manhattan and seem shocked they cannot get there by subway.

What is there about Maui that causes its partisans to shout its praises? Perhaps it all stems from the god whose name the Island bears, for it was this mighty god who pulled the islands from the sea, who later, to please his mother, caught the sun on a rope and forced him to slow his pace, and, like Prometheus in another mythology, delivered to man the gift of fire.

On Maui is Haleakala, the world's largest dormant volcano and House of the Sun, where thousands trek annually at an ungodly early hour to glimpse the first rays of the sun. We rate this as one of the high points of a trip to the Islands. Others might consider the drive to Hana as the high point of their vacation.

While Mauians boast of the best of everything, we freely admit they have the best potato chips, the best onions, the best wine made in Hawaii, and incredibly beautiful scenery and beaches that rival the best. However, some would say that Maui along with Waikiki serves as the best example to the other Islands of what to watch out for, uncontrolled, poorly planned growth that has created more high rises than Hawaii ought to have.

Our view is that there is really no *best Island.* Each Island has its charm and its appeal. Too often neglected on any of the Islands are the non-tourist areas. So if Maui is your choice, be sure to experience Kahului, Wailuku, Paia, and the Upcountry of Makawao and Kula as well as all those white sand beaches.

LUAUS

MAUI LU
The Maui Lu Resort in Kihei has a Wednesday and Friday night Prime Rib Dinner Buffet with a Polynesian Show. Dinner is from 6 - 8 pm and the Show is at 8 pm. $29.95 for adults, $16.95 for children under 12. Show only is $10.

OLD LAHAINA LUAU
Located in Lahaina at 505 Front St. The luau starts at 5:30 and is held Monday through Saturday on the beach in front of their restaurant, Old Lahaina Cafe. The cost is $46 for adults and $23 for children ages 3-12 years, and is all you can eat and all you can drink. At that rate children should be less that half price, shouldn't they? For more information call 667-1998.

MAUI INTER-CONTINENTAL WAILEA
They advertise this as the Maui's Merriest Luau. This is held Tuesday through Friday at the Maui Intercontinental Hotel at Wailea in Kihei. The cost is $47 for adults and $23.50 for children 12 and under. Dinner is at 5 pm and the show starts at 6 pm. For more information call 879-1922.

ROYAL LAHAINA LUAU
This is the Kaanapali area and the cost is $44.27 for adults, $20.78 for children ages 5 - 12. Happening every night, Dinner is at 6 pm and the show begins at 8:45. Call 661-3611.

SPECIAL EVENTS

ANNUAL ASAHI BEER GOLF TOURNAMENT (EARLY FEBRUARY)
Professional men and women golfers vie for 15,000,000 yen. For more information call Marsha Wienert at 808-879-4465.

LPGA WOMEN'S KEMPER OPEN GOLF TOURNAMENT (LATE FEBRUARY)
For a while this was held at Princeville on Kauai but has returned to Maui and is held at the Wailea Golf Course.

ART MAUI (MIDDLE TO END OF MARCH)
One of the most prestigious juried art shows in Hawaii, admission free. It is held at Hui No'eau Visual Arts Center at Kaluanui, Makawao. Even if you don't visit in March, stop by there are exhibits all year round. For more information call 808-572-6560.

ANNUAL ZOO FEST (LATE MARCH)
A day of entertainment held at the Maui Zoo in Kahului featuring both Hawaiian entertainers, contemporary bands, and other groups. For more information call 808-244-3771.

MAUI/O'NEIL INVITATIONAL (LATE MARCH/EARLY APRIL)
Windsurfer contestants from 12 countries compete for $30,000 in prizes. It is held at Ho'okipa Beach, call 808-579-9756.

SEABURY HALL COUNTRY CRAFT FAIR (EARLY MAY)
Arts and crafts, food booths, games and entertainment, 9 am to 4 pm at the Seabury Hall, Olinda, which is Upcountry, Maui. Call 808-878-6246.

KAUPAKALUA ROPING CLUB'S RODEO (LATE MAY)
Full schedule of rodeo events, call 808-572-9689.

ANNUAL BARRIO FESTIVAL (LATE MAY)
A community cultural event with a Miss Barrio Fiesta Contest, arts and crafts, contests, food booths and more, sponsored by Binhi Filipino Community and held at the War Memorial Gym Complex in Wailuku.

ANNUAL UPCOUNTRY FUN FAIR (EARLY JUNE)
Old fashioned farm fair featuring 4H farmers' products, a fun run, sports tournaments, entertainment and food booths. Call 808-572-8883.

MAKAWAO STATEWIDE RODEO (LATE JUNE EARLY JULY)
An oldtime upcountry rodeo-one of the best held at Oskie Rice Arena in Makawao. Call 808-874-0315.

GREAT KALUA PIG COOK-OFF (JULY 4)
A competition with a $1,000 prize for the best pig roaster in the state. Spectators can watch contestants prepare pigs and imus (underground ovens). A full day of entertainment with a Pua'a Parade (costumed pigs) at noon, held at the Royal Hawaiian Hotel in Lahaina. Call 808-661-3611.

PLANTATION DAY (AUGUST)
Includes annual Portuguese Bean Soup Contest, Keiki (kids) fishing contest, cultural demonstrations, and more. Held at the Maui Tropical Plantation in Waikapu. Call 808-244-7643.

MAUI COUNTY FAIR (OCTOBER)
Held at the fairgrounds in Kahului. Call 808-244-3242.

MAUI COUNTY RODEO (NOVEMBER)
Paniolos (cowboys) from Molokai and Maui compete at the Oskie Rice Arena in Makawao. Call 808-572-9689.

NA MELE O MAUI FESTIVAL (NOVEMBER)
A festival of Hawaiiana through arts, crafts, dances, music, and a luau, held at hotels is Kaanapali and Lahaina. Call 808-879-4577.

MAUI HOSTS

WAILUKU AREA

M-14
This comfortable home is only a few minutes from the Kahului airport. Two bedrooms, each with private entrance. Full bath is shared by both rooms. One room has two twin beds, and the other has a queen size bed. Outdoor patio is shared by all, including use of the pool. Guests can enjoy a dip in the pool or a nice two block walk to Kahului Bay in the mornings or evenings. This B&B is so centrally located it's a great starting place to explore all of Maui. No children. Non smokers, only.
RATES: $45 single, $50 double Two night minimum.

UPCOUNTRY MAUI

PAIA

M-12
Right on the beach and centrally located for sightseeing all of Maui, this large, plantation style home is also in an exclusive neighborhood adjacent to the Maui Country Club. While one cannot see the beach from the home, a short walk (100 yds) will take you to a stretch of white, sandy beach good for walking. Usually the hosts' friendly dog will accompany you! The ocean is calm enough to do laps. The accommodation offered is a large guest room with a private adjoining bath and a queen sized bed. No smoking in the house, please. Two night minimum.
RATES: $60 single, $70 double.

HAIKU

M-4A
A charming Inn that was built in 1870 for Maui's first doctor with the old pineapple cannery. Newly refurbished by the owner/host within the past two years, it sits among nearly one and a half acres of pineapple fields and pine trees. Located just 700 feet above sea level and just down the road from Hookipa Beach. Full breakfast is included each morning and guests have a choice of Twin beds or a Queen size in any of the four guests rooms each with it's own private bath. The host is presently open from October thru May as he owns and operates another Inn each summer in the Adirondacks, called Moose River House.
RATES: $65 single, $80 double. 20% discount for 5 or more day stay. 20% Kama'aina discount for 2 or more day stay.

M-9

A delightful B&B with an ocean view setting, this studio attached to the host's home is private and quiet. The accommodation offers a separate entrance and private bath and is furnished with double bed, rattan furniture, ceramic tile floors and features a mini-kitchen which includes a microwave, toaster, coffee-maker and refrigerator. Your tropical breakfast is served outdoors in a setting of bamboo and palms overlooking the sea. Off the beaten path and on the way to Hana, the rural location and proximity to fresh water pools make this hideaway a memorable one.
RATES: $55 single, $65 double

M-15

For the free spirited, this ocean front, one room, guest cottage known as the "Gazebo" is perched at the edge of a 300 foot cliff with spectacular views of Waipio Bay where whales swim and nurse their young in the winter months. The "Gazebo" is fully carpeted with a queen sized foam mattress on the floor for sleeping and offers a CD player/stereo, small refrigerator, hot plate, toaster oven, microwave and coffee maker. The 1/2 bath is hidden behind mirrored sliding doors, while the hot and cold shower is outside, sheltered from the rain and hidden by tropical plants and flowers. Guests are welcome to use the beautiful swimming pool landscaped with a waterfall as well as the tiled patio with hot tub. Hosts live in the main house and sometimes can rent out the entire home and "Gazebo" for larger parties.
RATES: $75.00 single, $85 double, Two night minimum.

M-18A

This accommodation in the Upcountry area is our recommendation for those who want a special experience and hang the cost. The host, designer and builder of this unique home, has done an outstanding job of creative design. As guests enter the home their first view is a huge mural wall of a surfer catching a big one. Then there are a few stairs down to the living area, past a small interior stream and small fish pond. The bedroom is so cleverly built, using glass to create an open feeling, that you will feel you are nesting with the birds in a tree house, and the view is a tree-top view indeed! Guests, of course, have their own private bath, with a shower that provides a view of the Kula landscape all the way to the blue Pacific. Located above that room at the end of a circular staircase is a small room called the "moon room." It is entirely glass enclosed, hence not for day use as it is quite warm. But imagine the view of the heavens from the bed that rotates 360 degrees. Guests breakfast by the stream that runs through the home or out on the cantilevered deck which hovers over a tropical paradise. Then when guests return after a long day of exploring the Island, your hosts ask them to relax in the hot tub.
RATES: $95 double for one night, $85 double for 2-4 nights, $75 double for 5 nights or more.

M-55
Real island-style living can be enjoyed while staying here   on the lower slopes of Upcountry Maui just about 5 minutes drive from Hookipa, the windsurfing beach of Maui. Overlooking pineapple fields, this studio has a separate entrance and sun deck landscaped with tropical flowers and fruit trees. Inside there is a queen sized bed plus a single bed for a child. Hosts are from Maryland and brought over a lovely armoire and old fashioned stove to complete the furnishings in the studio. The art work on the walls was done by a famous Maui artist, a good friend of the hosts. Three night minimum. Smoking outside, only.
RATES: $50 single, $55 double, Three night minimum

M-56
Your hostess came from the Mainland in 1978 after retiring from a career as psychologist/management consultant with the Navy. Her home is a modern cedar chalet built on two acres, about 17 miles from the airport, on the beautiful green slopes of Haleakala crater in paniolo country near Makawao. While active in community affairs, her hobbies include music, art and environmental issues. The home is tastefully decorated, offering the accommodation of either a bedroom with twin beds or one with a double bed, both adjacent to the guest bathroom. A hearty breakfast is served. No young children or smoking please.
RATES: $60 single or double

M-63
A Maui hideaway in a private setting just about 10 minutes from Hookipa beach. Hosts own their own windsurfing company on Maui so they can offer guests a discount on equipment. The cottage is spacious and with open beam ceilings and sits away from the main house on 2 1/2 acres of palm trees, fruit trees and tropical flowers. Queen sized bed in one bedroom and two high poster twin beds in the other, one private bath with a shower, and a full kitchen with indoor private washer/dryer, TV, cassette stereo (bring your own cassettes). Your hostess spoils her guests with a wonderful basket of goodies for their arrival,. **however no breakfast is served or provided here.** Hosts require a one week minimum. They have a crib for infants at no extra charge.
RATES: $90 single, $110 double, $115 two couples.

KULA

M-1
In Kula experience million dollar views of West Maui, the ocean and the islands of Lanai and Kahoolawe! No wonder your hostess, who has a love for the environment, flowers and nature, lives atop this dormant volcano they call the House of the Rising Sun. Breakfast is brought up to the studio each morning and either served on the private deck or in the room. The large studio has it's own entrance, queen sized bed and private bath tastefully decorated in Laura Ashley prints and white wicker.   There is a counter, sink and refrigerator so that picnic lunches can be prepared, however no cooking is possible. Non smokers please.
RATES: $75 single or double two night minimum.

M-6

Kilohana Bed & Breakfast "Plantation Style". Gather your own macadamia nuts, watch a melodious Chinese thrush build her nest, hike Haleakala, enjoy the panoramic view of Lanai Island, Freshly ground Kona Macadamia Nut Coffee, homemade whole wheat toast or banana bread, fresh fruit compote is a great way to start the day in this spectacular upper Kula home. It is located at 3,300 foot elevation on the slopes of Mt. Haleakala, just a short walk to the Kula Botanical Gardens. From this home it is around a 45 minute drive to the top of Haleakala. There are four accommodations offered here. Two bedrooms upstairs with a bathroom between. One room has a queen bed and single bed in the room while the other room offers a queen sized bed. Also a tiny room downstairs with it's own entrance off the garden and another queen bedded room and private bath facing the flower garden with lovely views. The hostess suggests you find her place before dark, at least on the first night, and that you keep in mind the elevation and wear warm clothes. From this home it is about 15 minutes to the nearest restaurant, 30 minutes to Hookipa beach, and about 2 1/2 hours to Hana. This is a great place for those who love quiet and solitude and want to experience more of Hawaii than the beach.
RATES: $65 single, $75 double. $85 for room with the private bath. Two night minimum

M-7A

This newly remodeled home located on one and a half acres of upcountry oceanview property can accommodate a family of three. The unit offered has a separate entrance and a private bath. Your host family is busy and bustling with two children and working parents. The host is a ranger at Haleakala National Park. Guests have limited refrigerator space for snack food and cold drinks in kitchen. Guests can usually count on fresh bread or rolls being served. Hosts desire non-smoking guests only.
RATES: $45 single or double, $5 extra for third person.

M-26

Named Halemanu which is Hawaiian for bird house, this home is perched at 3,500 ft elevation up on the slope of Haleakala in the town of Kula. An awesome view of the island of Maui away from the mosquitoes and bugs, with quiet and cool nights. The home is brand new and has lots of windows with knock out views as well as various decks, covered or not for outside sitting. The guest room has it's own entrance and private deck, private full bath and queen sized bed. Your hostess is single and is a writer for the Maui News. She looks forward to sharing her home and sometimes will guests hiking or snorkeling . Breakfast is served in a sunny spot on the deck or in the dining area.
RATES: $70 single or double.

M-52

Enjoy cool evenings and relax on a sunny hot deck in the daytime. This lovely home in Kula offers two rooms to guests who enjoy the quiet surroundings of the slopes of Haleakala. Wild birds and exotic flowers greet you in the morning. A great breakfast in the dining room will start your day right. The master bedroom has twin beds with an adjoining fill bathroom. The second room features a queen size bed also with a private bath. A 20 minute drive will get you to wonderful beaches or windsurfing spots and there are many excellent restaurants within a 10 minute driving distance.
RATES: $55 single or double.

M-53

Enjoy an elegant and comfortable stay with charming, gracious hosts in Kula. Up on the slopes of the dormant volcano, Haleakala, guests can enjoy a bedroom with a queen bed, a private full bath and separate entrance to the sunny courtyard where breakfast is served. Hanging plants adorn the courtyard for a very cozy atmosphere. The home is new and specially designed with B&B in mind. Beautiful landscape surrounds the home and there are many unusual plants and shrubs to be found in the yard. About 30 minutes by car to the beaches and 40 minutes to the airport, this is truly a quiet, relaxing place from which to enjoy Maui.
RATES: $57 single or double, Three night minimum.

M-61

One bedroom cottage nestled in the quiet and coolness of upcountry Maui. Modern, fully equipped with all the conveniences of home, including a kitchen stocked with breakfast fixings, it's perfect for those who want a cozy retreat. Queen size bed in the bedroom, private bath and a wood burning fireplace in the living room to warm the cool evenings. The beach and windsurfing are only 1/2 hour away and restaurants are just 5-15 minutes by car. Enjoy the exclusive retreat and view of the West Maui mountains and the ocean. You'll never want to leave! The cottage was built for two, however, hosts can offer a futon on the floor for one small child.
RATES: $85 single or double, $5 for futon.

KIHEI/WAILEA AREA

M-10

Since this one bedroom condo on the ground floor of a small complex does not have a host living in the home, it is not really B&B. We offer it for guests at an attractive rate, just in case they need more than a room in a home. The condo is fully furnished, has all the appliances for cooking including dishwasher, color tv, washer/dryer. There are two pools and a tennis court for guests to enjoy. The unit could accommodate a family since there is a queen sized bed in the bedroom and a queen sofa bed in the living area. There is a white sandy beach right across the street.
RATES: $55 single or double, $10 each additional person up to four.

M-16

What a view from this large home situated at the very edge of Ulapalakua Ranch on Haleakala and totally surrounded by decks. Enjoy lounging around the pool area while working on your tan in this sunny Kihei location, eating breakfast from the upper deck, whale watching. In the main house accommodations include two bedrooms one with an ocean view while the other one has tropical garden views both decorated with Japanese antique furnishings. They both share the bath across the hall and have cable TV, a queen bed and separate entrance to their own private deck. A studio with kitchenette and private entrance, a private bathroom with shower offers a little more privacy for a longer stay. For a family of four or two couples the best choice might be the one bedroom thatched roof cottage on the same property featuring mosquito netting on the beds,a private bath and kitchenette.
RATES: Main house bedrooms $55 single or double; Studio $75, Cottage $85 double.

M-17

Years ago these hosts decided that as nice as it was in San Diego, California, it was nicer yet on Maui, and since the host is a professional tennis instructor, one of the first things they did was build two tennis courts on their property. Tennis buffs could not ask for a better place to vacation than sunny Kihei with courts available right outside their door. The host has been a musician all his life, and he took a job playing piano part time at one of the finest restaurants on Maui, Raffles, in the Stouffer Hotel, Wailea. The hostess has been selling real estate for five years. She works for Chaney Brooks Realty in Kihei. The accommodation is a full apartment available for B & B guests: one bedroom, private bath, kitchenette with dining area, living room with queen hideabed, cable T.V. The home has a great ocean view, and it is just a short drive to beaches, golf, and restaurants on the Kihei coast. No smokers, please.
RATES: $65 single or double, three night minimum.

M-19

Two beautiful studio apartments for guests are offered here, just 3 blocks away from the sunny beaches of Kihei. Lots of thought and care went into furnishing guests with all the comforts of home. Each studio has a separate entrance, large bedroom area with a firm queen sized bed, private bathroom, sitting area with TV, full kitchen stocked with all kinds of breakfast fixings and dining area. Sliding glass doors open out to a large covered lanai shared by both studios and is meticulously landscaped by the host. Each unit has comfortable outdoor furniture for outdoor dining. A washer/dryer and BBQ are shared by both units. Both units have air conditioning, ceiling fans, and beautiful art work on the walls done by the hostess. Hosts are delightful and will do everything they can to ensure you have a memorable vacation! Smoking outside only, please.
RATES: $75-$85 single or double. Three night minimum.

M-20

Overlooking the ocean and other islands guests have a choice of accommodations when they stay with these busy hosts. The guest cottage is a totally separate building from the main house and can sleep four people comfortably. There is a large room that is part bedroom and part living area with a queen sized bed and a fold out futon couch-bed plus a full kitchen and private bathroom. Sliding glass doors open out to a nice deck with views. The other unit is part of the host's house and is downstairs. It has it's own entrance, kitchenette and private bath and can sleep two people comfortably with the queen sized bed in the living room area. Since the hosts are always on the go pretty early, they leave the breakfast foods in the units for guests to prepare. Children over 12, ok. Three night minimum.

RATES: Cottage: $100 double, $120 for four. Unit: $75 single, $80 double.

M-28

Retreat, Restore and Renew by leaving behind the busyness of your life, and luxuriate in the privacy of this large home. Three bedrooms are available for guests. A suite that can accommodate two couples has a shared sitting room, with a mini kitchenette and two bedrooms each with a queen sized bed. One of the rooms has a private half bath adjoining it while the other bedroom has a full bath and the shower is shared by both bedrooms. A third bedroom with a king sized bed that can convert to twins if needed has a wonderful bathroom with a gigantic all tiled bath and sunken tub and separate entrance. Hostess has a healthy lifestyle which is reflected in her home with all cotton sheets and towels, purified water, a large screened meditation room and garden, healthful breakfasts and other meals if guests would like, plus a great library of books and videos. Three night minimum.

RATES: $85 single, $110 double.

M-32

This comfortable home in Maui Meadows offers a bedroom with a private bath and a private entrance off the deck for B & B travelers, so that guests come and go with privacy assured. The host and hostess, however, urge guests to join them on the front deck for fantastic sunset views. The accommodations offer a large private bath. The room has a king sized bed that can convert to two twin beds, a color TV and small refrigerator. Ideal for a child or young adult is a loft with a double built in bed. Breakfast is usually served on the front lanai where guests can enjoy a panoramic view of the ocean. Three night minimum.

RATES: $50 single, $55 double, $30 for additional room.

M-32A

This accommodation is a large apartment on the garden level of the home mentioned before. It has a fully equipped kitchen and two bedrooms with one bath. It would be ideal for a small family who wished to eat some of their meals in and would make a good accommodation for long or short stays. The unit has lots of windows which afford an excellent ocean view. The hostess serves breakfast on the lanai upstairs.

RATES: $80 double, $100 for four. One week minimum.

M-32B

A large and private two bedroom cottage is available on the same property as the two before. This cottage also has panoramic views of the ocean from a private deck as well as garden views. Inside is a   full kitchen and full bath, one bedroom offers a queen bed the other has two twin beds. Breakfasts can be brought over by the hosts or guests may join the hosts on their front deck for breakfast each morning. Four night minimum preferred.
RATES: $100 double, $120 for four.

M-38

This B&B accommodation offers two bedrooms on the 2nd level of this two story cedar *ocean front* home, located on historic Makena Landing. Each bedroom has a private entrance, full private bath, small refrigerator, color TV and a queen sized bed. Each room opens out to a   shared, covered deck which overlooks the picturesque islands of Kaho'olawe and Molokini, a sky blue ocean, and a 360 foot volcanic cinder cone. Guests can enjoy breakfast with the hosts downstairs. The native Hawaiian hosts have retired on Maui and are anxious to share their aloha with guests. Also, since the rooms are on the second level, guests must be able to handle stairs. Hosts have a friendly Golden Retriever.
RATES: $70 single or double, three night minimum, two week maximum, no smoking, children over twelve, ok.

M-62

Panoramic ocean views, beautiful landscaping, and lots of room highlight this house and separate cottage. Guests have a choice of 4 rentals. Upstairs in the house there is a one bedroom, 1 bath suite with double bed and an extra spacious 1 bedroom, 1 bath master bedroom complete with king size bed and whirlpool bath. Both include breakfast which is served in the dining room or out on the deck and the views are magnificent. Downstairs, there is a private 1 bedroom apartment with a queen size bed, bath, kitchen, dining area and outside entrance. Separate from the house is a 2 bedroom, 2 bath cottage with complete kitchen and living room. One bedroom has a queen sized bed and the other has a double bed. The apartment and cottage do not include breakfast since they have kitchens. However, for $4 extra per person, you can join your hosts for an "all you can eat" wonderful breakfast if you wish.   Amenities include cable TV, telephone, washer/dryer facilities, beach towels. Hosts are from Marin County, California. They fell in love with Maui and enjoy sharing their new home with guests. Smoking outside only, please.
RATES: Suite: $55 single or double, Master Bedroom: $65 single or double. Apartment: $65 single or double, Cottage: $90.

It is a good idea
to let your host know
the time of your arrival.
The more communication between
host and guest the better.

LAHAINA AREA

M-2A

Right in Lahaina town and right on the ocean! Your host has two different accommodations to fit your needs. In the main house there is a room with private bath, small refrigerator and TV. This room is furnished with a queen sized bed and daybed which serves as a couch by day or an extra sleeper by night. The window overlooks the ocean just steps away with easy access to the sea-wall through your own private porch. The other accommodation called "Ohana House" is attached to the main home and although has no ocean view, guests are just 50 feet to the ocean. This cottage offers a private entrance and has room for four adults with sofa-bed in living room and queen bed in large bedroom. Kitchenette and private bath plus TV included. Breakfast is not included in the Ohana House, but the refrigerator will be stocked with fresh island fruit and juice for the first day to get you started to a grand vacation! Two night minimum.
RATES: Room in house $55, "Ohana House" $75, $10 extra per person.

M-5

This guesthouse is a private home created for those who appreciate a restful, relaxed holiday. A swimming pool and deck are featured. Guest rooms offer optimum luxury - all have remote color TV, refrigerator, and air-conditioning. Each room has its own character: the Alii Room features an inside jacuzzi tub, queen and twin bed and private bath; the Wyland room has queen and twin bed with a private bath, entrance and enclosed lanai with Jacuzzi; the Bamboo room offers a queen bamboo canopy bed and a private bath plus an enclosed lanai with jacuzzi. The Makai room has a queen and twin bed, private entrance, enclosed lanai with Jacuzzi and the Mauka Room has a queen bed with a private bath. The spacious family room offers a VCR and comfortable seating for all to share as well as the living room which has a 350 gallon marine aquarium. Hosts are licensed divers and own a dive business.
RATES: Alii Room, Bamboo Room, Wyland Room and Makai: $95 single or double; Mauka Room $75.

Please keep in mind that our office
is anxious to help with all your travel needs.
Also, while we have inspected every host home
to insure they are reliable, sometimes things change.
Please let us know if
you find anything unsatisfactory.

KAHULUI

When you land in Maui you will, no doubt, land at Kahului. Maui has three airports, Kahului, Hana, and Kaanapali, but only Kahului handles the larger planes. Most tourists' experience of the Kahului/Wailuku area consists of arriving and leaving Maui, places to drive through on the way to Kaanapali, Kihei, or Kapalua.

Kahului is the business and commercial center of Maui, with the only deep water harbor on the Island. The downtown area, all along Kaahumanu Street, consists mainly of three shopping centers: Maui Mall, Kahului Shopping Center, which is the oldest and funkiest of the three, and Kaahumanu Center, the newest, largest, and in many ways the nicest Center. Each Center has a number of restaurants, many of them in the fast food category. We have tried to point out those that in some way seem a little special. While this area is little frequented by tourists, there are good restaurants and several places of interest here.

MAUI MALL
As you enter Kahului from the airport the first Center you come to is Maui Mall, which is newer than Kahului Center but older and smaller than Kaahumanu. Woolworths is the largest store in the complex. There are some half dozen basically fast food restaurants including Woolworths Harvest Home Snack Shop. All are moderately priced and seem adequate for a quick snack, but none is of particular note. One interesting shop is Sir Wilfred's Coffee Shop. Last year we mistakenly listed this as a LOCAL restaurant on the advice of one of our hosts. While you can get a snack there, it is mainly a coffee house. Tour buses sometimes stop at this Center to let their passengers take advantage of the good bargains that Woolworths offers.

KAHULUI CENTER
There are no large stores in this Center which obviously has been around for a long time. In the middle of the Center there is a tree lined mall with benches which makes a nice place for the local folk to sit and chat and watch the world go by, and based on our observation, many take advantage of it. If you decide to join them you will be one of the few tourists who do.

KAAHUMANU CENTER
This is the largest and in many ways the nicest of the three Centers in Kahului. There are about fifty small shops, several nice restaurants, and two major department stores, Sears on the east end, and Liberty House on the west. There is a theater that shows first run movies and gives a senior citizen discount.

RESTAURANTS

LOCAL STYLE

ICHIBAN-THE RESTAURANT
At the west end of the Kahului Center facing Kaahumanu Ave. Ichiban in Japanese means "number one" so maybe they were the first restaurant in Kahului. The decor as well as the food served is pitched to the locals, but tourists are certainly welcome. It is clean and neat and the prices are low-lunch for around $5 and dinner around $5-9. They are open for breakfast, lunch and dinner, closed Sunday.

NOODLE KITCHEN
At 251 Lalo Place. If you like the local style, this is a good chow down place with very reasonable prices, which is mainly set up to serve lunch to the workers in the area.

RESTAURANT MATSU
A small Okazu style place in the Maui Mall. Most of the plate lunches are under $5.

SUI'S KITCHEN
Right next door to Matsu, Chinese cafeteria style. We had a chat with Eric Sui, the owner's young son, and he assured us the food was great.

SONGS KITCHEN II
A new Korean restaurant located in a small shopping center as one leaves Kahului for Kihei or Lahaina. We did not sample their wares but one interesting item on the menu was Intestine Stew. It did not specify where the intestine came from.

local Style

CHINA CHEF
In the Kaahumanu Center. This used to be Ma Chan's Okazu-ya, which was a good place to sample many different kinds of Oriental food. It is very different now, featuring a very extensive Szechuan and Cantonese Menu. Most dishes run around $6-8. They are open for lunch from 11-2 and for dinner from 5-9 daily.

HARVEST HOUSE
Located in the Maui Mall and part of Woolworth's. The food is fixed for local tastes and priced accordingly.

local/Tourist Style

ORANGE JULIUS
Located in the Kaahumanu Center. This would be a good place for a quick snack.

KOHO
In the Kaahumanu Center on the corner next to Liberty House. The menu is very middle America, open for breakfast, lunch, and dinner with modest prices. (Shrimp Scampi $9.25, Top Sirloin $9.45). The menu is extensive and they have several Cajun dishes.

MING YUEN
At 162 Alamaha St., which runs along the east side of the Maui Mall. It is open for lunch and dinner every day but Sunday and then only for dinner. The fare is both Cantonese and Szechuan, very tasty, good service and moderate prices. If you like Chinese food be sure to give this one a try.

LOPAKA'S
Located just across the street from Ming Yuen, this small restaurant opened in May of 1986. Lopaka is how you say Robert in Hawaiian. They are open from 11 a.m. until 10 p.m. with the same menu served all day. The food is reasonable and the atmosphere is O.K. They have a happy hour from 3-6 when drinks are reduced to $1.25.

MICKEY'S
Just west of the Kahului Center, behind the bank. This used to be called Island Fish House and is not much different now. They are open for lunch Monday through Friday from 11 until 2 p.m., with lunch in the $8- $12 range with sandwiches a little less. Dinner is served from 5 p.m. until "closing" daily and prices go from $15 for chicken to $34.95 for lobster. They almost always have local fresh fish and it is all enjoyed in a very stylish atmosphere. Recently they have added an early bird special of Prime Rib/Chicken/Scampi for $12.95 from 5-6:30.

CHART HOUSE
On Puunene St. which runs along the east side of the Maui Mall, makai of Kaahumanu, the main street. This is a fairly large chain with several locations on Hawaii and the mainland. If you are familiar with them, this one will present no surprises. They have an adequate salad bar, fresh local fish, and most of the entrees run around $15 with several chicken dishes for under $10.

SIZZLER
This is located just east and behind Maui Mall. Since this is familiar to most of us it needs no explanation.

IHOP

Just the same as the Mainland chain. One of the advantages of knowing about this is it is open late. Monday-Thursday until midnight and Friday, Saturday, and Sunday until 2 am. They are located in the Maui Mall on the far east side.

LUIGI'S PASTA AND PIZZA

There are several of these on Maui. This one is located in the Maui Mall. The menu is extensive, not just pasta and pizza but many different Italian dishes. They have different specials each night and they also have different entertainment each night with several nights a week devoted to Karaoke, where patrons sing on stage with the words flashed on a screen. Very interesting.

AURELIO'S

Located across the highway from Maui Mall, they are open for lunch and dinner. In spite of the Italian sounding name, the food is quite varied with only one Italian dish, Shrimp Fettuccine. They serve a plate lunch for $5.95. They also have entertainment nightly. When we visited this time, we got the feeling they were more interested in the tavern aspect of the business than the restaurant aspect.

PINATA'S

A new Mexican Restaurant located at 395 Dairy Rd. in the Dairy Center which you will see as you leave Kahului on the way to Kihei. Their prices are very reasonable, combination plates from $5.65-$6.95. While we did not get a chance to sample their food, we must confess that the aroma was tantalizing. This would be a good place for a quick lunch.

ARCHIE'S MEXICAN

Also located on Dairy Rd. just past Pinata's. They were not open when we passed by but it looked clean and neat and the prices are even less than Pinata,s. If you do try it, let us know what you think.

MAUI BEACH/ MAUI PALMS HOTEL

On the makai side of Kaahumanu as one enters Kahului from the airport. In the Maui Beach there are three different restaurants: Rainbow Buffet Lunch room, Red Dragon Chinese, and Prime Rib & Seafood. The Rainbow Room is open for lunch from 11:30 a.m. until 2:00 p.m. and is an all you can eat buffet at a fairly modest price. The Red Dragon Room is open every night except Monday from 5:30 to 8:30 p.m. Service is buffet, all you can eat, price moderate. Prime Rib and Seafood on the regular menu is more expensive. On Monday through Saturday the Maui Palms features the Imperial Japanese Buffet, which is excellent and the price is right. On Sunday they have the Hawaiian Buffet.

We hope you try one of the
restaurants in this area.
The owners will appreciate it
for except for the restaurants directly above,
they don't see many tourists in this area.

POINTS OF INTEREST

MAUI POTATO CHIP FACTORY

At 295 Lalo St. If you haven't tried Maui Potato Chips you have missed a treat. You will really impress your friends if you stop by here and pick up a case of chips to take back home. Because of insurance liability they do not give tours, they are open for business from 7 am to 2 pm.

MAUI ZOO AND BOTANICAL GARDEN

To find take Kaahumanu St. east toward Wailuku and just before it starts to go up the hill, watch for Kanaloa Ave. on the right. Turn right on Kanaloa and go about 1/4 mile and you will find the Zoo on your right, across from the high school playing fields. While this is not much of a Zoo, it might make a nice break, especially if you have small children. They have several animals, monkeys, goats, a raccoon, and pygmy donkeys. Perhaps of more note than the Zoo is the Botanical Garden where an attempt is being made to preserve some of the plants once abundant on Maui.

HAWAIIAN TROPICAL PLANTATION

To find go east on Kaahumanu St. to the town of Wailuku, turn left on High Street past the State and County buildings and go six miles to the town of Waikupu. You will see the Plantation just past the town on the right. This is not a bad place to shop for that gift to take home since the prices are not out of line. Every 1/2 hour there is a tour of the Plantation, which grows most of the Hawaiian crops: sugar, pineapple, papaya, banana, coffee, taro, avocado, mango, macadamia nut, guava, and even fish and prawn ponds. The cost of the tour is $8 for adults and $3 for children. The trolley stops half way around where fresh fruit and juice are served. We did not take the tour, but several guests have reported they found it very informative. The restaurant serves either an all you can eat buffet for $11.50 or ala carte counter style. On Tuesday, Wednesday and Thursday they offer a Hawaiian Country Barbeque and Revue from 5:00 to 8:00 pm at a cost of $46.95 per person, $19.95 for children.

BEACHES

While Kahului is not thought of as a beaching area, there are some nice spots if you know how to find them. Keep in mind, however, that the north and east of all the Islands is the windward side and that the surf, especially in winter time, can get quite rough. If you see one of the local boys riding the waves some half mile out, do not jump to the conclusion that all is safe. Off shore there are dangerous rips that can carry you away from the beach as if you were in a river. Swimming against them is useless. When drownings occur, it is usually under some such circumstances. That is not to say that one cannot enjoy playing in the surf. Also, these north shore beaches because of the prevailing winds tend to be a bit cooler than the south and west side beaches.

KANAHA BEACH PARK

Just east of the airport. To get there take the airport road and turn left at the car rental area. Look carefully and you will see a sign pointing the way to the beach. Once you make the turn off the airport road, you should not have much trouble finding the beach. This is a great favorite with the residents of the area and on the weekends all of the tables go early. There are picnic tables, rest rooms, and showers.

ALA KAPA BEACH
To find go east from Kahului to Ala Kapa Rd., turn makai to Laulea, turn left on the dirt road and go to the end. There are no facilities here. This is a great favorite with the windsurfers and you will see some good action at this spot.

SUGAR COVE BEACH
This is our name for this little secluded beach, which is much used by the residents. To find, take Nohehe Place makai to Paani St. and turn left to the Sugar Cove Condos where you will find a beach access path. No facilities.

GOLF COURSE BEACH
Again, the name is our own invention as we have no idea what the beach is called. To find, take the road to the Maui Country Club and turn makai on Kealakai. No facilities.

BALDWIN BEACH
Seven miles east of Kahului. This has the facilities, picnic tables, rest rooms, showers, but did not appeal to us at all.

NIGHT LIFE

There are two theaters in Kahului, one theater in the Kaahumanu Center which shows first run movies and gives a good senior citizen discount, the other in the Maui Mall. Sometimes there is something going on at either the Maui Beach or the Maui Palms Hotel.

BALDWIN MINI THEATER
Located at Baldwin High School 242-8521. Live theater, call for schedule.

KAHULUI COMMUNITY CENTER
This is a new building, now under construction to be completed by 1993, in the Kahului Park area near the Kahumanu Shopping Center. Call for directions, 244-8762.

SPORTS

GOLF
The Maui Country Club, which is listed as semi-private, guests can play there on Monday only. The cost is $45 per person for nine holes. This price includes a cart, but carts are not mandatory. For more information call 877-0616.

Waikapu Valley Country Club is also a private course, however, they welcome tourists. $65 per person for 18 holes includes a cart. 242-7090

TENNIS
There are two lighted courts at the Kahului community Park and two unlighted courts at the Kahului Salvation Army.

WAILUKU

Wailuku, the County Seat for the county of Maui, is just west of Kahului. *Wai* in Hawaiian means fresh water; *luku* suggests death and destruction. The name suggests that bloody battles were fought here, and that is exactly the case. In fact, in one big battle the river which runs through Wailuku turned red with blood from dead and dying warriors. Much more peaceful now, Wailuku gives the tourists a clearer picture of how life is lived in Hawaii today. Shops are geared for the Maui resident. Along Main St. and along Market there are several little stores with good prices. If you are in the market for and eel skin products, you can save money here. The restaurant prices also tend to be lower than in tourist areas. One must keep in mind, though, that most of the restaurants cook for local taste.

RESTAURANTS

LOCAL STYLE

SAM SATO'S
From Main St. turn right on Market and proceed north about 1/2 mile down the hill and you will see Sam's on the right at 318 N. Market St. Open for breakfast and lunch, Sam's specializes in Japanese and American with food mostly for local tastes. This is a good place to eat if you are budgeting.

FUJIYA'S
At 133 Market St. Several editions ago this was a funky little place that did not seem to encourage tourists to enter. Now, however, there has been some remodeling and they have added a sushi bar that is not expensive and it is our opinion that you will not feel out of place. In fact for lovers of Japanese food this place is a good deal with lots of local flavor. Also, if you are a saimin lover this is your spot.

TASTY CRUST
One of our readers told us about this spot, and when we checked with our hosts they confirmed that the food, especially the Hot Cakes for breakfast, was good. The prices are very low, but do not expect a fancy atmosphere. They are open for breakfast, lunch and dinner from 5:30 a.m. until 11 p.m. They are located on Mill Street just off Central Ave., which runs north off Main St.

AKI'S
Located at the foot of Market St. on the left hand side across from Sam Sato. If you want some Hawaiian food, chicken hekka or lomi lomi give this place a try. It is not much to look at from the exterior but it is neat and clean inside.

KEN-SAN
If you want chow-down local you might try this fairly new place on Main St. Open weekdays from 10-2.

BENTO'S & BANQUETS
Located on Church St., a take-out lunch for $5-6.

local Style

SIAM THAI
Makai of Main St. on Market St., about a block from Main. We ate here and were pleased with the prices and the food.

SAENG'S THAI
Located on Vineyard above Market. The menu is not much different from Siam Thai, which is logical since it is the same owner; they also have a Saeng's Thai in Lahaina. They are not open for lunch on weekends.

TSURU
This is a new restaurant in town and is absolutely worth a try. *Tsuru* is the Japanese word for crane and the crane represents long life in Japanese folklore. The menu is eclectic (Chicken Teriyaki, Rigatoni with Sausage and Peppers, Asian Stir Fried Vegetables) and all made with fresh, high quality ingredients. It is located at 2080 Vineyard St. just west of Market St. One thing we noticed as we enjoyed lunch is the great view of Haleakala. We happened to hit it on a very clear day.

GOLDEN JADE
South of Main St. at 301 Kalawi. Go one block above Market, turn left and go two blocks south, turn left and go east to Kalawi St. and turn right. To us this was the best restaurant in town for Chinese food. It is not much to look at either inside or out, and you will probably be the only tourist there. When we ate here we made the mistake of ordering three dishes when two would have been ample. A good meal will run around $8 a person. They are closed on Sunday and Monday and they close early for dinner, 7 pm.

NAOKEES
Most tourists just do not find this, which is fine with the locals; that way they don't have to wait so long for a table. If you are coming into Wailuku from the airport, just after the bridge, turn right on Central, go one block to Nani, turn right to the bottom of the hill. Naokees faces the Main Street Bridge, but you enter from the back. As you enter the sign says, Sorry, we're open. The prices here are not as low as Hazel's and the food is not as local. Lunch for two will not be much over $10 and dinner not over $20. In fact, they offer a one pound steak for $8.95. (unfortunately Naokees was destroyed by fire in May of 1992. We were not able to ascertain when or if they will re-open.)

117

local/ Tourist Style

CAFE KUP A KUPPA
This little espresso bar serves breakfast and lunch located on Church St. between Main and Vineyard. Their motto is *FIT///FRESH///FAST*. They claim to have the "best salades" (sic) in Maui for $5.75. They also serve an excellent sandwich for $5. They include tax in those prices.

TOUCH OF GLASS
This is an interesting looking new Studio/Cafe located on the left side of Main St. as one enters Wailuku from Kahului. For the most part the menu is sandwiches but they also have one hot special dish daily.

MAUI BAKE SHOP & DELI
Not a sit down restaurant, but if all you want is a sandwich or sweet you might give this a try.

CHUMS
This is a new place located on Center St. just off Main just as you cross the bridge coming into Wailuku from Kahului. They also have a much larger restaurant in Kihei, but the owner assured me the prices were a little lower in Wailuku. Since they serve Loco Moco, we might have put this in a different category, but they also serve Hot Turkey/Beef/Pork Sandwich so the menu is varied.

PAR FIVE
Four miles west of Wailuku, at the Public Golf course, you get there by taking Market St. off Main and driving four miles to the town of Waihee. In the center of town you will see a ball field on the right. Turn right and proceed to the end of the road. Kind of a snack/bar/restaurant, it is open from 11 a.m. until 2 p.m. for lunch, and from 2:30 - 6 p.m. for pupus (light snacks). Prices are very moderate, chicken and fries $3.95, BLT $3.75, burger with fries $2.95.

LOWER MAIN STREET RESTAURANTS

We had a little problem finding Lower Main Street so perhaps directions will help. If you are heading east on Main St., follow the sign at the bridge which points to the right and proceed until the road dead ends. Turn left and you are on Lower Main no matter what the signs say. There are several restaurants in this area worth finding, and they are all LOCAL or local style. Few tourists eat in these restaurants and in our opinion many are missing a good deal, at least if the local style food appeals to you. We will list them in the order you would come to them if you were driving down Lower Main.

local Style

ARCHIES
On the left side of Lower Main. Don't be fooled by the name, this is not the local pub even though it may have that look. It is local Japanese style food with several American dishes on the menu also. We recently had lunch there and enjoyed it very much. The bill was around $8 for the two of us. It is open from 10:30 a.m. until 2 p.m. for lunch and from 5 p.m. until 8:30 for dinner.

VIETNAM CUISINE
New to this location but not new to Lower Main, we just missed it last time. They also have a few Chinese dishes.

LA PASTARIA
This place is new and seems like it would be worth a try, but it would have to be a nice day since seating is outside. They are open for breakfast and lunch and the menu is limited, Quiche or Croissant for breakfast, sandwiches for lunch priced from $3.95 to $4.50. If you are staying at a place with cooking facilities, you might try some of their fresh pasta made on the premises daily.

TIN YING
On the same side as the above, open for lunch and dinner from 10:30 until 9 p.m. The food is Cantonese style, not much atmosphere, but a real experience in *local* dining.

NAZO'S*
As you drive down Lower Main you will see a large series of buildings on your right called Puuone Plaza. Nazo's is located on the upper level. You can either park below or drive up to it. Not many tourists find this so you may be the only tourist here. Almost all entrees are below $6 and features such things as fried chicken, roast pork, corned beef and cabbage, and mahi mahi, even New York steak for $5.50. They are open for breakfast, lunch, and dinner seven days a week.

TOKYO TAI
In the Puuone Plaza on the lower level at the opposite end from Nazo's. This is really excellent food at very reasonable prices. Lunch is served from 11 a.m. until 2 p.m. and almost all dishes are under $6., with salad and rice included. Dinner is served from 5 p.m. until 9 p.m. and unless you want steak the bill for two will run around $12.

KALEO'S KAU KAU
As the name suggest's, Hawaiian food available here.

MOON HOE
Just down and across from Tokyo Tai. The cuisine is Cantonese and Scezhuan, the prices are modest and from the looks of things when we were there, you won't need a reservation.

POINTS OF INTEREST

IAO VALLEY STATE PARK

Most tourists pass through Wailuku for only one reason, to get to Iao Valley State Park and see the Iao Needle, a pinnacle which reaches to an elevation of around 2200 feet, with the Iao stream flowing at its feet. Iao State Park is about three miles west of Wailuku and is not difficult to find. Just proceed up the hill on Main St. through the town of Wailuku and when the road divides, take the one to the right and you will dead end at the parking lot for the Park.

The walk from the parking lot to the lookout at the top is about a five to fifteen minute walk, depending on how you go about it. Iao Valley is very lush and if there has been some rain, you are apt to see several water falls on the cliffs above. The best time to see the valley is in the a.m. since the needle can be obscured by clouds in the afternoon. However, the local residents say you haven't really seen the Valley until you have seen it on a clear full moon night.

When you reach the top lookout you will see a dirt trail going beyond. We took it for about a 1/4 mile but could see no reason to continue since our view was not improving. When you return to the parking lot, you might like to return by the path which goes along the stream. That will give you a better view of the many tropical plants which grow along the stream.

KEPANIWAI PARK or HERITAGE GARDENS

Very easy to find since you pass it just before you reach Iao Valley State Park. This is a series of gardens representing the heritage of the people of Hawaii. There is a Japanese, Chinese, Filipino, Portuguese and Hawaiian garden. Since there are many picnic tables and barbecue pits, all of the tables covered in case of showers, this makes an excellent place to have a picnic. Perhaps while you are there, you will get a chance to see a wedding as the Chinese Garden is much favored for this.

HALE HOIKEIKE

Maui Historical Society Museum. This was once the home of Edmond Bailey, a 19th Century missionary. It is not extensive and will not take long to see, including the art works of Mr. Bailey housed next door, but it is definitely worth the stop. You will see many artifacts from before the arrival of Captain Cook plus some fine examples of koa furniture which at one time was fairly common in Hawaii. It is open Monday through Friday from 10-4 and costs $3.00, seniors $2.50, $1 for children.

KAAHUMANU CONGREGATIONAL CHURCH

Since this the oldest church on Maui, it is of some note. To see the inside, however, one must attend the Sunday service as the church is not open during the week.

TROPICAL GARDENS OF MAUI

If you go the Iao Needle you can't miss it. If flowers are your thing, especially orchids, you will enjoy this. The cost to tour the gardens is $4. They ship orchids all over the world and their prices are not out of line.

WEST OF WAILUKU

If you play golf on Maui's Municipal course, you will become familiar with the four miles west of Wailuku. Most tourists, we feel sure, never venture out this way, and we feel they are missing something. Just the drive from Wailuku to Waihee four miles to the west can be quite nice. We took it on our first trip to Maui trying to find a cool spot and it worked, for along this lush north west coast the trade winds do their best work. As you leave Wailuku you will be in the middle of a rather large macadamia nut orchard. On our first trip down this road these now mature and producing trees were newly planted.

It is beyond Waihee, however, where the road really gets interesting. One can, if so inclined, drive from this point all the way around to Napili and the west shore of Maui. From Wailuku to the good paved road above the Napili/Kapalua area is 17 miles. If you take this drive, be prepared for the last two miles which are unpaved and very rutty. In fact if there have been heavy rains or it looks as if there might be while you are driving, you probably won't make it without four wheel drive. Having said all that, we still want to encourage you to take the trip, since some of the views are spectacular. Even if you do not go the entire way, drive far enough, about 12 miles from Wailuku, to get a view back to the Kahului area. As we drove out there on this trip we noticed a sign several miles past Waihee which said, "road closed to all but local traffic." How seriously one should take that message we are not prepared to say. We turned back at that point, but had we not already traveled past that point we imagine we would have continued.

BEACHES

West of Wailuku is a good spot for ocean views but not for ocean activities. However, this year we did discover a little beach behind the golf course that has a little sand and looks safe for swimming and snorkeling. Most of this coast line is steep and rocky, with a small beach here and there. The surf even at the best of times is strong, with dangerous rips, and at its worst, it is awesome. There are so many safe places to enjoy beaching that it would be foolish to try it most places along these shores.

SPORTS

GOLF

Waiehu is Maui's only municipal course. The green fee is $25. Carts are available for $14 for two but they are not mandatory. It is difficult to get a starting time here so call ahead or try late afternoons. For more information call 244-5934. See additional golf listings under Kahului.

SANDALWOOD GOLF COURSE & WAIKAPU VALLEY COUNTRY CLUB

There are two new courses located on Honoapiilani Hwy. several miles south of Wailuku. Sandalwood is public and the green fee is $65, cart included. Waikapu is presently open to the public but sometime in the future will become private. Their green fee in $80, cart included

TENNIS
There are five lighted courts at the Maui War Memorial Center that are open to the public.

NIGHT LIFE

The only thing going on in Wailuku at night that we could discover was the Maui Community Iao Theater on Market Street. This group puts on plays about once a month. To find out what is going on call 242-6969.

Isn't the traffic on Maui a pain?
Remember, if you have to catch a plane,
give yourself plenty of time.

To book a reservation or
for any other travel need
write
B & B Hawaii
Box 449
Kapaa, Hi. 96746
or call 808-822-7771
Visa-Mastercard-American Express accepted.

UPCOUNTRY MAUI

On the slopes of Haleakala, which rises to a little over 10,000 feet, are several little towns and communities, all known as Upcountry Maui: Pukalani, Makawao, Kula, the little town of Kokomo, and, for our purposes, the town of Paia, which is eight miles east of Kahului on the road to Hana.

Upcountry is the farm/ranch area of Maui where the somewhat famous Maui onion is grown. On Maui they are called *Kula Onions* and though they are expensive, as much as $1.50 a pound, those who try them feel they are worth the price. Also grown in this area is Protea, a unique flowering shrub imported from Africa. Many of the carnations so popular for leis are grown in the Kula area. Upcountry even boasts of a winery, the Tedeschi Winery, which is known for pineapple wine and is in the process of producing grape wine.

If you go to the top of Haleakala you will go through part of this area, but you will not see it all unless you take a few side roads. When it gets too hot in the low lands, a drive up to Kula is most rewarding.

PAIA

As stated above, Paia is on the road to Hana so most visitors to Maui have at least been through it. In fact, many who are Hana bound stop for a bite to eat since once past Paia there is not much civilization until one arrives at Hana. In Paia there are several little shops, most geared for tourists. We were not impressed with what they had to offer or the prices charged. But there are several antique/junk stores that are fun to browse through, and there are several restaurants mentioned below that are worth consideration. Many residents of Maui think of Paia as a Hippie type area that is getting a big economic lift from the wind surfers who come from all over the world to windsurf this coast. We could not see where things had changed much except that some restaurants had changed hands and one new one was being constructed when we were there.

RESTAURANTS

LOCAL STYLE

KIHATA

On the left side of the Hana Highway just opposite Baldwin St. This used to be Larry's, a landmark place in Paia. It has been fixed up a bit and now specializes in Japanese cuisine. The prices are modest and hosts tell us the food is good.

local/Tourist Style

PICNICS

On Baldwin St., which is the main street in Paia and goes mauka of the main highway, on the right hand side as one heads for Makawao. If you ask the people who live in the area where to have lunch, chances are they will say Picnics. Health food people love it for the specialty of the house, a Spinach Nut Burger, which consists of peanuts, spinach, and soy bean meal all ground together and broiled like a hamburger. We asked the girl at the counter if it tasted like meat. She assured us it tasted like spinach and peanuts all ground up together. We had a club sandwich on a Kaiser roll ($3.95) and a Chef Salad ($4.50). They are open for breakfast, lunch, and dinner.

WUNDERBAR

As we said above, some of the restaurants have changed hands. This used to be Dillon's, which had been in Paia for a very long time. The new owners are really fixing up the place and going upscale. The menu is distinctly European (Bavarian Hunter Steak-$16, Piccata Milanese-$12, Hungarian Goulash-$12, Paella Andalusia-$32 for two. These and many more dishes are on the lunch menu. They did not yet have the dinner menu finalized, but one can get the drift from the lunch menu. They are open for, breakfast, lunch, and dinner. One thing is for sure, their menu, be it breakfast, lunch or dinner is not ordinary.

CHARLIE'S

Just past Baldwin on mauka side of highway. Especially noted for their pizzas, but sandwiches and other dishes available. They are open for breakfast, lunch, and dinner. The food is very good and the prices moderate. What makes their dinners special is that they offer five different specials every night.

PEACH'S & CRUMBLE

Located on Baldwin just up from the highway. This is a little take out place that has some interesting offerings. Everything is made fresh daily. If you are driving out to Hana, you might want to pick up a "Hana Box Lunch-Choice of one of seven gourmet sandwiches, a bag of Maui Chips, three Fresh Baked Cookies, and choice of soda, all packed in a convenient lunch box with condiments-only $6.95."

FISH MARKET
On the corner of Baldwin and main highway. This is a good place for fresh fish at reasonable prices. Counter style and take to table. Most meals go between $4.75 and $6.95

VEGAN REST
Up Baldwin toward the end of town. As the name implies vegetarian. They are open from 11 am to 8:30 pm, closed Monday and Tuesday.

MINUTE STOP-GAS & GO
All the food offered here is take out, but we had to include it when we saw that they offered a foot long sandwich for $4.99 or a six inch one for $3.29. They also offer a foot long Veggie Sandwich for $3.19. At the price of vegetables in Hawaii that is an unbelievably low price.

MAUI GROWN
This is a small take out stand located about 7 1/2 miles east of Paia. One can pick up a box lunch to take out to Hana for $6.95. If you call ahead, 572-1693, they will have it boxed and ready to go.

PARADISIO RESTAURANT
In our very first book we wrote about a great little restaurant called Pierro,s Garden. Unfortunately, it was short lived and until now nothing opened in its place. However, by the time this goes to press, Paradisio should be in full swing. The cuisine will be Mediterranean and on most nights there will be live music.

MAMA'S FISH HOUSE
Just east of Paia on the makai side of the Hana Highway. This is a popular spot for residents and tourists alike and often the only restaurant in Paia mentioned in most guide books. Mama's has been serving delicious local fish for about eleven years now. They are open for lunch from 11-2:30 and for dinner from 5-10 with a happy hour from 2-4. Most entrees run over $15. Some of our hosts feel their prices are just too high.

BEACHES

HOOKIPA PARK
Located right at the town of Paia, convenient but not too appealing. Swimming is not recommended because of the strong currents. Rest room facilities, picnic tables available. Camping allowed with a permit. Up the road a bit is Hookipa Beach- World Class Windsurfing Competition.

MAKAWAO

Seven miles mountain side of Paia, up Baldwin St. is the cowboy like village of Makawao. Unless you stop here to eat at one of the places mentioned below, you will not be here long. Like Paia, there are some shops which seem to be geared toward tourists, fun to browse through and you might find the unusual gift to take home. There is a small shop which specializes in cowboy boots, which is appropriate for this area.

As you drive toward Makawao watch for the Hui No'eau Visual Arts Center, located on the Kalunaui Estate. We believe the estate belonged to the Baldwin family, and you will see it on the left several miles up the road. The Center has various exhibits throughout the year from local artists and is worth a visit just to see the home and the grounds.

RESTAURANTS

LOCAL

KITADA'S
On the left side of the road as one enters Makawao from Paia. This is very local saimen spot. Try it for real local flavor.

local/Tourist

POLLI'S MEXICAN RESTAURANT
In the center of Makawao Town Polli's is one of the most popular spots in Upcountry and for good reason; the food is good, the portions are large, and the prices are moderate. They are open for breakfast, lunch, and dinner.

MAKAWAO STEAK HOUSE
On the right hand side of Baldwin as one enters from Paia. Nothing outstanding here, much like Chart House/Spindrifter restaurants. The food is good, nice salad bar, with most entrees between $15 and $25. They are open for dinner only from 5-9:30.

CASANOVA'S
Italian cuisine open for dinner only from 5:30 to midnight. Prices range from chicken dinner for $15 to a 16 ounce steak for $20. Disco with live music.

CASANOVA DELI
Next to Casanova's. This is a good spot for a light lunch, very tasty sandwiches on a variety of rolls or bread at reasonable prices. Counter service.

THE COURTSIDE DELI
A new little restaurant located at 3620 Baldwin Ave. at the rear of a new small mall. They are open for breakfast and lunch. On their menu is a quote from one Alice May Brock. "It's a lovely thing-everyone sitting down together, sharing food. So take a moment before you begin, to smile at your friends." Evidently the young lady working there the day we visited either had not read the quote or did not subscribe to the concept. Mostly they serve soup and sandwiches at reasonable prices.

HALIMAILE GENERAL STORE Do not be fooled by the name. This is one of the most talked about restaurants on Maui and we are ashamed that we failed to include it in our last edition since it has been in business for over four years. They are open for lunch and dinner every day but Monday and for brunch on Sunday from 10-3. Dinner is ala carte with salads around $3-$6 and entrees from $12 (Bow Tie Pasta) to Rack of Lamb Hunan Style $24. The setting is elegant and the food is superb. One of the reasons we missed it is that it is out of the way, located on Halimaile Rd. several miles from Pukalani. To get there watch for Hailemaile Rd., which runs east off the Haleakala Highway below Pukalani. Everyone we have talked to has assured us that this is a DON'T MISS SPOT. For a reservation call 572-2666. This is so good we put it in twice.

PIZZA STOP
Located in a small mall half way between Makawao and Pukalani.

PUKALANI

Pukalani, about eight miles up the Haleakala Highway, is the first community one reaches after leaving Kahului, and unless you want to stop here to eat or play golf at the Pukalani Country Club, you will pass through in seconds.

RESTAURANTS

LOCAL STYLE

MIXED PLATE
In the Pukalani Shopping Center on the right as you enter Pukalani is a Japanese cafeteria style restaurant where the local folk like to eat. A good sized lunch runs around $5, it is all tasty Oriental style food, served cafeteria style.

FU WAH CHINESE
Also in the Pukalani Center. They are open for lunch from 10:30- 3:30 and for dinner from 5-9 pm.

local/Tourist

LUIGI'S PIZZARIA
In the Pukalani Shopping Center. They have entertainment on Friday night.

BULLOCKS
On the right as you leave Pukalani. This is a good place for a quick lunch. Prices are low and the food is not bad. The specialty of the house is moonburgers and guava shakes. They are open from 7:30 a.m. until 8:30 p.m.

UP COUNTRY CAFE
This little restaurant located on the left side of the highway just past the Pukalani Center is under new ownership since our last visit and from the crowd we saw the day we were there, they must be serving pretty good food. They are open for breakfast, lunch, and dinner, closed Tuesday. No doubt one of the things attracting people are the very low prices here with the most expensive item on the menu being Caesar Salad for $5.95 or with "morsels of smoked chicken" for $7.50. Since they have Loco-Moco on the menu, one should think they cater to local folk.

GOLF COURSE
Go down the road that the shopping center faces and it will take you to the golf course, which has a nice little restaurant with modest prices. From here there is an excellent view of Kahului and the valley.

HALIMAILE GENERAL STORE
Do not be fooled by the name. This is one of the most talked about restaurants on Maui and we are ashamed that we failed to include it in our last edition since it has been in business for over four years. They are open for lunch and dinner every day but Monday and for brunch on Sunday from 10-3. Dinner is ala carte with salads around $3-$6 and entrees from $12 (Bow Tie Pasta) to Rack of Lamb Hunan Style $24. The setting is elegant and the food is superb. One of the reasons we missed it is that it is out of the way, located on Halimaile Rd. several miles from Pukalani. To get there watch for Hailemaile Rd., which runs east off the Haleakala Highway below Pukalani. Everyone we have talked to has assured us that this is a DON'T MISS SPOT. For a reservation call 572-2666.

KULA

Whether one takes the high road which continues on to Haleakala or the low road that goes to Tedeschi Winery, one is in Kula, for Kula is an area not a specific location.

RESTAURANTS

local/Tourist Style

KULA LODGE
On the right side of the Haleakala Highway about six or seven miles beyond Pukalani on the way to Haleakala. The best thing about eating at the Kula Lodge is the magnificent view of most of Maui below: from Kahului and the west Maui Mountains, to the Kihei coast line in the south. They are open for breakfast, lunch, and dinner.

KULA SANDALWOOD RESTAURANT
Across and up from the Kula Lodge, this used to called Silversword. In December of 1991 it opened under new management, the Loui family, and have been going great guns ever since. At the present time they are open for breakfast and lunch, and when we asked Mrs. Loui if they would soon be open for dinner, she merely shrugged. We had breakfast there and were very pleased, especially with the way they prepared the potatoes, simple but tasty.

POINTS OF INTEREST

TEDESCHI WINERY
On the Ulupalakua Ranch on the southwest slopes of Haleakala. To find the winery take the Lower Kula Rd. after passing Pukalani. Or if you are taking the road from Hana south, you reach it soon after you hit paved road. If you do come the Hana way, it is likely to be closed since the drive takes so long and the winery is open from 10 a.m. until 5 p.m. The Winery has long been known for its pineapple wine and is now making a reputation with its grape wine. They may have a new red wine in late 1992. 878-6058.

CLOUD'S REST PROTEA
The road to this is off the upper Kula Rd. as one nears Kula Lodge. Watch carefully and you will see a sign pointing to the left. Take that road and continue on until you come to the Protea farm a mile or so up the road. On the way you will pass several small carnation farms, beautiful when the flowers are in bloom. If you have not seen protea before, you will find this an interesting stop. This was formerly Protea Farm, the name was changed by the new owners, former B&B hosts, Clark and Denise Champion. Feel free to ask questions as they are ready and willing to talk. You can buy flowers and they will ship them to the mainland. Protea makes a nice arrangement either dried or fresh. They are not native to Hawaii, but they do very well in the Islands at higher elevations, and there are some that do well at sea level. At times you can buy the flowers on special. Plants can be shipped. For more information call 808-878-2544.

PROTEAS OF HAWAII
Former owners of the farm above, these farmers moved to 210 Mauna Place in Kula and have six acres of proteas. Their main business is wholesale and mail order. Located just across from the Dept. of Agriculture Experimental Station, visitors may tour both. The best time to visit is on Mondays, harvest day. 878-6015.

HALEAKALA
To visit Maui and fail to drive to the top of Haleakala, the House of the Sun, is in our view a big mistake. In fact, do yourself a favor and go there to see the sun rise. The distance from Kahului to the summit is around 38 miles, but you need to allow around two hours for the drive, and keep in mind that sunrise at the top is around fifteen minutes sooner than at sea level. At any time of the year it can be cold, so bring warm clothes, especially in the winter, or you will wish you were somewhere else. From the rim of the crater you will view 19 square miles of awesome moon-like landscape.

Haleakala is one of the favorite hiking places in Hawaii, and short hikes down into the crater are possible. Remember, the elevation is 10,000 feet and the air is much thinner so hiking can be more difficult.

Near the top is Haleakala Visitors Center with models and illustrations of the geological history of the dormant volcano. If the day is clear, the view cannot be surpassed anywhere in the world. To check on the weather conditions call 572-7749.

SPORTS

GOLF
Pukalani is an eighteen hole course open to the public. Except during the height of the tourist season (January-March) starting times are not hard to get. Since the winds become quite strong in the afternoon, play is much better in the a.m. Green fees are $60 carts included. On Wednesday and Sunday nights they have a Karaoke Bar. For more information call 572-1314.

TENNIS
There are two lighted courts at the Eddie Tam Memorial Center, one lighted court at Halimaile Park, and one lighted court at the Pukalani Park. All of these are open to the public at no charge.

If you have explored this area
you are one up on most
of the tourists who visit Maui.
On all of the Islands
there is more to do than lie
on the beach and soak up the sun.
Of course that's not such bad duty, is it?
But when it gets too warm in the lowlands,
head for the hills.

HANA

In spite of all you have heard about the difficulty of driving to Hana, we feel this is a must trip. A trip to Hana should be started with a full tank of gas and possibly a picnic lunch, as there are no gas stations or stores once you pass Paia. You will hear all sorts of stories about how rough the drive is, depending on how long ago the person telling you made the trip. When we first made the trip in the fall of 1984 the road had recently been improved so the drive was not all that bad. When we drove out to Hana this year we felt that parts of the road had been improved and that vegetation on the roadside was cut back to make the drive easier. The distance from Kahului to Hana is about 50 miles. The first 20 are good, the next 15 not bad, while the last 15 gets a little bumpy and the road gets narrow. If you move right along with a minimum of stops, it will take about two or two and a half hours. Then again, if you want it to, it can take all day, as there are many places along the way to stop and sight see.

One of the do not miss spots on this drive is the little village of Keanae. At approximately 0.9 miles past the 16 mile marker, turn left and proceed around 1/2 mile down the road to Keanae. Several varieties of taro, the source of poi, are grown in this valley.

Hana itself is a delightful, sleepy little place with not much going on. Be sure to spend some time on the beach there, where the water is calm and swimming is easy. Some of the beaches both before and after Hana can be rough, especially in the winter months. Also, visit the Hana Maui Hotel, which is the center of everything in Hana.

About ten miles beyond Hana is the famous Seven Sacred Pools. To us the Pools were a disappointment. While the getting there was beautiful, the pools were muddy and did not look inviting; though many people swim there, it is not recommended because of bacteria from the animals living above the pools. The walk over to the pools and down to the ocean was pleasant. One of our hosts has told us that there is a wonderful bamboo grove above the Pools that is delightful to walk through.

Past the pools the road really gets rough, and if you are in a rented car you are not supposed to drive it. Mauians will tell you that it is no big deal and that they do it all the time in their little old whatever it might be. Well, we have good news and bad news. The bad news is that it is a big deal, and while the views are spectacular, to say the road is rough does not do it justice. We made the trip during a dry time, and we could not go much more than 10 to 15 miles an hour for the 10 miles of unpaved road. The good news is that you won't run into any traffic jams. If you tend to be timid, do not make the trip. But if you like to take chances, go for it. You might ask, would we do it again? Absolutely!

One of our readers questioned why we would recommend this road and not the Saddle Road on the Big Island. We have taken the Saddle Road and enjoyed it very much. However, if one has not driven up through Waimea or down through Volcano and around to Kona, we feel they would get the short end of things just to save a little time. If a person has already travelled these roads, then we suggest taking the Saddle Road; just don't tell the car rental places we said so. It is very isolated - Don't run out of gas.

RESTAURANTS

LOCAL STYLE

TUTU'S
At Hana Bay, home style cooking, open for breakfast and lunch. Open seven days a week, prices low for plate lunch specials. You can buy it here and picnic on the beach.

local Style

SNACK SHACK
Located just past the 17 mile marker and 18 long miles from Hana, this just might give you the break you need. Do not count on seeing many of these along the road for this is, as far as we know, the only one.

local/Tourist Style

HANA RANCH
If you have worked up a big appetite by now, you might give this a try, as they serve an all you can eat buffet lunch for $12.95 for adults and $6.50 for children. Or if a salad bar would suffice that is offered for $7.95. If you are spending the night in Hana or want to have dinner there, Hana Ranch serves on Thursday (Pizza), Friday, and Saturday.

HANA RANCH TAKE-OUT
This is a little take out window right next to the restaurant. There are tables outside for dining. They are open from 6:30 am to 4 pm.

HOTEL HANA MAUI
Open for breakfast, lunch, and dinner. The prices are high, but the service is elegant and the food is good.

POINTS OF INTEREST

KEANAE ARBORETUM
On the Hana Highway after you pass Paia. You may want to walk around here to see taro under cultivation. The view overlooking Keanae is one of the most picturesque in Hawaii.

HELANI GARDENS
Located just a short distance past Waianapanapa State Park on the right. Open from 8 am to 4 pm. The gardens are under new management. The plan is to charge a minimal entrance fee or donation and set up a flower and fruit stand and add more picnic tables. Right now you can walk the lower gardens only, five and a half acres of tropical and sub-tropical plants including a koi pond and a bamboo grove, and tour the upper garden in your car. The new owners are in the process of opening the upper garden for walking tours also. 248-8274

BEACHES

HONOMANU BAY
Located off the Hana Highway about 30 miles east of Kahului. To find take the dirt road just past Kaumahina State Park and follow it to the beach. This is a beautiful, secluded black sand beach in a tranquil setting. There are no facilities, and like many beaches on the north and east shore, not always good for swimming. Because of the high waves, the surfers love it.

WAIANAPANAPA STATE PARK
This black sand beach is a great place for a picnic, and the swimming is O.K. if the ocean is calm. There are picnic tables, rest rooms and showers.

HANA BEACH PARK
At Hana Bay in Hana. As mentioned already, this is a great place to swim since the bay is almost always calm. Also, there is good snorkeling by the lighthouse. There are rest rooms and picnic tables and the snack bar is across the street.

KOKI PARK
To get there go about two miles past Hana and watch for the loop road which leads to privately owned Hamoa Beach. You will come to Koki on the left before you reach Hamoa. This is a good place for a picnic, but do not swim there as the currents are treacherous.

SPORTS

TENNIS
There are two lighted courts at Hana Park that are open to the public at no charge.

KIHEI

Before Maui was developed for tourists, the Kihei area must have been one of the most beautiful in Hawaii. Located along the south west shore of Haleakala, about eight miles south of Kahului, Kihei is now one of the most developed places in the Islands, and now whenever a development is proposed for any of the neighbor Islands, protesters shout, *Are we going to become like Waikiki or Kihei?* Many people feel that what was once one of Hawaii's pristine areas has been ruined forever by poorly planned, concrete monstrosities that block the view of the shore line.

The distance from the beginning of Kihei, which starts with the Suda Snack Bar, probably the cheapest food on the Kihei coast, to the posh Wailea development on the south end and the new Prince Hotel, Grand Hyatt and Makena Golf Course, is about seven or eight miles. And in those few miles, there are more high rise condos than in any area of Hawaii save Waikiki. Still, all is not lost and there are still nice beaches and open spaces.

As stated above, Kihei ends at the Wailea Resort, a beautiful example of what the Kihei area might have looked like with better planning. Wailea is not, though, for the budget minded, whether it is golf at one of their Robert Trent Jones Jr. designed courses or accommodations at the luxurious Westin Wailea Beach Hotel. Golf, for example, is around $100, while accommodations at the Stouffer Hotel run from $185 to $300. Well, maybe there is a need for the Waikiki/Kihei condos after all.

Since the new Prince Hotel and Makena Golf Course are now complete, getting to the famous Makena Beach is a little easier since most of the road has been paved. Past the Hotel, however, the road is unpaved but in very good condition. It is just a few miles past Makena to La Peruse Bay where a very extensive lava flow can be seen.

A DIGRESSION CONCERNING BOOKINGS.
Hosts lives' change
and on occasion a booking made
cannot be completed.
These events are beyond our control.
Every attempt will be made
to place you in a comparable Host home.
Our experience has shown that the
more communication between
host and guest the better.

RESTAURANTS

Most of the restaurants in the Kihei area depend mainly on tourists for their survival, and normally in a tourist area prices tend to be on the high side. However, competition is keen in Kihei and some of the restaurants have early bird specials. Also, there a few new, very reasonable places as well as one or two more elegant high priced ones. Perhaps the main point to make is that Kihei has enough variety to satisfy just about anyone.

LOCAL STYLE

SUDA'S SNACK SHOP
You will see this on the left as soon as you reach the Kihei area. Very low in price, heavily frequented by locals. This is a good place if the budget is tight, or you like the local style food and are not looking for atmosphere.

SURFSIDE DELI
In the front of the Surfside Hotel on the mauka side of the highway. This is a good place to get a snack of local style food at reasonable prices.

local style

SURFER JOES GRILL & BAR
You will find this, if you are so inclined, just as you enter Kihei from Kahului. The atmosphere is what the name implies. Here you can get Dukes Fried Zukes or Gnarly Fries or even Hang Ten Tempura Fish. Nothing on the menu was over $6.

local/Tourist Style

SAND-WITCH
This can be found at Sugar Beach Resort which is one of the first resorts you come to in Kihei, if you are arriving from Lahaina. If coming from Kahului side, turn right when you reach Kihei and you will come right to it. Good home cooking, sandwiches, at reasonable prices. They are open from 11 am until 11 pm.

MARGARITA'S BEACH CANTINA.
Formerly called Polli's on The Beach. It is located upstairs by the fitness center at Kealea Beach Club, which is just next door to Sugar Beach. The menu is not much changed from Polli's and the setting is great.

MAUI LU RESORT
Open for breakfast, lunch, and dinner. On Wednesday and Friday nights they have a Prime Rib dinner and a Polynesian Show.

PERRY'S SMORGY
This is a new restaurant located in a fairly new shopping center, Kukui Mall. You may be familiar with Perry's from the mainland. This is definitely the chow down restaurant of Maui. Right now the prices are low, all you can eat lunch from 11:30-2 for $5.95 and dinner from 5-9 for $8.95. Perhaps they will stay that way if all the hungry surfers stay down at Joe's. The cuisine, and we used the word loosely, is typical smorgy. However, the roast beef, sliced individually off the biggest roast beef we have ever seen looked great. How they would treat a guest who just wanted to fill up on roast beef is anyone's guess.

CHUCK'S STEAK HOUSE
In the Kihei Town Center. Prices here are reasonable and the food is good. Very mainland style. Early Bird special $8.95, 879-4488.

CHUMM'S
On the mauka side of the highway upstairs at the Rainbow Mall. Food here has a decidedly local flavor and they are attempting to make this one of the night spots in Kihei. They have a Karaoke Bar (Japanese sing-a-long), which is bringing in a pretty good crowd.

ISLAND FISH HOUSE
In the south Kihei area on the mauka side of the main road. This is a good splurge place. The prices are high but the food, service, and atmosphere are excellent. Early bird special $9.95. (When we were there this year they were closed for remodeling, but will be open when this goes to press or shortly after.)

FERRARI'S
Located behind Island Fish House and, as the name implies, Italian cuisine. They offer an early bird special. Their regular menu goes from pizza ($10.95) to pasta (from $12-$19) to Roasted Duck Ferrari's ($20). They are open nightly from 5:30 to closing. For reservations call 879-1535.

ALEXANDER'S
This is a small fast food place that serves fish and chips served with corn bread for very reasonable prices. They are located on the mauka side of S. Kihei Rd.

NEW YORK GOURMET DELI
Located at the rear of the Dolphin Plaza at 2395 S. Kihei Rd. This is an excellent place to grab a quick sandwich for lunch. They have several small tables outside or eat it on the run. All of their sandwiches are $5.95 or less and very, very good. Or maybe all you want is a bagel with cream cheese and lox, $5.95.

KIHEI'S PRIME RIB HOUSE
At the Kai Nani Village above the La Bahia (formerly La Familia). The good deal here is the early bird prime rib for $8.95 between 5-6 p.m. Other than that this restaurant is much like mainland places, salad bar, with entrees between $10 -$16. Most of our hosts rate this as one of their favorites. 879-1954.

LA BAHIA
Located below Prime Rib House. The menu and prices have not changed much from when it was La Familia. The cuisine is, of course, Mexican, and it is one of the busiest spots in Kihei.

ERIK'S SEAFOOD
This is a fairly new restaurant in the Kamaole Center that is open for dinner from 5-10 pm. They claim to have the largest selection of fish in Kihei and the menu is extensive with prices $15 and up. They offer an early bird special from 5-6 pm. for $12.95. 879-8400.

DENNY'S
Also new in the same Center. Just like all other Denny's as far as we could tell. They seemed to have most of the action when we passed by.

CARLOS & ROSSI
Next door to Denny,s and run by the same owner. Mexican food at fairly low prices.

CANTON CHEF
Also in the Kamaole Center open for lunch from 11-2 and for dinner from 5-9:30. They offer both Cantonese and Szechuan dishes, 879-1988.

INTERNATIONAL HOUSE OF PANCAKES
In the Azeka Shopping Center. Like IHOP's everywhere else, its strong point is that the food is familiar, reasonable, and they are open Sunday-Thursday from 6 a.m. until midnight, and on Friday and Saturday from 6 a.m. until 2 a.m.

LUIGI'S PASTA & PIZZA
On the highway at the Azeka Center. Much the same as the one in Maui Mall in Kahului. The only difference would be that the entertainment might not be the same. They also have a Karaoke Bar but not necessarily on the same nights. They are open for lunch and dinner, 879-4446.

ROYAL THAI CUISINE
In the Azeka Shopping Center and open for lunch weekdays from 11-3 and for dinner every evening from 5 9 pm. We tried it and found it O.K. but not outstanding. Prices are moderate with most dishes around $7.

THE GREEK BISTRO
Located behind La Bahia and a little hard to find but if you like Greek food it is worth the hunt. Their prices are moderate, Prawns Island Style $12.95 or Spanakopita for $8.95. They also serve Gyros, a favorite of people who know Greek cuisine. They are open for dinner only from 5:30-9.

OCEAN TERRACE

On the ocean in one of the condos on the south end of Kihei just before you get to Wailea. The setting here is one of the nicest in the Kihei area in our opinion. Ocean Terrace is owned and operated by the same people who own Island Fish House and Ferrari's's. They are open for breakfast, lunch and dinner, with lunch between $6 and $8 and dinners between $16 for Chicken and $21 for Steak and Scampi. They offer a special dinner for two for those in a splurge mood, two kinds of fish, broiled lobster, New York Steak, deep fried shrimp and scallops ($64.95). They also have an early bird special. 879-2607.

CARELLI'S ON THE BEACH

Located next door to Ocean Terrace. If you are looking for a really romantic setting and price is no object this is the spot for you. It is a good idea to call ahead for a reservation, 875-0001.

SAND CASTLE

In the Wailea Shopping Mall. This is not low priced but the food, service and setting is good, all first class as one would expect in a resort of this caliber. 879-0606.

BEACHES

As you drive the Kihei coast you will see many beaches that in the morning offer the calmest, warmest water in all of Hawaii, with a great view of the little Islands of Lanai and Kahoolawe. Since several of them are County Parks, showers, change rooms, rest rooms, and picnic tables are available. What will not be as obvious are the beaches developed by Alexander & Baldwin, the developers of the Wailea Resort, and since turned over to the County. Easy access is available by paved road and parking is ample.

MOKAPU/ULUA/WAILEA BEACH

These three beaches are controlled by Maui County. Access to them is easy once one arrives at Wailea.

PO'OLENALENA BEACH PARK

You will come to this beach just after you pass the Prince Hotel. Swimming and snorkeling are good here.

MAKENA BEACH

This is one of the most spectacular beaches in Hawaii. To get there, go through the Wailea development past the golf course, and then through the new Makena development and that golf course to where the paved road ends. Continue on past the road which goes to the left to the Makena Golf Course. Go about one third of a mile and you will come to a road which goes makai to the beach. You will know you have arrived when you see all the cars. There are no facilities so if you intend spending time here, bring food and drink.

SPORTS

GOLF

Wailea has two eighteen hole courses, both championship caliber. The green fee for non-guests on the Blue Course is $125 and the Orange Course is $95, cart included and mandatory. Another 18 holes named the Gold Course is under construction. For more information call 879-2966. The Makena Golf Course is located south of Wailea. Green fees are $100 cart included and mandatory for 18 holes. One of things we noticed at this course, however, is that at times they offer reduced rates. We suggest you call ahead just in case. 879-3344. The newest course in this area is the Silversword Country Club located on the highway on the way to Wailea. The green fee is $65 cart included for 18 holes of golf. They offer a summer special. 874-0777.

TENNIS
There are fourteen courts at Wailea which are open to the public.

MAALAEA

This little community located between Kihei and Lahaina does not have much there other that a couple of restaurants and a marina where the Coast Guard is located and several condos. If one wanted to go deep sea fishing or snorkeling one could find a choice of 15 charter boats here. One smaller 40 passenger boat called Adventure 1 offers a morning snorkel trip to Molokini State Park, 7 am to noon, 7 days a week. $49 per person includes breakfast, lunch and drinks. Call 242-7683.

RESTAURANTS

BUZZ'S WHARF
Open for lunch and dinner. Mainland style food with moderate prices. The best thing here is the location which has a terrific view.

WATERFRONT
Located in one of the condos and open for dinner only in spite of the sign which says breakfast. At least that was the case when we were there. It is a little on the high side but the view is fantastic and they offer a very good lobster chowder.

MAALAEA FISH HOUSE
This is located right at the marina just past the Coast Guard Station and open for lunch from 11-4 and for dinner from 4:30- 8. When we were there they had a pretty good deal on lobster tail

LAHAINA

At one time Lahaina was a haven for whalers, and during the winter months it is still a great place for whale watching. Located on the south shore of the West Maui Mountains, Lahaina is fully protected from the winds that often whip the Kaanapali/Napili area. It is fairly teeming with tourists and with shops and restaurants to serve their every need. Since our last visit many new art galleries have opened making Lahaina an art lovers paradise. It is from Lahaina that one can catch a glass bottom boat that gives a good glimpse of the coral reef, rife with sea life, or hop on a sail boat to cruise to one of the nearby Islands. Visitors can find most anything they like here for Lahaina lives for and on the ubiquitous tourist.

We will not mention every restaurant and shop, for to do so would be close to a book in itself. As you walk down the main drag, appropriately called Front St., you may be a little overwhelmed by shops, many having sales, and after a while the next store tends to look just like the one you were just in. And yet if you are really looking for bargains, Lahaina, because of the intense competition, might be a good spot.

Restaurants, however, are another matter. Almost all restaurants in town cater to tourists. That and the fact that rents are astronomical (one shop keeper told us it was not uncommon for a new shop located on Front St. to pay up to $60,000 to the landlord just for the privilege of opening the door) work to keep the prices up.

The newest thing in our last edition in Lahaina was a large shopping center called the Cannery located at the west end of town. It is completely enclosed and air-conditioned, making it a great place to cool off from the hot afternoon sun. There are many little shops and several fast food restaurant types as well as a Safeway Store that is open 24 hours a day. If you drive through Lahaina you cannot miss this center as it fronts both on the main highway and Front St. When we first wrote about this center it was not yet complete. Now all the stores are occupied and we feel this is a good place for shopping and is going to give the older shops in town a run for their money.

The new thing in Lahaina this trip is a large shopping complex located between old Lahaina and the Cannery. Very few of the stores were occupied when we passed by but by the end of 1992 they should be in full swing. They even have a night club, Blue Tropix Nightclub, located on the second level above Chili's Grill & Bar. The key stores are Liberty House and Woolworth and by the time it fills up they will have around 75 shops.

Would you agree that the big thrill
in Lahaina might be getting a parking place?
Crowded, eh what?
Well, it must have something good to offer
or people would not flock there.
Maybe our tip about hanging a red cloth
from your car aerial would come in handy here.

RESTAURANTS

LOCAL STYLE

SUSHIYA DELI
On Prison St. off Front. A definite two scoop rice place where you will get filled up for low cost. It is clean and if you like local style, you will feel right at home.

SONG'S ORIENTAL KITCHEN
Located in the center across from the Pioneer Hotel. The food served Okazu-ya style (cafeteria) is very much for local tastes and priced accordingly.

OLD FASHION SAIMIN
Located a few doors down from Musashi (see below). They are open weekdays from 10am to 2am and weekends from 11am to 3am. This must be the place that all the locals go when everyone else closes. Those hours are more like New York than Hawaii.

local Style

GREAT JANE'S EATERY
This is a little off the beaten track but not that hard to find. It is located at 888 Wainee St, which parallels the main highway toward Front St. They are open for breakfast and lunch only from 7-4 weekdays and 7-2 Saturday, closed Sunday. Here you can get a sandwich anywhere from 4 to 12 inches long, ranging in price from $2.65 to $17. Their motto is Get it by the Inch.

GOLDEN PALACE
In the Lahaina Shopping Center off Front St. at the west end of town just before Longi's restaurant. Open for lunch from 11-2 and for dinner from 5-9. They specialize in Cantonese food. Prices are moderate.

THAI CHEF
In the same center mentioned above. Since we are fond of Thai food, we had lunch hear and found it very good. They are open for lunch Monday-Friday from 11-2:30 and for dinner every night from 5-10.

MUSASHI
In the rear of the shopping center mentioned above. This used to be called Fujiyama's. Those who enjoy Japanese food tell us this is the best value in town. The food is good and the prices are moderate. They are open for lunch and dinner and do a brisk business with the local crowd.

local/Tourist Style

SUNRISE CAFE

We did not experience this place ourselves so we are reporting from one of our guests, Jeanne, from Lima, Ohio. She assures us this is a must spot as their food is prepared by one of the fancy French restaurants. It is located next to Lappert's Ice cream in the middle of Lahaina, makai side.

** LONGI'S**

On the mauka side of Front St. on the west end of town. In spite of the prices, this is our favorite spot in Lahaina. Not only is the ambience good, the food and service are great. Do not be surprised when the waiter grabs a chair, turns it around backwards, plunks himself down, and proceeds to rattle off the menu, which is all in his head.

JJ'S

This and the next four places are all located at 505 Front St. in the Whaler's Shopping Center, at the other end of town from Longi's. Many different restaurants have opened and closed in this center over the years, some of them quite good. As busy as Lahaina is, for some reason anything east of the Pioneer Inn seems to have a tough time making it. Now with all of the action on the west side of town things may not get any easier. However, people keep trying, and who can blame them since the setting here is as good as it gets in Lahaina, right on the water. JJ's is owned and operated by the same people who own Chez Paul's, which has been successful for years. At JJ's they told us the food was just as good but less expensive, figure around $20 per person.

OLD LAHAINA CAFE & LUAU

Next door to JJ's. They are open for breakfast, lunch, and dinner. Lunch runs from $7-$10 and dinner between $12-$22. They also offer a Luau dinner for $16.95.

BETINNO'S

At the east end of the center.

JUICE'S TROPICAL BAR

If you are looking for a health food lunch or breakfast you might want to give this a try. Or maybe you want to cool off with a tropical fruit smoothie.

VILLAGE PIZZERIA

You can't miss this if you find Whaler's Village. They are open every day for lunch and dinner.

GILL'S

If you looking for a great little place in Lahaina called Tasca that a guide book, including our last edition, said you just have to try, stop looking. The bad news is that they did not make it. The good news might be that someone is going to try again. They had not yet opened when we were there so we can not vouch for it yet. When open they will serve *Italian* food; the new owner, of course, is French. "But," he exclaimed, "my grandmother was Italian.

LAHAINA COOLERS
For some reason we missed this in our last edition. Perhaps because it is a little out of the way, at 180 Dickinson St, which runs between Front and Wainee. They are open for lunch and dinner from 11:30 to midnight. They have an extensive menu with the most expensive item being Prime Rib at $15, or you might try Evil Jungle Pasta at $9.90.

BENIHANA OF TOKYO
This is on the third floor of the shopping center across from the Pioneer Hotel. Since they are a major Mainland chain, no explanation is needed.

HARBOR FRONT SEAFOOD
On the 2nd floor of the same center, they claim to have the largest selection of seafood in Lahaina. Our memory tell us that someone else in Maui makes that same claim.

LANI'S PANCAKE COTTAGE
This is at the rear of the same center. When we visited Lahaina things were relatively slow and this place was packed to the rafters, which is a indication that folks like it.

PANCHO AND LEFTY'S
Located at the Wharf, Mexican food with prices a bit on the high side (Fajitas Supreme-$15.95, Enchilades de Marisca's-$12.95).

PIONEER INN
Stop by here even if you've eaten, for it is more than an Inn; it is an institution. Recently we heard a visitor comment that it was like staying in a museum. Old and funky, yes, but as a fine wine it seems to improve with age. The main restaurant, located on the south east end of the Inn is open for breakfast, lunch, and dinner. The prices are moderate. Do not give up if there is a crowd. They are used to that and can handle lots of people.

MOONDOGGIES
Across the street from the Pioneer Inn. A new restaurant in Lahaina serving an assortment of soups, salads, sandwiches, pasta, and pizza plus their special dessert, Chocolate Volcano.

CHEESE BURGER MAUI
They claim to have the best burger on Maui, served hot and gooey on a sesame and whole wheat bun. For vegetarians they have Tofu Burger (ugh) or Spinach Nut Burger (we can hardly wait). One thing for sure, they have the number one view in Lahaina.

MOOSE McGILLYCUDDY'S
This one is easy to find since it is located right on Front St. They have an early bird special for $7.95 and their regular menu is not all that high priced.

ALEX'S HOLE IN THE WALL

We just do not understand how we left this out of our last edition. Was it being remodeled? At any rate, since it is one of our favorite places, we will not leave it out this time. They are open for dinner only and a reservation is recommended. They serve excellent Italian food for anywhere from $17 to $24. Or one can have a pasta dinner for $12. We are sure either way you will not be disappointed.

AVALON RESTAURANT & BAR

In our last edition we promised we would give this a try next time through Lahaina, and lucky for us we were true to our word. They call their cuisine Contemporary Asian, and the menu is varied and interesting. Since Thai food is one of our favorites, we felt sure we would be pleased, and we noted the menu had food for many tastes. Evie had the Thai Chicken Salad, excellent and more than she could eat. Al had Stir Fried Chicken served over noodles or brown rice, which is prepared mild, medium, or spicy. We chose spicy. While it was very tasty and full of great ingredients, it was not spicy at all. However, they provided us with chili to spice it up. To make up for the fact that we had to request extra spice, they gave us each a complimentary dessert; one of the best desserts we ever had: a dish of hot caramel with a large dollop of macadamia nut ice cream in the middle, surrounded by raspberries, blackberries, blueberries, cherries, banana, and mango. They are open for lunch and dinner every day from noon to midnight.

HAPPY DAYS

If you want a hamburger in what is trying to pass for a '50's setting you might give this a try. What caught our eye was the juke box. When we first visited here it had a "Do not touch" sign. We were glad to see it had been removed. They are open for breakfast, lunch, and dinner and serve a 1/2 lb. burger for $4.75, each add on $1 extra. Located on Lahainaluna St.

LAHAINA BROILER

Across from Longi's and the best part of this place is the setting, right on the water. They are open for breakfast, lunch, and dinner. Lunch costs between $6 and $10 while dinner goes from $13 for chicken to $20 for steak.

DENNY'S

Needs no introduction to Mainlanders or locals. It is located in the Lahaina Square Center on Wainee St.

COUNTRY KITCHEN

In the same center as Denny's. This owner and operator used to own La Bretagne (see below under Splurge Restaurants) so should know what he is doing. They have a full dinner for $13.95 with different gourmet dishes every night except Sunday.

HARD ROCK CAFE

Located in the new Lahaina Center just west of Longi's on Front St. Since this is a rather large chain, you may be familiar with their menu. If not, let us assure you it is mainstream America, reasonably priced. If the size of the crowd is any indication of things, they must be doing something right.

CHILI'S GRILL & BAR
Next door to Hard Rock. If you must have Mexican food you can choose between this and Pancho & Lefty's. Here you get fajita for $10.95. However, the only other Mexican dish we saw on the menu was chili. Visitors from San Francisco will be thrilled-not to see Chicken Frisco on the menu.

MARIE CALLENDERS
Located in the Cannery Center. You may be familiar with this since they our a mainland chain with several locations in Hawaii. If you do not know them, take our word for it, they are Main Street America, especially popular for their pies and cakes.

ATHENS GREEK RESTAURANT
A little fast food take out in the Cannery mall that serves a couple of interesting dishes such as Spanakopita (Spinach-Cheese Pie) or Baklava (a tasty dessert made out of filo dough and honey syrup).

SAENG'S THAI
On Front St. west of the Cannery. Open for lunch and dinner, owned by the same people who own Saeng's Thai in Wailuku.

CHART HOUSE
The last place one comes to heading west on Front St.

SPLURGE RESTAURANTS

KOBE JAPANESE STEAK HOUSE
This is located in the center of Lahaina, one block away from Front St. This is the same owner as the one in Waikiki and since that has a very good reputation we would think this as good. They are open for dinner only from 5:30. For a reservation call 667-5555.

GERRARD'S
Several of our hosts rave about this spot. The prices are fairly high but if it is as good as they claim, it is worth it. They are in a new location at 174 Lahainaluna Road at the Plantation Inn, a new Bed & Breakfast Inn created for those who desire casual elegance, call us for a reservation 1-800-733-1632. We noticed this year that they were open for lunch, and it seemed that their prices were not all that high. 661-8939

LA BRETAGNE
Across the street from Lahaina Shore Village, facing Maul-ulu-o-lele Park. There are several French restaurants on Maui, and we have been told that this is the best. If you are in a splurge mood and do not mind spending between $50-$100 give this place a try, 661-8966.

CHEZ PAUL
This excellent French restaurant is located east of Lahaina right at the 15 mile marker. We had dinner here and even though the bill was in the neighborhood of $100 for two, we feel it was worth it. Most dishes go between $27 and $30 a la carte. Let's face it, though, this is not the place to bring the kids and you have to be in an expensive mood, 661-3843.

DAVID PAUL'S LAHAINA GRILL
This may be the best value of the higher priced Lahaina Restaurants. Located just off Front St. on Lahainaluna St. in the Lahaina Hotel and open for dinner every day. Prices run between $20 and $35 salad included, 667-5117.

POINTS OF INTEREST

Not only is Lahaina swollen with tourists of all ages, since it was the State Capitol until 1843, it is full of valuable historical landmarks. The East Indian Banyan Tree, just across from the Pioneer Inn, is the oldest and perhaps the largest in Hawaii. The building in front of the tree, once the Courthouse, is now the Police Station and the Center for the Lahaina Art Society.

Lahaina Boat Harbor is filled with private and commercial craft of all sizes and descriptions and any number of purposes from glass bottom sight seeing to whale watching in a sailboat to a dinner cruise on a larger boat or a catamaran to one of the smaller islands. While not as famous as the Kona Coast for marlin, plenty of big fish are brought in to the Lahaina Harbor.

BALDWIN HOUSE
Baldwin House was the original home of Medical Missionary Dr. Dwight Baldwin and his family. He was responsible for saving the people of Maui from the small pox epidemic of 1853. Now completely restored, the home is open for tours from 9 a.m. to 4:30 p.m. Admission $3 adults, $2 seniors, $5 families.

HALE PAAHOA
Hale Paahoa, which translates *Stuck in Irons House*, is located aptly on Prison St. Behind its stone walls were thrown the town drunks and other wayward souls. No admission charge, open 9-5.

DAN'S GREENHOUSE
Located on Prison St. one block off Front St. Do not miss this plant nursery with exotic baby birds and marmoset monkeys, especially if you have kids that are getting a little hot and tired of all the shopping and sightseeing. We are sure this place will pick up their spirits. 661-8412.

TAKE HOME MAUI
At 121 Dickinson St. around the corner and west of Dan's. Stop by and get a sample of local pineapple and perhaps you will decide that the folks back home might like a little taste. If so, no problem, they will sell it to you there and make sure it is ready for you at

146

the airport when you are ready to depart, or you can have it mailed to the mainland. You will pay more per pound than if you were to consume it on Maui, but keep in mind that all fruit sent to the mainland has to be specially treated. They also sell and ship Kona coffee beans, Kula onions, coconuts, papaya, etc. 661-8067

WO HING TEMPLE
On the mauka side of Front St at the west end of town. It is open Monday through Saturday from 9 a.m. to 5 p.m. and on Sundays from noon to 5 p.m.

DOMED THEATER
This is located right in the heart of town at 824 Front St. Shows are held on the hour from 10 am to 10 pm and last for around forty minutes and cost $5.95 for adults and $3.95 for children under 12 (under 4 free). While in some ways the movie is enjoyable, if you have a tendency toward motion sickness you might want to skip this as one really has the sensation of flying. 661-8314.

FOUNDATION GALLERIES
Ordinarily we do not include art galleries as places of interest, but we make an exception here because Naomi Rubine, publicity director for the Gallery, pointed out what we thought might be a unique feature. The policy of the gallery is "Art for Conservation" and buyers are asked to deduct 10% from the purchase price and write a check directly to the conservation society of their choice. This gallery of some 30 artists is located at 143 Lahainaluna Rd., just off Front St.

BEACHES

LAHAINA BEACH
There are no facilities here, in spite of the fact that except for Kaanapali beaches, this is the most frequented in the area. To find, go north from the middle of Lahaina until you come to Puunoa Place. Turn makai to the beach. Swimming is good on any beach in the Lahaina area; snorkeling is fair and very easy since the water is shallow along this coast.

WAHIHULI STATE PARK
There are picnic tables, rest rooms, and showers here and a little lawn too. Located just north of Lahaina off the main highway.

PUAMANA PARK
Two miles south of Lahaina, this is a good place for picnicking, not so hot for swimming or snorkeling.

LAUNIUPOKO STATE PARK
Since there is little beach here, this is more a place for picnicking as there are tables and rest rooms. Swimming is safe but not appealing. It is located about a mile south of Puamana.

KAANAPALI/NAPILI/KAPALUA

As you leave Lahaina heading north, you enter the area that many mainlanders consider the premier spot in the Islands. Long ago if you took this drive you would have looked down on seemingly endless white sand beaches. The beaches are still there, of course, but hidden behind the many hotels and condominiums that line this area. At one time this was the dumping ground for the waste product (bagasse) of the Pioneer Sugar Mill.

There is excellent swimming and snorkeling at the Kaanapali beaches. On the rare occasions that the surf is too high for safe swimming, the hotels fly a red flag to warn their guests. Since private beaches are not allowed in Hawaii, feel free to stop by and enjoy the water whether you are a guest of the hotel or not. Some people think a stop by the Maui Hyatt is a must.

Keep in mind that this area is totally devoted to tourism so restaurants and shops reflect that. Hotels in this area are all on the posh side, starting at Kaanapali, where there are several hotels, and ending at the elegant and expensive Kapalua Bay Hotel. We would venture to say that there were no bad restaurants here, and no doubt some are excellent. All are going to be more expensive than they would be if they were in another location. We have not spent as much time in this area as we have elsewhere since it is not really a Bed and Breakfast area. At the present time we have only one host homes here. A few of the restaurants we have tried and liked are mentioned below.

A REMINDER ABOUT OCEAN SAFETY

While the ocean along this area
can be very safe for swimming,
it is a good idea to exercise care.
If there is no life guard,
check the conditions.
Do not go in if the waves
are obviously too high,
and never turn your back on the ocean.
We do not mean to alarm,
but believe us,
it pays to be cautious.

RESTAURANTS

local

RICCO'S PIZZA
This is just beyond Fat Boy's and good if all you want is a snack.

DOLLIES
Located in the Kahana area which is between Kaanapali and Napili. It is a little sandwich place, order at the counter and take to a table. We felt that the sandwiches priced between $5 and $6 were not a very good deal compared to what you can get at the Grill and Bar mentioned below.

local/Tourist

EL CRABCATCHER
Located in the Whalers Village at Kaanapali. Full dinners go for around $18, light supper around $10. They are open for lunch from 11-3 and dinner from 5:30-10:30, with the happy hour from 4:30-6:30. There is Hawaiian and contemporary music from 5:30-7:30 pm. Reservations are usually needed, 661-4423.

CHINA BOAT
This is a new venture located at 4474 L. Honoapiilani Rd. The cuisine is mostly Szechuan but they do have a few Cantonese dishes. Prices are somewhat on the high side with most of the house specialties between $8-$13.

ERIK'S SEAFOOD GROTTO
Located in the Kahana villa Condominium and open for dinner only from 5-10 pm. They have a large selection of seafood including fresh oysters and clams, 669-4806.

KAHANA KEYS RESTAURANT
This is located in the Kahana Keys Resort. They offer an early bird special until 7pm for $9.95.

SEA HOUSE
Located at the Napili Kai Resort. While they do have a great setting, we felt their breakfast and dinner prices were on the high side. Lunch prices, however, were more reasonable.

ORIENT EXPRESS
This is billed as the first Thai and Chinese restaurant on Maui and is located at Napili Shores. It is up-scale, expensive, and very good, 669-8077.

GAZEBO
For breakfast or lunch in a really nice setting give this a try. It is located at Napili Shores.

KOHO GRILL & BAR
This is a new restaurant located in the new Napili Plaza. They are open for lunch and dinner. Prices here are very reasonable, with the highest priced item being New York Steak at $12.95. The menu is extensive, middle American food.

THE GRILL AND BAR
Or as the locals call it *the Gorilla Bar*. Whether for lunch or for dinner this is good value. Not only is the setting great, the service excellent, the food good, but the prices, especially for lunch, are not out of line. Lunch goes for about $8 or $9 while dinners go from $14 to $29.95 for lobster. It is located at the Kapalua Bay Golf Course.

PINEAPPLE HILL
This is a former plantation manager's home in a lovely setting high up behind the Kapalua Golf Course. The view is spectacular, looking over to Molokai and Lanai. The prices are high. We suggest that you at least stop by here for a cool drink. They open at 4:30 for dinner only, 669-6129.

BEACHES

KAANAPALI RESORT BEACHES
Access to this long stretch of beach is through any of the hotels. Swimming and snorkeling are ideal especially at the north end in front of the Sheraton Maui. All of the equipment can be rented at the beach.

NAPILI BAY
The easiest access to this beach is through the Napili Kai Resort. Swimming and snorkeling are good here.

D.T. FLEMING PARK
About ten miles north of Lahaina, this beach has all the facilities except food. Most of the time swimming is good, but from time to time the surf gets rougher than at Kaanapali or Kihei. The main problem we experience every time we go north of Kaanapali is wind. Surfers and windsurfers paradise.

NORTH OF FLEMING PARK

There are several beaches beyond Fleming that are beautiful to behold, but none have facilities and all are a little difficult to get to. Also, swimming can be tricky when the surf is up. For privacy, however, they are tops on Maui for obvious reasons. The first, Oneloa, is about a mile north of Fleming Park. Stop at a safe place off the road and hike down the steep trail to the beach. When you have gone three miles north of Fleming, watch for a dirt road which will take you to Ponakupile Beach. Snorkeling is great here when the sea is calm. Around six miles north of Fleming you will come to a rocky little beach called Honokolau.

For most visitors who even get this far, the road stops here, but for the really adventurous, going beyond this point might prove irresistible. (see *WEST OF WAILUKU* in earlier section). If the weather is nice, we urge you to continue. For two miles you will think you are crazy and that we are crazy for suggesting it. Then you will come to a fairly good road, sometimes paved, sometimes dirt, that will take you all the way to Wailuku.

SPORTS

GOLF

There are five courses in this area, two at Kaanapali and three at Kapalua. The Village course at Kapalua, finished in 1975, was designed by Arnold Palmer. At the Kapalua Bay Course Palmer assisted architect Ed Seay. Green fees here are $110 per person for non-guests, including cart. At the Royal Kaanapali North or South, fees are $110 per person including cart.

WHAT HAVE WE MISSED?

Plenty, we feel sure!
If you have made some discovery,
drop us a line, or give us a call.
One of the girls, Patty, Nancy, or Elvrine
will be happy to talk to you.
Or you may even catch Evie or Al
on one of those rare days they are not out exploring.

call or write

B & B Hawaii
Box 449
Kapaa, Hi. 96746
808-822-7771
1-800-733-1632
or fax us at 808-822-2723

Chapter VII...KAUAI

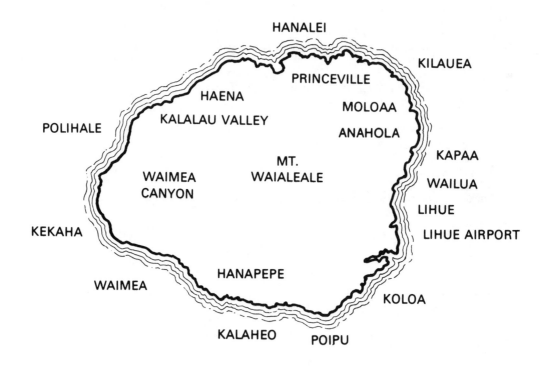

KAUAI.....THE GARDEN ISLAND

.....DRIVING TIMES....

From Lihue Airport to: (approximate)

Wailua......................7.5 miles, 15 minutes
Kapaa.......................... 9 miles, 20 minutes
Hanalei..................... 35.5 miles, 45 minutes
Poipu..........................12 miles, 20 minutes
Hanapepe...................17 miles, 40 minutes
Kalalau Lookout...........45 miles, 90 minutes

KAUAI

the Garden Isle

That Kauai is called the Garden Isle is no surprise to anyone who has been there, and yet the name is in one sense of the word a misnomer. It really depends on what one imagines when one hears the word *garden.* If one comes to Kauai expecting to see a profusion of flowers neatly arranged in some sort of a nursery fashion, disappointment will be inevitable. Often we have been asked the question, "When do the flowers bloom?" The first time we heard this question, we were surprised since flowers are always in bloom on Kauai: bougainvillea, plumeria, African tulip, hibiscus (the State flower), just to name a few. But what really strikes any visitor to Kauai is the lushness. Perhaps it should have been called the Emerald Isle, or as Mark Twain once suggested for Oahu, Rainbow Island.

Located north and west of Oahu, Kauai's beauty seems never ending. Whether one prefers the lush verdant tropics of the Hanalei Valley or the stark, sharp beauty of the arid Waimea Canyon, or the many-meadowed valleys of the Na Pali Coast, beauty is never lacking. Nowhere in the Islands are beaches more plentiful or more beautiful.

At the center of this Jewel rises Mt. Waialeale, which means *rippling on the waters,* where rainfall is not measured in inches but in feet. Can you believe an average rainfall of thirty-seven feet? And just a few miles away, in the Waimea/Kekaha area, desert conditions prevail. If any tourist has had a stay on Kauai during one of its rainy spells, it would be hard to convince him that those of us who live here do much more than grow moss. We remember one particularly rainy time when we were having lunch at the Sheraton Coconut Beach Hotel. The rain came down so hard that the pool overflowed. Suddenly the Fire Department rushed in, dropped large hoses in the pool, and began pumping the water toward the ocean. Seeing this Evie exclaimed, "Kauai is the only place they call the Fire Department to put the water out." Yes, we do get a little rain on Kauai, and yet since most of the rain comes at night or in the early morning, one need not be too concerned. Visitors can be assured they will see more shades of green than they thought existed, and there are few days the sun cannot be found.

Of all the outer Islands Kauai has had the most growth in the last ten years. Long time visitors are often shocked at the congestion. Development on Kauai is somewhat different than on the Mainland. Our experience in California was that a housing development would go in and a shopping center would be built to service those homes. The size of the center would be determined by the number of homes serviced. Honolulu grew in much the same way. On Kauai, however, shopping centers are built to service basically the same number of homes. To be sure several new hotels have been constructed to accommodate visitors and these visitors frequent the new centers to a degree. But the pressure for housing and roads that these new hotels and centers have created is intense. Hence, Kauai is not the sleepy little place it was years ago.

Since much of Kauai cannot be seen from the main highway, which traverses three quarters of the way around the Island, we recommend visitors take a helicopter ride. Such a trip is not inexpensive, around $146 ($20 discount for B & B members); however, our recommendation is to take the ride, for unless one is a strong hiker, much of the Na Pali Coast, Waimea, and Waialeale cannot be seen. The hike to Hanakapiai Beach, the first two miles of the Na Pali Coast, is not that strenuous and should be attempted unless walking is a problem. To get the best deal on a helicopter ride, be sure to call our office (see below) and have one of the girls book it for you; they are quite knowledgeable about the best deals.

Kauai is, for that matter, a hiker's paradise, with many miles of trails not only along the Na Pali Coast but in the Waimea Canyon and Kokee State Park and in the interior of the Island above the Kapaa area. Hiking to the top of Sleeping Giant is far more ominous in appearance than in reality, but the reward at the top is not diminished.

Ever the land of enchantment and romance, Kauai was and still is in some people's minds the home of the Menehunes, that diminutive race of people who never took a task they could not complete in one night. It is the Menehunes who are credited with the construction of the Menehune Fish Pond outside of Lihue and the Menehune Ditch off the Waimea River. Legend has it that the Menehunes are still living on Kauai, deep in the valleys along the Na Pali Coast.

How much time one takes to explore Kauai depends on how one goes about it. Our first visit was two weeks, and that did not give us the time we needed. We have lived on Kauai since 1979 and are still discovering our new home. After all, we have not even been able to catch up with the Menehunes, yet.

*For assistance
with all your
travel needs
call our office
(808)-822-7771
1-800-733-1632
FAX 808-822-2723*

KAUAI'S LUAUS

The Luaus listed below are the professional ones. At times churches and other organizations have luaus and if you are fortunate enough to attend one of these, you will get much more of the local flavor of a luau without all of the tourist oriented hoopla. But if you have never been to a luau, by all means go to one of the ones below if you are not able to find a more traditional one.

SHERATON COCONUT BEACH
This luau is held every day but Monday. At 10:45 a.m. they hold the Traditional Hawaiian Imu Ceremony. At 6:30 p.m. there is a Tropical Shell Lei Greeting and the bar is open from 6:45-9 p.m., with the buffet starting at 8 p.m. At 8 pm entertainment by the Victor Punua Polynesian Revue begins. Adults $45, children under 12 $27.24, children 5 and under free. Friday night is Senior Night, $36. On Wednesday and Saturday, family nights, a family of four pays $90. For reservations call 822-3455, ext. 651.

TAHITI NUI
We give a lengthy description of this luau in Hanalei Restaurant section and we suggest you check it out as this is our favorite luau spot on Kauai.

POIPU SHERATON
Every Wednesday there is a luau and Polynesian show. The Buffet features American, Hawaiian, Japanese, and Chinese cuisine and starts at 7 p.m with an open bar and dinner. The show starts at 8 pm. The tab is $42 for adults and $24 for children. 742-1661

SMITH'S TROPICAL PARADISE
Located just south of the Wailua River. There is a luau every weekday night. The cost is $43.75 for adults, $26 for children seven to thirteen, $17 for children three to six and under three are free. The cost includes the entrance fee to the park, a luau, cocktails, and a Polynesian show. Everyone we talked to who has gone has felt they more than got their money's worth. 822-4654.

STOFFER WAIOHAI HOTEL
Every Thursday they have a buffet dinner and the show South Pacific. Much of the talent used is local and it is really great fun. The cost is $48 for adults, $24 for children 5-15, under 5 free. You get quite a bit for your money; they have an open bar starting at 6pm which runs right through the show. For more information call 742-9511.

SPECIAL EVENTS

KAUAI MUSEUM FOLK ARTS EXHIBIT (JANUARY TO DECEMBER)
An on going rotating exhibit celebrating the folk arts of Kauai by honoring master crafts persons. Such arts include quilting, hula, woodworking, lei making and more. Every six weeks the focus of the exhibit changes. Call 245-6931 for additional information.

BROWN BAGS TO STARDOM (MID JANUARY)
A celebration of talent as "stars to be" compete at the Kauai War Memorial Convention Hall for prizes. Kauai's own Glen Medeiros was discovered at this very event. Call 245-4355 for more information.

HANAPEPE RAFT RUN (EARLY FEBRUARY)
A 2 and 5 kilometer event. Held on the Hanapepe River and sponsored by the Garden Island Road Runners. 338-1475

CAPTAIN COOK CELEBRATION (THIRD WEEK IN FEBRUARY)
Waimea's Annual celebration with entertainment, hula exhibition, street dances, food, games and craft booths. Parade. Call 245-9696.

MIRAGE PRO-AM GOLF (MID FEBRUARY)
With a $10,000 purse this event is held at the Prince Course in Princeville. Televised. Call 826-3580 for more info.

PRINCE KUHIO FESTIVAL (AROUND THE 26 OF MARCH)
This festival includes songs and dances from the era of Prince Kuhio. Ironman/Ironwoman Canoe Race has been held annually for over 20 years from Kealia to Wailua Beach. Activities held at different resorts around the island. Call 245-3971

PRINCE KUHIO RUN (AROUND THE 26 OF MARCH)
5 & 10 kilometer races beginning early in the morning in Poipu. Call 742-9391.

PRINCE KUHIO DAY (MARCH 26)
State Holiday honoring Hawaii's Prince Kuhio with a special observance on Kauai where the beloved Prince was born.

POLO SEASON (APRIL)
Begins in April and runs throughout Spring and summer. This sports event attracts players from the around the island as well as visiting sportsman. Events held at the polo field at Anini Beach. For more info call Ken Anderson at 826-9210.

LEI DAY (MAY 1)
With a traditional emphasis on flowers the Garden Isle especially celebrates this day. Watch the papers for specific celebrations at the various grammar schools where children put on a May Day/Lei Day program for their parents and friends with lots of flowers and hula dances.

SPRING FESTIVAL (MID MAY)
Annual Ke Ola Hou Hawaiian arts and crafts, hula, food, games, a Tahitian competition, contests and a variety of entertainment. Hanapepe Town Park. Ca;; 335-5765 or 335-6466.

POOKU HANALEI STAMPEDE (END MAY)
A state wide rodeo held at Pooku Stables with music and dancing. 826-6777.

KING KAMEHAMEHA DAY (JUNE 9)
This state wide celebration in honor of the ancient king is a uniquely Hawaiian festivity. There are celebrations, canoe races and a parade.

O-BON SEASON (JULY THROUGH AUGUST)
Kauai's Buddhist missions in Lihue, Kapaa, Waimea, Hanapepe,and Koloa are the sites for colorful O-Bon dances. These happy celebration are in honor of Japanese ancestors and include a floating lantern ceremony. Cultural songs, dances, food booths, games etc. For more info call on the of the Hongwanji's island wide.

KAUAI HOSPICE FUND RAISER (JULY 4)
The Annual Fund raiser for Kauai Hospice is a family affair celebration held at Vidinha Stadium in Lihue. Main highlights include a magnificent fireworks display synchronized with music, food booths, local and Honolulu entertainment, contests and a fanfare of exciting events. Call 245-7277.

POIPU PRO-AM SURF MEET (EARLY JULY)
Hawaii's surfers compete for $2,500 in prize money at Prince Kuhio Beach. Watch the local papers for times and water conditions.

KING KONG ULTRA TRIATHLON (MID JULY)
A swim across Hanalei Bay and back (2 miles) bicycle from Hanalei Pier to Waimea and back to Wailua (90 miles) and run Powerline Trail to Princeville (18 miles) Call Larry King 826-4393.

KOLOA PLANTATION DAYS (END JULY)
Celebrating the birth of sugar plantations in Hawaii. An historic parade depicts ethnic cultural heritages of early plantation workers. Entertainment, crafts, games, food, luau. Parade begins at 10:00 am with festivities immediately following. The Aloha Queen Contest ends the celebration.

TROUT SEASON OPENS (AUGUST - SEPTEMBER)
Kokee State Park. Call the Division of Aquatic Resources for permits and restrictions. 335-5871

NO HOLO KAI (MID AUGUST)
Celebrating the renaissance in Hawaiian culture, outrigger canoes equipped with sails will bring paddlers across the 86-mile Kauai channel. Festivities and entertainment, booths brimming with local food and everything else imaginable will greet the weary paddlers upon their arrival sometime in the afternoon.

KAUAI FETE (MID AUGUST)
An annual festival of both group and solo competition. Celebrating Tahitian arts and crafts, Hawaiian wood carving jewelry, coconut weaving, haku leis and flowers. Kapaa soccer field.

FARM FAIR (LABOR DAY WEEKEND)
This Hawaiian fair has everything from cotton candy to malasadas. The local 4-H shows off their finest in livestock along with rides, contests, and just plain island fun. This event draws families from all over the island. There are prizes for everyone for orchids and anthuriums to home baked goods. Join the fun in Lihue at the War Memorial Convention Hall.

MOKIHANA FESTIVAL (SEPTEMBER)
Celebrating the Hawaiian arts in a week long celebration sponsored by the Garden Island Arts Council. Festivities are scheduled throughout the week. Call 245-6931 for a complete schedule of events.

KAUAI RENAISSANCE FAIRE (BEGIN OCTOBER)
Jugglers, jousters, dancers, actors, musicians and artists will perform representing the 16th century at Kilohana Estate in Puhi. 245-6684

ALOHA DAYS (THIRD WEEK IN OCTOBER)
The Aloha week tradition is a celebration of Hawaii's people and a way to perpetuate all things Hawaiian. Colorful pageantry, street dances and special events. There is always a parade and lots of "Aloha Spirit."

KAUAI LOVES YOU TRIATHLON (MID OCTOBER)
An APT world championship (LD) super series event. a 1.5 mile swim, 54 mile bike ride and 12.4 mile run. Begins and ends in Hanalei. Call 825-9343 Larry King.

HALF-MARATHON/5-10KM (BEGIN NOVEMBER)
Starts at Sheraton Coconut Beach Hotel in Kapaa. Call 245-7255 for more info.

KAPAA CHRISTMAS PARADE (BEGIN DECEMBER)
This festive occasion is held in Kapaa with entertainment, drawings, hula contests, food and craft booths. Keiki Christmas Hula and Miss Christmas hula contests. Enjoy a day filled with beautiful floats and ono food. Sponsored by the Kapaa Business Association.

KILOHANA CRAFT FAIR (BEGIN DECEMBER)
Kilohana Estate in Puhi. Call 245-6684

TREES OF HOPE (BEGIN DECEMBER)
Sponsored by the Association for Retarded Citizens. A display of beautifully decorated trees, wreaths and centerpieces along with evening entertainment. ARC 245-4132.

KAUAI MUSEUM HOLIDAY FESTIVAL (BEGIN DECEMBER)
A Christmas sale of hand crafted gifts and baked goods at Kauai Museum. 245-6931.

FILM FESTIVAL
To obtain information on this festival, call the County Information office, 245-2313. In years past there have been some very interesting films shown at this festival.

KAUAI HOSTS

KAPAA AREA

K-1

A secluded ocean front home on beautiful Anahola Bay where   guests can enjoy the peaceful serene environment of a country setting right on the beach. Guests sleep to the sounds of the ocean and wake up to the sounds of nature in this large, airy detached studio complete with mini-kitchenette for total privacy with breakfast fixings provided. Amenities include a garden shower, sky light, it's own lanai, a queen sized bed, cassette player, TV, plus your own private phone.

Occasionally, hosts will offer a 'honeymoon room' in the main house that features a big deep jacuzzi surrounded by mirrors and hanging ferns in it';s own private bathroom. This beautiful room has sky lights and doors that open to a private lanai overlooking the ocean. Accommodations are a queen sized bed, cassette player and TV. A continental breakfast is served on the lanai or you are welcome to use the kitchen as well as the other amenities of the main living area.

RATES: Detached Studio: $85/day, $500/week.

Honeymoon Room: $125/day, $775/weekly. Three day minimum.

K-3

Stay in a new one bedroom guest cottage nestled in the lush and country mountain side of Wailua Homesteads. Views of the wettest spot on earth can be seen from the deck. The bedroom can be either twins or a king bed and there are futons for extra people. The kitchenette is great for preparing light meals and a welcome fruit basket is provided A gas barbeque grill is available to guests. Breakfast is not served or provided at this accommodation. Private bath, color TV and phone with a private line. Hosts live in the main residence away from the cottage on the same property and can help with information about Kauai. No smoking, please. Children welcome.

RATES: $70 single or double, $80 for three, $90 for four. Weekly and monthly rates available.

K-3A

Cloud Nine Holiday is a newly decorated spacious apartment that is completely private with its own entrance. The master bedroom has a king size bed and off the living area is a queen size bed. It comes equipped with a cable color TV, a microwave, a small fridge and all the breakfast fixings. The lanai overlooks a beautifully landscaped "Bird of Paradise" tropical garden perfect for romantic sunrise or sunset strolls. Opaeka'a Stream which crosses the property turns into Opaeka'a Falls just a mile down. This the most photographed water fall on the island. On the other side of the stream and a short walk away is a public tennis court. Cloud 9 Holiday is located a short drive from the beach. You will have a great view of Sleeping Giant mountain and since it is at an higher elevation, nights are a little cooler. During the day ceiling fans do the job. Non smokers, only, please.

RATES: $60 double, $80 three, $100 for four persons. $5 extra for 1 night.

K-4

Enjoy traditional B&B in this lovely two story cedar home. Guests have a choice of three rooms each with their own private bath and queen sized bed and TV. The suite has a large soaking tub in the bathroom. Each morning wake up to the smell of fresh baked bread and Kona coffee which is served in the glassed-in lanai area offering views of tranquil countryside with Mt. Waialeale in the background. Just 5 minutes by car to warm, sunny beaches and excellent restaurants, this home is also a central location for sightseeing all of Kauai. Smoking outside only, please.
RATES: Suite: $60, B&B Rooms: $40 single, $45 double

K-5B

Makana Inn offers two separate units. It is centrally located in Wailua Homesteads, a tranquil country setting with beautiful mountain views. Three miles from beach, golf, tennis, shopping and dining. A generous continental breakfast is stocked in your kitchen upon arrival: fresh fruit, juice, coffee, tea, milk, muffins, butter, jam and honey. Also available is washer/dryer shared by both units. The one bedroom Guest Cottage has a king sized bed and private bath with a tub and shower. There is a double sofa bed in the living room area for extra sleeping. Light cooking in kitchenette. Color cable TV with HBO, Cinemax & Showtime, telephone with a private line. Outside, the private lanai overlooks Mt. Waialeale and green pastures. Located downstairs of the main house with a private entrance is the Downstairs Apartment which has queen sized bed in the bedroom plus a double hideabed in the sitting area for one extra person. The private bath with shower adjoins the bedroom. Kitchenette offers light cooking. Color cable TV with HBO, Cinemax and Showtime plus a telephone. Smoking outside, please. Two night minimum.
RATES: Guest Cottage: $75 double, $85 for 3, $95 for four.
Downstairs Apartment: $65 double, $75 for three.

K-6

These three fresh and comfortable accommodations overlook a horse pasture skirted by Opaekaa Stream in a tranquil country setting on three acres. Waterfalls are often visible in the distance from the lanai. Private entrances open in to suites graced with traditional island furnishings. The KING is a large 2 bdrm/1 bath suite with ceiling fans. It includes a living room, dining area and full kitchen. One bedroom has a king bed while the other has a king bed or extra long twins. The QUEEN has one bedroom with a queen sized bed and private bath along with a sitting area that offers a queen murphy bed for a third person. The dining area adjoins a small kitchen for light cooking. The PRINCE is a master bedroom suite with private bath, king sized bed and ceiling fan. A tiny kitchenette area holds a small refrigerator, microwave and coffee pot for preparing picnic lunches or midnight snacks. Smoking outside only, please. Hot springs spa available.
RATES: King $100 for 1-4 people; Queen $75 double, $7.50 each for additional persons; Prince $50 single or double.

K-7

On a quiet country road in the hills of Keapana Valley your hostess offers guests rooms in a quiet pastoral setting. Although this home is just a five minute drive to great restaurants and beaches, guests feel transported to a secluded place far from civilization. Beautifully landscaped and architect designed by the hostess herself, the property offers panoramic views of the ocean and mountains. This is a perfect place to relax. Choice of three rooms are offered: A room with double and single beds and adjoining full private bath; a room with a queen bed and single bed for up to three persons that shares bathroom in the hall with the third room furnished with a single bed. Guests may use the solar hot tub as well as a refrigerator for cold drinks or picnic fixings. There is a spacious lanai with rattan furniture and hammocks for guests relaxation in a tropical, non-smoking, adult only environment.
RATES: Room with private bath: $60, $350/wk. Other rooms: $40.

K-7A

A romantic, rustic private cottage is nestled in a setting of ginger and hibiscus flowers under the shade of two huge monkey pod trees. A chance to experience simple living in this natural setting which includes bathing outdoors. An outside shower with hot and cold water is surrounded by tropical foliage for complete privacy. The bedroom is upstairs and has a built-in bed with a sky light above it for viewing the moon and stars. Light kitchen and living area downstairs, plus a deck for outside sitting. Non-smokers only, please. Three night minimum preferred.
RATES: $75/day, $450/wk.

K-16

Hosts offer three rooms on the coconut coast of Kauai and just two blocks inland from the beach. The Aqua Room is totally separate from the main house and is next to a coconut grove. Inside is furnished with a double sized bed, two comfortable chairs and TV. The private bathroom offers tub and shower. Guests are welcome eat their breakfast out in the yard under the mango tree or inside the main house kitchen. The Jade Room is off the living room of the main house and has it's own kitchenette and separate entrance. Furnished with two double beds and cable TV, the bedroom is large and has plenty of closet space. The kitchenette/dining area is all screened in and is fully equipped for light cooking. The kitchenette is stocked with breakfast fixings daily. A uniquely designed shower with two shower heads is featured in the adjoining private bathroom. The Hibiscus Room offers a double bed, cable TV, adjoining private bathroom and a private courtyard with it's own entrance. All the rooms have hand painted art on the walls done by your hostess who is a homemaker and is originally from Oregon. Your host comes from a local family of entertainers on Kauai. They have a son in grade school. Their home is special and they enjoy offering their hospitality. No smoking in the rooms, please.
RATES: $50/ night per room, single or double. $60 for three $70 for four in the Jade Room only.

K-26A

Serene, pastoral setting with panoramic views of mountains, waterfalls and the ocean. Upcountry, central location. Want to hear more? Set apart amongst the trees is the private guest cottage. It features bright and spacious private island-style antique filled rooms. There is a queen sized bed in the bedroom and a sleeper sofa in the living room. The bathroom has a bathtub and shower combination. There is a fully equipped kitchen should you care to prepare meals and snacks. Cable TV, ceiling fans, gas barbeque, beach gear and all amenities are included. Relax at your own pace from the wrap-around deck. The lovely island decor suite accommodation is the first level of the main house. It is self-contained with private entrance and lanai with a beautiful view down through the sugar-cane fields to the ocean. This one bedroom unit has a queen bed, a sleeper sofa in the living room, a breakfast and snack center with refrigerator, microwave and light cooking appliances. The full private bathroom has a tub and shower combination. Cable TV, ceiling fans, gas barbeque grill and beach gear are included. Aloha Breakfasts are Home-grown and served to you by your hostess. Home-baked breakfast breads and muffins with jams and marmalades from the fruit of the trees and vines are served along with freshly harvested fruits of the season. Guests are invited to enjoy their stay at this smoke free environment. There is an outdoor jacuzzi to add to your enjoyment. Three night minimum.
RATES: $85 single or double, $10 extra per person.

K-30

For the discerning traveller, the Fern Grotto Inn is perfectly situated on the only private property in the middle of the Wailua River State Park. Breakfast is served on elegant English china in the Plantation Dining Room with its many windows providing a view of the Wailua River. Drift off to sleep in one of the three bedrooms on the finest queen size beds available, complete with designer sheets and comforter, and piled high with white goose down pillows. Also provided are European down/feather beds for your added luxury and comfort. Pamper yourself in the private adjoining bathroom complete with full bathtub, goldtone fixtures, glass shower doors, fine linens and quality skin and hair care products. Each bedroom is beautiful, they are priced according to size of the room and bathroom. The hosts at the Fern Grotto Inn will do their utmost to assure that you enjoy an intimate connection with the island of Kauai.
RATES: Serena Room: $70 single, $80 double, Isabella Room: $80 single, $90 double, Tara Room: $90 single, $100 double.

K-33

This home is located about eight miles north of Kapaa on Moloaa Beach in one of the most beautiful settings in Hawaii. The host and hostess are sure they have found Paradise and want you to experience it with them. The accommodation offered is a little rustic cottage, not at all fancy with a tin roof, screens instead of glass panes in windows and a bathroom that is attached to the cottage, however, is accessed by going outside along the covered porch to the bathroom door. A full kitchen with a gas stove and full refrigerator and dining area is in one room while the other room has a queen sized bed. The cottage is nestled at the edge of a tropical rain forest whose inhabitants are your neighbors. There is a cool spring that the owners have made into a shower outside the cottage that is very nice after one returns from the beach. Pick this if what you are looking for is a beautiful, secluded beach spot, but not all the amenities of a resort hotel. If you really want to get away from the hustle and bustle and enjoy the "real Hawaii" this is the place.
RATES: $50.00 single or double, three night minimum requested.

K-36

Experience Kauai living in this A-frame cottage on the hosts' 1/2 acre property in Wailua. Set back from the main home there is plenty of privacy and plenty of space. A large deck fronts the cottage. Inside through french doors is an oversized all glass family room. The kitchen is well equipped and breakfast fixings are stocked for the entire stay. Two bedroom areas are featured to sleep up to four comfortably. Twin beds that convert to a king size bed plus an upstairs loft with a queen sized bed. The bathroom has a tub and shower. Children are welcome, two night minimum.

RATES: $75 double, $85 for three or four.

K-47

A spectacular 360 degree view of ocean, Sleeping Giant, and Mt. Waialeale can be seen from this bi-level cottage that can easily sleep up to six people. Built by the hosts, this cottage has all the comforts of home including a private bathroom with tub and shower. Breakfast fixings stocked mostly from the garden: fresh fruit from their trees and fresh eggs from their chickens. The bedroom has a queen sized bed and there is a queen sofa bed in the living room plus a color TV. Adjoining the living room is a large screened-in lanai for lounging and dining. Upstairs the loft offers two twin sized futons for adults or children. The unit is private and away from the main home where the host and hostess live with their two children on their 10 acre parcel of land. Children are welcome and hosts have equipment for babies. Smoking outside only, please.

RATES: $65 single or double, $5 for each additional person up to six. Three night minimum.

K-53

A lovely one bedroom cottage in a secluded lush and private tropical country setting. The home overlooks several acres of what once was part of a nursery specializing in exotic tropical plants. Many of the ferns, fauna and trees were allowed to mature and now provide a tropical garden view from the guest cottage. Although under the same roof as the home, the cottage is separate and has it's own entrance and lanai. The living room is nicely furnished including color cable TV with VCR and stereo. Light meals can be prepared in the kitchenette or BBQ. The bedroom is air conditioned and is furnished with a queen sized bed. The bathroom is private. Children are welcome, comfortable futons can be provided on the floor for sleeping. Less than ten minutes to beaches to shopping.

RATES: $65 single or double, $5 extra for child

K-62

The Orchid Hut is a modern, brightly decorated cottage located in a lush, romantic setting less than 10 miles east of the Lihue Airport. With a complete kitchenette (fridge, microwave, hot plate, toaster oven, etc.), sitting room with color TV, bedroom with double bed and bathroom with marble floor and oversized shower, you will find all the comforts of home. The sitting room and bedroom both have ceiling fans. There is also an outside shower (hot & cold) for after the beach. Take your breakfast fixings from the fridge whenever you please (no regimentation at all here and expect to be serenaded by the many birds as you enjoy your morning meal in your own private tea house while taking in the spectacular scenery on the very edge of the Wailua River Canyon. Perfect for couples and honeymooners. Beach mats and beach towels are provided. Non-smoking adults only, please. Three night min.

RATES: $75 single or double,10% discount for 7 days or more.

K-63

Only a few minutes drive from the ocean at Coco Palms Hotel beach, situated behind Sleeping Giant Mountain, this home offers travelers more for their money with a choice of three bedrooms. All have them have color TV and private adjoining baths and tubs with showers. The entrance takes you into a cozy and comfortable recreation room with a fully equipped central kitchen plus a fireplace for those cool mornings and evenings. Keyed locks for your security are provided. A continental breakfast is served at your wake up time in the lovely garden gazebo next to a stone waterfall. Enjoy fresh fruit, right off the trees on a lovely, landscaped 1/2 acre. Centrally located on Kauai with a scenic drive past Opaeka'a Falls. Lots of light provided for late nighters with off road parking.
RATES: $45 single, $50 double. $10 additional for 1 night stay.

K-67

Wake up in beautiful tropical surroundings at Anahola Beach Bed & Breakfast abundant with flowers, fresh fruit, singing birds and sounds of the ocean. Enjoy beautiful views and rural, beach atmosphere in this bright airy downstairs studio with private yard and entrance, full bath and breakfast facilities. The two story redwood home is set back from the road and just across the street from a romantic, secluded, white sand beach great for swimming, snorkeling, boogie boarding and windsurfing. Conveniently located to all the pleasures of Kauai, amenities include queen size bed, color cable TV, ceiling fan, breakfast facilities, tile floors, white rattan couch and chairs, dining table and three sliding glass doors to private yard with outdoor table, chairs and lounges. Tropical continental breakfast fixings are provided. Ideal for couples. Three night minimum preferred.
RATES: $75 single or double.

K-73

Enjoy a room and private bath in the rambling home of these hosts who have plenty of space since their five boys have all gone off to college. This two story Victorian house sits against the backdrop of Sleeping Giant Mountain and has been beautifully landscaped since the host is a landscaper by trade. Downstairs guests may sleep in the screened lanai turned bedroom for balmy nights. Upstairs the king sized bedroom has adjoining private bath with sunken tub. For parties of three, the east room has queen bed and two twins with the bathroom in the hall. This is a central location for sightseeing all of Kauai and is just 10 miles north of the airport. Good beaches are five minutes drive. No smoking please.
RATES: $45 single, $50 double, $10 extra for third person in same room.

K-76

Guests who stay here will find themselves nestled in a little valley where hostess and her son, who lives next door with his family, keep a plant nursery. Accommodations are just for two and include a bedroom with king sized bed and a private bath. Also provided is a coffee maker and small refrigerator. Breakfast can be enjoyed in the dining room or out on the patio. Smoking is OK. Three night minimum.
RATES: $55 single or double.

K-78

A one bedroom condo on the water with ocean views is not really a B&B. However we can offer it to guests as the owners live nearby and do a lot of added touches such as a welcome basket of breakfast fixings. Queen sized bed in the bedroom and private bath plus the living room can sleep two more on the queen sized murphy bed. Full kitchen and a private lanai with a great ocean front view. The beach is just a few steps away. Guests can use the pool and jacuzzi as well as the tennis courts and can actually get by without a car since restaurants and shopping are within easy walking distance. $20 cleaning fee. Three night minimum.
RATES: $72 per night up to four people plus a $20 cleaning fee.

K-79

Rainbow Valley is the name of this brand new home in the hills of Kapaa. Guests can enjoy an ocean view from their queen sized bedroom with shared bath. Amenities include a small refrigerator, color cable TV with remote control and ceiling fan. Sliding glass doors open out to a large deck where breakfast is served each morning overlooking the valley and Kealia beach. Guests are encouraged to use the outside gas cooking grill with a handy side burner as well as the bicycle, beach mats and chairs. Your host, a builder and originally from Massachusetts, designed and built this two story four bedroom, three bath home on a secluded hill top setting on three acres.
RATES: $39 single, $44 double, weekly rates available.

K-82

Hosts built an extra two story house on their mountain view plateau property just for B&B guests. Upstairs is a cozy sitting room and breakfast nook where guests can enjoy their breakfast and the view. Another special feature is the gazebo with a sauna and jacuzzi. Accommodations consist of two separate units downstairs. Kapaa Unit: Bedroom with a Queen sized bed, private bathroom, living area with a queen sized sofa bed, color TV, wet- bar, fridge & microwave. Lihue Unit: a larger unit with a bedroom with twin beds that can be converted to a king size bed, large private bathroom with a shower stall, spacious living area with a queen size sofa bed, color TV, wet-bar, fridge & microwave. Each unit has own entrance and lanai area.
RATES: Kapaa $75 double, Lihue $95 double, $10 each extra person. (children under 5 years, no charge)

NORTHSHORE

K-13

Overlooking Hanalei-- Your hosts' brand new and beautiful house is built on 1 1/2 acres. This resort community offers a 45 hole golf course, clubhouse, athletic club, tennis, swimming and driving range just minutes from the house. You may prefer a peaceful day reading on the lanai, then walk a few steps to another deck and see the fabulous sunset behind "Bali Hai" and Hanalei Bay. Breakfast is served in the dining room or on the decks overlooking the blue Pacific. Distant waterfalls are seen on mountain slopes. All rooms have private entrances and baths, ceiling fans, refrigerators and color TV's and decks. The lovely tropical breezes generally make use of the air conditioning unnecessary. Charming fireplace in the guest living room with Hawaii decor in pastel wicker. Choose a spacious queen bedded room with view or the luxury king bedded honeymoon room and

bath with whirlpool tub. The panoramic, 1,000 square foot penthouse featuring open beams, private balcony and a glamorous bathroom also with whirlpool can accommodate a party of four. Three night minimum, no children, smoking outside only, please.
RATES: Twin Bed Room $80, Queen Bed Room $85; King Room $120; Penthouse $190.

K-20

Heart Song Inn welcomes you to the magical, healing, beauty of Kauai. When you enter through the door you will feel loved and cared for. There is a large, thickly carpeted living area where you may simply relax or you may chose to read from a wide assortment of books that line the bookshelves, enjoy music from the stereo as well as a 45 inch colored cable TV. Breakfast is served out on the deck through sliding glass doors where the view of the valley is breathtaking. A lower deck offers hot tub and view of the Kilauea waterfalls. Two bedrooms are offered for guests with a private bath in the hall so from 1 to 4 in a group could be accommodated with a choice of twin beds or a queen bedroom. No smoking please. Three night minimum is preferred.
RATES: $65 single or double, $10 extra for child under 18, $115 for two rooms.

K-21

This hostess offers to share her beach house right on Anini Beach with visitors in the event she is "on Island." Since she is a world traveller, she is not always available. She recently returned from a trip to Burma and then made a trip to the Far East. It is her love of travel that makes B & B interesting to her as she has a natural affinity for travelers. Her home is halfway between Kilauea and Hanalei just a few steps from the ocean at Anini Beach. The room offered has a double bed, guests share the bath with the hostess. There is a large covered porch for relaxing and viewing the magnificent sunsets of the North Shore. Smoking outside, please.
RATES: $45 single, $50 double, Two night minimum.

K-28

This home is built on the edge of a mountain with views of the Kilauea River and the ocean. Outside, guests can use the hot tub or lounge on the patio. The house a two story split level with the guest accommodations downstairs. A private entry leads into a living/sleeping area with plate glass windows facing the view. A queen sized bed and private bath are featured. Light cooking can be done as there is a microwave and small refrigerator in the room. Smokers, OK. Three night minimum preferred.
RATES: $75 single or double.

K-28A

Nestled in the small community of Kilauea guests have the pleasure of staying in a cheerful brand new home at the River's Edge. French doors lead into a large foyer with open beam ceilings. The bedroom is in a separate wing, with it's own balcony that views the river. When the sliding glass doors are left open the soothing sound of the water will lull one to sleep. The bed is queen size plus there is a fold out sofa bed in case there are more than two in the party. Hosts have a young child, so a small family would find this an ideal place to stay. Adjoining private bath with tub and shower plus a counter with appliances for light cooking makes this accommodation perfect for longer stays.
RATES: $70 single or double, $10 extra person.

K-31
A spectacular Northshore, Kauai Guesthouse is the perfect setting for getting away from it all. Accommodations include a full kitchen, full bath, queen size bed and a sitting area with a pull out double couch. The view overlooks the beautiful Kilauea River and valley. A private trail takes you down to a secluded, sandy beach, where you can swim and surf in the ocean and lagoon. Your hosts live on the same property in the main house, which has a lap pool that guests may use. Ideal for honeymooners and couples with children.
RATES:$115 per night

K-32
This accommodation is a little backwards which is great as the hosts live in the apartment above the garage while the guests stay in the main house designed for total comfort and casual beach style living. Situated in the sleepy town of Hanalei just steps away from the beach, a beautiful 2 mile crescent shaped bay surrounded by lush mountains and waterfalls. Included are two bedrooms, one with queen bed the other with two twins, one and a half baths inside, plus an outdoor shower for after the beach, living room has open beam ceilings, wood floors, rattan furniture, cable TV and a complete library. Five night minimum is required.
RATES: $100 per night up to four people.

K-35
You are invited to come and enjoy this tropical paradise overlooking the Kilauea Valley. Your bedroom looks over one of the most spectacular views on the island. Newly remodeled, the room is bright and airy with its own private bath and entrance. Wake in the morning to the sound of a waterfall and exotic birds. Stepping out onto your cedar deck, you will be greeted by a panoramic view of mountains, mist and the lush valley below while enjoying continental breakfast of Kona coffee, baked goods and fresh local fruits.
RATES: $65 single or double. Two night minimum.

K-39A
On the North shore of Kauai in Kalihiwai hosts offer a beautifully appointed suite with private entrance on their 3 acre country estate. Their home, complete with horses, cats and two golden retrievers, is at the edge of a 600 acre guava orchard. Enjoy long walks in the well maintained groves, lounge on the covered deck in the two-person hammock or relax in the outdoor hot-tub. At night the sky is covered with stars, no neighboring lights can be seen and yet it's only a quick drive to a number of beaches. The bedroom is elegant and spacious with double insulated walls and is furnished with a King size bed, color TV & VCR, double head tiled shower and features a bay window with a view of the grounds. Hosts are very hospitable and enjoy sharing their acreage. They encourage guests to explore the area; you can walk for miles and find streams and waterfalls and not see another soul. No smoking, please.
RATES: $75 single, $90 double. Three night minimum.

K-45
This B & B accommodation is located just 100 yards from the gorgeous Hanalei Bay. The house is a stylish two story home with 1000 square feet of deck surrounding the second floor and providing a partial ocean view and a spectacular mountain view of majestic waterfalls. Since the house faces west, often times the sunsets from the lanai of the house are breathtaking. The interior decor is a unique blend of oak antiques and island style furnishings and hardwood floors. The living room may be used by guests for TV, games, cards or reading. Country Cedar Room is a small room on the second floor nicely furnished a queen sized bed, bathroom located just 3 steps from the room and private. Makai Studio is on the ground floor with a private entrance and lanai, queen sized bed and wetbar with a microwave. The private bathroom has an outdoor hot shower for the more adventurous! Pualani Room is lovely and airy with a private balcony, queen sized brass bed and adjoining private bath. Upstairs on the third floor is the Bali Hai Suite featuring a 360 degree view of the mountains and ocean. One queen bed and a twin bed plus a private bath. Also available is the Garden Lanai Apartment on the ground floor with a full indoor bath and additional outdoor shower. The bedroom has a queen sized bed and the living room offers a futon couch. Kitchenette, TV.
RATES: Country Cedar $60, Makai $65, Pualani $70, Bali Hai $75, $15 for third person, Garden Lanai $80 double, $15 for extra person up to 4.

K-46
This spacious newer country home and separate guest quarters offer both comfort and one of Kauai's most spectacular views from an agricultural site overlooking Hanalei Valley. Guests can enjoy the sunsets, the mountain waterfalls, and the peace of this special location which is still just five minutes away from the amenities of Princeville or Hanalei town. The best view, in fact, is from the guest bedroom as is it built on the second floor, which has a king sized bed, a microwave oven, a small sink, and a refrigerator. The private bath is just at the foot of the staircase. The hosts are in the process of creating a beautiful natural environment of gardens and horses on their 5 acre property and look forward to sharing it with their guests.
RATES: $70 per couple, three night minimum.

K-48
You can spend your days looking for shells or snorkeling while staying in this small separate studio just a 30 second walk to the beach. The building is totally separate from the main house with a little porch for outside sitting and is set back from the road across the street from the ocean. Inside the king sized bed takes up most of the space. To prepare snacks, there is a wet bar with a small refrigerator on one side of the room. The tiny 1/2 bath has a door leading to the private, enclosed, outside shower which has a view of the jungle. Two night minimum.
RATES: $65 single or double.

K-57
This little cottage reminds us of something out of the Swiss Family Robinson. It is nestled in the trees behind the main house just about a block to Tunnels beach and is a bit rustic with a tin roof and screens. Inside is a cozy living area with double sofa bed and TV. There is a kitchenette for cooking light meals that's stocked with breakfast fixings. The bathroom has an extra large shower with smooth stones resined into the floor for a natural effect. Upstairs in the tree tops is the bedroom with a queen sized bed surrounded by screened windows where one is awakened by the singing of birds each

morning. They enjoy sharing this bit of paradise with guests.
RATES: $80 single or double, $5 extra for one person. Three night minimum.

K-60

Brand new and spacious, this completely separate accommodation is just a block from the beach and almost to the end of the road on Kauai's Northshore. Sit out on your own private deck and see Bali Hai Mountain or enjoy breakfast in the dining area with an ocean view. Full kitchen complete with microwave plus a bathroom with a jacuzzi tub are featured. The bedroom with queen size bed can be found up the romantic spiral staircase to the loft where guests can cuddle in front of the TV or gaze at the stars through the two sky lights. The living room has a Queen sized sofa bed for a third person. Three night minimum. No smoking inside.
RATES: $100 single or double, $25 for third person.

K-60 Bedroom

Another accommodation on the same property as the above description is a separate bedroom with it's own sliding glass doors entrance and patio area. The bedroom is on the first floor of the hosts' own two story house. The patio faces the ocean. The room is furnished with a queen sized bed, TV, small refrigerator, microwave and coffee maker to prepare light snacks. The "surprise" bathroom is unique and was designed and built by the hosts as was the entire house. When the bathroom door is opened the entire bedroom is flooded with light because the tub/shower wall is completely made out of large glass blocks that reach to the ceiling, only there is no ceiling! The toilet and vanity are under cover, but the tub/shower is open air. Two night min.
RATES: $50 single or double.

K-64

Vacation on Kauai's lush north shore in a private, hand-crafted redwood guest cottage, separate and unattached from the hosts' main house. North Country Farms is surrounded by thoroughbred and Arabian horse farms and is itself an organic fruit, vegetable and flower farm. Just a hike or a drive to beaches, your cottage is completely and comfortably equipped for any length of stay, including a kitchenette for snacks and light meals as well as a private full bathroom with tub and shower. The bedroom offers queen sized bed. The living room is furnished with a large L-shaped futon couch for extra sleeping. French doors open out to the deck which offers distant ocean, mountain and sunset views. For guest's convenience, there is an outside shower for after beach. Hosts have three young children. Smoking outside only, please. Children welcome.
RATES: $85 single or double, $5 extra up to four.

K-74

A comfortable accommodation on a working organic vegetable, orchid and tropical flower farm is a great way to relax on Kauai. The bed & Breakfast, in a building separate from the main house, has a large, airy second story bedroom with great views, comfortable king bed and sleeper sofa. On the first floor is an efficiency kitchenette with continental breakfast fixings provided, as well as a private bath. Guests can enjoy picking their own papayas off the trees and enjoy fresh eggs from the chickens. Hosts encourage guests to explore the grounds which include a pineapple patch and orchid green house. Children are welcome and smoking outside, please.
RATES: $60 single, $65 double, $5 each additional person up to four. Children under 16 free.

K-81

Enjoy a relaxing stay in Hanalei town. This full apartment can be found in a quiet area of Hanalei just 200 feet from the bay. Hostess lives in the upstairs half of a new two story house across the street from the ocean and on a dead end street. The down stairs portion of the home is for guests with all the comforts of home, the rooms are light and airy and nicely decorated. Guests have a private entrance, Queen sized bed in the bedroom, private bath with tub and shower. Fully equipped kitchen and comfortable living room. Guests can cook all meals in, including breakfast. **No breakfast is served or provided here.** Three night minimum, preferred.
RATES: $90 single or double, $600/week.

POIPU AREA

K11A

Enjoy a luxury 1 bedroom B&B with first class accommodations in acres of gardens and tropical flowers just a short 5 minute walk to Poipu Beach and the ocean. Guests have use of the main bedroom with a king size bed, color TV, sliding glass doors out to the lanai and private adjoining bathroom with tub and shower. Hosts have their own bedroom and bath upstairs. A delicious breakfast is served out on the lanai overlooking lush tropical gardens and the Waikomo Stream. Since this accommodation is part of the hosts' condominium home, guests may take advantage of the amenities such as pool, tennis courts and jacuzzi. For total privacy and a full kitchen plus breakfast, too, hosts also have two one bedroom condo units in the same complex. Each one has a kitchen, bedroom with queen sized bed and private bath. Since each living room has a sofa bed, too, each condo can accommodate four.
RATES: B&B Room $75 single or double. Condos $95 single or double, $5 extra person. Three night minimum.

K-22

Now at Poipu Plantation, two B&B rooms are available in the plantation house. One has a king size bed while the other one has a queen bed each with it's own private adjoining bathroom. There is space to relax in the large, screened-in lanai area where guests can lounge while planning their sightseeing excursions or in the living room where guests can share experiences and get to know one another. Tropical continental breakfast is served in the dining room or on the lanai. The ocean is just across the street and Poipu Beach is one and a half blocks down the coast. TV in each bedroom and a house phone is available. Two night minimum is preferred and smoking outside only, please.
RATES: King room $75 single or double, Queen room $65.00 single or double.

K-23

Right in Poipu and just two blocks from Shipwreck Beach are two accommodations in one. The entire downstairs of this architect designed home is devoted to B&B. Mauka Room is really a two room suite with private bath with a queen sized bed in the bedroom and a queen sofa sleeper in the living area. Also featured is a kitchenette with dishwasher, microwave, stove and refrigerator for fixings snacks or light meals. The Makai Room has a queen sized bed with sliding glass doors out to a sitting area. Plus adjoining private bath includes a walk-in closet with a small refrigerator, for storing cold drinks and a microwave. Resort pool, spa and tennis are free to guests. The hosts live upstairs and serve breakfast each morning. Both rooms offer TV.
RATES: Mauka Room $85 double, $5 extra person; Makai Room $65 double.

K-24
This is Evie and Al's Poipu Plantation, which is not really a B&B accommodation since a total of twenty people can be accommodated, a bit more than will fit around the dining room table. There are nine units altogether three that face the garden, and the rest face the ocean. Seven of the units are one bedroom, each fully furnished with a queen sized bed in the bedroom, private bathroom, full kitchen, dining room, living room with a TV and private telephone with your own number. The other two units are two bedroom, two bath with a queen bed in each bedroom. Guests are welcome to pick any fruit in season, mango, papaya, guava, banana, and citrus. There is a barbeque and sunning area as well as a laundry area.
RATES: One bdrm units $75 garden view, $80 partial ocean view, $85 full ocean view; Two bdrm units $90 partial ocean view, $95 full ocean view. $10 extra for third or fourth person.

K-25
This is available to B&B guests at a favorable rate but is not really a B&B since there is no host on site. It is a two bedroom condo at Makahuena on the second floor. The complex is ocean front on the cliff at Makahuena Point, the condo has a deck and ocean view. Walk along the cliffs to Shipwreck Beach or down the street to Poipu Beach Park only three long blocks along the coast. This is perfect for two couples or a family of four since there are two bedrooms, one with a double bed the other with two twin beds each with it's own bathroom. Downstairs there is also a 1/2 bath in the hall off the living room. The kitchen is fully equipped, however, **no breakfast is served or provided.** Amenities include TV in the living room and each bedroom, telephone and use of the lighted tennis courts and swimming pool. The owners don't live far away, just down the street.
RATES: $85 double, $10 each extra person.

K-71
Japanese decor is the theme for this separate 900 sq ft cottage in Poipu. Guests will enjoy the shoji screen doors throughout as well as the Japanese gardens and waterfall. Full kitchen, laundry and queen sized bedroom are offered as well as a sunken bathtub in the private bathroom. Ceiling fans in the living room help the trade winds cool the cottage as well as the large trees that surround it. A pleasant five minute walk takes you to the Poipu Beach park as well as fine dining and shopping. Your hosts live on the property in the main house. **There is no breakfast served or provided at this accommodation.** TV and telephone are furnished. Non smokers only, please. Children over 10 years can be accommodated on the sofa bed in the living room.
RATES: $100 per night double. Four night minimum.

K-75
Enjoy a relaxing stay practically ocean front on Brennecke's beach in sunny Poipu. Your hostess offers one bedroom in her quaint two bedroom plantation cottage. A king size bed and private adjoining bath with separate entrance and private lanai with ocean view awaits singles or couples. Your hostess prepares breakfast every morning and serves it either in her dining room or on your lanai. A small refrigerator is provided to keep cold drinks.
RATES: $75 single, $85 double Two night min.

K-80

A new attraction in Poipu is a Dinner Show at the Stouffer Waiohai. The host at this B&B helps direct this professional dinner theater as well as other civic drama productions throughout Kauai including working with the Department of Education. Guests are welcome to enjoy the house which is a Japanese style older home with a patio for outside sitting, as long as you clean up the kitchen after. The guest bedroom is small and has a double bed with a private adjoining bathroom. The bathroom has a tub but no shower. The home is just about 1/2 mile from Poipu Beach at the end of a quiet cul-de-sac. A perfect walk in the early mornings and late afternoons.
RATES: $50 single, $60 double.

KALAHEO AREA

K-10A

An extremely comfortable and nicely furnished apartment is attached to this host family's private residence. Hosts have two school aged daughters. They live in the quiet country side of Omao just 5 minutes by car to Poipu Beach. The suite includes a small kitchen, with microwave, double burners, coffee maker, table and four chairs. The bedroom has a firm four poster queen sized bed and a private bath with shower. The sitting area has a cable TV and telephone as well as full size couch/futon to accommodate two additional guests, if needed. Off the sitting room is an 8'x12' deck which overlooks the backyard, reservoir, forests and distant ocean. The unit will be continually filled with fresh island flowers and is decorated in new island motif linens and art.
RATES: $65 single or double, three night minimum.

K-18A

A completely furnished and self-contained apartment awaits guests here in the hills of Kalaheo with a sweeping ocean view. This second story one bedroom apartment offers a firm queen sized bed in the bedroom and a single roll away for third person can be set up in the living room, a private bath with tub and shower plus a full kitchen. There is a TV. Only 5 minutes from the golf course and 15 minutes drive to Poipu Beach. Your hosts are a married couple who have lived in Hawaii for over 20 years. They built the apartment for their parents to come and visit them various times during the year and enjoy meeting new people and hosting B&B the rest of the time.
RATES: $60 single or double $10 extra per night for third person. Two night minimum.

K-19

Three bedrooms open onto a swimming pool flanked by flowering hibiscus, gardenias and bougainvilleas in this home nestled in the hills of South Kauai. Out back, a second story wooden porch (known as a lanai) overlooks sugar cane fields, jungle and the National Botanical Gardens. It is a short 7-20 minute drive from popular, or if preferred, more secret beaches that the hostess can direct guests to. One room offered is barrier-free (with ramp) and has twin beds (or king). All rooms have private baths. Hostess prides herself on pampering guests with home-made bread and hot muffins several Hawaiian fruits and Hawaiian coffee! Non-smokers and no children, please.*"Victoria's Other Secret" A studio apartment with a separate entrance on another level has king sized bed, bath, a kitchen area and laundry privileges. Available for $95.00 Guests can join the others for breakfast or dine 'alone'.*
RATES: $75 twin (or king) room, $65 queen room, $55 single room. $10 increase on all

rooms Dec15-Jan15.

K-29
This newly built, spacious one bedroom apartment overlooking the south shore of Kauai is conveniently located in Omao just minutes from Poipu Beach. Hosts have lived on Kauai nearly 20 years and can share information about beaches, dining, shopping and island adventures. The apartment is a private upstairs unit, tropically furnished, with a large kitchen, telephone and cable TV. The bedroom offers queen sized bed and private bath with entrance from bedroom and living room. It can sleep four with a sofa bed in the living room. Guests can enjoy ocean and mountain views from their own private deck. Continental breakfast fixings are stocked in the kitchen. Smoking outside only, please. Three night minimum.
RATES: $60 double, $10 each extra person.

K-43
Nestled in the scenic hills of Kalaheo, this Bed & Breakfast offers one the most spectacular views of Kauai's South Shore & Poipu. The mountain, ocean and lush valley views are one of the trademarks. The three suites offer you all the comforts of home with daily linen service, private bath/shower, color TV, plush carpeting, private entrance and continental breakfast. One of the suites is extra special, with a living room and its own kitchen. Home is very private but close to all the activities that the Garden Island has to offer. The resort amenities of Poipu and beaches are all within a 10 to 15 minute drive. Kokee Mountain and Waimea Canyon are two of Kauai's don't-miss-attractions and are only 20 miles to the West.
RATES: B&B Suite $55.00, One Bdrm Suite $60.00, Addtl pax $10.00

K-61
Enjoy a quiet, relaxing stay in lush surroundings on the Southshore of Kauai in a beautifully furnished room with king size bed, reading area and breakfast nook, complete with coffee maker, small refrigerator and microwave for light snacking. The room is cool and airy, very comfortable with adjoining private bath. Guests are invited to use the lanai with breathtaking distant view of the Poipu coastline with coffee orchard in the foreground. The home is situated on a quiet cul-de-sac within walking distance of the National Tropical Botanical Gardens, hence the name, "Pacific Gardens Bed and Breakfast". Since your host is third generation Hawaii born and both hostess and host are athletic they can offer information on where to swim, hike, bike and run. They have an infant son. Hostess is a homemaker and host works for Kauai Electric. One night stays are accepted for $5 extra.
RATES: $65 single or double

K-84
A serene landscape in Lawai is the setting for this separate little one room cottage set apart from the main home on seven acres. Inside is a little kitchenette and private bathroom. The living room/bedroom features a brand new Serta queen size sofa bed and a full size futon in case there are two singles travelling together. Hosts have pets, a cat and Dalmations. Hostess is an activities desk director so she can give great sight seeing tips. One night is OK.
RATES: $65 single or double, $10 extra for one nighters.

K-85
Mango Hill Cottage is situated on 2 1/2 acres in Kalaheo overlooking the ocean and many acres of coffee fields. The cottage is nestled near a magnificent mango tree, hence the name. The hostess has been a professional interior designer and her attention to details is apparent from the freshly arranged flowers to the cheerful furnishings. **Fresh fruits, muffins, juice and coffee are provided for the first day.** The living room has a pull out queen size sofa, cable TV and an adjoining full kitchen with counter seating. The bedroom has a mountain view and is furnished with a queen sized bed. The adjoining bathroom has a shower. This host and hostess have a creative lifestyle with a home in Hawaii in the country, and home in the city in Seattle. The host is a commuting dentist with a practice in both states. He is an avid diver and sailor and is happy to share information on both. The hostess presently leads personal and team achievement seminars for businesses and is a volunteer at the Pacific Tropical Botanical Gardens. Swim in the pool or read a favorite book in the hammock under the flowering trees. Smoking outside, please. Three night minimum preferred.
RATES: $65 single or double, $10 extra for third person.

WAIMEA

K-42
In the heart of old Waimea town and within walking distance of the store, pier, restaurants and shops, this home is perfect for those who want to get an early start for hiking the Waimea Canyon and exploring Kokee State Park. A path around the back of the house leads guests into a tiny garden with lanai under the shade of a large old mango tree. Guests have a private entrance to their cozy bedroom and sitting area just for two furnished with a double bed in the bedroom plus cable TV and light cooking area in the sitting room. The private bath room has a tub and shower. The hosts leave early for work each morning and leave a prepared continental breakfast in the refrigerator for guests to find at their leisure and enjoy out on the lanai.
RATES: $60 single or double. Three night minimum.

A REMINDER
Let your host know
the time of your arrival.
The more communication
between Host and Guest
the better.
Children under 4 must be in a car seat
and be sure to buckle up.

LIHUE

In the early 1800's there is no record of the name Lihue, which may have meant "cold chill," and there was little activity in the area. It was not until one of the early missionaries, Reverend Dr. Lafon, moved to Lihue from the Koloa area to start a church and school in 1839 that Lihue began to grow. In 1854 William Harrison Rice, a former missionary, took over as manager of the fledgling Lihue Sugar Plantation. Due to his efforts, mainly the digging of an irrigation ditch to bring the plentiful mountain waters to the Lihue sugar fields, the Lihue Plantation became one of the most successful in the Islands. Rice died of T.B. in 1862 at the age of forty-nine, but the success of the Rice family was assured, and they played a major role in the development of Kauai.

Now all visitors to Kauai know about Lihue; it is the place you have to go through after you leave the airport to get to wherever it is you are going, and as one drives from north to south and south to north one again goes through Lihue. To those of us who live on Kauai, however, Lihue is the center of things, for it is the County Seat as well as the center for State Office Buildings on Kauai. It is also the main shopping center for Island residents, since Kukui Grove, one of the largest shopping centers on the Neighbor Islands, has most of the big stores: Penney's, Sears, Liberty House.

The newest development in Lihue is the new Westin Hotel, developed by Chris Hemmeter, located at the site of the old Kauai Surf. With little doubt this is going to be the premier hotel in Hawaii, let alone Kauai. Rooms start at $180 and go as high as $1500, that's right, $1500. While prices this high may discourage some from staying there, we would encourage all to stop by for a visit.

Another spot tourists like not to miss is the Kilohana Shopping Center, located just south of Lihue at the old Wilcox mansion. This and the Westin make an interesting study in contrasts. The attempt at Kilohana is to emphasize Hawaii, while there is little of Hawaii at the Westin. That is not meant as a value judgment but as a simple statement of fact. In our opinion each has excellence but differ greatly. Both are certainly worth visiting.

Since Lihue exists mostly for residents, it is an excellent place for visitors to discover a truer picture of local life. Stores and restaurants, while delighted when tourists visit, are not dependent on the tourist trade. A good place to pick up bargains is at Gem Department Store in the Big Save Shopping Center. While not a full line department store, they have a good selection of things and prices are lower than shops in resort areas. Also, if you are going to camp on Kauai, you will need to secure a permit in Lihue. It is possible to obtain a permit through the mail so you could have it before your arrival. Write to the Division of State Parks, P.O. Box 1671, Lihue Hi. 96766. You will need to send a copy of your driver's license, name of camp site, and dates of use. There is no charge for a permit. For more information call 808-245-4444. If you put off obtaining a permit until the time of your arrival, you may not be able to obtain one, as there is a limit as to how many are issued for any one time.

RESTAURANTS

LOCAL STYLE

KAUAI SUASAGE COMPANY
Located just south of Lihue in Puhi, across from the Community College. They serve hamburgers and sandwiches. There is just one table inside, but several tables outside.

HAMARA'S SAIMIN
2956 Kress St., which runs off Rice St. They serve probably the best saimin to be found in the Islands.

MA'S PLACE
4277 Halani St., which runs off Kress St. Good food at low prices, mostly Hawaiian food. Tripe stew is a specialty of the house. They are open for breakfast very early and for lunch until 1:30 pm. From the outside it does not look appealing, perhaps, but give it a try if you like to try different places with local flavor. Inside it is very nice and the food is very good and low priced.

KUN JA'S KOREAN
4252 Rice St. Easy to find, once you are on Rice St. If you judge this from outward appearances you will pass it by, but if you like Korean food be sure to try it out. Very LOCAL, low priced.

TAMMY'S OKAZU-YA
Located in the Pay & Save Center on Rice St. Strictly takeout. One can choose from a dozen or so items, all priced under $1 and put together a pretty good lunch to take to the beach.

O.K. BENTO
Takeout box lunches. Next door to Tammys.

KAUAI KITCHEN
Located in the Rice Street Shopping Center back by the bowling alley. For lunch you can choose one dish for $3,95, two for $4.50, or three for $4.95.

SAMPAGUITA'S (Pikaki Flower)
Located a few miles north of Lihue on the mauka side of the highway, just next door to Planters Restaurant. Filipino take out. Very ethnic, an interesting place to visit.

local style

KALAPAKI BEACH BURGERS
This is located at the foot of Rice Street just past the Westin and across the street from Pacific Ocean Plaza. If you like burgers, do not miss eating here. The owners are the ones who started Ono Char Burgers in Anahola and subsequently opened Ono Family in Kapaa. They have brought the same skills and devotion to good eating that they exhibited at there other stores. Remember, it is just burgers-ham, buffalo, chicken, or mahi-mahi. There is a great crow's nest, open aired, above the cooking and ordering area. Window service.

KIIBO'S
Japanese food at fair prices, located at 2991 Umi St., which is just off Rice St. This is our favorite spot in Lihue for lunch. The portions are not large, but ample. Try their teriaki chicken, really good. Open for lunch 11-1:30, dinner 5:30 - 9 p.m. Closed Sundays. They have added a sushi bar. Beer and saki served, 245-2650.

KAUAI CHOP SUEY
Located in the Harbor Center across from the Westin. This is high on the list for the local folks. You get lots of food for a modest price, (dinner will run around $8-10 a person) Cantonese style. Open every day but Sunday and Monday for lunch from 11-2 and every day for dinner from 4:30-9.

BARBECUE INN
2962 Kress St. off Rice St. Open Monday-Saturday for breakfast, lunch, and dinner. This is where the county takes the jurists; either the prices are right or the judge is a silent partner. Wide variety of entrees, modest prices.

TIP-TOP CAFE
3173 Akahi St. off Hardy. Great ox-tail soup and excellent macadamia nut cookies.

DANI'S
4201 Rice St. across from Pay and Save. Heavily frequented by locals, but some dishes to appeal to all. Modest prices

LIHUE CAFE & CHOP SUEY
2978 Umi St. off Rice St. Cantonese style food but also some Japanese food served. Not much atmosphere but the food is good.

local/Tourist Style

KALAPAKI BEACH DELI-CAFE
Located in the Anchor Cove Shopping Center, around the back over on the south side. Open every day from 8 am to 7 pm. Mainly soup, sandwich, chili, salads, with a daily special. This is a good place to get a quick snack or take a sandwich out to Kalapaki Beach.

EGGBERT'S

4481 Rice St. across from the Big Save Shopping Center. As the name suggests, breakfast is the specialty and at one time when they were called The Egg & I that is all they served. Now they have enlarged and serve all day. Prices are modest for this category and the entrees will all be familiar to you, 245-9025.

J.J.'S BROILER

Newly located in a new shopping center at Nawiliwili at the foot of Rice St. They are open for lunch and dinner. A very spiffy place set on Kalapaki Bay. The specialty of the house is still Slavonic Steak, described to me as a very this steak dipped in a garlic/butter/wine sauce, in the $20 range. Sandwiches at lunch time range from $6 to $9. We like to eat down stairs where light meals are served.

CAFE PORTIFINO

This is a new restaurant located in the Pacific Ocean Plaza, across from the Westin. We have tried it for both lunch and dinner and can recommend it highly. Lunch is served out on the porch affording an excellent view of Kalapaki Bay. While the dinner menu is not extensive, everything we ordered was quite special, from deliciously prepared ahi to rabbit and stuffed calamari. Pastas are as good as you will find anywhere served with bread that is outstanding. So far they have weathered the storm of opening and a fairly slow winter season, so we hope and trust they are here to stay. Dinner prices are from $12-16 for entrees, everything ala carte.

TOKYO LOBBY

A new addition to Kauai, located in Pacific Ocean Plaza at the foot of Rice St. They are open for lunch and dinner and their menu seems very authentic Japanese. Lunch prices between $6 and $8, while dinner prices are from $10 to $15, unless you go for the *Tokyo Love Boat Special* which is $25 a person.

HANAMAULU RESTAURANT & TEA HOUSE

In Hanamaulu two miles north of Lihue on the mauka side of the highway. This is almost in a category of its own. If a local family is having a special occasion they would probably have it here, since the Tea House can handle groups up to 300. The food is a mixture of Chinese and Japanese with a few other ethnic dishes thrown in. For plenty of atmosphere, make a reservation for the Tea Room, where you can sit on the floor Japanese style. Now don't let that turn you off; all of the tables though low have a well to put your feet, so it seems you are on the floor, but it is quite comfortable. They also have a sushi bar. They are open for lunch from 9 a.m. to 1:30 p.m. and for dinner from 4:30 to 9:30, 245-2511.

PLANTERS RESTAURANT

Located two miles north of Lihue in Hanamaulu. At the present time they are open only for dinner, with special drinks and pupus from 3 pm to 5 pm. The prices are modest and the specialty of the house is ribs. They serve an early bird special from 5 to 6:30: chicken or mahi for $9.95, or prime rib for $11.95.

GAYLORD'S AT KILOHANA

This is one of the favorite spots for Kauai residents. The food is consistently good. The setting is very nice, the courtyard of the old Wilcox mansion. They are open for lunch and dinner. We recommend this highly and in our humble opinion this is one of the better eating spot on Kauai. It is expensive but we think you will find it worth the price. The service is, in our opinion, the best on Kauai. All we have spoken to rave about the Sunday brunch.

KUKUI SHOPPING CENTER RESTAURANTS

SIDEWALK CAFE
Located in the Kukui Shopping Center on the north side. The food is served cafeteria style and is mostly local fare but also hamburgers and sandwiches. Recently they have added some Hawaiian dishes: lau-lau, lomi lomi, etc.

GREAT GOURMET
In the Kukui Center just behind Liberty House. They have recently started serving soup, salad, and sandwiches in this gourmet food shop. For a quick snack while you shop either this or the one below would be our recommendation. Also, if you are craving some good cheese, this is about the only place you will find it.

STONE'S GALLERY
In the Kukui Center. No heavy meals here, but great for a light snack or a tasty dessert. They also have all kinds of coffee. Since it is located in Stone's Gallery, you will have plenty to view while you snack.

JONI-HANA
Located in the Kukui Shopping Center. Sit down or box lunches to take out. Low prices, interesting Japanese dishes, but beef chop suey is also served. (can you see the problem with labels?). It looks much different this year as it has been remodeled. They have added a buffet table; one plate, one fill, $4.95. It might be fun to see just how much one can pile on one plate.

SI CISCO'S
This used to be called Rosita's and we did not tout it very highly. New owners have taken over and done a great job of remodeling. The food is good and very reasonable. The new owners are working hard and it seems they always have something special going on. There is a bar also, so if you like margaritas after a hard day's shopping, stop in here.

HO'S CHINESE KITCHEN
If you are a long time Kauai visitor you may remember them when they were up on Umi St. in Lihue. We used to eat there once in a while and found the food acceptable and low priced, most dishes under $6.

KINOS KAUAI KIM CHEE
This is a bit hard to find and is probably one of the reasons that so many have failed to make a go of this place. Several years ago Brick Oven Pizza of Kalaheo opened here and they did not make it in spite of their great reputation. If you like Korean food at very reasonable prices (stuffed shrimp $6.75 or BBQ chicken for $4.75) you will find them around the corner to the north of Ho's Chinese Kitchen.

JV SNACK BAR
Filipino plate lunch.

WOOLWORTHS
At the other end of the center from Liberty House.

KAUAI CINNAMON
While this is not a restaurant, one might like to try one of their delicious cinnamon rolls.

POINTS OF INTEREST

KAUAI MUSEUM
44208 Rice St. Open Monday-Friday from 9-4:30 and Saturday from 9-1. Adult admission $3.00, children free. A good collection of Hawaiian history, with changing exhibits. They have a 1/2 hour video taken from a helicopter which gives an overview of Kauai. There is also a gift shop and book store which carries most of the books about Kauai. For information call 808-245-6931.

GROVE FARM HOMESTEAD
There is a two hour guided tour every Monday, Wednesday, and Thursday starting at 10 a.m and 1:15 p.m., which gives a flavor of early plantation life. Since the tours are limited to twenty people and by reservation only, call or write in advance. (P.O. Box 1631, Lihue, Kauai, Hi. 96766: 808-245-3202). It is located on the south side of Nawiliwili Rd. Admission is $3.00 for adults, $1.00 for children 12 and under.

MENEHUNE FISH POND
To get to the Fish Pond overlook take Rice St until it dead ends at the Harbor, turn right and proceed on the road that goes by Matson which will be on your left. You will go across a one way bridge and the Fishpond overlook is a mile or so up that road. There are many fishponds in the Islands but I believe this is the largest. Legend has it that this one was built by the Menehunes, a diminutive race that lived on Kauai prior to and with the Hawaiians. At the present time the fish pond is for sale.

SUNSHINE MARKET
Held only on Friday starting around 3 p.m. We think this is a must see if you are interested in Island life. Here local people bring their garden goods and offer them for sale. Some of the produce you may not be familiar with unless you know Filipino and other Island food. Located at Vidinha Stadium on Hardy St., which runs off Rice St. about in the middle of Lihue.

THE KAPAIA STITCHERY
Just north of Lihue at the bottom of the hill past Wilcox Hospital on the mauka side of the highway.

WAILUA FALLS
To get here take the highway from Lihue north. When you pass the hospital, you will start down the hill. At the bottom of the hill, watch for the sign on the left that points the way to Wailua Falls. Take this road about four miles where it ends at the falls. If you get tempted to hike to the bottom of the falls, forget it! It is far too dangerous. Also, crossing the river above the falls is very dangerous. One slip and you better be in a barrel. There is talk about extending the road from the falls all the way to Highway 480 in Kapaa. If they ever do it will be a very scenic drive.

HANAMAULU MUSEUM
Right in Hanamaulu, you can't miss it. No charge to see this. Some artifacts, but mainly the sugar story. Since none of the sugar mills on Kauai allow tours, a stop here will answer some of your questions.

BEACHES

KALAPAKI BEACH
Right in front of the new Westin Hotel. You can get access to it by parking at the Oar House and walking between the shops. Kalapaki Bay is very calm, and while the water is not as clear and blue as in some other places, swimming is good. Keep in mind that beaches in Hawaii are all open to the public and are not owned by the hotels that front those beaches. Some hotels like to set things up in such a way that suggests the beach is for their exclusive use.

HANAMAULU BAY OVERLOOK
This is not a beach but an interesting ocean/bay overlook. To get there take the airport road and go past the airport where the road ends at the overlook. In hot weather, this is a great place to catch the cooling trades. You are bound to see local fishermen trying their luck.

HANAMAULU PARK
When you reach Hanamaulu, around two miles north of Lihue, watch for Hanamaulu Rd., just beyond the Shell Station. Turn makai and this drive will put you right at Hanamaulu Bay, where you can swim, picnic, and fish.

NIGHT LIFE

CLUB JETTY
Disco/Rock N' Roll music every Thursday, Friday, and Saturday night and they sometimes go until 4 a.m. It gets pretty lively when the cruise ships are in.

PARK PLACE RESTAURANT AND NIGHT CLUB
Located at 3501 Rice St. This could be listed under restaurants but mainly it is a disco spot with dancing until 4 a.m. They do have a pupu menu and a seafood bar. For more information call 245-3617.

LIBRARY
Located on Hardy St. Every Tuesday night from 7 to 8 there is a free movie on some facet of Polynesian life or on a subject appropriate to Hawaii. For more specific information call 245-3617. (see Poipu section for the one in Koloa Town).

SPORTS

GOLF
At the Westin there are two courses, the Jack Nicolas designed, championship Kiele, with five tee locations on each hole and the easier Lagoons Course (also designed by Nicolas). Either course is a real treat in spite of their expense, Kiele course $145 a person which includes cart, free use of range both before and after golf, and use of the spa. The Lagoons course is $100 per person and includes all of the above.. Of course, if you can afford to stay at the Westin, who cares how much the cost.

TENNIS
Public courts with no charge are located at the War Memorial Convention Center just past Wilcox School on Hardy St.

WATER SPORTS
The best place to rent equipment is at Kalapaki Beach where one can rent from Kauai Windsurfing. Such things as windsurf boards, glassbottom kyaks, surf boards, wave skis, rubber raft, Hobie Cat are available. From Aqua Bikes you can rent aqua bikes, snorkeling gear, and boogie boards. Lessons on the use of any of these are available. Try *Sea Fun* if you would like to go on an organized snorkel tour. They will pick you up in a van, from a convenient location, supply all the equipment, and take you where the snorkeling is best at that time. They also provide a lunch. For more information call 808-245-6400.

KAUAI BY KAYAK
From all we have heard, this is really a fun trip. A guide takes a group by "royak", a cross between a kayak and a canoe, which makes them very stable, up into the Menehune Fishpond. They make two trips a day, one at 8:45 and the other at 12:45 and the cost is $39. We suggest you call ahead for a reservation, 245-9662, and for directions since it is a little difficult to locate. The best way to book this is to call our office and let the girls handle all the arrangements.

BOWLING
In the middle of Lihue on Rice Street at the back of the rice Shopping Center you will find a modern 28 lane Bowling Alley. One need not know how tto keep score as it is all automatic.

WAILUA

WAIPOULI/KAPAA/ANAHOLA

To the ancient Hawaiians Wailua was an important area, a place special to the Alii, those born of Royal blood. Commoners lived here at the behest of the chiefs. When chiefs from the other Islands visited Kauai, they most often came to the Wailua area, where there were several sacred temples and special places of worship.

Now, except for Lihue, Wailua is the main business center on Kauai as well as being a major tourist destination. The oldest major hotel on Kauai, the Coco Palms, is a Kauai landmark for most people who have visited here. The newer Plantation Marketplace, a tourist shopping mecca, houses the Sheraton Coconut Beach Hotel, the Beach Boy Hotel, and several condo complexes. There are also many small eating places and several large restaurants.

From the Wailua river to the end of Kapaa, a drive of about four miles, there are well over forty restaurants, which run the gamut from the posh new Pacific Cafe to funky little Fast Freddies, where lunch is around $3.00. Excluding fast food and resort restaurants, we cover most of them. With this many restaurants, competition for business is keen, and restaurant owners keep prices down in an effort to attract customers. To some extent the same is true for the little shops. Because of location, they cannot command the same prices as the more heavily used shopping centers.

Kapaa town seems to be a curious mixture of the old, the older, and the oldest. Like many small towns in America, Kapaa Town has no where to go but up, but it does it very slowly. Yet progress is being made and not at the expense of historical considerations, since the buildings that have been built and restored are in keeping with the old Hawaiian architecture. Let us hope that as Kapaa Town modernizes it does not lose its charm.

The latest addition to Kapaa is Kauai Village which has many new shops and restaurants with the key lease being a very large (for Kauai) Safeway. It will take some time to fill all the stores in this center and one can only wonder where all the workers will come from to man these stores, let alone all the shoppers to keep them in operation. Long time Kauai residents and visitors cannot believe the congestion that all this development has caused.

It is a little easier to get in and out of the three major shopping centers as each one has a stop light. Just think, the sleepy little town of Kapaa which ten years ago had no stop lights now has around half a dozen. Now that's progress! Isn't it?

RESTAURANTS

There are so many restaurants in the Kapaa area that organization becomes difficult. This year we have decided to group them in the following way: we will follow the Local, local, and local/tourist classification and also within these categories they will be placed south to north, ie. the first LOCAL spot one comes to driving north is Wha Kung Chop Suey, located in the Kinipopo Shopping Center, the first local the Waipouli, and the first local/tourist the Wailua Marina, which is also the first restaurant one comes to as one enters the Wailua area. We hope that makes them easy to locate.

LOCAL STYLE

WAH KUNG CHOP SUEY
A little Cantonese style counter service spot in the Kinipopo Shopping Center. Prices here are very low, which is fitting for the atmosphere.

MANILA
This is a new restaurant located across the street from Kinipopo. Unless you are fond of Filipino food, you can pass this one by. If, however, you just have to have some Adobong Atay At Ballumbaluman (chicken liver and gizzard deep fried and mixed with adobo sauce) or Pinakbet Na Baboy At Hipon (mixed vegetable with chunks of pork and shrimp sauteed in a special shrimp sauce) don't miss this spot.

ALOHA DINER
In the Waipouli complex on the mauka side of the highway. All Hawaiian food (kalua pig, lau-lau, lomi lomi salmon, haupia, poi and much more). You will get the same food here that you would get at a luau for a much lower price. This is a good place to try out Hawaiian cuisine.

BIG SAVE
In the shopping center in Kapaa. Inexpensive plate lunches. This spot is popular with locals.

BARBEQUE HOUSE
Located in the Big Save Center, back by the Post Office, and right below our office. Our office girls (Elvrine, Nancy, Patty) tell us they eat there often and it is pretty good. You can take our word for it, when it comes to LOCAL food these girls are expert eaters. How do they stay so slim and attractive?

VIOLETS PLACE
A new restaurant in the Kauai Village Center around from Safeway. Open for breakfast, lunch, and dinner, mostly Filipino food.

FAST FREDDIES
Located in the center of Kapaa on makai side of the highway, just past the Ono Family restaurant. We tried the Chicken Teriyaki and it was pretty good, plenty of rice and potato salad for $3.50. It's not much on atmosphere but clean and comfortable. Elmer Dills, who has a TV Show in Los Angeles related to travel, loved the place.

HIGASHI'S
Next to the Bank of Hawaii in the center of town across from the ball field. Very LOCAL, lots of rice, low prices. Some of the locals think they have the best teriyaki beef on the Island.

local Style

WAIPOULI
In the Waipouli/Foodland Shopping Center behind McDonald's next to Foodland. Open Monday & Tuesday from 7 am to 2 pm and from Wednesday-Sunday from 5:30 am to 9 pm. Frequented mostly by locals; however, one can get a good meal for a very reasonable price. They now have a $1.99 breakfast special.

S & R RESTAURANT
In the Waipouli Complex, which is between the seven and eight mile marker. Open for breakfast, lunch and dinner. Very low prices and for what you pay the food is good, but fixed to please locals. Closed Monday.

EL CAFE
The old place next to the Roxy Theater is now called the BBQ Pit, a LOCAL bar. El Cafe is now open at their new location just around the corner on Kuhio Highway. Norbert is running things as before so we would imagine that the food will be as tasty as before. They are open for dinner only and this is a good place to get a good meal for a low price.

BUBBA'S
Located across the steet from El Cafe. You can get a pretty good hamburger and fries here for around $3. You can eat at the outdoor counter or at one of the tables by the sidewalk. Just like Paris, right?

local/Tourist

WAILUA MARINA
Located at the mouth of the Wailua river where the boats to Fern Grotto dock. This defies a label since almost everyone eats here. When we first visited Kauai, we stopped here for breakfast one morning and someone in the party asked for an Irish coffee. "I'm sorry," the waitress replied, "we only serve Yuban." They are open for breakfast, lunch, and dinner. Prices are moderate to low for a place that has so much tourist business. For example, an extra thick cut of Prime Rib for $15.50 or Mahi Mahi for $9.50.

SEA SHELL

Excellent location right on the ocean's edge, open only for dinner. They have mostly seafood, as one might expect, but a few other dishes also. Prices range from $13.50 to $25.

SIZZLER

Just like back home. The thing is that this really is one of the least expensive chow down places on Kauai. The food is not much different than Mainland; they have a very good soup & salad bar.

MEMA

Just across from the Sizzler in the same little Center. This has just opened and if the food is good it is a welcome addition as we love Thai food. Their sign says Thai and Chinese but the menu is mostly Thai.

KINTARO

Across the street from the Coco Palms as you enter the Waipouli/Kapaa area. More expensive than most of the other places in town but we think it is worth it if you like Japanese food. Excellent sushi and sashimi and other authentic Japanese dishes. Since last year they have expanded and now offer Tappanyaki style (food cooked in front of you). The decor is interesting and the service is good. Open every day except Sunday from 5:30-9:30, 822-3341.

AL & DON'S

This is a little hard to find. It is located in the Kauai Sands Hotel, which is just south of the Plantation Marketplace. Open for breakfast and dinner only. About the only tourists who find this are the ones staying at the hotel, but the locals have found it because it is such a good deal. The atmosphere is good, right on the water, and the prices are low. 822-4221.

BULL SHED

The entrance road is just across from McDonald's in Kapaa. Very nice setting, right on the ocean, especially if you have a window table. Open for dinner only. This has long been a favorite with tourists. Broiled steak and fish, and prime rib, salad bar included with all meals. Prices are mid to upper teens. Reservations accepted only for parties of six or more.

PANDA GARDEN

A new Szechuan Chinese restaurant in the Safeway Center. They are open for lunch and dinner.

PAPAYA CAFE

A great place for health food lovers. You will find it at the far north west corner of Kauai Village under the clock tower.

GINGER'S BAR AND GRILL

Located in the new Kauai Village Shopping Center. At the present time the menu is limited (hamburgers, sandwiches, fish & chips, salad) but they intend expanding the menu to include seafood and steak. We had a very good hamburger served with French fried potato curls.

A PACIFIC CAFE
In our last edition Pacific cafe had just opened and we had not had a chance to try it. We since have had several meals there and must say that it might just be the premier dining spot of Kauai. If it were in a more luxurious setting it would absolutely be so. The food is outstanding and the service is excellent. This excellence, of course, is reflected in the prices. Most dishes are in the $20-$30 range and the wines are not cheep, the lowest priced white around $25. But if one wants a special occasion spot, be sure to give this a try.

PARADISE HOT DOGS
In Kauai Village Shopping Center. If all you want is a quick lunch, this is a possibility. You will feel right at home.

THE KING AND I
Located in the Waipouli Plaza on the mauka side of the highway. As the name suggests, Thai food and very authentic. We have eaten here often and have never been disappointed. They are open for dinner only from 4:30-9 every day.

DRAGON INN
Also located in the Waipouli Plaza on the second floor. Pretty good Cantonese food at reasonable prices. They are open for lunch and dinner.

ONO FAMILY RESTAURANT
In the center of Kapaa on the makai side of the highway. Open for breakfast, lunch and dinner. Moderate prices, good food. Good spot for a fresh fish dinner under $10. Be sure to try their Portuguese Bean soup.

JIMMY'S GRILL
Fairly new in Kapaa, located on makai side of the highway just where Highway 581 meets the main Highway. Mainland type food at reasonable prices. Since it is on the second floor it is a good place to view life in Kapaa.

MICHELLE'S CAFE AND BAKERY
You must try this new little spot because it they are not successful Evie will be very disappointed. She has eaten there several times and loves it. They are open for breakfast (Mon-Fri 7-11, Sat-Sun 8-11), lunch (daily 11-4) and dinner (Wed-Sun 5-9). They are located at 1384 Kuhio (main) Highway in the center of Kapaa. There is ample parking in the rear.

HANA YA
Another new restaurant just a few doors up from Michelle's. We tried this and were very pleased. One can have a very authentic Japanese meal or all the sushi one desires. They are open for lunch and dinner.

MAKAI
Try this if you like Greek food since they have a few Greek dishes but plenty of other selections also.

KOUNTRY KITCHEN
Toward the end of Kapaa, about a mile past Ono Family Restaurant on the mauka side of the highway. Open for breakfast, lunch and dinner. Moderate prices and good food, much like a Mainland cafe. Home made corn bread.

KAPAA FISH AND CHOWDER HOUSE
At the north end of Kapaa on the mauka side of the highway. They are open for dinner only with entrees in the $12-$18 range, and offer free Karaoke in the bar. 822-7488.

POINTS OF INTEREST

KAMOKILA HAWAIIAN VILLAGE
This is a restored ancient Hawaiian village located on the north bank of the Wailua River on the site of an old village. Guided tours are provided and visitors get a chance to see some of the old Hawaiian crafts. To find take Highway 580 toward the mountain and watch for the sign on the left just opposite the falls. The charge is $5 for adults, $1.50 for children between 6 and 12. They are open from 9 a.m. until 4 p.m. Monday through Saturday. For more information call 822-1192.

FERN GROTTO
To get to the Fern Grotto one must take one of the river cruises from the mouth of the Wailua River, either Smith Motor Boat Service or Waialeale Boat Tours. It costs $9 for adults and $4.50 for kids and some people feel it is too touristy but we have enjoyed it the two or three times we have done it. Try not to get on a boat with all Japanese tourists because the guides will speak Japanese.

OPAEKAA FALLS
Take Route 580 from the Coco Palms and go about two miles up the hill. You will see a large parking lot on your right. Once there be sure to cross the street to look over the Wailua River and the valley below.

ALEXANDER'S NURSERY
Continue up Route 580 for another mile or so and you will come to the nursery on the right. It is closed Sunday and Tuesday. It is lots of fun to look around here at all the tropical plants. Richard and his wife are very helpful in answering questions.

STATE PARK

If you continue up 580 for another few miles, past the University of Hawaii Experimental Station, you will come to the Wailua River up near its source. You will be about seven miles from the Coco Palms. Depending on the rainfall, the river will be going either under or over the road. Most of the time it is safe to drive to the other side of the river to the parking area. This area is not kept up as it once was, and yet it is a great place to enjoy some of Kauai's natural beauty. You can walk down along the river bank, and, if you like, you can swim in one of the swimming holes along the way.

COCONUT PLANTATION SHOPPING CENTER

Retrace your route down to the Coco Palms. At the main highway turn left and go about one mile and you will see the entrance to the Marketplace on the makai side. On Thursday, Friday, and Saturday, starting at 4 p.m., there is a free hula show. There are all kinds of shops and restaurants. One shop you should not miss is the Kahn Gallery, which features many of the local craftsmen. While many of the items they carry are expensive, the quality merits the price. Not everything in the store is high priced. There are koa chop sticks by Troy Lydgate and baskets by Theo Morrison, but even here the quality is obvious.

SUNSHINE MARKET

Every Wednesday starting at 3:30 local folk sell produce (see Sunshine Market under Lihue section). To find, take route 581 (Kukui St.) and head mauka for a few blocks. You will come to a park and some tennis courts on your right. The sale takes place in the parking lot.

SLEEPING GIANT

When we first visited Kauai, we felt that the top of this mountain was inaccessible. In reality it is not too strenuous a hike, with the trail beginning on either side of the mountain. To hike from the east side, turn mauka just north of the Coco Palms on Haleilio Rd. and continue toward the mountain, bearing to the right until you come to the trail head marker. To hike from the west, go mauka on 580 until you reach 581, turn right and drive a little over one mile where you will see the trail on the right.

FRUIT FARM

This is the best place to buy papaya, banana, and pineapple, especially if you are here for a long stay. To find, take Kawaihau Rd., which runs into the main highway at the north end of Kapaa, and drive a little over three miles. Just after you pass the ball field on the left, watch for a driveway on the right which may have a keep out sign. Ignore the sign, drive in past the house to the garage where you will see all the fruit. If no one is around, weigh the fruit and leave the money on the bench at the back of the garage. The cost is $.45 a pound.

BEACHES

NUKOLII

Starting behind the Wailua Golf course and going south, almost to Hanamaulu are beautiful, almost unused, white sand beaches. If you walk along here, yours may be the only footprints you will see. This is a good place for beaching and getting away from crowds, and maybe doing a little fishing, but it not so good for swimming. Waves tend to be rough with lots of rip tides.

LYDGATE STATE PARK

Just past the Wailua Golf course you will come to the Kauai Resort. Turn makai at the resort and go past it to Lydgate. Once a place of refuge and sacred to the ancient Hawaiians, this is a great spot if you have children. Many residents bring their children here where the water is safe. If you are a beginning snorkeler, this is the place to start.

COCO PALMS BEACH

Just across from the Coco Palms, parking can be found at either end. Swimming is good and safe if you do not venture too far out. At times you can watch the surfers at the north end. If you walk around the point at the north end, you will come to a secluded section , good if you want to be alone.

KEALIA BEACH

Just past Kapaa you will come to one of the most beautiful crescent beaches in Hawaii. Be careful here, for the waves can be awesome and the rips treacherous. At the far north end of the beach is a little cove used by locals and a safer place to swim. This is also an excellent place to body surf.

DONKEY BEACH

Closed to all but those who have a Lihue Plantation sticker.

ANAHOLA BEACH

North of Kapaa, just before you reach Anahola as you go down the hill, you will see a Hawaii Visitors Bureau marker on the right. Take this road and after one half mile you will see a sign pointing down a dirt road to the beach. Swimming is fair here, but if the surf is up, best to stay out. Beachcombing here is excellent. If you are early enough or lucky you may find a glass ball off one of the Japanese fishing boats. These are getting rare as other material is being used to make the floats, mainly plastic. If you miss the first road, you can take the road just past the store. Watch that you do not swim into the coral at the left side of the river. You can also find beach access by turning makai at the 14 mile marker on Aliomanu Rd. and going about 2.3 miles. This is a good place to go if you really want to get away from it all. Just past the 15 mile marker on the main highway you will come to the other end of Aliomanu Rd. Don't get confused, the two roads no longer connect. If you turn makai here and go about two miles to Kukuma Rd. and then left for about .2 of a mile you will find access to a very small, secluded beach.

MOLOAA

We think this is the most beautiful beach in Hawaii. Swimming is safe here unless the waves are very big on the north shore. To find, turn in at the fruit stand which is on the makai side of the highway just past the 16 mile marker. Take the road behind the stand which goes off to the left and proceed for 1.2 miles until you come to Moloaa Rd. on the right. Take that road and proceed to the beach. There is not much parking, but few people use this beach. When you come out you can get back to the main road by continuing on Koolau Rd. for 2.3 miles. The road is a little rough but certainly driveable.

NIGHT LIFE

COCO PALMS

Every night starting at 7:30 there is a torch lighting ceremony at the Coco Palms. There is no charge. Everyone who comes to Kauai should see this at least once, if for no other reason than to hear the talk that goes along with it. People react differently to the ceremony, but see it for yourself. To some it is the highlight of their trip.

BEACH BOY

Located in the Marketplace, there is sometimes some action here.

KAUAI RESORT HOTEL

Sometimes the Kauai Resort will feature entertainers from Honolulu. To find out what is going on, call 245-3931.

PLANTATION CINEMA

At the south end of the Marketplace. There are two small theaters here which show first run movies.

BRIDGE

There is a duplicate bridge game in the Kapaa Library every 2nd and 4th Thursday at 9:30 am and every 1st and 3rd Friday night at 7:30 pm. For more information call Patti Ficker, 742-1816.

SPORTS ACTIVITY

GOLF
Wailua golf Course, County owned and operated, is one of the best deals in Hawaii. Green fees for non-residents are $18 weekdays, $20 on weekends and holidays. Carts are available, both hand and power for $4 and $11, but not mandatory. Clubs can be rented from the pro shop located next to the sign-up window for $12. Larry Lee Sr., the pro, is most helpful. They also handle the hand cart rental. If you rent clubs, a hand or power cart is mandatory. The driving range is open every day except Sunday until 10 p.m. Small buckets are a $1 and large buckets are $1.75. *Golf Digest* once rated Wailua one of the ten best Municipal courses in the Nation. For a starting time call 245-2163.

TENNIS
The Coco Palms has three clay courts which are open to the public for $10 for one confirmed hour and longer on a space available basis. They also have six hard courts available at $7. Raquets are available at $5. Sheraton Coconut beach Hotel has courts available for $7 per person but if you have your own raquet the fee is $5. Public courts with no charge are located in three places in the Kapaa area. 1.) Wailua Houselots, just past the Coco Palms take Haleilio Rd. until you come to Nonu St. on the left. Turn on Nonu and go several blocks to the courts. 2.) Kapaa Town, turn mauka on route 581 (Kukui St.) and go about 1/4 mile and you will see the courts on your right. 3.) Wailua Homesteads Park, take 580 mauka for a little over two miles, turn right at 581 for about 1/2 mile and you will see the Park on your right.

GYM
Next door to our office in the Kapaa Shopping Center, upstairs, is a new Gym called Silent Thunder. They have been in business since early 1991 and have exercise and weight lifting equipment. They have a good rate for visitors. Open daily 6 am to 10 pm. 822-BOOM.

WATER SKIING
At the mouth of the Wailua river on the north side. To get there go up 580 one block and turn left to the river. For more information call 822-3577 and ask for Ken, or just go there to see what is happening.

DIVING & WINDSURFING
In the center of Kapaa is Sea Sage Dive Shop. Equipment is available for purchase or for rent and dive trips are available.

BICYCLE RENTING
Bikes can be rented at Rays Rental located in downtown Kapaa for $20 a day. At times he has coupons in the tourist magazines which offer two for one. 822-5700.

BLUE WATER SAILING
They offer several different trips from half day, $75, to exclusive hourly, daily, weekly rates. For more information call 808-822-0525.

NORTH TO HANALEI

Several years ago *Sunset Magazine* did an article on Hawaii in which they said, "It is the Hanalei Valley that most people see when they close their eyes and dream of Hawaii." The drive from Kapaa to the end of the road at Kee Beach, especially the ten miles past Princeville, is one of the most scenic in Hawaii. The question of how long this drive takes is a difficult one to deal with since there are many little side trips one can take to get the full impact of this area.

The first community you come to after leaving Kapaa is Anahola, which is not much more than a store, Post Office, and Duane's Ono Burgers. Before you reach the Anahola turn off, you might want to check the little lei stand, which is located just before the 13 mile marker. Richard, the owner, is a fascinating gentleman to talk to and will sell you a plumeria lei for $4 or an orchid lei for $5. All of the flowers are grown on his property behind the lei stand. Since the stand is not always open, you might try calling ahead, 822-5691. Just after the lei stand you will see Kukuihole Rd. If you take this road to the right and proceed .9 of a mile and then turn right on the dirt road you will be at Anahola Bay beach, an absolutely beautiful crescent shaped beach. On most days you will not find many people, local or tourists, on this beach. When you leave, continue on Kukuihole Rd. for .6 of a mile and you will be back on the highway just south of the Anahola Post Office.

The next town you come to is Kilauea Town, and unless you pull off the road, you will go right past it. Turn right when you see the sign for the fruit stand (Mango Mama's- a good place to get a smoothie). Past the fruit stand, turn left to get to the main section of Kilauea. You will cross a little stream where the makers of *South Pacific* built the slippery slide. When we first came to Kauai in 1978 one could still venture down this slide, an unforgettable experience, take our word for it. Several years ago the land was purchased and rumor was that it was going to be developed into a tourist destination spot. The present owner submitted plans to the Planning Department of Kauai but his plans of turning it into a tourist attraction came to naught. It seems that many of the people who live in Kilauea are against development of the area. Under consideration now is a new golf course but there is much opposition from some of the local folk. If people in Kilauea favor tourism it seems they do not favor it in their area.

One thing you do not want to miss is Christ Memorial Episcopal Church, located on the road that takes one to the main highway and out of Kilauea. Be sure to go in to see the beautiful stained glass windows and be sure to take one of the brochures and read the history of this church.

Kilauea is mainly a residential town, but it has one of our favorite stores in all Hawaii, the Kong Lung Co. When they first opened they had a sign in the window *Gumps In a Cane Field.* We were told that one of the Gump family happened to see the sign and asked that it be removed, so it was changed to *Gifts in a Cane Field.* We noticed this year that sign had been removed. Evidently, most tourists now find them and they feel less isolated. If you could use a little snack, stop by the *Kilauea Bakery and Pizza,* found behind Kong Lung, and try one of their sweet rolls or take home a loaf of bread. Here you will also find Crater Hill, an art and furnishing gallery with a new and different look. Owner, Margaret "Gritt" Benton has put together a unique collection of exotic bamboo furniture from South East Asia and hard to find antiques and collectibles from many parts of the world. Another interesting business in this town is Jacques' Bakery, which has bread so good that most of the better restaurants on the Island use it.

Also new to Kilauea is the Guava Plantation, a C. Brewer enterprise, located on the left side of the highway as you leave Kilauea, attempting to diversify agriculture on Kauai. They have set up a very nice Visitors Center, where guests can sample their products. They have a little snack bar with sandwiches and juices.

Just past Kilauea, as you go down the hill and just before the bridge that crosses Kalihiwai Stream, look to your left and you will see a fairly sizable waterfall. One can judge from this how much rain is falling in the high country. If you park by the bridge, you will get a good view of Kalihiwai Valley.

At about the twenty eight (28) mile marker, just past the Princeville Airport, you will come to the entrance to Princeville on the right. This planned development is made up of many homes, condo complexes, the Hanalei Bay Resort, the new Princeville Sheraton Hotel, and the Princeville Golf Course, a twenty-seven hole, Robert Trent Jones Jr. designed course that has vistas unsurpassed anywhere. One does not need to be a golfer to enjoy a walk or ride around this course.

The Prince Golf Course, which operated for a few years as a nine hole course, opened in July 1990 as a championship 18 hole course and is one of the most scenic courses we have ever played. Since our last edition their clubhouse has been completed and it is truly something. Even if you are not golfers, stop by here to see true opulence.

Just past Princeville is the overlook for Hanalei Valley, where fields of taro grow in all stages of development. It is from taro that poi, a staple to the Hawaiian people, is made. When you reach the bottom of the hill, you can drive into this area to get a closer look. A very good dirt road goes only a few miles.

Next is sleepy little Hanalei Town nestled between the Hanalei River and Hanalei Bay. Change comes slowly here and is sometimes resented by the long time residents. Several years ago the Ching Young Village Shopping Center, made up of Big Save Market, a number of little shops, and several small restaurants, all vying for the tourist dollar, was the new thing in town. Then the Old Hanalei School was moved to the center of Hanalei, renovated, and turned into shops and one restaurant.

The seven mile drive from Hanalei town to the end of the road is of unparalleled beauty and charm. One crosses a number of one-way bridges, where small streams flow to the sea. The road rises and falls and constantly there are beach vistas hard to believe. One passes what is perhaps the most famous beach in Hawaii, Lumahai, or Nurse's Beach from the movie *South Pacific*. All of this ends at Kee Beach, the setting for the love scene in *The Thorn Birds*.

RESTAURANTS

ANAHOLA

DUANE'S ONO BURGER
Located next to the store and post office in Anahola, this small take out restaurant has become kind of a fixture on Kauai. It is not the same owner, however, and the hamburgers are not the hand made patties of old. One has to go to Lihue, to Kalapaki Beach Burger, where the original owners of Ono Burger now reside. We recently stopped by Ono Burger and we are hoping that they return to the home made patties.

KALALEA'S HALE AINA
You will find this just past the Anahola Store, sort of across the street from Ono Burger. The specialty here is BBQ Chicken for $3.50, and while we have not tried it, our friends tell us it is delicious. They also have a plate lunch for $5, shave ice, or ice cold coconut for $3. Window service with tables under the trees outside. Closed Monday.

MOLOAA FRUIT STAND
Just past Anahola and before Kilauea, you will see it on your right. It is possible to get a sandwich or a cold drink here.

KILAUEA

CASA 'D AMICI
This opened either late in '86 or early '87. As the name implies, the food is Italian. Several years ago a new owner took over and we certainly noticed the difference in the food. We had some of the best pasta we had ever eaten. Everyone of our friends who has tried it raved. The only reason we do not eat here often is that it is a far piece from Poipu.

FARMER'S MARKET STORE & DELI
At the store just past Casa 'D Amici one can get a sandwich or a small salad.

PRINCEVILLE RESTAURANTS

CHUCK'S STEAK HOUSE
Prices are moderate to high and the food is what one would expect in a tourist restaurant; that is, very reliable. Lunch runs between $6 and $10 while dinners are in the mid-teens. They are open for lunch and dinner, and offer a salad bar lunch for $6.25. 826-6522.

BEAMREACH
To find, turn in at Princeville and go past the golf course to the last condo complex on the right. Open for dinner only from 6-10. The food is good; their prices range from $12 to $20. 826-9131.

BALI HAI
This restaurant is located at the Hanalei Bay Resort. At our last visit, prices were reasonable. There is new management and they are open for breakfast, lunch, and dinner. At one time we used to go there just to order their Monte Cristo sandwich. It is still on the menu and we can only hope it is still as good. The outstanding thing here is the fantastic view of Hanalei Bay. 826-6522.

LANAI RESTAURANT
Located above the Pro Shop at the Princeville Golf Course. When we went to press they had been closed for remodeling. We are not sure when they will re-open.

CAFE ZELO'S
Located at the rear of the shopping center. They feature Fajitas, both chicken and fish, lox and bagel, and stuffed potato. The menu is varied, not only the above but pasta, Cajun hamburger, tarragon chicken burger.

PIZZA-BURGER
Next to Zelo's, just what the name implies.

HANALEI RESTAURANTS

LOCAL STYLE

HANALEI MUSEUM SNACK SHOP
Behind what used to be a museum on the mauka side of the road when you enter Hanalei. Take-out only. Plate lunch specials including fresh fish when available for under $5. Hamburgers and other sandwiches are offered.

BLACK POT LUAU HUT

We have never been able to find this place open, but we keep trying because we get good reports from some of our guests. It is pretty local in orientation and probably serves some good ono Hawaiian food. We had the same luck finding them open this year as last. We arrived at lunch time but it said they had gone to Kapaa to shop for supplies.

THE VILLAGE SNACK AND BAKERY SHOP

In the Ching Young village. Good food at low prices, try the home made pie.

HAWAIIAN DELIGHT

A little take out place located in Ching Young Village.

local Style

U.S. BARBEQUE & SUB

A little take out window on the same side of the street as Ching Young Village but on the highway. One can get a slab of baby back ribs for $10.95 or 1/2 a slab for $5.95 or 1/2 a mesquite smoked roasted chicken for $5.95.

PIZZA HANALEI

In the Ching Young Village. You can get small-$7.58, medium-$10.40, large-$15.68 and then add your own toppings from over a dozen choices (small-$1.10, medium-$1.65, large-$2.25). One could run up quite a bill at that rate.

FOONG WONGS

In Ching Young village, on the second floor. Cantonese style, with plate lunch specials of a Hawaiian flavor. It is the plate lunch specials that make this a good deal. If one orders several dishes a la carte as we did, their price will be high for what you get. 826-6996.

local/Tourist

HANALEI WAKE UP CAFE

This is a new little restaurant just next door to Black Pot. They serve breakfast only from 7 am until Noon. It is cute and clean, and the local folk rave about the Custard French Toast.

TAHITI NUI

In the center of Hanalei. The Tahiti Nui really defies description and in spite of the enlargement and modernization it remains a unique spot in Hawaii. We are not great promoters of the Hawaiian luau, but if it is a luau you are looking for, this is the most interesting we have been to. The price is up to $35 for adults, $15 for children aged 5-11. Those under 5 are free. No drinks are included. There is a good sampling of Hawaiian food and plenty of dessert. The show is the best part of the evening and always a special treat is hearing Louise Marston, the owner-operator of the Nui, sing one of her Tahitian songs. The entertainment is very "local" and can be a delight. To quote one of our guests, "This luau had a family flavor. The songs were mostly about the North Shore, Hanalei, and the beautiful scenery of that area." Luaus are held on Wednesdays and Fridays, but

197

call ahead for information. If not a luau, stop by for lunch or dinner, or just a cool drink in the bar. 826-6277.

THE DOLPHIN

On the makai side of the highway as you enter Hanalei. Open for dinner only. Good food, with prices in the $14 to $22 range. The setting is nice, right along the Hanalei River. 826-6113.

SHELL HOUSE

On the highway just past the Tahiti Nui. Open for breakfast, lunch, and dinner. If you have tried this before and were not pleased, give it another try, as there is new management and the food is very good and the prices are not too high. We recently had lunch there and were pleased. 826-9301.

HANALEI GOURMET

Located in the old Hanalei School building, across the street from Ching Young Village. They are open for breakfast and lunch and from the looks of things do as much business as the other restaurants combined. They serve mostly salads and sandwiches for lunch but they must be very creative as they are popular with the locals.

CHARO'S

Past Hanalei between the thirty-five and thirty-six mile marker at the Colony Resort. This used to be called the Sandgroper but has since been purchased by Charo, completely remodeled and in many ways improved. We had lunch there and the food and service was very good but the menu was limited to a few items: hamburger, chicken sandwich, and several salads. The best part is a very pleasant setting. We were told that Charo spends as much time on Kauai as she can and when on Island visits her restaurant daily, taking much care with the menu. 826-6422.

POINTS OF INTEREST

THE LIGHTHOUSE

Take the main road into Kilauea and go past Kong Lung Store. The Light House area is a sanctuary for a large number of marine birds (the Red footed Booby, the Frigate, the Albatross). There is a small museum in the Light House that has pictures of all the birds. It is also possible to borrow binoculars to watch the turtles. The gate to the Light House opens at 10 am and closes at 4 p.m. and has a $2 admission charge. The museum is closed on Monday.

CHRIST MEMORIAL CHURCH

This stone edifice is not as old as it looks. It was built during World War II in 1942. The church is left open so visitors can enjoy viewing the hand-carved altar and stained glass windows imported from England. There is also a small graveyard behind the church that is interesting to visit.

HANALEI MUSEUM
In the center of Hanalei Town. Fee for adults in $1.00, children free. The museum has a small collection of artifacts. It is open on Tuesday, Thursday, and Saturday only.

WAIOLI HUIIA CHURCH
On the mauka side in Hanalei Town. This church is over a hundred and forty years old and holds services every Sunday. The unique thing is that the hymns are sung in Hawaiian.

WAIOLI MISSION HOUSE
Built in 1836, this old home gives one an idea of life long ago. There is no charge and visiting hours are from 9-12 and 1-3.

WET & DRY CAVES
Near the end of the road past Haena Beach Park. Legend has it that this was once the home of Madam Pele, the volcano goddess. When the caves filled up with water, Madam Pele, liking a warmer climate, moved on to the Big Island.

KALALAU TRAIL
The trail head begins at Kee Beach on the mauka side of the road. Hiking the entire eleven miles is strenuous and should only be done with planning. Usually this hike takes a couple of days in and out and a camping permit is required. The two mile hike to Hanakapiai Beach, however, is not that tough. In fact, the hike from Hanakapiai Beach to Hanakapiai Falls, a distance through the valley of about two miles, is also not that hard. We would urge anyone who is a good walker to at least try the first two miles, and if they felt up to it to try the hike to the falls. Under no circumstances should anyone try swimming at Hanakapiai Beach as the rip tide is fierce. Strong swimmers have been swept out and drowned at this spot. It may look inviting but it is a definite no-no!

BEACHES

The North Shore of Kauai is one beautiful beach after the next. People debate which beach is best. In actuality they are all "best" depending on weather conditions, wave conditions, one's mood, or whatever. We would encourage you to spend some time at one of the less accessible beaches to get that "away from it all" feeling. Also, none of the beaches mentioned below are difficult to get to, and if hiking is involved, it is very little. It is possible that at some of the beaches you will be the only ones there.

KALIHIWAI BEACH
Just past Kilauea, before the road descends, you will see Kalihiwai Rd. on your right. Once on this road you will see a "No Outlet" sign. That means that the road dead ends at the beach. The swimming here is safe, especially in the lagoon where the river meets the ocean. Things can get rough way off to the right as you face the ocean. If the surf is up, be careful. There are no facilities here, so if you intend to stay awhile, pack a lunch.

ANINI BEACH
About one mile past the first Kalihiwai Rd., you will come to another Kalihiwai Rd. At one time they were connected by a bridge over the lagoon. Once again you will see a "No Outlet" sign. As soon as you can, turn left on Anini Rd. and proceed to the beach. You can stop anywhere along here you like, but a mile or so up the road you will come to a public park where there are picnic and rest room facilities. The water is shallow, making this a perfect place to snorkel, especially for the beginner. Also, windsurfing is good here.

HANALEI BEACH PARK
Hanalei Bay is surrounded with beach, but the most popular place is by the pier on the far east side of the Bay. To find, turn makai off the main highway at the Tahiti Nui and go one block, turn right and this road will take you to the park. There are picnic tables, rest rooms, and showers.

LUMAHAI
Near the thirty-seven (37) mile marker, at an obvious vista point, you will find a small trail leading to the beach. Unless the waves are small and the ocean is calm, this is not a good place for swimming.

TUNNELS BEACH
This beach is located near the end of the road, just before you reach the wet caves. Watch for the beach access sign, turn makai and the beach is about 100 yards ahead.

From Hanalei to the end of the road at Kee Beach there are numerous other beaches to enjoy such things as sitting in the sun or shelling. No doubt you will see surfers at various points. Do not conclude that this beautiful water is perfectly safe. North Shore water on each Island can be dangerous. There are so many safe places to swim on Kauai that it is silly to take chances in dangerous places. Keep in mind that this is an isolated area and should one get in trouble, it would take some time for help to arrive. Kee Beach at the end of the road is safe for swimming and snorkeling in the summer months, but when the surf is up, do not venture out here or your next stop might be Mid-Way Island.

NIGHT LIFE

There used to be music at the Hanalei Bay Resort, and perhaps when the new management takes over they will have some evening activity in the Happy Talk Lounge. The Tahiti Nui has shows when they have a luau and sometimes even when there is no luau they have music in the bar. Also, often there is some special thing going on and these will be mentioned in The Garden Island newspaper.

KILAUEA THEATER
Located a few doors from the Kong Lung Co. Store. They started out showing old movies but lately have started to show some first run movies. They are open Friday through Tuesday and have a magic show on Saturday evenings at 5pm.

BRIDGE
On the first, third, and fifth Thursday of the month there is a duplicate bridge game at the Hanalei Bay Resort, and at the Pahio Clubhouse in Princeville every Saturday at 6 pm. For information call Lolita Horney, 826-6805.

SPORTS

GOLF
Princeville Golf course at the Princeville development is one of the most photographed courses in Hawaii, and a favorite with many of Kauai's visitors. Unless one is staying within the Princeville Development, green fees are $90 including the cart which is mandatory. A husband and wife would pay $180 for a round of golf. For those staying at Princeville, the fee is somewhat less. Since B & B has accommodations within the Princeville development, B & B members who choose one of these should check with the Princeville Pro Shop. For more information call 826-3580.

The Prince Course is $110 per person ($85 if staying in Princeville) and offers free use of driving range and Spa. Club rental is $20. The course is one of the most beautiful courses we have seen but very difficult for the hacker. It is cart paths only, and you can take our word for it, you will not desire to play more than 18 holes in one day. The course is continuous (no break after nine) so take along something to eat and drink. You will not be sorry. For more information call 826-5000.

TENNIS
There are courts open to the public at the Princeville Golf and Tennis Club, (826-3620) $12 per person per hour, court rules. They also offer weekly rates of $40 single, $75 per couple, $100 for family which includes free clinic and 15% off all merchandise in the pro shop. There are also courts at the Hanalei Bay Resort. They charge $30 per court for as many players as one likes for two hours, but they are not strict if they are not busy.

POLO
Polo is played down at Anini Beach probably on the weekends around 3 in the afternoon.

If you have taken this drive all the way to the end,
we feel sure you will agree
that this is one of the most
beautiful places on earth.
If you happen to catch it on a rainy day,
you must come back in fairer weather
to get the full sense of its spendor.
Do not hesitate to take
at least part of the Kalalau Trail.

SOUTH TO POIPU

Most of the tourist activity on Kauai takes place in the Poipu area, on Kauai's south side, about twelve miles from Lihue, where beaches are big and the sun shines brightly. The first place you come to after you leave Lihue is the little community of Puhi, where Kauai Community College is located. Across the street from the college, on the makai side of the road, is the People's Market Fruit Stand. Stop by here for a visit or to pick up some fresh papaya or pineapple, or maybe an orchid spray or a few anthuriums.

A few miles south of this you will see a sign pointing to the left for Kipu. If you take this drive, do not expect to come to a town or anything resembling a town. Two and one-half miles after leaving the main road you will reach a monument to William Hyde Rice, who died in 1924. He was the son of William Harrison Rice, one of the first managers of the Lihue Plantation. William Hyde Rice was born and grew up on Kauai and had a great knowledge and love of the people and legends of the Hawaiians. Not only did he speak Hawaiian, it is said he understood it on a multiple meaning level that even some of the Hawaiians failed to grasp. His book *Hawaiian Legends* is considered one of the most important of its kind. The monument in his memory was erected in 1925 by his many Japanese friends. You can drive past the monument on dirt road and all you will see are some little Hawaiian homes and plenty of cats and chickens.

Perhaps during your stay on Kauai you will hear about the tunnel in this area that goes to the Poipu/Koloa area. Local folks insist that if you try to go through this tunnel carrying pork your motor will stall and you are apt to see Madam Pele. We have been through this tunnel, but alas no Madam Pele appeared. Since this is private property, belonging to one of the sugar companies, we do not recommend using this route.

When you return to the highway, you proceed south to one-half mile past the six mile marker where you will come to the road to Koloa. The first part of this road is called the *Tunnel of Trees* because of the huge eucalyptus trees that line the road. Before the hurricane in November of 1982 these trees were so thick they blocked the sun, hence the name. This is a much safer tunnel to use to get to Poipu/Koloa. We have heard of Madam Pele making appearances here too, but usually after mid-night, and by then we are fast asleep. At the Tunnel of Trees, turn left and three miles later you arrive at Koloa Town, the oldest plantation town on Kauai. If you look to the right at the end of the Tunnel of Trees road you will see a monument to the first sugar mill in Hawaii. Just to the left of the monument is a small planting of sugar cane with all the different types identified. Since sugar is such an important crop in Hawaii and the real cause of all the different ethnic groups in the Islands, you might like to stop and look this over.

202

In the last few years Koloa Town has been receiving a face lift, making it an attractive tourist center, and this development continues. The most recent addition is a few new shops just west of the Koloa Ice House restaurant at the east end of Koloa. When you turn right as the road dead ends in Koloa, you will see a cluster of small shops on your left. Across the street from the existing buildings in Koloa there is a shopping center being built. It was started late in 1988 but evidently they ran in to a problem and not much has been done since the initial grading. If and when that center is finished Koloa will be a fair sized little town.

After you make the jog in the road at Koloa town, you proceed three miles and you are in Poipu, the tourist mecca of Kauai. Poipu is an area, not a town, and in a sense the center of Poipu is Poipu Beach Park at the foot of Hoowili Rd. off Poipu Rd. Just west of Poipu Beach are the hotels: the Waiohai, Poipu Beach Hotel, the Sheraton, and the Kiahuna with its complete tennis complex and an eighteen hole Robert Trent Jones Jr. designed golf course. To the east are a series of condos, available for vacation rentals. To the north of these condos is Poipu Kai development, made up of four condo complexes with many lots for private homes. Much care has gone into the planning of this area, and while there are one or two unattractive condos just above Brennecke's Beach, when this area is compared with others in Hawaii, it is obvious that someone deserves credit for making sure Poipu stayed attractive.

In October 1989 the Kauai Planning Commission approved an 800 acre development that will go all the way from Poipu Rd. out to Spouting Horn. This development will add some 1200 homes along with shopping and restaurants. The Hyatt Hotel, located just east of the Poipu Kai development was completed late in 1990. At one time it was thought that another hotel would be built west of the Hyatt, but instead of a hotel condominiums have been built. they should be complete near the end of 1993. Tourists who have been coming to Poipu for years will probably be disappointed to see so much development but let's face it, Poipu is getting to be a popular place and as demand increases so will supply. The question we local folk have is how are the roads going to accommodate the extra traffic when they barely can handle the present load?

If you are a long time visitor to Kauai,
there is little doubt that you
have noticed much change
in the Poipu area.
As stated above, there is much more to come.
And yet, Poipu is still
one of the more plesant spots in Hawaii.

RESTAURANTS

LOCAL STYLE

BIG SAVE
In the Big Save Market at the east end of Koloa Town, you get lots of chow down food at low prices.

SUEOKA'S MARKET
Just to the right and alongside Sueoka's market. Every day is bargain day at this little take out stand. Hamburgers are only $.80 for plain and $1.10 for deluxe. Feed one to the kid and if he makes it, order up. Just kidding, the food is very good for the price. Try the plate lunches, tasty and cheap. Or for a snack, five won ton for $1.00.

local Style

TAQUERIA NORTENOS
Next to Kukuiula Store. The owners describe this food as *Sonoran style Mexican.* Morgan, who moved to Kauai from Tucson, Arizona, was raised by a Mexican Nanny, who taught her that style of cooking. The service is from a take out window but recently they have acquired the store next door to provide a place for patrons to sit and eat. Lots of food for a low price. Open every day accept Wednesday from 11 a.m. until 11 p.m. This is about the only place in the area that you can get a snack after 10 p.m.

KOLOA ICE HOUSE
At the east end of Koloa Town, just before Big Save. Very good sandwiches for a modest price. Also special dishes such as chili & rice for under $2.00. Shave ice served. When you see shave ice with beans, do not worry, it is not the ones they use in chili.

TAISHO
This is the newest restaurant in Koloa Town and it is a welcome addition. The cuisine is Japanese, moderately priced and very tasty. It is located on the east end of Koloa just next to the Ice House. Give it a try and we are sure you will like it.

KOLOA BROILER
In the middle of Koloa. If you do not like the cooking, there is no one to blame but yourself since you are the cook. There is a good-sized broiler in the room where one can broil a steak, fish, beef kabobs, or a hamburger. This along with a salad bar with rice and beans, priced between $8 and $10 makes this one of the livelier spots in the area. It can be crowded, but be patient, they eventually get everyone served.

Tourist

HOUSE OF SEAFOOD
In the Poipu Kai development. We have tried this several times and each time it improves and now we recommend it especially to seafood lovers. They have come up with some really interesting seafood recipes. Most entrees run between $20-30 and salad is included. The setting is nice. 742-6433.

BRENNECKE'S
Right at Poipu Beach Park, and as their ad says "Right on the Beach, right on the price." Open for lunch and dinner. Mainly tourists eat here. All of the entrees come with pasta in a white sauce. Very good fresh fish starting at $16. What we like here are the "starters" ie., ceviche, tomatoes and onions vinigarette, etc. We often make a meal of just "starters". Also, since it is right on the ocean, it is an excellent place to watch the sun set. They have a long happy hour in the afternoon and the drink prices are reasonable. 742-7588.

COURTSIDE CAFE & BAR
This fine little restaurant is at the Kiahuna Tennis Club and plenty of tourists who would love it unfortunately never find it. They are open for breakfast and lunch, and lunch goes to pretty late in the afternoon. Every day different specials are offered at modest prices. We feel sure that even those who are not tennis buffs will like this spot. 742-6696

KIAHUNA CLUBHOUSE RESTAURANT
At the Kiahuna Golf Course. Open for breakfast from 7 am until 11 am and lunch from 11:30 until 3 pm. 742-6055.

THE BEACH HOUSE
On the road to Spouting Horn. The original Beach House was destroyed by the hurricane but they have built it back bigger and better than ever. The setting is perfect, right on the water. They are open for dinner only and a reservation is suggested. The food is O.K., very much what you would expect, and the service is good considering the crowds they handle. Prices range from $16 to $30, 742-7575.

PANCHO AND LEFTY'S
In Koloa Town right next to the Chevron Station. 742-7377

KEOKI'S PARADISE
This restaurant is located in the new Kiahuna Shopping Center at the entrance to the Kiahuna Golf Course. They are open for dinner only. As far as most local folk are concerned, this is the best deal in the area. They are the largest restaurant in the area, and if you have to wait it probably will not be long. You could have dinner in the bar if you don't want a large meal, 742-7534.

POIPU BEACH HOTEL
Next door to the Waiohai Hotel, in fact the same owner, but not nearly as expensive for either food or accommodations. At lunch time you can broil your own hamburger by the pool.

PLANTATION GARDENS
Located in the Kiahuna development next to the Waiohai. If you are looking for the nicest restaurant in the area, this is probably it. The atmosphere is excellent, the service is good, and the food can be great. Price wise, it will be around $20 to $30 a person depending on wine and dessert choice. Everything is ala carte, but for a special occasion this would be our choice. 742-1695

FLAMINGO CANTINA
Mexican style and very good value. It is located where the Aquarium used to be, just east of Poipu Beach turn left when you see Nii Kai Villas or the sign for Flamingoes. We usually order the fajita, very good. Our only negative here is that their house wine, served in a carafe, is $16, which we feel is overpriced for a bulk wine. 742-9505

POIPU BAY GRILL & BAR
While we do not cover every restaurant that caters mainly to tourists, we include this because it is really excellent. It is by far the best place in the Poipu area for breakfast, and one of the best for lunch. They are also open for dinner and while we have not tried their regular menu we have had most of their appetizers. If you like things spicy try their Buffalo Wings. 742-8888

POINTS OF INTEREST

SPOUTING HORN
To find, just stay to the right on Poipu Rd. after you pass Kukuiula Store and you will come to it. We enjoy seeing and listening to Spouting Horn since it is always a little different depending on the mood of the ocean. It is fun to calculate which swell is going to produce the highest fountain. One of our friends dubbed it *the god's bidet*. This is a good spot to pick up a gift for someone on the Mainland as the vendors are pretty competitive. At one time these vendors paid no rent, but now they are controlled by the County and bid for their spots.

PLANTATION GARDENS
At the Kiahuna, all around the Plantation Gardens Restaurant. At one time there was a charge to go through these gardens, but no longer. Unlike some botanical gardens, you won't always know what you are looking at, but it is all beautiful. Of special interest is the cactus garden.

OLD KOLOA TOWN
Koloa is the oldest plantation town on Kauai. Some time around 1835 Ladd & Company, made up of three men, William Ladd, Peter Allen Brinsdale, and William Hooper, started a sugar plantation in Koloa. Hooper was made the manager of the operation and in spite of his lack of knowledge about sugar, the plantation became successful, and no doubt this success encouraged others to go into the production of sugar. Koloa was also a place for whaling ships to stock up for their long journeys to and from the North Pacific.

FARMERS MARKET
This got started in July of 1986 and is a welcome addition to the Koloa area, since residents had to drive all the way to Lihue before. The market is on Monday, starting at noon at the ball park next to the Fire Station in Koloa. One must be on time as things are sold off quickly.

BEACHES

KOLOA LANDING
To find, take the middle road where Poipu Rd. divides just past the Kukuiula Store and go over the little white bridge. Watch for a dirt road on the right. This is not really a beach, but if the ocean is calm and you are a confident swimmer, this is a good place for snorkeling. Often the dive shops bring people here for lessons or for certification. This is the spot where ships docked and cargo was loaded and unloaded in the early days.

POIPU BEACH PARK
With little doubt, this is the most popular beach on Kauai and for good reason. First, it is almost always sunny, and if a shower comes, do not panic and leave, just wait a bit and very likely the sun will return. Also, the facilities are excellent: picnic tables, rest rooms, showers, a store and a snack bar across the street. Then, the swimming and snorkeling is excellent. The best snorkeling is in the cove to the right, out around fifty feet. It is only three to five feet deep in most places and many varieties of fish can be seen. Surfing is out in front of the Poipu Beach Hotel.

BRENNECKE'S BEACH
Once known as the best body surfing beach is Hawaii, Brennecke's was damaged by Hurricane Iwa. It is, however, coming back and hopefully its reputation will be restored. It is located a hundred yards or so east of Poipu Beach Park.

SHIPWRECK
To get to this beach it is necessary to drive through Poipu Kai. Continue on Poipu Rd. into Poipu Kai past the main entrance to the Hyatt. You will see a beach access road to the beach between the hotel and the golf course that goes makai. Take this to the beach. Although this beach is beautiful and great for sunning, it is not so good for swimming. Many of the expert body surfers who once used Brennecke's now use Shipwreck. If you beach here do a little exploring east of the beach. There are some beautiful little coves along these cliffs. Look for the petroglyphs along these cliffs.

MAHAULEPU
To gain access to this beach one must get permission from McBride Co. by going to their office which is located on Highway 540 between Kalaheo and Hanapepe. It is located east of Shipwreck about three miles. Just continue on the cane road from Poipu Kai until you come to a road lined with power lines. Turn right. Do not take the forks to the right or the left. When this road turns sharply to the left, you are almost there. Drive straight ahead until you see a parking area. This is where the locals go to picnic and fish and enjoy a day of relaxing. There are no facilities so if you intend on staying, pack a lunch.

NIGHT LIFE

HYATT REGENCY
There is disco dancing every night.

POIPU BEACH HOTEL
After 9 p.m. there is a band for dancing. Since the band is not there every night, call ahead at 742-1681.

SHERATON HOTEL
Sometimes the Sheraton has entertainment but it is not on a regular basis so it is best to check in advance. They offer a luau with the usual show attached. 742-1661.

THE LIBRARY
On Wednesday night starting at 7 p.m. the library in Koloa shows a movie once a month. For time and date call 742-1635.

BRIDGE
Every Tuesday night starting at 7 p.m. there is a bridge game under the House of Seafood restaurant in Poipu Kai. It is a very low key game of Chicago or Country Bridge. You do not need a partner since if there is an odd number, they will make up a team of three or have the dummy play with the spare. Coffee is served. For more information call Carl Steinhart at 332-9610.

SPORTS

DIVE SHOPS
The Fathom Five Dive Shop in Koloa offers boat dives every day and they rent all kinds of equipment. There is also a little store at Poipu Beach that sells and rents equipment. 742-6991.

TENNIS
The only public court is on the left as you enter Koloa on the Tunnel of Trees Rd. The Kiahuna has courts for $15 per person per day depending on how busy they are, 742-9533. Poipu Kai also has courts at $6 a person a day, court rules. It is best to call ahead to reserve a court (742-6464). They also rent racqets for $5 each (742-6464). Also, there is a court at Poipu Sands in the Poipu Kai development that is seldom used. The new Hyatt Hotel is open to the public, $20 per person for one hour with complimentary use of the ball machine and racquets.

HORSEBACK RIDING
A new and welcome addition to the Poipu area. For reservations and information call CJM Country Stables, 742-6096. There are all sorts of rides available, from a one hour scenic ocean ride for $27 to weddings and celebrations on horseback at quoted prices.

GOLF

You can't miss the Kiahuna Golf Course as you drive down Poipu Rd. The fee is $70. Carts are included and mandatory and they have recently changed to cart paths only. From what we have seen you will not have much trouble getting a starting time. There is a twilight rate starting at 2 pm for $45. For more information call 742-9595. By far the best course in the area is the new Hyatt Poipu Bay Resort Course. The fee is higher, $115, but in our opinion it is worth the difference. Players have full free use of the driving range which is excellent. It is all around first class. For a starting time call 742-9489.

WATER ACTIVITIES

More and more sea trips are being offered and we do not list them all. When you arrive on Kauai you will find their flyers on any of the Information Racks. If you need more information or would like to book in advance any activity on Kauai, be sure to call our office and have one of our staff take care of all the details. With them taking care of the details, all you need worry about is having a great vacation.

A REMINDER
Poipu Beach is a very safe
place to swim or snorkel.
Shipwreck Beach, which fronts the Hyatt,
is in our opinion less safe.
Keep in mind that the ocean
is very unforgiving
to those who do not
treat her with respect.

For all your travel needs,
call or write to
BED & BREAKFAST HAWAII
PO BOX 449
KAPAA, HI. 96746
808-822-77711
800-733-1632
FAX 808-822-2723

KALAHEO

Kalaheo, a quiet residential community, is little visited by tourists since there are seemingly no attractions in this area. However, we will be pointing out several things we feel all visitors should see, and since these will take you off the the main highway, we suggest you take a little time and enjoy the scenery.

When you get to the center of Kalaheo, turn makai on Papalina St. and go up the hill until you see Puu Street on the right. This road will take you through some of the residential and farm area of Kalaheo and will return back to Papalina St. at the entrance to the Kukuiolono Golf Course. Along this drive you will get some good views of the south Kauai Coast, all the way to Niihau, the so-called Forbidden Island.

When you reach Papalina St., if you turn left you will return to the main highway. If you turn right and go down the hill you will come to Waha Rd., where a left turn will take you to Lauoho where a right turn will take you back to the road that runs between Koloa and the main highway. Most of the locals who drive from the Poipu-Koloa area use this road as a short cut to the golf course.

RESTAURANTS

LOCAL STYLE

LAWAI RESTAURANT
This is located on the main highway just before you come to Kalaheo, in the town of Lawai. The owners of this restaurant used to run the Waipouli Chop Suey in Kapaa. The food is Cantonese style, moderately priced (most dishes under $5), and in our opinion pretty tasty. As in most local style restaurants, it is possible to get Japanese dishes also. The atmosphere is local.

local Style

THE BREAD BOX BAKERY
While this is not a restaurant, we mention it for those of you who really like great breads. It is located on Papalina Rd. across from the Kalaheo Steak House (see below). One must get there in the am as they usually sell out by noon.

MUSTARD'S LAST STAND
This is a little take-out place located at the junction of the main highway and the Koloa Rd. To find it you must pull off the main road and head toward the Poipu area or else be driving from the Poipu area. The specialty here is all kinds of sausages, bratwurst, knackwurst, or Polish.

BRICK OVEN PIZZA
If you like pizza be sure to eat here. Maybe we have been in Hawaii too long, but we think this is the best pizza we have ever had anywhere. Try their whole wheat pizza with the garlic rubbed crust, topped with Portuguese Sausage. They have recently opened in a new building across the street from their old location. They are now in the first commercial building on the right as one enters Kalaheo from Lihue.

KALAHEO STEAK HOUSE
Back in the '70's one of the more popular local eating spots was the Steak House. Nothing fancy, mind you, but good food for a good price. They closed in 1982 and four or five restaurants have tried to make a success at the same location with out any luck. But since they have reopened they have been very successful and we think it is one of the best values on Kauai: Cornish game hen for $11.50, Top Sirloin $14.50, or a bucket of clams $5.95. They are open only for dinner from 5 to 9 pm.

CAMP HOUSE GRILL
The specialty of the house is Broasted Chicken, which they call Huli Huli Chicken. It is a bit spicy but very good and you can't beat the price, around $5.95. The highest priced item on the menu is the 9 oz. steak for $9.95. They are open for breakfast, lunch, and dinner. You can't miss seeing the place since it is right on the highway.

POINTS OF INTEREST

KUKUIOLONO GOLF COURSE
Be sure to visit here whether you golf or not. The Japanese garden here is delightful. Nowhere on Kauai, unless you climb Sleeping Giant, will you get better views, from the Poipu shoreline all the way to Kekaha and Niihau beyond. This year they have added a small snack bar where one can get a good sandwich, nothing fancy but a great place to enjoy the view. The gate closes at 6:30 p.m., so if you are there to watch the sunset, keep one eye on the clock or you may spend the night.

OLU PUA GARDENS
Located about a half mile beyond Kalaheo on the mauka side of the main highway. There are guided walking tours every day on the 1/2 hour starting at 9:30 and ending at 1:30. The tour lasts an hour and the charge is $10 for adults and $5 for children. Inquire about special events such as weddings. For information call 332-8182.

PACIFIC TROPICAL BOTANICAL GARDENS
This is a guided tour by appointment only on Mondays, Tuesdays, and Thursday starting at 8, 9, 10:30 and 11:30. The charge is $10.00. Since part of the tour is by Jeep on narrow dirt roads, the tours are called off if it is rainy. For more information call 332-8131.

SPORTS

GOLF
If Wailua isn't the best deal for golf then Kukuiolono is. It is a nine hole course and not quite as nice as the other courses on the Island, but it is still a challenge. As stated above, the setting and the views make one forget the dubbed drive or the missed putt. Daily green fees are $5, but for those on extended stays, a yearly ticket can be purchased for $100 which allows unlimited play. For more information call 332-9151.

HANAPEPE

The last time we updated our book, we received quite a shock as we drove in to Hanapepe to see what was new. We did a very large double take, for right before us was a new night club offering dancing girls and private booths. What was even worse was that on either side were smaller clubs offering the same thing. What, we mused, was Kauai and the previously sleepy little town of Hanapepe up to? One expects to see this kind of thing on Hotel St. in Honolulu, but in Hanapepe? Have no fear, Kauai has not gone to the dogs, yet. Hollywood hot shots were just giving Hanapepe's main street a face lift for a new movie being made partly on Kauai. Nor is this the only movie being shot on Kauai. It seems as if Kauai's charm and beauty is being discovered by the movie moguls. The curious thing is that they always seem to want to make Hanapepe older and funkier than normal and we locals would never have dreamed it possible.

As you drive in to Hanapepe, just as the road forks, look to the right, up the hill, and you will see a rainbow of bougainvillaea. (We must point out that this year the bougainvillaea was sparse due to the lack of rain). Hanapepe is a most colorful little town, in more ways than one. When we first moved to Kauai in 1979, Koloa looked about the way Hanapepe looks now. We would not be surprised in the next few years to see Hanapepe targeted for the kind of renewal and development that has been going on and continues to go on in Koloa. At one time, when pineapple was king, it was a thriving, bustling community with several hotels, a movie house, and even a taxi service. All of the buildings, some now in a state of disrepair, housed profitable businesses.

While not quite the same since the demise of the pineapple industry on Kauai, Hanapepe is not dead yet. A few years back it was used by the makers of *The Thorn Birds* as the setting for the honeymoon scene. If you look to your left just after you enter town and start to round the first corner, you will see the Dungloe Hotel, which formed the main scene. As you drive through town, keep in mind that the movie makers had to work hard to make Hanapepe look older.

There are several art galleries in town. One is located in the hotel mentioned above and is owned and operated by James Hoyle, a local artist of some note. Over the years several new galleries have opened, and this year we counted six on just one street of little Hanapepe: McLaren Woodwook, Dawn M. Traina, Lele Aka, Andy Lopez, and James Hoyle. Finding any of the galleries open at any given time is another matter. After all, these are artists first and business people second.

Whatever you do in Hanapepe, be sure to stop at the Feed Store located at the end of town after you cross the bridge. Shimonishi's is a grower of orchids, and if you walk behind the Feed Store you will see orchids of every size, color, and type. In fact, Mr. Shimonishi has created at least one new type of orchid, we have been told. Some, but not all, of the orchids are for sale, and you cannot beat the prices. Most of the orchids you see displayed at the hotels or for any special occasion come from Mr. Shimonishi.

The new rage in Hanapepe is Lappert's's Ice Cream, which is located on the main highway on the mauka side in the middle of Hanapepe. Now there are several outlets for this very tasty confection and we wouldn't be too surprised to see franchises popping up on the Mainland. At any rate, this might be a good place to stop for an afternoon refreshment.

One new shop we discovered several years ago that we found interesting was Longi's Crackseed, located right in the center of Hanapepe. We were very happy to see they are still serving up delicacies. Check this out especially if you have children along. It won't be a waste of time and you will discover a bit about Hawaiian culture.

RESTAURANTS

LOCAL STYLE

LINDA'S
In the center of Hanapepe on the makai side of the street. Open from 7-1:30 for breakfast and lunch, with breakfast served until 10 a.m. Good local food at low prices, a good spot for lunch either going to or coming from the Canyon. Closed Sunday

OMOIDE DELI & BAKERY
Located on the makai side of the highway across from Sinaloa (see below). This is a real chow-down place with food served cafeteria style. The food is Chinese, Cantonese style, where you can select three dishes with rice for around $5. They also make excellent pies.

local Style

SUZIE'S ALL KINE BURGER
Formerly Susie's Cafe, it is now under new management and serves all kinds of burgers, including mahi-mahi and chicken. They are open every day from 10:30-7:30 and their burgers are well priced; nothing over $5.

PORT ALLEN BAR AND GRILL
Located in the Eleele Shopping Center where the Pasta Pub used to be. We have not tried this place yet, but from the looks of they place it is pointed more toward locals than tourists, but one would not feel uncomfortable here. They are open for breakfast and lunch, except for the bar, which goes until midnight.

local/Tourist Style

SINALOA MEXICAN FOOD
Located on the mauka side of the highway. This place is new and when we tried it they were still in the process of making some changes. For example, when they opened they served food on paper plates. However, the night we were there they were trying out their new china. By the time this goes to press that, of course, will be standard. The food we had was very good and the prices were not too high. Also, they made a good margarita.

GREEN GARDEN
Probably more has been written about this restaurant than any other on Kauai, and it has long been a favorite with locals and tourists alike. They are open for breakfast, lunch, and dinner, closed Tuesday evening. There is a very nice garden atmosphere. Keeping in mind that this is considered a "tourist" restaurant, prices are not too high and the portions are ample. We have been getting some great reports lately, especially about their mahi mahi. One of their specialties is box lunches, called bento in Hawaii, for those who would like to picnic in the Kokee area, 335-5422.

ESPRESSO BAR
If you just want a snack or perhaps a waffle with real maple syrup, try this new little place located in the Hanapepe Book Store. They are open every day except Sunday from 7:30am to 6pm. They are strictly vegetarian.

POINTS OF INTEREST

HANAPEPE VALLEY LOOKOUT
After you pass Kalaheo and start toward Hanapepe, you will come to the lookout on the right. There is quite a bit of farming done in the Hanapepe Valley.

PORT ALLEN
To get to this turn makai at the Eleele Shopping Center and drive right out to the pier. Sometimes in the afternoon it is possible to buy a fresh fish from one of the local fishermen. Unfortunately, such times are getting very rare.

BEACHES

SALT POND

As you reach the west end of Hanapepe watch for a road on the makai side of the high-way with a sign for Salt Pond. About one-half mile down this road you will see a sign pointing to the right for Salt Pond Park. Swimming here is very safe. Rest rooms, showers, and picnic tables available.

WAIMEA/KEKAHA

It is from either Waimea or Kekaha that one goes to Waimea Canyon and Kokee State Park. Since both of these towns are mainly residential and not tourist oriented, spending a little time here gives the visitor a truer picture of life in Hawaii than some of the more familiar tourist areas. Waimea is the larger of the two, and you might find it interesting to walk around. Check the Thrift Store and you might get a great buy on an aloha shirt. You might also enjoy a picnic at the park located at the mouth of the Waimea River. To get there, turn left on Ala Wa just after you cross the bridge. Recently a small Pedi-cab business has opened up which gives an hour and a half tour for $50. They would have to pedal pretty slow to make a journey through Waimea last that long, but maybe that is the idea. After all, when you are in Paradise what's the hurry? We wish this new venture much success.

In Kekaha it is fascinating to watch the huge sugar cane trucks unloading at the Kekaha Sugar Mill. As the cane goes into the hopper, it is washed, and before it is ground it is washed again. What comes out the side and is dumped into the trucks is called bagasse and is used for cattle feed or for fertilizer. The syrup from the cane is processed into a brown sugar, unrefined, stored in a huge tank which you can see from the road. It is then sent to Lihue, where it is processed into molasses to be shipped to California for refining.

You may also enjoy browsing through Kauai's Hidden Treasures, a gift and curio shop, where you may find an Island souvenir. While it is a bit of a tourist trap and some-what garish, they do have Niihau shell necklaces at lower prices than you will see in the stores. The quality of Niihau shells varies greatly, however, and lower price is not always best value.

Isn't this area an amazing
contrast to the Hanalei area?
Here they do not get yearly
the amount of rain Hanalei gets monthly.
In the space of a few hours driving time
one goes from rain forest to desert.

RESTAURANTS

LOCAL STYLE

DA BOOZE SHOP
This used to be called Nothing Fancy, but, from what we could see, nothing has changed. They are open only for dinner and we have not had a chance to try it. What a great name, though. It is located just east of the Big Save Market in a little corner spot.

YUMI'S
In Waimea on the right side of the main highway if you are heading west toward Kekaha, just past the twenty-three (23) mile marker. The specialty here is home made apple, pineapple, and coconut turnovers, as good as we have eaten. Get there early as they usually sell out by noon. Also, the owner makes excellent sushi. All of the food is low priced.

BIG SAVE
In the Big Save Market. Local food, low priced, plate lunch specials.

THE GOODIE BARN
Not a full restaurant but a good place to have a hot dog and a bowl of chili or a Lappert's Ice Cream Cone. It is located at the far end of Kekaha on the inside road.

PASTRY SHOP
This is also not a restaurant but a good place to have a cup of coffee and a pastry. It is located in the center of Waimea on the makai side of the highway.

C & K CAFE
Next door to the Pastry Shop. Open for sandwiches from 11-3. All of their sandwiches are under $5.

local Style

TOI'S THAI
This fairly new Thai restaurant is located behind the Traveler's Den bar in Kekaha. The atmosphere is not much unless you like quaint, but the food is good if you like spicy and the prices are moderate. They are open every day except Saturday for lunch and dinner.

local/tourist

WRANGLERS RESTAURANT
Located in the center of Waimea on the makai side of the main highway. This is a new restaurant and from our experience there, it should be around for a long time. The menu is quite extensive, from plate lunch to Mexican to sandwiches, with very good deals on their plate lunch specials. Their dinner prices are for the most part under $10 with just a few over. 338-1218.

INTERNATIONAL MUSEUM CAFE
This is a most intriguing little place that adventurous people will want to check out. The menu is not extensive but they have imaginative dishes that should satisfy all but those who insist on meat and potatoes. Vegetarians will be delighted, but they have chicken and fish dishes also. They are open for breakfast, lunch, and dinner.

KOKEE RESTAURANT AND GIFT SHOP
Located above Waimea Canyon. They are open every day for breakfast and lunch from 8:30 to 1:30 and for dinners on Friday and Saturday. If you are going up to Waimea Canyon and you certainly should unless you have several times before, this is a good place to have lunch. Getting there for breakfast requires an early start from most places on Kauai.

POINTS OF INTEREST

KASHUBA FINE ARTS GALLERY
Located right in Waimea next to Da Booze Shop. They were not open when we passed through, but we peeked in the window and it looked interesting.

RUSSIAN FORT
Located just before you cross the Waimea River, you can't miss it. One needs a little imagination for this, as there is little left but piles of stone, attesting to the fact that the Russians tried for a foothold in Hawaii in the early 1800's. In actuality all of this was the work of one man, Georg Scheffer, an employee of the Russian American Co., who acted on his own without the sanction of the Russian Government.

MENEHUNE DITCH
You will see signs for this in the center of Waimea. Perhaps one needs an engineering degree to see the significance of this ditch, which runs along the Waimea river. Legend has it that the Menehunes built the ditch in one night. More fun to us is the little foot bridge which spans the Waimea River.

NIIHAU
No place on Hawaii causes more wonderment that the little island of Niihau, the so-called *Forbidden Island*. The simplest explanation for Niihau is that it is privately owned, hence visitors must be invited. In 1863 a family headed by a widow, Elizabeth Hutchinson Sinclair, bought the Island of Niihau for the price of $10,000. With her were her two daughters, Helen Robinson and Jean Gay. With Helen was her son Aubrey Robinson. Jean had married Thomas Gay, a widower with a five year old son. At the

time they purchased the Island, there were about 300 Hawaiians living on Niihau. The importance of this extended family on the history of Kauai is significant and too extensive to be covered here. A good book for further study would be *Kauai, A Separate Kingdom* by Edward Joesting, University of Hawaii Press and Kauai Museum Association, Limited. Now some 250 people, almost all pure Hawaiians, live here. There are no modern facilities: no T.V, washing machines, in fact no electricity. The children of Niihau are educated on Kauai and have the advantage of speaking both English and Hawaiian.

WAIMEA CANYON
Called *the Grand Canyon of the Pacific*, the beauty of the Waimea Canyon can hardly be over-stated. Take Canyon Rd. from Waimea and proceed up the mountain. Be sure to stop along the way before reaching the Canyon to enjoy the view of Kauai's west shore. From here you will get the best view of Niihau you are likely to get. There are two official lookout points where you park the car and walk to the lookout. Along the way there are several unofficial lookout spots, no guard rail, so be careful.

KOKEE STATE PARK
A little ways past the last Canyon lookout you will come to Kokee State Park, where there is a small restaurant, gift shop, and museum. From this point there are many hiking trails: out to the Na Pali coast overlook, into Alakai Swamp, to Waimea Canyon overlooks, and down into the Canyon. Or one can simply enjoy being around the Park, picnic on the lawn and watch the wild chickens cavort.

KALALAU LOOKOUT
Several miles past Kokee is the Kalalau Lookout. No matter how foggy it might be, spend a little time here. One of the most beautiful sights in Hawaii is the fog invading and retreating in Kalalau Valley. Too often visitors see the clouds and decide it is the wrong day, when just a little time later all the clouds might be gone.

BEACHES

There are beaches all along the south coast and they are little used except by surfers. The waves along here are big and rough and the undertow and rip tides can be extreme. Playing in the surf may be O.K. when it is not too rough, but swimming is very dangerous.

POLIHALE STATE PARK
To find, go to the end of Highway 50 and you will see a sign pointing to the left for Polihale. You will go about five miles on cane road but do not give up. You will end up at the Park. There are picnic tables, rest rooms, and shower facilities here but no food, so stop by in Kekaha or Waimea to buy food. The swimming is fairly safe in the summer months, but dangerous in winter or when the surf is up.

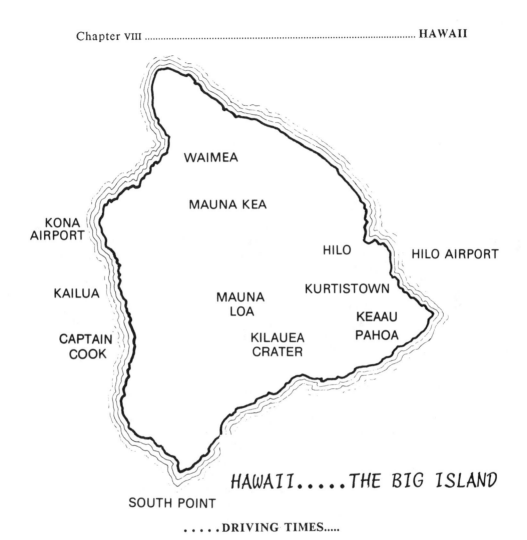

KONA
AIRPORT

WAIMEA

MAUNA KEA

HILO

HILO AIRPORT

KAILUA

MAUNA
LOA

KURTISTOWN

KEAAU
PAHOA

CAPTAIN
COOK

KILAUEA
CRATER

HAWAII.....THE BIG ISLAND

SOUTH POINT

.....DRIVING TIMES.....

From Hilo Airport-South: (approximate)

Kurtistown.....................12 miles, 20 minutes
Kilauea Volcano.............40 miles, 60 minutes
Kailua/Kona....................120 miles, 3.5 hours

From Hilo North:

Waimea............................63 miles, 1.5 hours
Kailua/Kona..................98 miles, 2.75 hours

HAWAII

the Big Island

Sometimes called the Orchid Isle or Volcano Island, but always referred to by residents of Hawaii as The Big Island, the island of Hawaii has about as much land mass as all of the other Islands combined. In some ways it is unfortunate that the State and the Island have the same name since tourists sometimes confuse Big Island with Main Island, which residents of Hawaii use to refer to Oahu. The Big Island has so much to offer that it puzzles us that it has not become the main destination point for tourists. A possible explanation for this is that the Big Island does not have as many white sand beaches as the other Islands. What often gets overlooked are the beautiful black sand beaches that abound on the Big Island and nowhere else in Hawaii. Yet, how often the comment is heard, "I could care less about going to Hawaii. Who wants to sit on a beach in the blazing sun and get skin cancer?" Too bad these people do not know about the Big Island that offers beaches but oh so much more.

As said above, Hawaii is the largest Island in the chain, and it is still growing. Two active volcanos, Mauna Loa and Kilauea, still spew out molten lava, which flows to the sea, building yet more land mass. This has really been striking over the last several years as lava has flowed down into the Kalapana area just west of Black Sand Beach and covered most of a small subdivision, closed the Chain of Craters Road, destroyed Queen's Bath and generally wreaked havoc. When one stands above the main caldera of Kilauea, even when the volcano is not at full steam, the view can only be described as awesome. When the lava is soaring thousands of feet in the air, the experience is unforgettable. Volcano National Park is truly one of the wonders of our Nation, and no visitor to the State of Hawaii should pass it by.

The Big Island is also the agricultural capital of the Islands, growing more sugar cane, papaya, macadamia nuts than the rest of the Islands combined. South of Hilo grows almost all of the anthuriums and orchids that Hawaii exports around the world. One need not go to a nursery to see orchids since fields of them grow wild in this area. On the Kona Coast, above Kailua Town, coffee grows in profusion, in fact, this is the only place in the U. S. where there are coffee plantations and along the Belt Road are several coffee processing and roasting places where one can stop and sample fresh brewed Kona coffee. Up at the north end of the Island there is the huge Parker Ranch, which is the largest privately owned cattle ranch in the U.S.

Over the last few years there has been extensive development in the Kohala area and more is anticipated. We have heard that a new hotel is planned for North Kohala, which few tourists have visited. The Waimea area has quite a bit of new development considering its size. There are several new shopping centers including the elegant Hale Kea, developed by the same people who did the Kilohana on Kauai.

Nowhere in the State is color more profuse and brilliant than on the Big Island. Stand on any tee at the Mauna Lani Golf Course to see jet black lava abut emerald green fairways dotted with white sand traps, and all of this along the bluest water imaginable, and if it is winter and the sky is clear, turn back to majestic Mauna Kea with its mantle of snow.

There are few places in the State where hiking is more spectacular, whether Volcano National Park, the gorges along the Hamakua Coast, up the slopes of Mauna Kea or Mauna Loa, through the Waipio Valley or Pololu Valley, or on the many trails behind Hilo Town.

However, it is not the size of Hawaii that makes it special. Maybe it is its diversity, for surely the contrasts are dramatic, from lush tropical rain forests to arid deserts, from rich fertile valleys to lava covered hillsides where pili grass and kiawe trees struggle to exist. We feel the Big Island is waiting to be discovered. Do yourself a favor, and no matter what you conceive Hawaii to be, set your course for the Big Island.

SPECIAL EVENTS

ANNUAL KILAUEA VOLCANO WILDERNESS MARATHON AND RIM RUNS (LATE JANUARY)
A 26.2 mile run that crosses the Ka'u desert and several other shorter runs. For more information call Phyllis Segawa at 9676-7676.

ANNUAL DR. RICHARD T. MAIYA GOLF TOURNAMENT (EARLY FEBRUARY)
A benefit for the Heart Association using the two man best ball format, held at Sea Mountain Golf Course, call 538-7021.

ANNUAL SADDLE ROAD RELAY AND ULTRAMARATHON (EARLY MARCH)
A 62.1 mile run across the rugged Saddle Road going from sea level to 6,500 feet back to 2,670, call 826-6981.

ANNUAL ALMOST GOLDEN LOBSTER HUNT (APRIL)
Scuba divers and snorklers look for a metal slipper lobster sculpture and colored lead weights for cash prizes, 329-8802.

MERRIE MONARCH FESTIVAL (MIDDLE TO LATE APRIL)
A week of hula competitions and festivities including a Royal Court appearance, arts, crafts, exhibits, musical entertainment and more. Tickets must be purchased well in advance. Call 808-935-9168.

'ILUNA LILO'MAUNA LOA HIKE (EARLY JUNE)
Experts only climb to summit cabin on Mauna Loa, call 935-9763.

HAWAII HIGH SCHOOL ASSOC. STATE RODEO FINALS (EARLY JUNE)
Culmination of monthly rodeos from all Islands, with winners going to the mainland to compete. Held at Paniolo Park, Waimea, 935-1191.

PUUHONUA O HONAUNAU ANNUAL CULTURAL FESTIVAL (LATE JUNE EARLY JULY)
Opens with the presentation of the Royal Court followed by three days of Hawaiian craft making workshops, hula, Hawaiian food tasting and a hukilau, held at Puuhonua O Honaunau National Park, call 328-2326.

KA 'IMA NA'AUAO O HAWAII NEI (JULY)
Hula performance at Volcano Art Center, 967-7179.

OHANA MUSIC FEST (JULY)
Big Island entertainers, games, pony rides, helicopter rides, a farmer's market and more, held at Paniolo Park, Waimea, 885-7987.

ANNUAL HILO ORCHID SOCIETY SHOW (EARLY JULY)
Butler Building, Affok-Chinen Civic Auditorium, Hilo, 935-5585.

ANNUAL BIG ISLAND BONSAI SHOW (EARLY JULY)
Wailoa Center, Hilo, 967-7360.

ANNUAL KARAOKE FESTIVAL FINALS (AUGUST)
Amateur singers and dancers performing in English the tradintional and modern Japanese folk songs to the accompaniment of pre-recorded music. Civic Auditorium, Hilo, 935-0505.

ESTABLISHMENT DAY CULTURAL FESTIVAL (MIDDLE AUGUST)
Annual festival offering ancient hula and workshops in lei making, Hawaiian lannguage, and other ancient skills, held in Kawaihae at the Pu'ukohola Heiau.

HAWAII STATE HORTICULTURAL SHOW (MIDDLE AUGUST)
Held at the Edith Kanakaole Multi-Purpose Stadium in Hilo, 968-6174.

10 TH ANNUAL KEIKI (KIDS) FISHING TOURNAMENT (LATE AUGUST)
A charity fundraiser
held at Kailua, Kona, 322-3823.

FROZEN PEAS BIATHOLON (EARLY SEPTEMBER)
A one mile swin and 10 K run open to atheletes of all levels, both individuals and relay teams, masks and snorkels allowed, 7:30 am at the Kailua Pier in Kailua Kona, 329-2023.

PARKER RANCH ROUND-UP RODEO (EARLY SEPTEMBER)
Cowboys Statewide participate at Paniolo Park, Waimea, 885-7311.

HAWAII COUNTY FAIR (LATE SEPTEMBER)
Old time country fair with food, music, and rides, held at Kailua, Kona, 329-6574.

ANNUAL INTERNATIONAL TRIATHALON (IRON MAN COMPITITION)
We almost left this out and we did leave it out which is unforgivable since this is one of the big events on the Big Island. We believe it is held in October, but we do not have time to verify since this is being typed just moments before this book goes to press.

ANNUAL KONA NIGHTINGALE RACE (OCTOBER)
A donkey race and other fun activities held at the Keauhou Shopping Center Field, 3293624.

ANNUAL WEST HAWAII MAKAHIKI FESTIVAL (OCTOBER)
A festival of Hawaiian games, goods, a parade, and musical entertainment, based on the ancient makahiki harvest time, held at Keaukou, Kona.

ANNUAL KONA COFFEE FESTIVAL (NOVEMBER)
Celebratesd harvest of only U.S. commercially grown coffee, held at Kailua, Kona, 325-7998.

FOOTSTEPS OF KAMEHAMEHA (NOVEMBER)
A tour for children and other interested groups through some of Hawaii's ancient sites including King Kamehameha's birthplace and Mo'okini heiaum a 1,500 year old temple, held at North Kohala, 337-5554.

YWCA FESTIVAL OF TREES (MIDDLE NOVEMBER)
Christmas crafts, ornaments, and decorated trees on display and for sale, held YWCA in Hilo, 935-7141.

**WE KNOW WE HAVE FAILED TO INCLUDE
SOME SPECIAL EVENTS
THAT YOU MAY HAVE ATTENDED AND
WOULD LIKE TO BRING TO OUR ATTENTION!
PLEASE DO. WRITE
B & B HAWAII
BOX 449
KAPAA, HI 96746
OR CALL 808-822-7771**

HAWAII HOSTS

HILO AREA

H-1
A large Hawaiian type home about two miles north of Hilo on the cliff overlooking Hilo Bay, this home has a yard so private that if you decide to take a swim in the lovely pool, only the birds will know. There are two bedrooms available, each with twin beds, both of which convert to king if desired, and for the B & B guests there are one and a half baths. Not only is the yard beautifully landscaped around the pool, there is a lovely mile walk past the surfing beach through the tropical forest.
RATES: $50 single, $55 double with $5 premium for less than 3 nights.

H-1A
This host home is located right next door to the one above and guests are more than welcome to use the pool. The home is perched on the cliffs overlooking Hilo Bay and the Big Island's premiere surfing spot. The house is small and guests can choose between the Honolii Room with private entrance and queen sized bed or the Hilo Room with two twin beds. The bathroom is shared between the rooms. The best part of the house is the outdoor patio where breakfast is served. Guests can enjoy watching sunrise, surfers, ships passing by on their way to Hilo Harbor and at night the city lights and the moonlight on Hilo Bay through the palm trees. The hostess also works part time in Volcano Park. The hosts' aim is to provide rest and tranquility to all their guests.
RATES: $45 single, $50 double, $5 premium for less than three nights.

H-2
"Hale Paliku" which means "House against the Cliff" is the name of this home originally built in the 1930's. Situated just three blocks from Downtown Hilo, guests enter through the lattice-enclosed front porch and breakfast room. Glass double doors invite guests into the living room where they are greeted with a spectacular view of Hilo Bay. Guests share the TV, tape deck, microwave and refrigerator. Two rooms are available for guests. The Mauka room has two long-twin beds, while the Makai has a king size bed with ocean and mountain views and private balcony. Each room has down pillows, comforters, shuttered windows and table for two. The shared bathroom displays an old fashioned brass shower with tub and double sinks. Hosts live downstairs in their own part of the house.
RATES: $55 Twin Room, $65 King Room.

H-3

Relax on a grand scale in this large, modern, Hawaiian style home, surrounded by nearly four acres of park like setting, on an ocean front bluff with a spectacular view of Wailea Bay. This is the perfect spot for anyone desiring a peaceful haven away from the cares of the world, yet close enough to everything to be convenient. A tennis court and a municipal beach park is within walking distance and the world famous Akaka Falls is just a short drive away. The accommodation is a separate one bedroom apartment, containing over a thousand square feet of space with a separate entrance. It includes a spacious bedroom (equipped with a queen sized bed), a private bath (shower only), a fully equipped kitchenette, a large living room with cable TV, a radio, a piano, and two day beds. This is a perfect accommodation for a small family. The host and hostess have lived in Hawaii all their lives and can offer valuable information on where to go and what to see on the Big Island.
RATES: $75 single or double, $20 for each additional adult.

H-3A

A charming little beach front cottage surrounded by swaying coco palms awaits guests. There is a nice beach and boat launch for guests to explore in a quiet, private setting. Guests can enjoy sitting out on the big lanai with ocean view or sitting on the rocks dangling their toes in the water while watching fisherman and sail boats pass by. The accommodation offers a room with twin beds and a private bath down the hall. Breakfast is served in the dining room by your hostess, who fell in love with the area. She is in real estate and has a dog. Two night minimum. Smoking outside, only, please.
RATES: $75 single or double.

H-4C

This B & B guest cottage on a lush tropical 9 acre estate is located just four miles south of Hilo Airport and just 20 minutes from Kilauea Volcano. The palm lined driveway takes you through a lovely macadamia nut orchard to the main house with the guest cottage 100 yards away. Guests enjoy a secluded private setting. The architect designed one bedroom cottage is fully furnished, has enough cooking equipment for the preparation of light meals. King bed, color cable TV and a glass fireplace for cool winter nights. An additional fold out bed is available in the living area. Continental breakfast is supplied and guests dine at their leisure. Accommodates four. Children are welcome. Three night minimum
RATE: $65 double, $10 per day extra for adults, $10 flat rate per child for entire stay. Long term rates available.

H-5

A charming B&B host home that offers guests views of Hilo Bay and Hilo town just 10 minutes for the airport and 10 minutes to Richardson Beach. Guests are offered a choice of rooms. Honokuhio room: Private entrance, King sized bed, ocean view, private bath with dressing room. Ehu'hoe Room: Private entrance, Antique four poster double bed, ocean view, private bath with a shower. Breakfasts are always a delight and are usually served in the breakfast nook or dining room tastefully furnished with antiques. Smoking outside, only. Children over 8 are welcome.
RATES: $65 single or double, $15 extra for child in the same room.

H-7

Right on a bluff overlooking the ocean, the home offers an ocean front pool with jacuzzi and a view of Hilo Bay. Large, covered, comfortably furnished decks face the ocean where you can watch the whales and cruise ships. This modern home, which was used for the University of Hawaii for display to raise scholarship funds and also by 20th Century Fox producer while filming the "Black Widow", is just 2 miles from downtown Hilo but quiet and private. Three accommodations are offered downstairs separated by a family room for guests' exclusive use complete with a TV and VCR plus a private entrance to the pool. Rooms #1 #2 are large and each have a King sized bed with adjoining private bath. Room #3, is smaller but nice with queen bed and sliding doors to the outside. The private bath is across the hall. Upstairs, the loft bedroom has a side window that overlooks the ocean, there is a private bathroom and queen bed. All rooms have cable TV. Your hostess is friendly, is a good cook and knows the island well. Your host is a native Hawaiian who can be induced to play the ukulele. Also on the property and attached to the main house is a Guest Cottage that can sleep three comfortably as it has one bedroom with a queen bed and a sofa bed in the living room area. This cottage has a kitchenette and private bathroom. Guests can either join the hosts for breakfast or have the fixings for breakfast provided.
RATES: Room #1 #2: $95 double, Room #3: $90, Loft: $85 Three night minimum. Guest Cottage: $105 single or double, $15 extra person. Five night minimum.

H-8

Paradise Place is on a rural acre just 1/2 mile from the ocean with views of Mauna Kea, the steaming volcano and tropical gardens. Accommodations are on the ground floor with private entrance and private bath with shower. The bedroom has a queen size bed and TV/VCR. There is a kitchenette with a full size fridge, microwave, coffee maker and a washer/dryer. The living room has a TV and queen size sofa bed. Your friendly host travels throughout Micronesia and has brought back many artifacts that decorate the rooms. Also included is a hammock, Ping Pong table, barbecue and picnic table. Centrally located to Volcanoes National Park and Hilo area attractions.
RATES: $50 single, $55 double. Stay 6 nights, get the 7th free.

H-33

A rain forest retreat just south of Hilo is waiting next to an orchid nursery. Your hostess tends the orchids and boards horses on her property as well as accommodating B&B guests in two different accommodations on her property: a private studio complete with king sized bed, private bath and light cooking appliances (refrigerator, hot plate, toaster oven) in the dining area is attached to the hosts main house with it's own private entrance. Or choose the Ohia house which is on the grounds of the orchid nursery and totally separate from the main house. It's fully equipped with a complete kitchen with microwave, king and queen sized beds, futons, has open beam ceilings and a large hot tub on the deck. This retreat is only 30 minutes from Hilo and Volcano National Park in a restful setting on 8 acres off the beaten path (gravel road) surrounded by native ohia forest and wild orchids. One night stays are accepted.
RATES: Studio: $45 single, $55 double. Ohia house: $60 single or double, $10 each additional person. $5 extra for one nighters. Three nights or more $5 discount per night.

H-45
This attractive two-story home in Keaau is designed with the idea of seeing as much as possible of the lovely gardens and ocean view. It is close to the highway and is 15 miles from Hilo and 24 miles from the Volcano. Accommodations include two bedrooms with twin beds and one private bath. A delicious breakfast is served in the dining room. No smokers, please.
RATES: $50 single or double.

H-42
Nestled in Leilani Estates in Pahoa, hosts offer two studios on their one acre property which has a swimming pool, abundant fruit trees and flowers and wild turkeys, wild pigs and squabbing pigeons. The studios can accommodate the handicapped. Each unit offers a Simmons Beautyrest queen sized bed, private bath, air conditioning, TV, radio, private patio, refrigerator stocked with goodies (cheeses, jelly, juices, soda, milk, coffee, tea, cereals, sweetbreads and butter.) Hosts were at one time Hoteliers on the mainland and aim to please.
RATES: $65 single or double, Two night minimum.

H-64
This is private cottage is attached to the main house only by a breezeway. Hosts love to garden and they keep their spacious grounds looking lush and beautiful. Just outside the private entrance to the cottage is a lanai with garden views. Inside there is a queen sized bed and private bath with tub and shower. A little kitchenette has a full sized fridge, stove and microwave. TV with VCR. Hosts can provide a double rollaway bed for a third person. Guests may use the above ground swimming pool.
RATES: $50 single, $60 double, $15 for third person.

VOLCANO

H-51
Conveniently located just two miles from Volcano National Park at 3500 ft elevation, helpful hosts offer a king sized bedroom with it's own entrance and private bath. A futon can be put down for a third person. Your hostess knows the latest Volcano information. Great breakfasts are served every morning to get you off to a good start for exploring the park. One stays accepted at $5 premium.
RATES: $45 single, $60 double, $20 extra person.

H51 Cottages
Also available to guests are the hosts' cottages. Guests still check in with hosts at their home and then are given the keys, the fridge and kitchens are always loaded with breakfast fixings, more than enough for a stay. The Dome: a dome-shaped guest cottage on the golf course with two bedrooms and two baths, fireplace and panoramic views of Mauna Loa. The Cedar One: a cozy two bedroom, two bath cedar cottage with full kitchen or choose The Grand Cedar: Brand new, a deluxe 2 bedroom, 2 1/2 bath and huge loft with five futons. The Master bedroom has a queen sized four poster bed and private bath with a whirlpool tub.

The other bedroom has twin beds and private bath. There is a half bath for the loft. Beautifully furnished, fireplace, TV with VCR, stereo. The Cedar Two: this one is great for reunions, groups or just a twosome. 3 bedrooms, choice of king, queen or twin beds, 2 bathrooms, huge living room with fireplace, 3 queen sized sofa beds in the living room area, plus a full kitchen.

RATES: Grand Cedar $125 double, $20 each additional person; Cedar Two $95 double, $20 each additional person. Cedar One and Dome $85 double, $20 each additional person.

HONOKAA/WAIPIO AREA

H-11

The hostess/caretaker of this large plantation estate enjoys having guests share the beauty, tranquility, warmth and friendship. With ocean views on three sides the estate is built on an ocean point at the 1200 foot level just outside of Honokaa which is 39 miles north of Hilo and on the way to Waimea/Kamuela, just about 8 miles from the Waipio Valley. Guests and friends have said it reminds them of being on the Robin Masters estate on Magnum PI, although it's the wrong island! The 5,000 sq.ft. main house offers guests three individual accommodations: the large suite with one room having a King size bed, adjoining a double bedded room via private bath between. The king room has one entire wall in mirrors, fireplace color TV, and private lanai. The bathroom is spectacular with an oval tub for two surrounded by mirrors and candles, a beautiful shower, two sinks and a panoramic ocean view. Also in the main house are two Queen bedrooms, one in many colors of blue; the other is done in royal colors of yellow and red. Both of these rooms offer a color TV and private bathroom. Twelve foot ceilings, T&G woodwork throughout. A den with color TV, wet bar, satellite control, adjoins the billiards/library overlooking the formal lawn and the ocean. Also there are three cottages on the property: HALE KONA sleeps four, one private bedroom, full bathroom, living area with two day beds, small kitchen, color TV. HALE HILO cottage can sleep six, one bedroom has a king sized bed, the other bedroom has two single beds, the living area has a couch that opens into a double bed, color TV, full bathroom, dining area and full kitchen. HALE MAUKA cottage, one bedroom with a queen sized bed, full bathroom, kitchen, dining room, living room with two day beds, sleeps four, large private lanai. Regulation lighted tennis courts with viewing gazebo, Macadamia orchard, fruit trees and lush tropical flowers throughout the estate. No smoking in any of the accommodations. Smoking outside is OK. High chair and portable crib available for guest cottages.

RATES: Hale Hilo: $75 double. Hale Kona and Mauka: $90 double, $15 each extra person. Suite: $140 double, $15 extra person. Queen Rooms: $105 double, $15 extra per person.

H-22

Step back in time and experience the gracious hospitality of a 1938 sugar plantation home, renovated and redecorated to preserve the character of old Hawaii. It provides a relaxing and peaceful retreat, catering to those who wish to unwind in a warm and comfortable atmosphere. Each bedroom is decorated with antique furniture, Chinese rugs, and exquisite hand-painted silk drapes done by a local artist. Choose the Moon Room with a full sized bed which shares the bathroom with the Plantation Room, which has twin beds. A private bath as well as a separate entrance is featured in the spacious Bird's Eye Room. Breakfast includes pure Kona coffee and fine Stash teas.

RATES: $85 single or double.

WAIMEA/KAMUELA AREA

H-27A

This host and hostess have a 4000 square foot home and have used about 800 feet of it for a completely separate apartment for B & B guests. Guest quarters include a bedroom, private full bathroom, a living room. The apartment also has a sink and a small fridge. The home borders a stream and has a 360 degree view of the Kohala Mountains, Pacific Ocean, and the famous Mauna Kea and Mauna Loa.
RATE: $80 one rate, $10 for each additional person, three night minimum.

H-41

In the historic area of North Kohala just about seven miles from lush Pololu Valley and the rugged coastline of beautiful Hawi, guests can enjoy the rural atmosphere and cooler climate. The home is set back from the road and is a modified A-frame. Accommodations include a self contained studio under the main house with a separate entrance, limited kitchenette, private bath and double bed. Hostess is originally from Honolulu and her husband hails from Connecticut. No smoking in the unit, please. This is a real get away spot.
RATES: $50 single or double. Two night minimum.

H-43

Still the best kept secret in the Big Island, this area above Waimea (Kamuela) is very peaceful and rural. Situated in Hawi, this b&b is a large 89 year old house set back in a secluded, rural landscape. This older style home with dining room and large living room and refreshing lanai provide a quiet atmosphere. The accommodations include two bedrooms with a private bath between. The smaller of the two rooms offers a separate entrance and double bed, while the other is larger and can sleep three with double bed plus a day bed. The hosts welcome children, however, will not accept smokers. They have outside pets, two cats and a dog.
RATES: $45 single or double, $6 children under 12 in larger room. One night stays are welcome.

H57

Newly built guest house with 1900 square feet of space and located at the top of Knob Hill. Just walking distance to Kamuela town and a fifteen minute drive from resorts and beaches. A beautiful view of Mauna Kea and Mauna Loa and Mt. Hualalai as well as about 25 miles of coastline. Since the accommodation borders Parker Ranch it is extremely peaceful and quiet. Country elegance on a private estate, this is a completely furnished two story house. It is ideal for a couple and can accommodate more guests as there is a a bed on each floor. First floor: Full kitchen, dining room, library, bedroom with queen bed, full bathroom with double sinks, tile and shower, washer/dryer. Second Floor: Open beam ceilings and large living room with color TV, king sized bed, fireplace and 300 square foot deck with views.
RATES: $125 single or double, $20 extra person. Three night minimum.

H-62

This B&B is part of a Swiss Chalet-style home just 3 1/2 miles outside of Kamuela and only 12 minutes from Hapuna Beach. Your hosts built their home in 1988 after 10 years of searching for this tranquil, majestic setting and look forward to sharing their knowledge and the beauty of this desirable area of the Big Island with guests. Accommodations consist of a two bedroom apartment. Each bedroom has a queen sized bed. There is one bathroom, a living room with a fireplace, TV and telephone. Breakfast is provided each morning and since there is a full kitchen, guests can cook. Enjoy views of Mauna Kea from the private sun deck. Three night minimum preferred.
RATES: $55 single, $65 double; Two couples $95; Family with two children $85

H-63

A detached studio apartment with private bath and kitchenette. Hosts own an eight acre lot at 1500 ft elevation above and three miles from Hawi. Hosts grow a variety of local fruit, ornamental and flowering plants which attract all kinds of birds, especially cardinals. The view is unobstructed to the ocean and across Alenuihaha channel to Haleakala on Maui. A perfect spot to distance yourself from the complexities of our civilization. Two rustic buildings built in 1977, are on the property, one is the main house and the other, 75 feet away, is for guests. The studio is furnished with a double bed and sofa bed, color TV, and radio. Sliding glass doors face the view. The kitchen is fully equipped for preparing all meals and breakfast fixings are stocked in the fridge. Non smokers only, please. Hosts can accommodate more guests if needed. Hosts can speak Swiss, German and French and spend their vacation time in Kirkland, WA and Switzerland.
RATES: $50 single, $55 double, $25 extra for adults, $20 extra for children under 16 yrs. $10 extra for one night stays.

KAILUA/KONA AREA

H-10

These friendly, warm-hearted hosts have a spacious home in Kailua Kona. It is surrounded by tropical foliage and yet about a five minute drive to the ocean. The downstairs accommodation offered includes a private lanai that looks out to the ocean with a separate entrance through sliding glass doors to the bedroom. Inside is a king size bed with a private full bath. The room is large and has a mini-refrigerator for storing cold drinks, a microwave for snacks plus TV and phone. The hosts serve a tasty continental breakfast either upstairs or downstairs. No smoking, please. Two night minimum.
RATES: $50 single, $65 double.

H-15

In a large homey residence on a hillside neighborhood of Kailua Kona guests are offered a bedroom with queen size bed and private bath. The view from the bedroom looks out over an exotic flower garden including gardenia, roses, night blooming jasmine and beyond that the expansive coastline of Kona. Fresh fruits from the garden are usually served in the sunny breakfast room or on the deck. These enthusiastic hosts are retired and devote their energies to their homes and their guests. Smoking outside, please. Hosts have a cat. Two night minimum.
RATES: $55 single or double.

H-23

Enjoy some Kona coffee and macadamia nuts while soaking in the hot tub on the lanai of this all cedar home. Marvel at the breathtaking ocean view surrounded by papayas, bananas and tropical flowers! The location, at 1600 ft, provides both guest rooms with cool breezes for happy sleeping. Each room has private bath, cable TV, microwave, refrigerator and coffeemaker. A hearty breakfast is served. The guest wing has its own entrance. The Hula Room with queen bed has a private, large lanai. The Garden Room is available with twin beds or a king bed. Two night minimum.
RATES: Hula Room $55 single or double, Garden Room $50 single or double, Weekly rates available.

H-26

Escape to the peaceful hillside of Hualalai Mountain, overlooking the beautiful Kona coast, to the lovely 2500 sq. ft. custom home of this host and hostess. The interior is meticulously furnished and quite spacious in its design. The B & B guest quarters are on the first level and have two bedrooms, one with king sized bed and the other with twin beds, private full bathroom and a complete kitchen and living area. There is a large deck for guests' exclusive use with a hot tub. The view here is magnificent. The hostess provides her guests with breakfast fixings since she and her husband leave for work early in the morning. They do, however, have plenty of time for getting acquainted and love to answer questions you might have about the Big Island. Both hosts have lived in Hawaii for many years and are there to share their aloha spirit with you. Two night minimum.
RATES: $55 single, $65 double, $15 each additional person.

H-29

Guests can stay in this peaceful B&B just 2 miles from the middle of Kailua-Kona town and the ocean. A large covered lanai offers ocean views and comfortable seating for breakfast. The accommodation is furnished with twin beds that can convert to king size and a private bath. Your hosts are originally from Santa Barbara, California and moved to Kona in 1989. They both work in Kona and enjoy meeting new people. Non smokers only, please.
RATES: $40 single, $55 double.

H-32A

Right on the beach in Kona! A luxurious and comfortable home where you can lounge in a hammock beneath palm trees, be served Kona coffee on the ocean front lanai and be lulled to sleep at night by the sound of the ocean. Two rooms are offered, one faces the ocean and has sliding glass doors out to a covered lanai. The other room has ocean view, although it does not face the ocean. Both are furnished with queen sized bed and TV and each has it's own full private bath with tub and shower. Host loves to play tennis and enjoys sharing her world with guests. Non smokers only, please.
RATES: Ocean Front Room $90, Partial Oceanview Room $70.

H-34

Located just 12 minutes from the airport and 15 minutes from Kailua Village in the cool Kaloko Mauka area is this beautiful new home on 5 acres. It offers an attractive separate apartment at garden level with two bedrooms (one double, one twin), bath and sitting room with TV and limited cooking facilities. Guests may choose to breakfast with their hosts or on their own. Non smokers please. The hosts have lived in the islands some 35 years and spent several years in the Orient. Their favorite sport is golf. After a busy day of sports, shopping or sightseeing come to cool Kaloko, sit on your lanai high above the Kona coast, with a magnificent sunset. There are well behaved pets. (1 dog, 2 cats) and several llamas.
RATES: $75 single or double, $25 each additional person. Two night minimum.

H-44

A charming guest cottage awaits guests just 1/12 miles above Kailua Bay and Village. Guests can relax in the private courtyard with a lovely garden view all nicely landscaped including a BBQ. Through sliding glass doors, the one bedroom cottage offers a bedroom with queen sized bed and private bath. The kitchenette offers a full refrigerator, microwave, coffee pot, toaster oven and blender. Great for a small family, the living room offers a queen sized hideabed. All the furnishings are brand new and include a color TV with VCR plus a stereo. Hosts have two children (3 and 8 yrs) and welcome families with children. Beach equipment is available and tennis courts are close by. Two night minimum.
RATES: $65 per night, $350 week double, $10 extra person up to four.

H-46

Elegance with an ocean view! B&B guests will enjoy this accommodation in Kona separate from the main house and with it's own entrance. One bedroom with a queen sized bed and full adjoining bathroom plus a sitting area complete with a color TV are decorated in off white with rose-colored accents. There is also a dining area with a refrigerator and wet bar for breakfast. Perfect for honeymooners! The view is breath-taking from the private deck. Nonsmokers only, please and no children.
RATES: $75.00 single or double. Two night minimum.

H-50

New home set on a hill overlooking Kailua-Kona combines 50's Art-Deco with Hawaiian comfort. The lush landscaped grounds frame a sunset view of the ocean. Two cozy bedrooms, one with queen size bed and the other with double bed, adjoin a large game room complete with wide-screen TV, wetbar, pool table, refrigerator, brunch table and, of course, your own private entrance. Master suite bedroom with King sized bed and private bathroom adjoins game room on the opposite end - a great honeymoon suite. Breakfasts include fresh Kona coffee, tropical fruits from the hosts own trees and pastries baked fresh each day. The perfect accommodations for two couples travelling together. Non smokers, only, please. One night stays are OK.
RATES: Queen Room: $60 Master Suite: $80 Double Room: $50

H-59

Guests can experience one of the many breathtaking sunsets from this B&B located on the slopes just above Kona Village situated on a 3 acre estate and overlooking the sunny coastline. The accommodations are very private and self contained. A separate apartment features one bedroom with queen sized bed, living room with a fold out sofa, queen sized futon couch bed, private bath and kitchen, TV, private entrance and a small lanai with BBQ. The building is designed like a dome with open beam ceilings so that the bedroom is separated by a wall that does not reach the ceiling and is perfect for one couple or a small family. Smoking outside only, please. Three night minimum is preferred.
RATES: $65 single, $75 double, $10 extra person.

H-60

For the traveler who seeks the comforts of a luxurious accommodation, Kailua Plantation House offers ocean front and oceanview suites each with a private lanai that overlook the ocean, spa and dipping pool. The house is elegantly decorated and air conditioned. Each of the five rooms is unique with queen bed or twin beds one has a whirlpool bathtub and bidet. All the rooms have TV, telephone, small refrigerator and daily maid service.
RATES: $120- $175 double.

HOSTS SOUTH OF KAILUA

H-28A

This B & B home is located about 30 minutes from the airport at the 1300 foot elevation. It overlooks the blue Pacific, Kailua-Kona, Kailua Bay, and the western slopes of Hualalai. The garden level accommodations are large and can accommodate a group comfortably. Hosts only accept one group at a time whether there are one or four persons so everything is private. Included are two bedrooms, each with a queen sized bed, a living room with cable TV, and a refrigerator. There is a bathroom with a shower/tub and a large dressing table. These rooms are located on a lower level than the main quarters and are very quiet. The unit has a separate entrance and a lanai for relaxing or sunbathing. Breakfast is served on the upper lanai, which is also available for guests who wish to enjoy the gorgeous view or sunsets. The garden always is colorful with tropical flowers as well as many of the tropical fruits. The hosts enjoy tropical gardening, hiking to beautiful isolated areas not available by car, Island hopping, and helping visitors plan an unforgettable vacation to beautiful Hawaii.
RATES: $50 single, $55 double. Two night minimum.

H-35

This B & B home is located above the little town of Captain Cook is hosted by a couple who are as interesting as their home is high, maybe more so. The host is a family practitioner with half a lifetime of service in Hawaii and the South Pacific; the hostess is an artist. They are both avid bicyclists who have led several bike tours through China, where the host was born and raised. They would be more than happy to assist those with a like interest who would like to be their guests. The accommodations offered are one of three bedrooms used for B & B guests. Two of the bedrooms have queen beds while the third has two twins. The bathroom is down the hall and is shared by guests. Their home is an expanse of emerald lawn with many palms and exotic fruit trees. Guests are more than welcome to use the pool or watch TV.
RATES: $45 single, $60 double.

H38

Five secluded acres with mostly avocado trees, overlooking and only 500 ft from Kealakekua Bay, great for snorkeling and swimming. The hosts have a school aged daughter and baby and live upstairs in the main part of the home. They are originally from the San Francisco Bay area and are both in the medical field. Host is a physician and hostess is a nurse paractitioner. Newly built, the home is a two story stucco house, 6,000 square feet, reflecting their southwestern roots - combined with polynesian openness. On the first level of the home there are two private guest bedrooms. Each room has it's own entrance, full private bathroom and a queen sized bed, guests can choose between a waterbed or a futon bed. There is a sitting room with TV, library and large covered deck for guest use. Each room has great views of the ocean and mountains. Children are welcome.
RATES: $75 single or double.

H-52

A privately owned Hawaiiana compound, fully contained on 8 acres of lush tropical fruit tree laden hills. The large rambling ranch house has an annex for guests with two bedrooms each with it's own entrance, TV and mini fridge. One room offers a queen bed while the other has two twins. The bathroom is shared between the rooms. Also offered are two more spacious completely furnished guest cottages. The one bedroom guest cottage can sleep four comfortably with a bedroom plus a queen sofa sleeper in the living room; the two bedroom guest cottage sleeps six comfortably with queen bed in one room twins in the other and a sofa sleeper in the living room. Both cottages have full kitchen, dining room screened-in lanais and TV. The grounds have outdoor BBQ pit, tropical grass huts for picnics, sand volleyball court, tennis courts and a large pool. A spectacular view of the ocean can be had from the hosts lanai where breakfasts are served. This property is in an area where the water is on a catchment system. Guests have filtered water available to them if they prefer. Two night minimum.
RATES: Bedrooms: $65 single or double, One bedroom cottage $75 single or double, Two bedroom cottage $100 single or double, $15 each extra per person.

Hosts love to hear from their guests.
Let them know what your interests are
and they can be very helpful
guiding you to particular places.
It is a good idea
to let your host know
your time of arrival
so they can make sure
you are greeted upon arrival.

HILO

One of the lines a travel writer used to describe Hilo was that it was more a place for travelers than for tourists. We are of a different opinion. Our experience has been that our stay in Hilo is never long enough, and this year was certainly no exception, for every time we are there we make new discoveries.

Hilo, located on the east coast of the Big Island, serves as the County Seat for the Big Island as well as the focal point of major transportation facilities into and out of the Island. With a population of around 40,000, it is the biggest city on the outer islands, and it is the banking and commercial center for Hawaii. It is also the oldest continuous city in Hawaii, having been founded by a religious revival in the 1840's when thousands of natives came to the Hilo bay to be baptized into the Christian faith and stayed to found a town. But in spite of Hilo's population, it lacks entirely the hustle and bustle of a city, clinging rather to older plantation traditions and slower Hawaiian ways.

Much of Old Town has been given a face lift, and a stroll up and down the streets of *Old Hilo Town* brings many pleasant surprises. There are several small shops worth a visit. A few we were particularly impressed with were the Most Irresistible Shop, the Chocolate Shop, the Futon Connection, and the Big Island Gallery. All of these shops are on Keawe St. There is much renovation on Kamahaneha St. and when we were there they were just completing the new Pesto Restaurant.

Hilo is also the home of the Merrie Monarch Festival, held every spring. This event gets sold out early, so if one is interested it is a good idea to call ahead for tickets, 808-935-9168. It is here that all the Halaus, Hula Schools, come to display their talent in the hula and maile chant. No where in the world can one see more authentic or accomplished hula dancing. An interesting note: during the 1986 competition there was a huge thunder and lightning storm over Hilo while the dancing was in progress. One of the Halaus took this as a sign and would not dance and some of the spectators also left.

In our last edition we mentioned the East Hawaii Cultural Center just across from Kalakaua Park in the center of Old Town. This former police station and District Court House has been restored as a cultural center. Eventually the upstairs will be used for plays and concerts (there are some events there now but the complete restoration is not yet complete) while the downstairs will house various art exhibits. They even hope to have a small restaurant on the upper level overlooking the park. However, they must be doing it on old Hawaiian time as we could not see much change from last year. We were assured again this year that progress was being made and that eventually they will have a restaurant. The main problem seems to be money. During the last three weeks of July Shakesperian plays are performed on the steps of the building or in the park across the street, no charge of course.

One item we feel must be talked about when Hilo is being discussed is rain since Hilo has an average rainfall around 140 inches. However, most of the rain is at night or early morning or in heavy downpours that do not last long. Let's face it, if Hilo did not get the rainfall it does it would not be as lush and beautiful as it is.

Using Hilo then as a home base, there is much to explore in the surrounding area. Since it is only about thirty miles from the Volcano and only a little over forty miles to Waipio Valley, day trips to these and all the sights in between are really no problem. Is Hilo then more for the traveler than the tourist, a spot better just to pass through? That can really only be answered by you, but remember, to answer properly, you should plan to spend time there. We cannot imagine you will be disappointed.

We hope you are not confused
by our method
of categorizing restaurants in Hawaii.
It is really very simple.
LOCAL STYLE means what indigenous
people might prefer,
two scoop rice, chow down spots, very cheap:
local Style would be
more like mainland
but out of the way where few tourists go,
local/Tourist would be
places much like mainland but
much more reasonable
for the most part than strictly Tourist spots

RESTAURANTS

LOCAL STYLE

HILO SEED AND SNACK

Located at the foot of Wainuenue Street on the left going up. If all you want is a snack and the budget is tight stop here and get a ham sandwich for $1.90 or a hamburger for $1.19 or five sushi for $1.39, delux for $1.79. The real specialty of the house, though, is their shave ice; they make a coffee flavor by soaking Kona coffee with a vanilla bean in a syrup. On top of this they put cream. Our mouths water just thinking about it.

KAWAMOTO TAKE OUT

On Kilauea Avenue across the street from Penney's. Strictly takeout and Oriental with low prices. All the food is prepared ahead, and you can just pick and point to your heart's or stomach's content.

KOW'S WUN TON & NOODLE

In the Penny's Shopping Center. Like KK's Place, low down prices, Oriental, cafeteria style. We have eaten here and while it is not gourmet it is not bad.

CAFE 100

On the makai side of Kilauea Ave. just south of the main part of Hilo. This is interesting because it is here that the Loco Moco originated, an invention of the 100th (Nisei) Infantry in W.W. II, so we were told.

THE PARKSIDE RESTAURANT

At 413 Kilauea Avenue is a little shopping center. This used to be KK's and that part is still there- real local chow down cafeteria style, with low down prices and plenty kau-kau. They are under new management and have expanded. Next door they have opened a sit down restaurant with very low prices (mahi-mahi $4.95, fried chicken $4.75). They must be giving Dick's (see below) some competition.

GWEN'S RESTAURANT

Located on Kalaianiole across the street from Harrington's try this if you want to experience LOCAL flavor. They are open from 6 am to 2 pm. Counter service and take to table.

LEUNG'S CHOP SUEY

On the mauka side of the main highway that goes to Volcano about a mile past Banyon Dr. in a sort of industrial area. We have been assured that this is the best Chinese food in town and the prices are low. It does not look like much, part of it is an old quonset hut, but those who know say do not judge by outward appearances. Open every day but Tuesday from 9 am to 8:30 pm.

SUM LEUNG'S
Located in Puainako Shopping Center, which is on the highway to Volcano. Cafeteria style, eat at tables outside.

MUN CHEONG LAU
In Hilo on Kilauea Ave. Very inexpensive, open for lunch and dinner. The atmosphere of this place turns us off, but every time we have been there they have been fairly crowded and the food, strickly Cantonese looked pretty good.

KIMO'S ONO HAWAIIAN
Located at 806 Kilauea Ave. If you want to try some authentic Hawaiian cuisine and you are not anxious to try a luau, you might want to give this little place a try.

local Style

KAY'S LUNCH CENTER
In spite of the name, they are open for breakfast lunch and dinner. Located at 684 Kilauea Ave. The menu is local Korean food, ie. anywhere for Loco Moco to Kalbi Ribs. All hot lunches and dinners include Hot Rice, Miso, Soup, Kimchee, Namasu, Namal.

DICK'S COFFEE HOUSE
In the Hilo Shopping Center on the makai side of Kilauea Avenue. Open seven days a week for breakfast, lunch, and dinner, locals consider this just about the best deal in town. There is little or no atmosphere, slightly reminiscent of a roadside diner, but there are few places anywhere that give so much for so little. Dinner comes with soup or salad, rice mashed potatoes or french fries, and rolls. All entrees are under $6.00, except for steak at $7,50, with spaghetti at $3.60. They have a cocktail lounge where you can dine if you want drinks or wine with your meal. The special the day we were there this year was Soup, Salad, Steak & Rice for $3.55. Master Charge and Visa accepted.

RESTAURANT OSAKA
Located on the mauka side of the main highway heading for Volcano about a mile or so from town. It is not much to look at from the outside but clean and neat inside and very reasonable. They are open for breakfast, lunch, and dinner every day except Tuesday when they are open only for lunch and dinner.

SACHI'S GOURMET
Located on the mauka side of Keawe Ave. We had lunch here and were pleased. The owners are from Japan so authentic Japanese dishes are available, but there are dishes to please those not used to Japanese food. Breakfast from 8 am to 2pm and dinner is from 4:30-8:30. Prices are not high.

TING HAO
In the Puainako Town Shopping Center, which is on the mauka side of the highway to Volcano. This is the only place we have found in Hilo that served Szechaun/Hunan cuisine. We ate there when they were located in the Lanikai Hotel and have not been to this new location. We liked the food and the price, 10 potstickers for $5.50 for example. They are open Monday-Saturday from 10:30 am to 2 pm and from 4 pm to 9 pm. Sundays from 4-9.

DOTTY'S
Also in the Puainako Center around the corner from Ting Hao. It is neat and clean with very reasonably priced American food and also a few Korean dishes. They serve a petite Top Sirloin (6oz.) for $4.55.

NEW CHINA RESTAURANT
Located at 510 Kilauea Ave. OPen from 11 am to 9 pm, closed Monday. Fairly standard Cantonese food at modest prices (most dishes are $5-6).

HILO SHOPPING CENTER
Located on the left hand side of the highway going toward Volcano. There are several fast food places along with Miwa, a Japanese restaurant, and Woolworth's, a local chow down place.

local/Tourist

ROUSSELS
This is still one of the hot spots in town for dining. The chef is from New Orleans; the cuisine is said to be creole style, but there are many dishes that more properly could be called continental. When we ate there the first time we found the creole dishes pretty authentic. On our next visit our Creole Shrimp was not spicy at all. The waiter told us that folks seemed to prefer it that way. Located on Keawe Ave. just north of Wainuenue Ave. 935-5111.

LEHUA BAY CITY BAR AND GRILL
Located at the foot of Wainuenue in the heart of Hilo in a refurbished building and new to Hilo. They are open for lunch and dinner. We had dinner there and it was excellent and reasonably priced. Most dinners are around $15 and salad is included. Lunches from $6.25-$15. They have expanded since last year and on Friday and Saturday night at 9 pm they become a popular night spot of Hilo. We must say, they place looked great.

RESTAURANT FUJI
Located in the Hilo Hotel in the center of town at 142 Kinoole. The food is good and the prices are moderate. This has long been a favorite with locals and tourists alike, closed Monday. 961-3733.

CAFE PESTO
This restaurant was just being completed in June of 1992. Their store in Kawaihae has been very successful and this also looks like a winner. Located On Kamehameha Ave in center of Hilo.

KK TEI
AT 1550 Kamehameha Avenue on the mauka side. If you try to find this at night it can be a bit tricky since the area and the restaurant are not well lighted. If you like Japanese style food that is not "to da max" authentic, you should like this. Prices are moderate to low. For example, a combination of tempura and teriaki chicken with miso soup, rice, and several pickled vegetables runs only $10., last year it was $9.95. The atmosphere is nice. Liquor is served and Master Charge and Visa accepted. 961-3791.

HILO BAY HOTEL/UNCLE BILLY'S
On Banyon Drive. As its counterpart in Kona, Uncle Billy's is somewhat of an institution on the Big Island and a definite favorite with the locals. Along with your meal, which is moderately priced from $8.00 to $16.95, you will get a free Hula show from 6-8. If you have never seen a Polynesian show, here is your chance and because it is free it is worth the money. 935-4222.

KEN'S HOUSE OF PANCAKES
On Kamehameha Avenue at Kalanikoa intersection. Are you getting homesick and lonesome for some good old mainland grub? Or are you a person who occasionally in the middle of the night has to have a snack? Do not raid your hosts refrigerator, just drive on down to Ken's and load up on blueberry pancakes or country fried chicken, 'cause Ken's is open 24 hours a day and in Hawaii that is rarer than a frog hair. Ken's will make you think you are right at home, until you look a little closer and see Loco Moco on the menu. The prices are low to moderate, the atmosphere is stainless steel clean and the food is pretty good. We think Dick's is better, but it could be a toss of the coin.

NIHON CULTURAL CENTER
(JAPANESE RESTAURANT)
On the north end of Banyon Drive. If you like Japanese food, this is the place to go. Local people who ate here when it first opened in late 1983 might put the knock on Nihon, but those who have tried it lately sing a different tune. We tried it for lunch and really enjoyed both the food and the price, and also a nice view of the harbor. Lunch is served from 11-2 and dinner from 5-9, closed Tuesday, and Sunday is dinner only. Liquor is served. Master Charge and Visa accepted. 969-1133.

BEAR'S COFFEE
If all you want is a cup of coffee and maybe some great dessert, stop by this little coffee shop, located on Keawe St. in the center of town. You can get espresso, capachino, or good old Kona coffee. This year they have started serving sandwiches.

HUKILAU
At 136 Banyon Drive. Open for dinner only from 4-8 Monday through Sunday, this is a big favorite with the residents of Hilo. Nice atmosphere and food for a variety of palates and prices in the moderate range; i.e., $8.95 to $17.95. Be sure to see the Tidal Wave marks recorded on the windows as well as the large koi pond. Liquor is served and Master Charge and Visa are accepted. 935-4222.

MIYO HOME STYLE JAPANESE
Located in the Hilo Shopping Center on the makai side of Kilauea Ave. They serve lunch and dinner Monday through Saturday and dinner is from 5:30- 8:30. The prices are very reasonable. This looks like a good spot if Japanese food is your thing.

JOHN MICHAEL'S
This is a new restaurant located at the Waiakea Villas Hotel, which used to be the Sheraton. They are open for breakfast, lunch, and dinner: 7 am to 1 pm for b/l and 5 pm-8 pm for dinner, closed Monday. The setting is fair and the prices were not high: lunch from $4-$6.50 and dinner from $7 to $12.95, 991-6624.

REUBEN'S MEXICAN RESTAURANT

At 336 Kamehameha Street in downtown Hilo and open for lunch and dinner from 11 am. to 9 p.m. Monday through Saturday, closed Sunday. Mamo Street, just a few doors away from Reuben's, is mentioned in one guide book as the sin center of Hilo. But be not dismayed, local folk assure us that it is perfectly safe here. At any rate, we tried Reuben's in Kona and found the food good and the prices low. Liquor is served and Diners, Master Charge, and Visa accepted. 961-2552.

FIASCO'S

A fairly new restaurant in Hilo that we are sure will be around a long time as it is really excellent for its type. It is not fancy or pretentious, and the prices reflect that fact. The menu however, is very imaginative. We had a delicious hot brie covered with macadamia nuts, and a chicken fajita (grilled chicken, onion, and bell pepper all rolled up in a tortilla). The meal was filling and well under $10 each. One of our guests liked it so much they wished they could stay another day just to eat there again. It is located in the center at the corner of Kamehameha and Highway 11. Recently they have opened a night club which has a comedy night on Monday and other entertainment Thursday through Saturday for 8:30 pm -2 am.

HARRINGTON'S

We were very pleased with the dinner we had here and our hosts say good things about it. It is located on Kalanianiole just past the Hukilau on Hilo's Ice Pond. Does that confuse you? It did us until we were told that the little pond in front of the restaurant was fed by underground springs, hence the water is very cold. Dinner only from 5:30-9;45 Monday-Saturday and 5:30-9 on Sunday. 961-4966.

PESCATORE

A new restaurant in Hilo on the corner of Keawe and Haili. They are open for lunch and dinner. Italian cuisine. We had lunch there and other than being very heavy on the garlic, it was good. They serve a very creative spinach sandwich, spinach sauteed with red onion, garlic, and mozzarella.

GLORIA'S GARDEN CAFE AND COFFEE COMPANY

A new little restaurant at 99 Keawe St. which specializes in coffee, creative breakfasts, soup, salad and sandwiches. Open for breakfast and lunch from 7 am 'til closing.

JASPER'S ESPRESSO CAFE

Located at 110 Kalakaua in Downtown Hilo, this new little restaurant serves an assortment of what might be considered health food items. You won't get a hamburger here, but you can get a chicken cashew salad or sandwich, or lasagne with salad and bread.

SOONTAREE'S THAI RESTAURANT

Located in the Hilo Shopping Center on Kilauea Ave. This is a new venture in Hilo and several of our hosts tell us it is very good and their prices are moderate, most dishes go for $6-7.

ROYAL SIAM THAI

Located on 68 Mamo St. We can vouch for this one ourselves. If you like Thai food you will love this little place. Prices are just about the same as Soontaree's. Closed on Sundays. 961-6100.

Special Category

UNIVERSITY OF HAWAII

To find go south on Kilauea Avenue to Kawili and turn mauka and you will see the University on your right as you drive up the hill. Open for lunch Monday through Friday, this is a good place to get an inexpensive, unimpressive, cafeteria style meal.

COMMUNITY COLLEGE

To find go south on Kilauea Avenue to Kawili and turn makai and you will see the college on your right as you drive down the hill. This year we did get a chance to try this and we recommend it highly. The menu is creative and the food is well prepared and the prices are very reasonable. The facilities are not large so lets hope not everyone discovers it. They are open for lunch from 11:00 a.m. until 12:10. Keep in mind that they are closed for the summer. The school trains cooks who to show their skills operate a restaurant for the public. Prices are low and the food can be great.

POINTS OF INTEREST

IN HILO

HILO ZOO

You can get here by driving Highway 11 toward Volcano. About five miles out of Hilo you will see a sign pointing mauka to the zoo. While it isn't the best zoo we have been to, it would be a fun thing to do for children.

LYMAN MISSION HOUSE AND MUSEUM

At 276 Haili Street which runs mauka off Kamehameha Avenue. We suggest you not miss this. At $4.50 for adults $2.50 for children we found this a real bargain. Built in 1839 by the Reverend and Mrs. David Belden Lyman, and restored in 1932 by the Lyman/Wilcox families, this home once served as a gathering place for Hawaiian Royalty as well as visiting foreigners. In the museum you will learn much of early Hawaiian history and later if someone tries to tell you that the Tedeschi Winery is the first in Hawaii you will know better. One of our Hosts who worked at the museum pointed out several things we were not aware of. Not only does the museum have one of the world's top Mineral collections, one of the top ten in the U.S., but also it boasts one of the best shell collections in the world. Also, at the Museum you can get a brochure that gives a walking tour of downtown Hilo that is interesting to anyone interested in architecture. On the third Saturday of the month the American Association of University Women leads a walk through the downtown Hilo area, starting at the Lyman Museum.

KAUMANA CAVES

On Kaumana Avenue about five miles from downtown Hilo. To get there take Wainuenue Avenue mauka and stay to the left as Kaumana Avenue branches off. These are lava tubes formed by one of Mauna Loa's eruptions. The lower cave is safe for exploring, but the other is considered dangerous.

RAINBOW FALLS
Several miles from downtown Hilo up Wainuenue Ave. The trick in finding the falls is that Wainuenue goes to the right and Kaumana Ave. to the left. The total distance from downtown Hilo is a little over two miles. Morning is the best time to see the rainbow as the falls cascade to the pond below.

BOILING POTS
About two miles beyond Rainbow Falls. The "pots" are a series of deep, round pools cut in the lava beds.

SUISAN FISH MARKET
An auction is held every morning on the north end of Banyon Dr. at 8 am. While there are bigger fish auctions in the world, we doubt they are as interesting or as easily seen as this one. The Honolulu fish auction is *pau* (over) by 5 a.m. Here every day but Sunday local fishermen bring in their catch, ahi (yellow fin tuna) for the most part, but also a sprinkling of akule, opakapaka, mahi-mahi, ono, ulua, and papio.All of this is auctioned off to the owners of restaurants and fish markets. Ahi brings the best price not only because it is served in all the better restaurants but also because it makes the best sashimi. Before the ahi is sold, a core sample is taken from each fish so the buyer can attest to quality.

LILIUOKALANI GARDENS
An exquisite 30-acre replica of a Japanese garden at the north end of Banyon Dr. You can spend minutes here just passing through or you could spend all day strolling along the footpaths and bridges to pagodas, tidal pools, and a ceremonial tea house, just lounging and watching the life of Hilo pass by. While we were there, we watched several men catching small shrimp in little nets which they used as bait to fish in the harbor across the road.

COCONUT ISLAND
Located via a footbridge from Banyon Dr, in Hilo harbor. A great place for a picnic or just to sit and view Hilo and the Harbor and on a clear day Mauna Kea.

HILO TROPICAL GARDENS
This is located about 2 miles down Kalanianiole, which is the road to Hilo's beaches. It looks like a Mom and Pop market at first, but behind the store is an exquisite two-acre garden of natural beauty. The bountiful orchid blossoms, colorful tropical flowers, shrubs and trees, together with natural tidal pools create a picturesque atmosphere. Visitors are welcome to wander through. The owners, who were most helpful, ship flowers to the mainland and Canada. They have a free hula show on Saturday at 10.

NORTH OF WAILUKU RIVER
If you would like to see some of Hilo's older large homes cross the Wailuku River on either Keawe or Wainaku Ave. and just drive some of the streets in this area.

FARMER'S MARKET AND CRAFT SALE
Every Wednesday and Saturday this is held at the foot of Mamo Street. It starts at 6 am and goes until things get slow around 4 pm or until a heavy rainstorm drives them away, we were told by one of the craft vendors.

SOUTH OF HILO

ORCHIDS OF HAWAII
Several miles south of Hilo at 2801 Kilauea Ave. It is free to visit this but like most "free" things you could end up spending a bundle since they do ship orchids all over the world. The day we visited they were working diligently on an order for Caesar's's Palace in Las Vegas: 1000 vanda orchid leis. Each lei consisted of 35 orchids, the smallest made. We asked if all the flowers used came from their nursery or whether for such a large order they had to call on other nurseries. The lady in charge, who was most helpful in answering all our questions, assured us their gardens were sufficient to fill the need. We urge you to visit here.

MAUNA LOA MACADAMIA NUT FACTORY
About six miles south of Hilo on Highway 11 you will come to the road which runs makai for about three miles to the Visitors Center and the factory where you can sample and purchase Mauna Loa's various products. Keep in mind, though, that when it comes to buying, it is hard to beat Long's Drugs or Pay and Save's prices. Mac nuts are grown all over the Big Island, replacing much of the sugar cane fields. From the time the tree is planted (actually grafted) seven years pass before fruit appears. Open every day 8:30 a.m. to 5 p.m. Recently they have added an ice cream/juice stand.

NORTH OF HILO

AKAKA FALLS
The turn off is 12 miles north of Hilo, past the scenic road.   Watch for the sign to Honomu where you turn left and proceed up the mountain through Honomu for about 3 and 3/4 miles to the end of the road. From the parking lot it is about a half an hour walk to Hapuna Falls and on past Akaka Falls back to the parking lot. Along the trail you will see most of the flora of Hawaii including coffee and golden bamboo. Akaka Falls with a vertical drop of 400 feet makes the trip worthwhile, but as one guest told us, "Send me back to Waikiki 'cause if I see another water fall I'll go bananas." Well, that's what makes horse races and why, thank goodness, not everyone wants to live in Paradise.

HAWAII TROPICAL BOTANICAL GARDEN
Located five miles north of Hilo on the four mile scenic road. The admission of $12.00 is tax deductible and is a bargain anyway (children under 12 free). About 1/2 mile down the scenic road you will see a church on the left. From here a mini-bus takes you into the garden, 45 acres of unspoiled beauty with over 1800 species od tropical plants, all labeled, where you will view not only most of the Hawaiian flora but also lily ponds, cascading water falls, streams and picturesque Onomea Bay.

BEACHES and PARKS

While the Big Island is not noted for its white sand beaches, do not conclude that Hilo is not a great place for beaching, snorkeling, and swimming. Most tourists fail to find what we found to be one of the loveliest spots in Hawaii. Access to this area is easy once you know where to go. As you come around Banyon Dr., Kalanianiole Dr. goes off to the left. Along this road are a number of parks (Onekahakaha, Kealoha, Leleiwi, and Richardson's Beach) all with picnic tables, where access to the water is easy and swimming is very safe.

RICHARDSON'S BEACH
We urge you not to miss this as we feel sure you will enjoy spending some time here. When we were there in October, 1987, they were in the midst of remodeling, but by the time this is published they should be finished. The plans for an Oceanography Museum and an excellent coastal trail adventure with a self-guiding brochure are on hold due to lack of funding.

REED'S BAY BEACH PARK
Located at the foot of Banyon Drive this is a good spot for picnicking and swimming is safe.

WAILOA STATE PARK & PICNIC AREA
To get here take Manono St., which is the continuation of Banyon Dr., to Hualani St. and turn right. This is a good place for a picnic.

NIGHT LIFE

BANYON HARBOR DRIVE
All of the hotels are along Banyon Drive and at times there is something going on there, especially at the Crown Room of the Naniloa Hotel. Most interesting to us on this trip was Rainbow Lodge at the Naniloa, which has a Karaoke Bar (where patrons pay $1 to get up and sing). The words are flashed on the screen so that one only need know the tune. These bars are the rage in Japan and people do not hesitate to participate we are told. While we were there a young Japanese man sang two songs in perfect English. Later we asked him if he spoke English and he said *Skosh* meaning very little. He had a very good voice. Several others could carry a tune.

BAY CITY BAR AND GRILL
There is entertainment here on Friday and Saturday nights. See Lehua Bay City Bar & Grill in Restaurant section for directions.

MOVIES
In the Waiakea Shopping Plaza there are three theaters which show first run movies. For more information call 935-9747.   Also, in the Prince Kuhio Shopping Center there are two theaters.

SPORTS

GOLF

Naniloa Country Club
   Located on Banyon Drive in the center of Hilo. A flat, fairly short, nine hole course. Green fees at $25 for eighteen on weekdays, and $35 on weekends, cart $7 for nine but not mandatory. For starting times call 935-3000.

Hilo Municipal Golf Course
   Located at 340 Haihai St. Green fees are $6 on weekdays and $8 on weekends except for seniors (55 and up) and then the rate drops to $3 and $4. Carts are not mandatory but available for $18 on a share basis. Call 959-7711.

TENNIS

   There are at least twenty-two (22) courts in Hilo located in nine different parks. Around half of these are lighted and indoor, located at Hoolulu Park.

KILAUEA VOLCANO

   In the first edition of our book we listed Kilauea Volcano as a point of interest under the section South of Hilo. This displeased our Hilo hosts who felt we were not as enthusiastic about Volcano National Park as we might be. Since our intention is to make sure that all of our readers visit this National treasure, we have decided to give it more emphasis.

   Volcano National Park is thirty miles, about a forty-five minute drive on excellent highway, from Hilo Town. If you simply make this a stop along the way you will miss much and end up wishing you had planned differently. It is our suggestion that you plan to spend at least one day visiting here. Of course, if you are lucky enough to arrive at a time when an eruption is in progress, we don't think you will need any special encouragement.

   One word of advice we would give is to bring along some warm clothes, long pants and a sweater will do, since the Park is at a higher elevation and at times can be chilly. Remember, it is easy to take a sweater off, but if you don't have one on, your stay might be a short one. That is just the mistake we made on our first visit here.

The amount of time spent here is up to you, it can be long or short, but it is hard to exhaust the wonders of this region. If you decide to hike the many available trails, check in at the Visitors Center for the information. Here you can view a short film about the history of the volcano. Across from the Visitors Center is Volcano House, a charming old hotel and restaurant, long a favorite with tourists and residents alike. This is an excellent spot from which to view the main caldera. Perhaps you will be lucky and Madam Pele will decide to favor you with a display far beyond man's ability to duplicate. *So far Madam Pele has been somewhat predictable, and even at her wildest presents no real danger to life. But as we know with the gods, one can never be too sure.*

When we wrote the above we had the tone of irony. Since that time the damage the lava has done is no laughing matter. Lava has flowed through the Kalapana subdivision destroying well over a hundred homes along with the general store down near Black Sands Beach. Some people actually carted off their homes and if you drive to Kalapana down through Pahoa to the Chain of Craters Road you will see these homes along the road as well as a little church. The potential for disaster in this area, as if what has happened is not enough, is very real. East of the vent that has spewed forth this lava are many other vents which could erupt and we were told by one man who is studying the Volcano that the possibility for lava to flow through Pahoa exists. Volcanoes are predicable up to a point. Keep in mind, though, that is has been property that has been destroyed, not human life. Visitors are able to get within a few feet of the lava which in the flat lands moves very slowly. Along the Chain of Craters Road (cut off on the lower end by the new lava flow) there are many scenic views, and visitors are able to walk out and stand right on the edge of the main caldera, an experience like no other we have had. There are other drives to take, such as the eleven mile drive up Mauna Loa. Even if you do not take this drive, be sure to take the short drive to the Tree Molds, which gives one a graphic idea of how deep lava flows can be.

One word of caution, under no circumstances should you pick up any of the lava to take home for a souvenir. It is not that the lava is in short supply. All of the lava is sacred to the goddess Pele and dire things will happen to you if you take the lava off the Island, or so we are told. At the Visitors Center you can read many letters from people who made that mistake and were forced to mail the lava back to stop the bad luck. We can attest to people sending back the lava having received several at our office from the mainland. In our cases not once did the people identify themselves, so we were not able to follow up on what happened. Of course, being at Volcano National Park and just looking at the lava is about as good luck as you can possible have.

RESTAURANTS

VOLCANO HOUSE
Open for breakfast from 7 am to 10:30 am, for lunch from 11-3, and for dinner from 5:30 -8, buffet style. The lunch is $11 for adults and $6.75 for kids. During the day there is a little snack shop for a sandwich or a sweet roll.

VOLCANO GOLF AND COUNTRY CLUB RESTAURANT
This opened in October of 1985 and we hear from our hosts and guests that it is good. The cuisine is American and Japanese. They are open daily for breakfast from 7 am- 10 am, lunch from 10:30-3 pm. On Friday and Saturday they serve dinner from 6-8:30.

VOLCANO STORE AND DINER
In Volcano Village on a frontage road which runs mauka and parallel to main highway. This is a little hamburger stand with window service and a room provided for eating open from 8 am to 5 pm. We were told that the hamburgers, $2.95-$3.25, were great, but the bun was unheated. They serve a plate lunch for $4.95.

KILAUEA LODGE AND RESTAURANT
Very nice dinner house with a fairly extensive menu and wine list with prices from $17-mid $20's. It is possible to split an entree for a charge of $7.50 extra. Our hosts prefer this to Volcano House. If you would like to spend the night at the lodge call B & B Hawaii, 800-733-1632.

NIGHT LIFE

The Kilauea Theater at times does plays but it is best to call ahead to see what is happening, 967-8222. The Kilauea Visitors Center publishes their activities a month in advance and these can be seen on any bulletin board in the area. Visiting scientists give free lectures (usually illustrated) almost every Thursday evening at the National Park Auditorium. Of course, if Madam Pele favors you with a display, that should be enough night life for anyone.

SPORTS

Volcano Golf and Country Club, located on the mauka side of the highway just west of Volcano national Park. The course is short but tricky and cannot always be played without long pants and a sweater. The green fee is $50 with a cart included. For more information call 967-7331.

The amount of destruction that has been done by Kilauea's latest flow is really remarkable. Well over a hundred homes in the Kalapana area have been destroyed along with the little convenience store that had been there for years. To view this area, go to Pahoa, which is just south of Hilo, and take the road to Kalapana and the Black Sands Beach area. Perhaps you will be lucky and get a glimpse of the lava as it flows into the sea. The gas that is produced by this has a special name which we have unfortunately forgotten. The haze that it produces is called vog, and is very evident in the Kona area most days.

SOUTH OF HILO

KEAAU

Where have all the flower children gone? Gone to Keaau everyone, and all the rest down the road a piece to Pahoa. About ten miles south of Hilo, where Highway 130 heads down to Black Sand Beach and the Kalapana area, nestles the little town of Keaau. When we first visited Keaau back around 1980 we were struck with how many hippie types there were wandering the streets or attempting to run little shops. Then when we visited a few years later it seemed as if things were picking up. There was a little group of shops being fixed up, mostly run by folks with an artistic bent, and it almost looked as if Keaau was going places. One year later and all of the shops were either closed or under a new and different type ownership. In previous editions we wrote about several particular shops. We hesitate doing so again since every time we return they are gone. One year we noticed a little sandwich shop where several years before there had been a local style restaurant called the Poi Bowl. We went in to find out what it was like and the owner was very disappointed when he found out we did not want to buy the place. He informed us that things were not so good in Keaau since the police had burned up all the money, pakalolo ie. marijuana that is. We got the impression that this particular shop keeper and maybe others depended on the growers spending money to keep things going. Sure enough, this year the store was boarded up. Well, just shows you what can happen when a market crashes. Imagine, those poor growers will actually have to go to work, unless they can survive on welfare and food stamps. At any rate, it is interesting to walk through Keaau just to see the changes from year to year. What we noticed on this trip was that Keaau seemed to be booming again.

RESTAURANTS

local/Tourist

MAMA LANI'S MEXICAN
In the main shopping center in Keaau. If you like Mexican food, this is absolutely worth the drive down from Hilo. Open Monday through Friday from 7:30 am until 9 pm. and Saturdays and Sundays from 11 to 9 p.m. Whether for lunch or dinner, the prices here are moderate to low. Dinner entrees are in the $5.00 to $6.00 range, while full lunches are under $5.00 with ala carte enchilada only $1.95. Liquor is served and Master Charge and Visa accepted.

TONYA'S CAFE
Located across from the Keaau Town Center. The owner assured us that this was the only all vegetarian spot available on all Hawaii. They are open for lunch and dinner Monday - Friday from 11 am- 7 pm. Entrees include such offerings as Vital Itals, brown rice smothered in Tonya's spicy stew at $4.50 with salad, or Dos Tacos Combination plate, two bean Tacos served with rice and beans, a small salad, chips, and salsa for $5.75. It looks like most little health food places we have been in on Hawaii.

MIU'S
In the Keaau Center, very LOCAL style.

SNAPPY'S PIZZA
In the Keaau Center.

ROSAL'S
This is a new little place just east of the road to Pahoa that opened in April of 1992. Mainly it is take out food but there are a couple of tables outside. They open at 6 am for breakfast and stay open through lunch. We tried several of their baked products and found them very good. If you want a picnic basket, they will prepare it for you and you can call ahead so they will have it ready, 966-6572.

PAHOA

In our opinion this is the funkiest little town in all Hawaii, a curious mixture of local folk and late '60 hippies who somehow or other found enough capital to open that business they had always dreamed of. Several years ago when we were there we eavesdropped on a conversation of several Pahoa entrepreneurs discussing the approaching opening of a new restaurant. "Serve good breakfasts, " he urged the prospective restaurateur. "Serve good breakfasts and you can't miss." This conversation went on for some minutes until the budding businessman shot back. "Well, I know the whole thing will be a great success. Unless I go broke before I get the damn thing opened." From the looks of things in Pahoa, a really good restaurant just can't miss. Walking around Pahoa is even more fun that walking around Keaau as there is a little more to it and, at least when we were there, a little more prosperous. Perhaps they are not dependent on the growers.

Several years ago one of the shop keepers, Robyn of the now defunct Not Jest Juice, asked to read what we said about Pahoa. We were a little worried that she might be offended, but when she finished she smiled and said, "Well, you folks really got a fix on Pahoa." We returned to see her this year, but her shop was closed. We heard she was around somewhere and we wish her well. Neither Pahoa nor our opinion of it has changed much over the years. If fact one shop keeper let us know that Pohoa was not the safest place to be once the sun set. During the day things seemed peaceful enough.

RESTAURANTS

LOCAL STYLE

CHOP SUEY HOUSE
On the mauka side of the road as you enter Pahoa from Hilo. If you like local food you will like this. We tried it and found it palatable and cheap.

local/Tourist

LUGUIN'S
In the center of town on the mauka side of the main road. Mexican cuisine with prices a little higher than at Mama Lani's and not as nice an atmosphere. But the people in town said it was very good. Open for and dinner every day from 3:30 pm to 9 pm. Maybe an early dinner would do.

RIB CAGE
We heard about this before we got to Pahoa. "Finger licking good!" is what we heard. Prices are moderate, $9.75 and lower and naturally chicken and ribs are the specialty. We have not tried it but several Hosts rave about it.

PARADISE WEST COFFEE SHOP
Well, the breakfast place has been opened and is doing very well, thank you. It is now open for breakfast and lunch from 7am until 2pm with breakfast served all day. At noon they close the breakfast restaurant and open the one next door for lunch and dinner. It's a little confusing but that's Pahoa.

HUNA OHANA CAFE & ESPRESSO BAR
On the main street, you can't miss it. Basically this is a small health food restaurant and book store

POINTS OF INTEREST/BEACHES

LAVA TREE STATE PARK
From Pahoa (and you must go through Pahoa or you will miss this since the new highway to Kalapana bypasses this) take Highway 132 toward Pohoki or Kapoho for a couple of miles and you will see the park on your left. The most amazing thing to us about this park is how few people visit it. Not only is it a beautiful tropical setting but the aspect of the lava sweeping through here and burning out what was once a lovely grove of ohia trees, leaving behind a fossil forest of lava, inspires us with awe. Wandering among these bizarre formations causes one to appreciate why the ancient Hawaiians created the myths and legends of the fiery goddess Pele.

KAPOHO
Just past Lava Trees take the turn to the left and follow the road to the sea and you will be at the eastern most point of Hawaii. Until 1960 Kapoho was a thriving little village, but, for whatever sins, Madam Pele did her in and now she is no more. We suggest you take this route because the drive from here down Highway 137 to Black Sand Beach is very scenic, going through mango groves, verdant jungle, a grove of iron wood that slightly resembles the pines of the Sierra Nevada Mountains, sparsely vegetated stark lava formations often skirting the bluest water in the Islands.

ISAAC HALE BEACH PARK & MACKENZIE STATE PARK
You will see these as you drive down 137. There are camping and picnic facilities at both. A permit is required for camping.

KALANI HONUA
As we drove down this isolated stretch of road toward Black Sand Beach, we were just a little surprised to come upon a sign "Kalani Honua Center" and could not resist driving in to see what it was all about. To our surprise we discovered a rather large retreat lodge which has the capacity to house over 50 couples. No one was staying there at that time, but they were actively getting ready for a church group arriving in a few days. This is by no means your typical resort; it caters to a specific segment of society, ie. those who wish to commune with nature, meditate, eat healthy, save the environment, etc. The rates are modest, $62 a night for 2 with a shared bath, $75 for 2 with a private bath. There are lower rates for weekly or monthly stays. For more information write to Kalani Honua Cultural Center, P.O. RR 2,Box 4500, Kalapana, Hawaii 96778 or call 808-965-7828. They have a tennis court which is unfenced, making a game of tennis strenuous but interesting. This year they were re-paving the court so perhaps they will put up a fence.

KALAPANA
After you leave Pohoa, take the fork to the right and go about 11 miles to the Chain of Crater Road. You will not be able to continue on this road as you once could due to the lava flow that has covered the road. Signs will tell you where to park and you will be able to walk right up to the lava flow. When we visited we could feel the heat from the lava. By all means take this trip. On the way you will see houses up on blocks that have been rescued from the lava. The flow has destroyed nearly 200 homes along with a little convenience store that had been there for ages. The total damage this flow will do is yet to be determined. After visiting here go back to the road to Black Sand Beach where you can park and then walk west to get a view of the lava flowing into the sea. If you have the time, return to Pahoa the long way by taking the 22 mile drive to Kapoho. If you do not want to continue all the way there is a turn off to Pahoa about half way.

NORTH OF HILO

HONOKAA

Forty miles north of Hilo, on what the locals call the belt road, you will come to the little town of Honokaa. You must, however, pull off the main highway or you will pass right by and go on to Waimea. Since doing that would cause you to miss Waipio Valley and the lookout above plus the other things Honokaa has to offer, look carefully for Highway 240, the Honokaa turnoff. Once considered the macadamia capitol of the world, Honokaa probably cannot even claim that distinction any longer, and as the highway has passed it by, its future is not bright. One can even get to Waipio Valley without journeying through Honokaa, but what's the hurry? Take a little time and wander around town. Believe us, the town folk will be glad to see you. One new thing to look for is Honokaa Town Western Week held the weekend preceding Memorial Day Week End. This gets started with a Portuguese Bean Soup contest, and is followed by a fashion show, steak fry, all with a two day Rodeo. This event was not held in 1992 because they did not get enough volunteers to run it. Hopefully in the future it will be revived.

RESTAURANTS

LOCAL STYLE

CC JON'S

On the makai side of the main street as you come into town, you are not likely to miss it. We ate breakfast here on our first trip to the Big Island in 1980 and were pleased with our meal and the price. If you do eat here, you will probably be the only tourist, but have no fear, they will treat you nice. Lunch will run you somewhere around $3.50 or so, and it is cleaner than it looks at first glance. It is just a little family run restaurant, those places that are getting more and more scarce as "Where's the Beef" gets more and more common.

HONOKAA HOTEL

A Honokaa resident told us he liked this better than CC Jon's since the prices were no higher and they had a salad bar with no restrictions on helpings. The food is a mix of Japanese and American with a little Hawaiian thrown in. Lunch is no longer served except on Saturday but they are open for dinner. This hotel, in existence since 1908 is for sale for only $890,000. Here's your chance to start a venture in Paradise.

local Style

TEX DRIVE INN

On the main highway at the Honokaa School intersection. Open for breakfast, lunch, and dinner, Tex's is more popular than the three mentioned above if for no other reason that it is on the main drag. Stop by here even if it is not meal time and try some of Tex's malasadas, Portuguese doughnuts without the holes. They have built a whole new building since our last visit.

HERB'S PLACE

This is a restaurant that we think 99% of the tourists that pass by would do just that, pass by. When we went inside we were pleased with what we found. They have fixed it up very nice and have a satisfactory menu with attractive prices. We wouldn't drive all the way to Honokaa just to eat here, but we would certainly give it a try if we happened to be in the area around hungry time.

POINTS OF INTEREST

KAMAAINA WOODS

On the road to Hawaiian Holiday Macadamia Nut Factory. If you want to purchase products made of local woods, koa, milo, monkey pod, mango, Norfolk Pine and be assured that what you are getting is authentic and not high priced, this is the best place we have found. The work is done on the premises, unless it is done by one of the other local artists, in which case you will be informed. They are very willing to discuss the different woods with you and even though we made no purchase they were very helpful and friendly. They specialize in making bowls.

HAWAIIAN MACADAMIA PLANTATION

As you drive through Honokaa watch for the sign on your right. It is hard to miss. We guess one could say, "If you have seen one Mac Nut Factory you've seen them all," but still we liked the free sample, which was very generous. There is also a self guided tour. They are open from 9-6.

WAIPIO VALLEY

Located some six or seven miles north of Honokaa on Highway 24, you cannot miss it as the road stops here. We urge that you do not pass this by. Best of all, make some time and take the shuttle down into the valley. The history of the valley is long and varied so we will not go into it here. Suffice to say that just as one should not miss Haleakala on Maui or Waimea Canyon on Kauai, one should not miss Waipio Valley on Hawaii.

KALOPA STATE PARK

Around five miles south of Honokaa a couple of miles mauka of Highway 19. This park made up of 100 acres of native rain forest and 515 acres of planted timber species makes a pleasant place for picnicking and short hiking, giving one a chance to see many of the trees endemic to Hawaii. Visitors can pick up a brochure at the bulletin board which gives good information about trails and what can be seen. The park has a picnic area, rest rooms, showers, and cabins. For information on reserving a cabin call 933-4200.

BEACHES

KOLEKOLE BEACH PARK

About sixteen miles north of Hilo watch for the sign on the makai side of the highway and it is a short ride down to the park. One can swim in the stream that comes in here but to swim in the surf would be foolhardy. There are picnic tables, rest rooms and showers, but no food sold.

LAUPAHOEHOE BEACH PARK

When you reach the twenty-five (25) mile marker start watching for the sign on the makai side of the highway. From the highway it is about one mile drive down to the beach. This makes a good place to picnic; rest room and showers available, but by no means try swimming here.

SPORTS

TENNIS

There are two lighted courts at Honokaa Park in Honokaa.

GOLF

In Honokaa there is a nine hole course, Hamakua Country Club, which was built by the plantation personnel and once was the site of the Macadamia Nut Masters Golf Tournament which was held in August. The course is short, 2520 yards, but since the greens are small, the fairways narrow, and the course hilly, it is by no means easy. The fee is $10 and one can play all day if desired. No carts are available. It is a little tricky to find but absolutely worth the effort if you have time for a game. To find look for Parts Plus on the makai side of the highway. Turn right if you are coming from Hilo. After you have turned right make a sharp left at first road. For more information call 775-7244.

On this visit we learned a little more about the now defunct Macadamia Nut Masters Tournament. The nuts were dipped in a resin to make them even harder and the heads of the golf clubs were covered with a rubber mat. Unfortunately, the Plantation owners stopped sponsoring the tournament and the folks have let it lapse. Let us hope some time in the future it gets revived.

WAIMEA/KAMUELA

If some of the terrain you have just passed through looks a little like West Texas that is as it should be for now you are in cowboy, oops, paniolo country. Waimea is in the heart of the Parker Ranch, which is the largest privately owned ranch in the U.S. As a matter of fact *Kamuela* is the Hawaiian equivalent of Samuel for Samuel Parker, the founder of the Parker Ranch. If you are ever going to need a sweater in Hawaii, this will be one of the places, for at night the temperature here can fall all the way into the fifties, and during the winter months even into the forties. But you will have little sense of being in the mountains since the climb from Hilo is so gradual. A stay in Waimea is a far different experience than a stay in most other parts of Hawaii. About the closest thing to it would be a stay in Kokee on Kauai. However, some of the most beautiful beaches in Hawaii are just a few minutes drive from Waimea. Our hosts tell us that it is great to be able to horse back ride in the mountains in the morning and then spend the afternoon relaxing at the sea shore. A vacation in the Kamuela/Waimea area settles the age old argument about which is better, the mountains or the seaside. Here one gets the best of both worlds.

We were impressed on this visit with the amount of development and restoration that was going on in Waimea. There is a new center just as one enters town from Hilo side called Waimea Center that has several new restaurants and many shops. On the other side of town on the way to Kona side in a new center called Parker Square. Past that is the new Hale Kea, a quite elegant arrangement of shops and a restaurant in what was once the Parker Ranch manager's home. It was built in 1897 and has long been a part of the Island's history. During the mid-sixties the property and some vacant beach land was purchased by Laurance Rockefeller. The beach land became the Mauna Kea Hotel and the home Rockefeller's private residence. It was during this period that the home expanded to its present size. It has been recently acquired by the developers of the Kilohana, the Wilcox estate on the Island of Kauai. This property has now changed owners once again. We encourage you to stop and visit here.

We would love to hear from you
about anything you have discovered
in this area
so we could share it with all our visitors.
Or perhaps you have a reaction to
or comment on the Kamuela area?

RESTAURANTS

LOCAL STYLE

DON'S PAKE KITCHEN
This is a little take out place where you buy by the pint or the quart, located on the left side of the highway as you enter Waimea from Hilo side. Stop here only if you want to eat on the run.

local/Tourist Style

EDELWEISS

Dining out in Hawaii is not always a great experience and unlike the metropolitan centers of the mainland such as San Francisco, New Orleans, and New York, interesting little restaurants at reasonable prices are rare. We stopped in for lunch here with no prior knowledge except that it had recently been taken over by a German fellow. One bite of just the potatoes so excited our taste buds that we had to know more of this "German fellow." Hans-Peter Hager was good enough to talk to us and when we exclaimed that he was a gourmet chef he modestly replied, "No, just a cook, but we enjoy what we do." Hans-Peter, we learned, had worked for twenty years at the famed Mauna Kea. Well, we hope Hans-Peter keeps up the good work in Waimea, unless he chooses to move to Kauai. Lunch prices were low last year ($4.50 for Edelweiss specialty, knockworst, sauerkraut, and potatoes) in spite of the elegant food and good service. Dinner entrees run higher, from $14.50 for Roast Chicken Diable to $41 for Rack of Lamb (for two).. However, a light meal is much less, $9.50. Since they do not take reservations and everyone we talked to on the Big Island considers this the best restaurant on the Island, you may have a little wait. A year or so ago was the first time we had heard negative comments about the Edelweiss. Several of our hosts reported they felt the food was too salty. They are closed Sunday and Monday. We were amazed when we visited this year that lunch prices had risen since our first visit. We again visited with Peter and after he read our comments he said, "Well, at least you are honest." They close for the month of September and for one week in April around the 15th.

WAIMEA COFFEE COMPANY
A small health food sandwich store across the street from Edelweiss that serves some tempting tidbits.

PARKER RANCH BROILER
In the Parker Ranch Shopping Center. This used to be the about the only game in town. It is either under new management or new ownership and the change is apparently for the better. Everyone we talked to said the food was excellent and the atmosphere improved. Long a favorite with residents and tourists alike as *the special occasion dining spot,* the atmosphere is not as formal as it once was. Open for lunch from 11-2 and for dinner from 5-10 with lunch around $5-$10.00 and dinner $10.00 to $15.00. From 4-5 free pupus are served in the bar during happy hour. They have live entertainment on Friday and Saturday night and a jam session on Sunday afternoon.

CATTLEMAN'S
You will find this at the back of a small center on the right as you enter Kamuela from the Hilo side. This is a mainland chain very well known for their large steaks and prime ribs.

CATHY'S KITCHEN
You will see this on the left side of the highway as you enter Waimea from Hilo. They serve pizza, sandwiches, and a daily plate lunch special. Prices are low, $4.25 for a pastrami sandwich or $4.10 for plate lunch.

GREAT WALL CHOP SUI
Now located in a new restaurant in Waimea Center. Buffet style Cantonese food, very filling, tasty, and reasonably priced. Their friendliness more than made up for the lack of decor.

YOUNG'S KALBI
In the Waimea Center and if you are in the mood for Korean food this is the place. Closed Monday.

AUNTY ALICE'S
Hosts tell us that this little pie shop has the best pie in the Islands. It is near the museum at Parker Ranch Center.

PANIOLO COUNTRY INN
They serve pizza but much more and their prices are good (for dinner 10 oz. Sirloin Steak $13.95 or Bar BQ Chicken $7.50 or for lunch same thing for $12.50 & $5.95). 885-4377

THE CAFE
Located in Parker Square way in the back. A good place to get a sandwich or light snack, perhaps an Asparagus Mushroom Crepe for $5.45 or a Vegetarian Delight sandwich for $4.25. Roast Beef, Ham, Turkey, Pastrami-$5.95.

MERRIMAN'S
With all the rave reviews posted in the lobby about the owner/chef, Peter Merriman, it looks as if they are out to give Edelweiss some competition. We had lunch there and found in very nice, a chicken sandwich covered with cheese. At this point we are not about to say it is better than Edelweiss. Their dinner menu was interesting.

A suggestion
From Waimea there are
two ways to get to Kona.
One could take the Belt road,
Highway 190, or drive down 19
to Kawaihae and then south to Kona.
We suggest You take Highway 19
which will take you past
the large hotels of North Kohala.

258

BREAD DEPOT

You will find this at the back of the same mall that Merriman's is located. Not only do they have fresh baked bread, they also serve a daily lunch special. The day we were there it was a vegetable curry stew for $4.50 or a variety of sandwiches at $4.50 or Chef Salad for $5.95. If we could judge by the crowd, they must be pretty good.

HARTWELL'S

In the Hale Kea Center which you will find on the right side of the highway as you drive toward Kawaihae. This is the elegant restaurant of Waimea. Hosts assure that the food is good and the prices are high.

KAWAIHAE

The following restaurants are located down by the ocean about 10 miles west of Waimea.

CAFE PESTO

If you happen to get through Waimea without trying one of the above and get to the coast and can not afford the Mauna Kea or whatever, you might like to give this little pizza and pasta place a in Kawaihae a try. They are open from 11-4. These are the same people who have opened the new place in Hilo.

TRES HOMBRES

Mexican food in a very nice setting. Their prices are moderate (Dos Combinations $9.95/Uno combinations $6.45).

BLUE DOLPHIN

The first place you come to as you enter Kawaihae. This is a little local style take out place where one can get a quick snack.

POINTS OF INTEREST

PARKER RANCH MUSEUM

In the Parker Ranch Center, admission $5 for adults, $3.75 for children. Some people feel this is little more than a glorified history of the Parker family and not worth the price. Perhaps we are easy to please. While we agree that it is not one of the high points of a trip to Hawaii, it is interesting enough if you have the time.

KAMUELA MUSEUM

At the junction of Highway 19 and 250. Not as slick, but in many ways far more interesting than the Parker Museum. It is open from 8 a.m. to 5 p.m. Founded by one of the Parker offspring, here you will find a potpourri of Hawaiiana, as well as other things from all over the world. We had a lengthy chat with Harriet Soloman who, as her card says, is the "Great-great granddaughter of John Palmer Parker, founder of world-famous Parker Ranch." $5 for adults, $2 for children under12.

NORTH KOHALA

Not a lot of tourists get up to the North Kohala district of the Big Island. Perhaps if and when the new hotel is built that will change. Until then we would encourage all to drive into this area via the high road, Highway 25 which goes north off 19 and to return down the coast via Highway 270. Called Kohala Mountain Road, it reaches an elevation of 3,500 feet. The vista of the plains and ocean below makes this one of the finest views in the Islands. A journey into this region gives one a good example of just how slow paced life in Hawaii must have been long ago. It was here that King Kamehameha, the great warrior who united the islands into one Kingdom, was born. At the little town of Kapaau you will see the original statue of Kamehameha. The statue in Honolulu is a replica, which was made when the original was lost at sea in 1880. It was subsequently found and returned to this spot.

If you take this drive, be sure to continue to the end of the road, past Kapaau, to Pololu Valley Lookout and, if time permits, hike the 1/2 mile into the valley. As you backtrack towards Kapaau, you will see a sign pointing makai for Keokea Beach Park.

As you travel south down Highway 270, watch for Lapakihi State Historical Park, an ancient Hawaiian Village. You get an idea of how the Hawaiians lived hundreds of years ago. The park closes at 4 p.m. From here on down to the town of Kailua, the scenery is stark and dry; the vegetation, mostly pili grass and kiawe trees and prickly pear cactus, fight for life among the jagged beds of lava.

When you reach Kawaihae you may be ready for food or drink. If it is budget time, stop by the Blue Dolphin, a little local take out place one can not miss. The menu is extensive and prices are low. Or you could go on down the street to Cafe Pesto, or the other restaurants mentioned above. If, on the other hand, the sky is the limit, stop by the Mauna Kea Beach Hotel. Brunch there is more of an experience than a meal. Eating there every day might cause your spread to match Mauna Kea. Further down the road you could stop at the new Ritz Carlton Mauna Lani Hotel and enjoy their elegant surroundings. A little south of here is the Sheraton Waikoloa, nice but not as elegant as the other two.

From here on south you will not see much except black lava and blue ocean. Before you reach Kona you will pass the Kona Airport.

BEACHES

POLOLU
It takes about a half an hour to hike down to the beach from the lookout. There are no facilities so if you plan to be there long, pack in food and drinks. Swim with caution.

KEOKEO BEACH PARK
You will see the sign on the makai side of the road between Kapaau and Pololu Valley. There are picnic facilities, rest rooms, and showers in this secluded little park. Swimming here is not advisable.

KAPAA BEACH PARK
There are picnic tables and rest rooms but no drinking water here. No sand beach but on a wind-free day, this makes a nice spot to picnic and to try your luck at shore fishing.

SPENCER BEACH PARK
If one is staying in the Waimea area, this is the spot for beaching. The swimming is excellent as is the snorkeling, even for the beginner. The facilities are good: picnic tables, rest rooms, showers, tennis courts, but no food sold there. Big white sand beach.

HAPUNA BEACH STATE PARK
Access to this beach is just south of the Mauna Kea, in fact the Mauna Kea is at the north end of this beach. Because private beaches are not allowed in Hawaii, the Mauna Kea must give access through their property to the beach and several parking places are reserved for that purpose. We prefer this beach to any on the Big Island. Swimming is great as is snorkeling. There are picnic tables, rest rooms, and showers, but no food sold.

SPORTS

TENNIS
There are two lighted courts in Waimea at Waimea Park and two lighted courts in North Kohala at Kamehameha Park.

GOLF
The North Kona Coast could be called the "Golf Capital" of Hawaii since there are four championship courses available and all of them are truly spectacular. However, all of them are privately owned and not inexpensive to play. The least expensive is the Waikoloa Village (883-9621) where green fees are $38 cart included (they have a twilight rate after 2:30 of $25)9. Waikoloa Beach (885-6060), located at the Waikoloa Sheraton, charges Sheraton guests $80 cart included and non-guests $95. The Mauna Kea (882-7222) is $130 for non-guests, cart included and $80 for guests. The Mauna Lani (885-6655) is $130 for non-guests and $65 for guests, cart included.

KAILUA/KONA

We once saw a sign on a Caribbean Island that read *sunny today - and for the next 364.* That sign could reside in Kailua and would not be much of an exaggeration. Up from Kailua, along the belt road, it is another matter. Here it rains almost every day at least a little, and in the evening the air moves down from Kualalai Mountain to keep things refreshingly cool. Kailua starts at the north end with the King Kamehameha Hotel and ends some eight miles south at the Kona Surf. In between along Alii Drive there is a smattering of hotels (Uncle Billy's Kona Bay, the Kona Hilton) many condos and more little shops and restaurants than we care to count. Almost all of the tourist activity takes place here, at sea level along Alii Drive in Kailua Town, with most things geared to tourism. If Kailua had the huge white sand beaches that exist on Oahu, Maui, and Kauai, there is little doubt that a high percentage of tourists would head here. Nowhere in Hawaii is the ocean more beautiful and warm, the sea life more plentiful, and all this with a backdrop of Mt. Hualalai.From the pier in the center of town, one can catch a fishing boat and try his luck at marlin fishing, for some consider Kona the marlin capitol of the world, and several tournaments with sizable purses are run each year. It is quite a sight to see fish of hundreds of pounds being hoisted from the boats and weighed in at the dock. But it is not only marlin they fish for, but ono, sail fish, ahi, and mahi mahi.

In October they hold the Iron Man Competition at Kona, and for weeks before triathletes train for the grueling event which starts with a two mile swim across Kailua Bay, a seventy five mile bike race, and ends with a marathon run, ending up in Kailua Town where thousands await the outcome. One must be in perfect shape to enter this event.

In years past we have been struck by how much Kailua seemed to want to be like Waikiki. On prior visits we noticed at least four hawkers of pearls from oyster shells and you could not walk by them with out getting the big insincere greeting. Also, they had little lights strung up everywhere making the whole place look like a Christmas tree with no presents. To us it just seemed to gaudy. However, on this visit we did not get the same impression. Sure, there are plenty of shops for the tourists and make no mistake, Kailua needs plenty of visitors to exist, but it just was not as glitzy, which we felt was an improvement.

262

RESTAURANTS

Because Kailua is so geared to tourists, much like Lahaina on Maui and Waikiki on Oahu, we will dispense with our usual method of classification, with the exception of including LOCAL STYLE. Since most restaurants in Kailua depend primarily on tourists and residents, they tend to resemble more closely mainland restaurants. After LOCAL we list lunch and snack spots, then American, Mexican, Oriental. We have included the phone number for those restaurants where it might be wise to have a reservation.

LOCAL

TERU'S BAR
Hard to find but if you want to get down and chow down this is the place. To find take Kuakini Highway extension from the north end of Alii Dr. and go one block (long) to Kaiwi, turn right and go 100 yards or so to Pawai Place, turn right and look for Teru's about half way up the block on the left.

KONA'S CHUCK WAGON
Not quite as LOCAL as Teru's and new to Kona at this location. However, the owner told us they had been in Kona for over five years. They are located in a new Center at the top of Kaiwi, which runs west off the airport highway just north of Kailua. They are open for breakfast, lunch, and dinner, all you can eat buffet style: breakfast $4.75, lunch $5.75, dinner $8.45.

BETTY'S CHINESE
In the Kona Coast Shopping Center which you pass as you drive into Kailua from the north. Fast food, cafeteria style, Oriental/Hawaiian fare at very low prices, choose four items for $4.85, little or no atmosphere.

KIM'S PLACE
This is a little take-out place in the Kona Coast Shopping Center just behind Mother India (see below) that serves Korean and Japanese food. Prices are low and the food looks pretty good.

AC'S CHINESE RESTAURANT
This one is really hard to find but make the effort it you want LOCAL. They are open Monday-Friday from 10 am to 6 pm with Friday being Hawaiian Food day, and on Saturday from 10-2pm. To find follow the directions to Teru's but go just a little farther up the street and you will see a chain link fence with a open gate. Go through the gate and drive down and between the building. When you can drive no farther, turn right to AC's. You can find this restaurant as we did from Kuakini Highway extension.

ROSIE'S KITCHEN
On Kuakini Highway. Either take out or dine in family style.

LUNCH AND SNACK PLACES

FAST STOP FOODS
Located in the Old Industrial Area at the corner of Luhia and Kaiwi. You can get a free cup of coffee if you get there between 5:30 and 8 am. This could qualify for the section above but there are plenty of sandwiches or burgers available and nothing is over $4.25 and a Cheeseburger goes for $1.59.

MOTHER INDIA
In our last edition this was Monster Burgers so this is quite a change. Service here is counter take out, but there are tables outside for dinning. Keep in mind this is in a very busy shopping center.

MCGURKS FISH AND CHIPS
Not quite as spiffy as they were last year but they are still going strong. They use ono or ahi for their fish and chips. Their prices are reasonable, six shrimp with chips for $8.75 or five fish and chips for $9.95. Counter service with a few tables provided. They also have have a store in the new Lanihau Center.

BIANELLI'S GOURMET PIZZA
This is located on Palani Rd. in the Kona Coast Shopping Center. They are open every day from 11 am to 10 pm. As with most other pizza places, they have other dishes available.

DON ALFREDO'S PIZZA & PASTERIA
This is a new little place located at 74-5467 Kaiwi St. You can get a large pizza for $10.95, a dinner for $5.95 and down and the aroma was tempting.

BUN'S IN THE SUN
This is a little place in the Lanihau Shopping Center which is on the left as you drive into Kailua from the airport. They are mainly a bakery but do serve sandwiches and coffee and patrons can sit at the tables outside.

SUZANNE'S BAKE SHOP
Since they open at 5am every day this is a good place for an early morning danish and coffee. They are right at the north end off Alii Dr. on Likana Lane. There are a couple of tables outside, but our suggestion would be to take your snack across the street along Kailua Bay.

DA BUS STOP or BOBBY'S "Q" SOUL FOOD
This is a little take out place at the rear of the Kona Marketplace where one can get a whole rack of BBQ Pork Ribs for $16 or if you like just a Rib Plate for $6.50. When we were there people were lining up.

AMERICAN/FRENCH/ITALIAN

STAN'S
Located on Alii Dr. next to the Ocean View mentioned below. The signs outside indicate low prices. Very tourist oriented spot and very competitively priced, mahi-mahi for $7.75 or New York Steak for $10.75. They are open for breakfast, lunch, and dinner.

GIUSEPPE'S
Located at 75-5699 Alii Dr. at the back of a little mall. They are open for lunch and dinner and their prices are modest with all of their pasta dishes under $10 and their dinner entrees from $9.75 to $15.25. If you like small tucked away little places this might serve you well. So far no one has made it in this location since we started writing this guide book.

LA BOURGOGNE
Located four miles south of Kailua on the Kuakini Highway and open for dinner only Monday-Saturday. It is best to call for a reservation since they have limited space, 329-6711. We highly recommend this if you want something special. The food and service was very nice and not all that expensive for what you get. Entrees go from $13.50 for Chicken to $26 for Saddle of Lamb.

BANANA BAY RESTAURANT
Right on Alii Dr. They have a dinner buffet for $8.95 and we are fairly sure that after the dinner hour there is entertainment of an Hawaiian flavor.

PHILLIP PAOLO'S
On the makai side of Alii Dr. upstairs from Jolly Roger. Fairly standard Italian cuisine with prices from $16 to mid $20's. They offer an early bird special for $9.95.

MARTY'S STEAK AND SEAFOOD
Right on Alii Dr. and upstairs so that with the right table one would have a nice ocean view. Entrees go from $10 to $20 and at times they have an early bird special.

DRYSDALE'S
On the makai side of Alii Drive in the Kona Inn Shopping Village. This is a good place for lunch if you want a little more atmosphere than the previously mentioned spots. Prices here are moderate, not as low as the ones above. They have a comfortable cocktail lounge with reasonable prices.

DRYSDALE'S TWO
Located in the new Keahou Shopping Center just before you get to the Kona Surf. Beautiful view and stylish surroundings.

KONA BROILER
Located upstairs in the Kona Marketplace right on Alii Dr. This is much like the Koloa Broiler of Kauai where you cook your own food. For $8.95 for Chicken or Mahi-Mahi or $13.95 for New York Steak one gets all the salad, rice, and beans one cares to eat.

KONA RANCH HOUSE
On the mauka side of Kuakini Highway, the one that brought you to Kailua from the north, just past Palani Road. There is a casual family section and a more formal *special occasion* section but they use the same menu. The food is good, the service is excellent, and prices are very reasonable, with a Barbeque Platter for $13.95 or ground beef steak for $7.95. They have an extensive menu, nothing over $20, 329-7061.

JOLLY ROGER
On the makai side of Alii Drive a little south of all the restaurants mentioned above. The best thing about this is the setting, right on the ocean. Our hosts tell us that this is a great place for early evening pupus. The food is typical Spindrifter/Chart House/Anybody's Broiler type, ie., broiled steak, fish, or lobster with the ubiquitous salad bar, with bronzed surfer type waiters who insist on telling you their name. The food is O.K. and prices run from $10.00 to $20.00. They do give seniors a discount (light dinner for $7.45) and they have an early bird special for $7.95.

KONA GALLERY
This is located in the Kona Inn and is one of the oldest restaurants in Kailua with the Inn going back to 1928. It is right on the water and has a very nice atmosphere. It is open for lunch and dinner. Prices for dinner run from $12.25 to $25.75 with salad included. Lunch, from $6 for a hamburger to $12.75 for a crab salad sandwich, 329-4455. One can either eat in the dinning area or in the bar.

ECLIPSE
On the mauka side just a few doors south of the Kona Ranch House. They are now open for lunch and dinner and there prices, considering the type of place this is, would be hard to beat. For example, there is nothing on their dinner menu over $10. In fact their prices this year were lower than last year. This is also one of Kona's night spots with dancing from 9 'til closing. 329-4686.

CALYPSO
Located on Palani Rd. just across from King Kamehameha Hotel. Entrees run between $12.95 for Chicken Florentine to $18 for Combination Seafood. The setting is nice, with a great view of the ocean.

FISHERMAN'S LANDING
Located next to Kona Inn and with as good a setting. They have been open for a couple of years and seem to be doing great. It is owned and operated by Uncle Billy's, who have been in Kailua for a long time. The menu is extensive and entrees are priced between $15 and $22. Lunch prices are under $10. 326-2555.

HUGGO'S
On the Makai side of Alii Dr. just before the Hilton. We have tried to eat here several times but we have never been able to. Our hosts say it is good but only if you are satisfied with either steak or lobster.329-1493.

JAMESON'S BY THE SEA
Located where Dorian's used to be and owned by the same people who used to run Jameson's on the north shore of Oahu so they must know their stuff. They are open Monday- Friday for lunch and dinner. Dinner prices run from $17 to mid$20's.

PALM CAFE
Open for dinner only, reservations suggested, 329-7765. Located in the Coconut Grove Marketplace on Alii Dr. Entrees between $14.50-$23.

CHART HOUSE
Located on the makai side of Alii Dr. just a short way south of all the Kailua action next to the Jolly Roger. Since this is a chain that most people are familiar with it really needs no explanation. If you do not know of it and want to get that feeling that you are back on the Mainland give it a try.

SIZZLER
Located in the Kona Coast Shopping Center, this really needs no introduction.

MEXICAN

REUBEN'S
Behind Crazy Shirts and run by the same family who runs Reuben's's in Hilo. We ate here and found the food acceptable and prices not high. One thing we did notice is that the people working there seemed to be of Mexican ancestry, which we can assure you is rare in the so called Mexican restaurants in Hawaii. We like the food here but on this visit we found the atmosphere in the restaurant depressing. However, there is table service outside and we feel sure you would like that better.

KONA AMIGOS
Formerly called the Kailua Cantina and under new ownership and according to the people we talked to much better. It is located at the north end of Alii Dr. They offer plenty of entrees with most around $10. They have a great view of Kailua Bay.

PANCHO AND LEFTY'S
Located on Kauakini Highway several miles south of Kailua where the Pottery Steak House used to be, if that is any help. There are several of these in the Islands and we are not sure if they are connected to a mainland chain. I guess we could have asked.

ORIENTAL

OCEAN VIEW INN
At the north end of Alii Drive on the mauka side. The Ocean View is the ultimate chowdown, two scoop rice restaurant in Hawaii, with a menu schizophrenic enough to be committed. One of our new hosts, a long time Hawaii resident who was born and raised in China, said it was the best chop suey place in Hawaii. The only place to go if you are looking for lots to eat at low cost. They must be doing something right because at times the action here is so fast that some patrons finally get discouraged with the wait and wander off to one of the nearby spots. But in spite of the long lines at times, they eventually get everyone served. They open for dinner at 5:15 or when they get around to it.

SIBU CAFE

At the back of Kona Banyon Court on the mauka side of Alii. We did not do justice to this little place in either of our last two editions. We had eaten there several times and always enjoyed the food since we are partial to Indonesian, Thai, or Indian cooking. Their prices are not low which is a bit surprising because of the location (from $10-$12) but if you are a devotee of Indonesian food, give this a try. They are open for lunch and dinner.

KANAZAWA TEI

On the mauka side of Alii Dr. across from the Hilton. This is authentic Japanese cuisine, not at all inexpensive, but very good if this is what you are looking for. You can get a seven course dinner for $35 or if you like Funamori, a wide variety of sashimi for $100.

KING YEE LAU

A new restaurant in the Alii Sunset Plaza which is also new. The cuisine is mainly Cantonese with a few Manderin dishes also. Prices are moderate and servings are ample.

THAI RIN RESTAURANT

Also located in the Alii Sunset Plaza. They are open for lunch from 11-2:30 and for dinner from 5-9. Their lunch special is $6.95. Their dinner entrees run between $7 & $9 and the menu is fairly extensive.

ROYAL JADE GARDEN

In the Lanihau Center on Palani Rd. One can put together a fairly inexpensive lunch of Cantonese cuisine from the food counter. No table service.

GOLDEN CHOPSTIX

A new restaurant in Kailua located in the Kaahumanu Plaza which is on Kaiwi St. off the Airport Highway. The chef is from San Francisco, so we were told. The style in Mandarin/Hunan, not too spicy, however. Most dishes run around $6 -$8, with the Chow Mein dishes in the $4-$5 range.

SU'S THAI KITCHEN

It is out of the way and a little hard to find, but from what one of our guests who ate there the day after we stopped by told us, finding it is worth the effort. Perhaps the easiest way is to call them for directions (326-7808). But if you are not near a phone follow these directions carefully. From Alii Dr. take the Kuakini Highway extension north until you reach a stop sign at Kaiwi St., turn right and go about 100 yards or so to Pawai Place, turn right and go about a block and you will find it on your right. Their menu is extensive with most dishes in the $6-8 range up to $16 for the combination sea food platter. They are open for lunch Monday-Friday from 11-2:30 and for dinner every night from 5-9.

ROYAL JADE GARDEN

Located it the Lanihau Shopping Center. The food is Cantonese style and the prices are modest.

POINTS OF INTEREST

You will not have to search out the interesting things to visit in Kailua since they are right there on Alii Drive. To us the most interesting place in town is the Kailua Wharf, where the action seems to go on all day, culminating in the middle afternoon with the return of the fishing boats, which fly different flags to herald their catch, either ono, ahi, or biggest of all, if not the best, the marlin. One place of interest we might mention is Hilo Hatties which is located across from the Kona Coast Shopping Center just before you enter Kailua Town. This is the closest thing to a department store on the Kona Coast. While the main emphasis is on Hilo Hattie products, there are several concessions in the store, such as Hill and Hill Kona Coffee, and one of the Mac Nut companies. Soon they hope to add seamstresses so patrons can see the garments being made.

For those captivated by the historical aspect of Hawaii there is the Hulihee Palace or the Mokuaikaua Church, the oldest in the Islands. There is a small fee to visit the Palace, ($4 adults, 12-18 $1, under 12 .50) now a show place for Hawaiiana. They are open every day from 9-4. Also, there is the Kamakahono Beach and the Ahuena Heiau, located behind the King Kamehameha Hotel, which is on the site of King Kamehameha's last residence. As you drive down Alii Drive toward Keahou Bay you will pass all the beaches that Kailua has to offer, including Disappearing Sands, which tends to wash away during the winter months.

One of the new additions to Kailua this year is a farmers market, which you will find on the mauka side of Alii Dr. several miles south of the main part of Kailua. We stopped by here and picked up a pound of pure Kona coffee for $7.50 from a little stand run by Hara and Alan. We do not think you will find it anywhere else that inexpensive.

BEACHES

HONOKOHAU BEACH
To get to this beach take Highway 19 north of Kailua for about two miles until you see the sign for the Honokohau Harbor. From the north side of the harbor, walk about a quarter of a mile north to the beach. There are no facilities here at all. Swimming is safe. The rest of the beaches in this area are along Alii Drive and quite obvious.

NIGHT LIFE
Most of the night life in Kona takes place at the various hotels, which often have entertainment and dancing. The *This Week* magazine, free at all tourist locations, lists the various entertainers appearing. Duplicate Bridge is played on Tuesday and Thursday night at Hale Halawai on Alii Dr. We hear that the hottest spot for dancing is at the Eclipse. At the Kona Surf there is a free Polynesian show daily at 7:45-8:30 p.m and we hear that now they have added a comedy club. The Spindrifter has live entertainment Monday through Saturday, starting at 8:30 p.m. First run movies are shown at the World Square Theater, 329-4070. We had lots of fun at the Hilton's Karaoke Bar and we feel sure that there several other Karaoke Bar's to choose from.

SPORTS

TENNIS

Many of the hotels in Kailua have courts that are open to the public. There are four locations where public courts are available. At Kailua Park there are four lighted courts. There is one unlighted court at Keahou Park. Kailua Playground and Greenwell Park each have one lighted court.

GOLF

The Kona Country Club, which used to be called the Keahou Golf Course, located at the south end of Alii Drive, is available to the public. The fee is $80 cart included for non-guests, $60 for guests of the Keahou Beach Hotel. It is an excellent course, where the wind is not as much a factor as on the North Kona courses. For more information call 322-2595.

Keep in mind that our office
is ready, willing, and able
to aid you in all your travel needs,
be it lodging, car rental, any activity
(and our reservationists
can make plenty of suggestions
about what activities are available).
Maybe you would like
to go after the big blue marlin?
Or make a starting time
on one of the many golf courses?
Whatever your vacation needs are,
Elvrine, Nancy, and Patti
are anxious to help.
Just call or write to
Bed & Breakfast Hawaii
Po Box 449
Kapaa, Hi. 96746
or call
1-800-733-1632
808-742-7771
FAX 808-822-2723

THE BELT ROAD

If you take Palani Road mauka from Kailua for about four miles up the hill, you will come to the Belt Road which runs above Kailua. Take this road south and you will join Highway 11, which continues on to South Kona and the Volcano area. Since this area is very different from Kailua, far older and less tourist oriented, we urge you to try this road. The scenery is spectacular, whether you are looking at the vegetation along the road or the awesome views of Kailua and the blue Pacific below. When we first took this drive, the growth of ginger, bougainvillea, royal poinciana and wild orchids was so over-powering that we failed to see the many coffee trees along the way. Should you be lucky enough to be there when the coffee trees are in bloom, you are in for a treat. Coffee trees are in the gardenia family and the blossom is as beautiful and as fragrant, but, alas, much more transitory, lasting only a few days.

As you drive this road, which starts at around 1500' elevation, goes to sea level at South Point, then to around 4000+' at Volcano and then down to sea level again at Hilo, you will pass through several old towns, still very busy little centers which serve the folks who live in this area. The first little town you come to is Holualoa. While there is not much there, you may find the Art Gallery interesting. We were told that this area has many working artists. We hope you see a small espresso bar on the left as you enter town. When we passed through the owner was working hard to open up but having much trouble with the bureaucrats. We wish her luck. Next you will come to Kealakekua, made famous in the song *Little Grass Shack*. After Kealakekua is Captain Cook. Once past Captain Cook you will not find much in the way of facilities until you reach the south end of the Island and the little villages of Naalehu, Waiohinu, Honuapoo, and Punaluu. (One thing we did notice on this trip was that the county has installed a spigot about 46 miles after you leave Kailua. So if you are thirsty make a stop here.) Before Kailua was developed mainly for tourists, all the action was in the higher elevation, which, when you think of it, makes much more sense for living due to the cooler climate. On the mainland we are more used to having our towns right on the water's edge on both coasts. In Hawaii, this is not always the case.

On our last trip we noticed that there were several new coffee roasting or processing places and there were even more this year so take your pick on where you would like to stop. What all this indicated to us was that coffee is doing well on the Big Island, so well in fact that the price is a little lower. Of course, one cannot be assured they will remain low.

RESTAURANTS

LOCAL STYLE

SANDY'S DRIVE IN
This is a new little place located just past the Kona Coffee Roaster. Prices are very low, fried chicken for $3.90. You order at the counter and take food to table. You will not find many tourists here but the place is clean and neat, a real chow down spot. They are open for breakfast, lunch, and dinner for 6:30 am to 8:30 pm Monday-Friday, and from 7:30 on Saturday and Sunday.

MANAGO HOTEL
This is located about 17 miles from Kailua in Captain Cook. We would urge you to stop by and pay a visit here, for such old hotels are becoming rare. We spent some time looking through the guest register and noted that few mainland people use this facility. While we think B & B is the best deal around, we would think anyone on a budget or with just a spirit of adventure would enjoy staying here. Rooms start at $18.00 for a single with a shared bath up to $27.00 for a private bath on the third floor accommodating three people. Meals are served: breakfast from 7-9, cost around $3.75, lunch from 11-2 from $5-$10, dinner from 5-7, priced from $6-$10. We imagine that after dinner one and all adjourn to the lobby where easy chairs are neatly lined for T.V. viewing.

CAPTAIN COOK INN
This is a new little restaurant in Captain Cook, just a few miles south of Aloha Theater. The place is clean and the prices are low. They have a salad bar for $2.00. Their plate lunch is $4.50. We did not eat there, but our guess is that food has a local more than a mainland flavor.

HONG KONG
In Captain Cook on the mauka side of the highway. They are open for lunch and dinner and it is buffet style, Cantonese with modest prices.

local Style

TESHIMA'S
Just past where Highway 180 joins 11 on the mauka side of the road. Even if you are staying down in Kailua Town, it is not much of a drive up here, and if you want Japanese food this is a good place. Not many tourists stop here, but plenty of residents do since the food is good and the prices are low. The menu is a curious mixture of Japanese and American, so you can choose hamburger steak, pork chops, or Nabe Yaki Udon. Prices run from $5-$10. They also fix a box lunch from $3.00-$3.50 in case you would like to picnic somewhere along the way. One of the things we learned this year was that the owner, Mrs. Teshima, has been honored by the Emperor of Japan for her fine tempura.

local/Tourist Style

ALOHA THEATER CAFE
This has long been a favorite breakfast and lunch spot for residents of this area, and now they are open for dinners too. We were told by some friends who live in Kona that the food is gourmet, one of the best in the area. Their menu is not extensive, some Mexican dishes, catch of the day, and a daily special on which the price varies. The day we were there the catch of the day was ahi and a full ahi dinner was $13.95. We had a bean soup on our visit this year that was outstanding. They bake all of their own cakes, pastries, and cookies. If you get there early in the evening you can have your meal on the lanai and watch the sun set.

CANAAN DELI
South of Teshima's on the makai side of the road. It seems that just about everyone in town has breakfast at the Canaan Deli. One orders at the counter, takes a table either inside of out and a short time later is served. The owners here must be from back east since one can get Philly Cheese Steak along with a whole host of sandwiches.

THE GALLERY CAFE
This is a new restaurant located in the Kealakekua Arts Center. They are open for lunch and dinner, Monday-Friday 10 am-7 pm and Saturday from 11-7. Dining after 7 is by reservation only. They serve a variety of sandwiches, salads, and pastas. They have a picnic basket to go, $17.95 for two and they provide cups, plates, etc. Several of our hosts told us not to miss this spot.

PEACOCK HOUSE
A new restaurant in Kealakekua serving Cantonese cuisine at very attractive prices. Their highest dish, Abalone with Black Mushrooms, is $7.50 but most dishes are in the $5-6 range, many less.

SHIRLEY'S
New and spiffy and food to please local folks. They serve a plate lunch for $3.65, but the specialty of the house is Chicken either to eat in or take out.

REAL MEXICAN FOOD
A take out window in the same little shopping center as the Hong Kong Restaurant.

KONA COFFEE ROASTER
If all you want is a cup of coffee and perhaps a torte or fresh croissant, stop by here and sit at one of the side-walk tables, and perhaps you can imagine you are in Paris. Perhaps while you are there they will be roasting coffee in the small roaster right in the front of their store. Open Monday-Friday from 8 a.m. to 5 p.m.

WAKEFIELDS GARDEN'S RESTAURANT
This is located on the road to the Place of Refuge. If you would like some health food you will find it here.

KONA COFFEE PLANTATION
Just past Captain Cook and the last place you will come to until you reach South Point. You can get a sandwich here, $4.95-$5.95, and, of course, a cup of coffee.

POINTS OF INTEREST

FUKU-BONSAI CENTER

We strongly recommend that you not pass this by. It is located between the 115 and 116 mile marker which is before you get to Kealakekua. There is a self guided tour, $5 for adults and $2.50 for children. This is a center for international artistic potted plants: Japanese bonsai, Chinese penjing, Hawaiian and indoor bonsai. There are nine themed gardens featuring the Hawaii State Bonsai Repository.

KAHANAKOU HAWAIIAN FOUNDATION (CRAFT CENTER)

We noticed this place located on the makai side of the road around 13 miles out of Kailua. This is a non-profit organization dedicated to teaching Hawaiian craft.

MAUNA LOA MAC NUT FACTORY

This is located just off the highway on a road that runs makai about 15 miles from Kailua in a new Shopping Center. They give guided tours every day. The nuts are harvested in September.

ROYAL KONA COFFEE MILL

Located on Route 16, which goes to Kealakekua Bay and the Captain Cook Monument. Open every day from 8 am to 4 pm. This is not a coffee mill but simply a coffee roasting station. They buy their beans from the co-op located next door, and it is here where the coffee cherries are processed. Believe us when we say that the whole process is complicated. We have several coffee trees on Kauai and have gone through the process of picking, pealing, drying, shucking, and roasting, and never will we complain about the price of coffee again. At the Mill you will read about this process and if you like you can buy some fine Kona coffee. Next door is a macadamia nut processing plant and when they are operating you can hear them for quite a distance. It might be possible to tour this facility.

KONA MUSEUM

Right after you pass Kealakekua and before you reach Captain cook, you will come to this small museum on the makai side of the road. To us the most interesting thing about the museum the building, which was constructed sometime last century. On this trip we did not spot it but perhaps it is still there.

ST. BENEDICT'S CATHOLIC CHURCH (THE PAINTED CHURCH)

As many times as we have made this trip, this year was the first time we stopped by here. You can find it by following the signs off the road to Captain Cook's Monument or the road to the Place of Refuge. It is called the Painted Church because Biblical scenes are painted in frescos all along the walls. This was the custom in the old country so that people who could not read could understand the Biblical stories.

CAPTAIN COOK'S MONUMENT

At the end of Route 16 you will come to Kealakekua Bay, where Captain Cook was done in by the Hawaiian Chiefs. Also, there is a heiau that was very important to the ancient Hawaiians. If you choose you can continue along the coast road for 4 miles to the Place of Refuge.

WAKEFIELD'S BOTANICAL GARDENS
It is located on the road to the Place of Refuge mentioned below. There are six acres of gardens to visit here and the price is right, free. They have over 500 varieies of bonzai trees. Open from 11-5. Their restaurant is open from 11-3.

PU'UHONUA O HONAUNAU or PLACE OF REFUGE
You can get to this by going on the small road which runs south from Kealakekua for about four miles. If you are traveling south toward Volcano, take Route 16 from here back to Route 11. There are other Places of Refuge in Hawaii, but none as large or elaborate as this one. At the Visitor Center you can pick up a self-guiding leaflet which will explain what it is you are seeing. Once called "the City of Refuge," the name was changed by an act of Congress at the request of the Native Hawaiians to *PU'UHONUA O HONAUNAU*. The Visitors Center will also provide you with a short history of the area. If you like, you can have a picnic lunch here. We spent quite a while exploring the ceremonial areas and looking for the petroglyphs.

FROM CAPTAIN COOK SOUTH

Once you leave Captain Cook, you will not see much civilization until the little town of Waiohinu some sixty miles south of Kailua. The stark, natural beauty of this area is unsurpassed anywhere we have travelled. Huge lava flows have in years past cascaded down the slopes of Mauna Loa to the ocean thousands of feet below. Unlike the slopes just behind Kailua Town, which are rich and verdant, here arid conditions keep some spots so bleak that at times one can imagine being on the moon. And yet in the middle of this seeming desert of lava, land developers ply their trade. Do people really look forward to building on these jagged lava stones? Already some homes have been built. As one wonders about homes built on earthquake faults, or along flooding river beds, one must wonder if Mauna Loa and goddess Pele are just dozing and will someday awaken to show man the folly of his ways.

As the road goes south along this coast line it passes through one of the largest macadamia nut plantations in Hawaii. Whatever this area looked like before the mac trees were planted, it is now a lush forest.

Just before the town of Waiohinu there is a sign on the right pointing the way to South Point, and if you want to be able to say you have travelled to the southern most part of the U.S., take this eleven mile drive that ends at sheer cliffs above the Pacific. This is a favorite fishing spot for the locals, so you are bound to see someone trying his luck. Just remember fishing is fishing and catching is catching. You may not see any fish.

In the town of Waiohinu you can sit under the Mark Twain Monkey Pod Tree, which he planted in 1866. This original tree, unfortunately, fell in high winds several years ago, and now a new "original" was planted; original, of course, because existentially it occupies the same space.

Just past Waiohinu is the little town of Naalehu and beyond that, Punaluu. From here to Volcano you pass through the southern edge of the Ka'u desert. Vegetation is sparse, with a sprinkling of sugar cane along the way. Unless you take the turnoff going mauka, you will pass the town of Pahala, a plantation colony where few tourists stop. We did stop here as we had heard of a Buddist Temple located somewhere in the area in a place called Wood Valley. Unfortunately, we were incorrectly informed that we needed a permit to drive that road. Evidently to get to the Monastery, you take the road that goes through Pahala to the right for about five miles. For more information you can write to Po Box 250, Pahala, Hi. 96777 or call 808-928-8539. Beyond Pahala you will rise slowly to around 4,000 feet at Kilauea Volcano.

RESTAURANTS

LOCAL STYLE

GREEN SANDS
In the Shopping Center in Pahala. Eating here would give you a good excuse to drive into town. You will most likely be the only tourists, but don't let that stop you since the locals are friendly, prices are low, and the food is good local fare.

NAALEHU SHORT STOP DRIVE IN
You can get a lunch here for $4.50, but do not expect to see other tourists. Plenty of local folks, however.

local/Tourist Style

NAALEHU COFFEE SHOP
When you reach Naalehu, the southern most town in the U.S., drive into the shopping center and you cannot miss seeing the Coffee Shop. We were told by the owners, Roy and Arda Toguchi, that the place has been there for forty years. If you are starved and can wait no longer, feast on the papaya fruit salad and banana bread for breakfast or on one of the tasty sandwiches for lunch. The prices are low and the service is friendly.

NAALEHU BAKERY
You can get a snack here or a loaf of freshly baked bread.

PUNALUU'S BLACK SANDS RESTAURANT
They are open for lunch and dinner and for lunch the have buffet for $10.95.

SEA MOUNTAIN GOLF COURSE DINING ROOM
At Sea Mt. Golf Course, this little restaurant is open for breakfast and lunch and makes a nice place to stop when driving the southern route from Hilo to Kona.

PLACES OF INTEREST

HOOKENA BEACH PARK
A few miles south of Captain Cook you will come to a road, marked with a sign, that leads to this Park. From the highway it is two miles. The park is not much, but there are bathroom facilities, picnic tables, and it looks as if swimming and snorkeling would be safe. In our opinion this is not worth the drive.

MILOLII
Around thirty-eight miles south of Kailua there is a road going makai to a fishing village that at one time we said was worth the five mile detour it takes to get there. Well, we took it again this trip and have changed our minds. The road is narrow and some what difficult to drive and we had the feeling we were intruding on local people. Unless one wanted to launch a small boat there is little reason to go there.

MANUKA STATE WAYSIDE
This botanical park has great ocean views and makes an excellent picnic spot on the way to Volcano. It is located about forty-one miles south of Kailua.

SOUTH POINT
(see above)

SPORTS

TENNIS
On the extreme south end of the Big Island there are two public tennis court sites, both lighted; 1) Naalehu Park, 2) Pahala School Grounds.

GOLF
Sea Mountain Golf Course is located at the southern tip of Hawaii, near Pahala. The fee for guests of Sea Mountain is $33 and that includes cart and tax. For non-guests the fee is $50. They also have a special on weekdays for seniors, $34. Look for a coupon in *This Week* and other magazines for other specials. The setting is beautiful and the wind is a very big factor here. For more information call 928-6222.

If you want to play golf in the southern most point in the United States play Discovery Harbor, located five miles from Naalehu. When we stopped by here the first time we thought it was some kind of a joke since the golf course looked more like a cow pasture. However, in 1985 the owners, American Showa of Japan, sent Mr. Katkuhiko Ando over from Japan to get the course in shape. The course is not pristine by any means but at least it is recognizable as a golf course. The green fee is $15 for Kamaaina, $20 for visitors cart included. We would suggest that you call first. For more information call 929-7353. Going here the first time reminded us of the time we followed a guide book to a course in Canada just outside of Hope, B.C. When we got there all we found was a cow pasture. All of those we talked to along the way for directions must have thought us foolish indeed.

CONCLUSION

We hope you enjoy reading this book as much as we enjoyed doing the research for it. No one guide book suits all visitors and all are written with a certain slant. Our book is slanted to Bed and Breakfast travelers, who we think differ slightly from the Hotel/ Resort guests. Staying in a bed and breakfast home sometimes takes more of a spirit of adventure than some people have. There can be more personal interaction, which some love and others shun. Also, many of the restaurants we suggest you try are frequented by few tourists. But that is the kind of travelers we are. We constantly search for funky little places and sometimes they are a delight and sometimes they are a disater.

In our minds we have combed the Islands fairly well, but we know we miss things worth seeing and doing. If you discover something we failed to find, please let us know about it. We will check it out and share your knowledge with our other guests.

It is our aim to be a full service travel aid. We want you to enjoy your stay in Hawaii in all respects. If you have a bad experience at any point, whether it be with a host home, car rental, bad service or meal at a restaurant, you can do us no bigger favor than letting us know. Such knowledge helps us protect future guests from the same bad experience.

If after using this book you feel it was not worth the money, simple send us your proof of purchase and we will refund your money. If you enjoyed the book, share it with a friend. One of the aims of this book is to ensure the growth of bed and breakfast travel. The growth of bed and breakfast during the last thirteen years we have been in business has been remarkable.

Aloha and mahalo for bearing with us. We look forward to meeting you somewhere in Paradise.

Call or write to
Bed & Breakfast Hawaii
PO Box 449
Kapaa, Hi 96746
808-822-7771
1-800-733-1632
FAX 808-822-2723

NOTES

NOTES